NEVER A SLOW DAY

For Bob —
The premier
off - road
warrior.

Frank
1-6-16

NEVER A SLOW DAY

ADVENTURES OF A 20TH CENTURY
NEWSPAPER REPORTER

FRANK A. AUKOFER

MARQUETTE
UNIVERSITY
PRESS

DIEDERICH STUDIES IN MEDIA AND COMMUNICATION

NO. I

BONNIE BRENNEN, SERIES EDITOR

LIBRARY OF CONGRESS CATALOGING-IN-PUBLICATION DATA

Aukofer, Frank.
  Never a slow day : adventures of a 20th century newspaper reporter / Frank A. Aukofer.
    p. cm. — (Diederich studies in media and communication ; no. 1)
  Includes index.
  ISBN-13: 978-0-87462-033-7 (pbk. : alk. paper)
  ISBN-10: 0-87462-033-3 (pbk. : alk. paper)
  1. Aukofer, Frank. 2. Journalists—United States—Biography. I. Title.
  PN4874.A845A3 2009
  070.92—dc22
  [B]
                                                    2009011924

Marquette University Press
Milwaukee, Wisconsin 53201-3141
All rights reserved.
www.marquette.edu/mupress/

FOUNDED 1916

⊗The paper used in this publication meets the minimum requirements of the
American National Standard for Information Sciences—
Permanence of Paper for Printed Library Materials, ANSI Z39.48-1992.

Association of American
University Presses

MARQUETTE UNIVERSITY PRESS
MILWAUKEE

The Association of Jesuit University Presses

TABLE OF CONTENTS

FOR SHARLENE

AND OUR FAMILY

INTRODUCTION

This is the story of a 20th century newspaper reporter.

I was in it for the fun and the front-row seat—and maybe the fame, if it happened, but never for money because everybody knew that reporters were poorly paid. The attraction was that you could watch and participate in events and situations that other people envied, even to the point of paying for them, and at the same time make a living at a craft that was not only useful, but made a contribution to society. I considered it an honor and a privilege to spend my working life as a newspaperman.

I was proud in 2000 when the "Biography" television program selected Johann Gutenberg as the most important person of the last millennium. Gutenberg was a printer, the inventor of movable metal type in the 15th century.

My grandfather, Frank X., and my father, Pat, were both printers, and I followed in the trade. They were pressmen, but I became a compositor and operator of a marvelously complex typesetting machine called the Linotype. It and similar machines like the Intertype are now museum pieces.

Though I loved the trade, I was happy to leave it. As a reporter, I covered the civil rights movement and the aftermath of the assassination of the Rev. Martin Luther King, Jr., interviewed presidents, covered two of history's three presidential impeachment proceedings and a dozen national presidential nominating conventions, went to war, wrote about Congress and the U.S. Supreme Court, covered disasters and parts of revolutions, pursued investigations, did profiles of the famous and, in my early years, wrote personal adventure stories.

I sat with presidents in the Oval Office, waylaid senators and congressmen in hallways, interviewed Supreme Court justices, rubbed elbows with celebrities, raced automobiles, motorcycles and go-karts, wrote about cars for more than 40 years, went spelunking and scuba diving, roared across the Saudi Arabian desert in a helicopter, took a ride on the battleship Wisconsin, blasted away at bowling pins with automatic assault rifles and shotguns in the basement of a gun manufacturer, and went through the Panama Canal on a British freighter.

Some of the stories were firsts. In June, 1965, I was part of the re-enactment of the Great Circus Parade, sitting high on the seat of an antique circus wagon lashed to a flatcar behind a steam engine as the train chugged its lazy way from Baraboo to Milwaukee. In 1976, I was aboard the inaugural flight from Paris to Washington on the Concorde supersonic transport, at more than three times the speed of sound.

I have used members of my own family as subjects for stories, in-cluding a Mother's Day piece about my mother, Wanda, with her eighth-grade education, becoming a published writer in her 60s; a story about a first cousin who put herself through college after rearing five children, and a magazine article about how, as a responsible grand-father, I taught my 5-year-old twin granddaughters to play poker.

After I moved to Washington, my horizons expanded. Shortly af-ter I arrived, I telephoned my brother, John, to tell him that I had stopped by the White House just to take a pee. Later I got involved in journalism politics and was elected to the Standing Committee of Correspondents and the presidency of the National Press Club. I also served as president and chairman of the National Press Foundation, president of the National Press Building Corp., and served one term as a board member of the Washington professional chapter of the Society of Professional Journalists. I won some awards, including the Sigma Delta Chi medal for Washington correspondence, became The Milwaukee Journal's Washington bureau chief and wound up in Who's Who in America for about 20 years, well into my retirement.

When I retired in 2000, I set out to write this book as a memoir, basically to share some of my extraordinary experiences in 40 years as a reporter. Eventually, I expanded it to an autobiography, reasoning that even if it were not a commercial success, it would be there for my grandchildren and their descendants, like an extended epitaph on a tombstone. I always thought I would have liked to read a memoir by my grandfather or any of my ancestors.

I originally intended to write this book in the same way that I would do a news story, with solid research and reporting. But I soon became convinced it would be an impossibly long and grueling task, even working with my own clips and notes. Then I recalled that a memoir, by definition, is what you remember. So I simply sat down and wrote the story, occasionally researching dates, facts and sequences. It still took a long time.

The result, I hope, is a reasonably accurate account of my years as a newspaper reporter, at a time in the 20th century when newspapers were at their peak. Obviously, I couldn't include everything, and I didn't try. I simply tried to hit some of the high points and show the incredible variety and fun I had as a newspaperman. If there are errors or misinterpretations here, they are unintentional but wholly mine.

With the advent of cable television, specialized publications and the Internet, the news biz has changed, and is changing, drastically and dramatically. It will never be the same as it was in my years. Reporters now are captives of something called convergence, which means they must not only report and write their stories, but also must do broadcasting, filing for web pages and blogging.

I'm not sure I'd enjoy it as much if I were starting as a reporter now. In fact, with all the help I had along the way, I'm not even sure that in these times I would be able to qualify for the job and carve out a niche similar to what I experienced. I can only hope that at least some of the young people going into journalism today will have as much fun as I did minding other people's business and basking in reflected glory and gore.

September 1, 2007

THE DEPRESSION BABY

My parents were optimistic enough to marry in 1934, in the midst of the Great Depression. I was born on April 6 the next year and was joined regularly by a new sibling until my parents, Wanda Mary Kaminski and Herbert Anselm (Pat) Aukofer, called it a family at seven.

Following family custom, I was named for my grandfathers, Francis X. Aukofer and Alexander Kaminski. Following church custom, I was named Francis after an official saint, but like Grandpa Aukofer I was always called Frank and it eventually became my legal name. My only brother, John Elmer, was followed by Cecile Catherine, Dorothy Ann, Therese Mary, Margaret Jean and Clare Elizabeth; each named for a Virgin Saint at Ma's insistence. Any hopes she may have had went unfulfilled; none felt the call of a Catholic vocation.

My father was a printer, a letterpress man, like his father. There wasn't much steady work in the grim years of the Depression but he worked whenever he could find it—a week here and there—to support the family. We were poor and at odds at the old cliché. We kids knew it. Some of our clothes were hand-me-downs from older cousins and our home seemed worn and dreary, even for those times.

My dad never had a decent car. They were always old clunkers that broke down with heartbreaking regularity. I helped push a lot of them, wishing, as I grunted against the heavy steel bodywork of a '37 Packard or a '36 Hudson Terraplane, for a kind motorist to stop and offer a push. Mostly they didn't.

The only mechanic Pop could afford was a geezer named Bill, who worked out of an old two-car garage in an inner-city Milwaukee neighborhood, a place where the floor was hard-packed mud. Bill's chief value was that he never charged very much. But he didn't fix very much either, though he tried. He'd somehow tape a leaky brake line or reverse a gasket, and the car would run for a couple of weeks or a month, and then it was back for another cheap repair.

When I was in second grade, my folks amazingly managed to buy a house. Actually, it was more like a barn. It was an old wooden structure, built over a hole in the ground. It sat parallel to the alley at the back of a typical 40-foot-wide Milwaukee residential lot, on the northwest corner of N. 37th and W. Concordia Streets. To the south was the asphalt playground for Peckham Junior High School. (Years later, reflecting the changing neighborhood, the school was re-named for Jackie Robinson, the first black man to play baseball in the major leagues).

The first floor was one room, undivided, with rough-hewn planks as flooring. It probably had been a stable or a shop at one time. The living quarters, kitchen, living room, two bedrooms and a bath were on the second floor.

If our house was less than ideal, the neighborhood was beautiful, especially in the summer when elm trees gave every street a cathedral-like canopy of green. Almost every house had fruit trees in the back yard, their branches often leaning over the alleys where kids could ride their bicycles at night and pluck plums and apples without stopping.

Because there was no basement under our house, we always had rats and mice. So we usually had at least one cat. We also had dogs, but they were a heartache to a boy because they never seemed to last. They'd get to be six or eight months old and they'd run away or get hit by a car, and we'd get another one. On my 10th birthday, I wished mightily for a baseball glove and figured I'd get it when Pop came home from work. But he didn't say anything. When we sat down to eat, he casually told me—as if it were an afterthought—that I needed to go get something off the front seat of the car.

I thundered down the steps, visions of a beautiful leather outfielder's mitt in my head. When I opened the car door, all I saw was a bunched-up white towel. I picked it up and inside was a tiny cocker spaniel puppy. I fell in love.

Thinking about getting a dog of my own, I had fantasized about a name. It always came down to something noble and brave, like Rex or Flash. But when I put the puppy on the floor and watched his tiny clipped-off tail wiggle, there was only one name possible: Stubby.

Despite the fact that there never seemed to be any money, my folks managed to send all their children to the nearby Catholic school—St. John de Nepomuc. It was an eight-room schoolhouse—one room for each grade. My third-grade teacher was a wizened old Notre Dame nun, less than five feet tall, whose name was Sister Mary Seraphim. She was very strict—as were most of the nuns—but I had a knack for mimicking the beautiful handwriting that all the nuns seemed to have. In fairly short order, I was writing papers in longhand that looked just like the letters posted above the blackboard. I was solid with Sister S.

ALCOHOL

When I was 10 and in the fourth grade, I was introduced to alcohol. It happened the day after my brother, John, was hit by a car. He was banged up, but not enough to be hospitalized. Bruised and bandaged, he lay in bed at home and couldn't come along when my dad, my Uncle Arthur H. Fink Sr., and my cousin, Art Jr., went out to Silver Lake on a Sunday in October.

Uncle Art was maybe the second wealthiest of our immediate relatives, behind Uncle Warren Gehrs, my godfather. Like Uncle Warren, he was a pharmacist and owned his own drug store. Uncle Art and Aunt Tess—my dad's sister—eventually had seven kids, just as we did, but they had money. They lived in a nice house and had a cottage on Silver Lake near West Bend, where they spent their summers. I was envious of my cousins, though with affection because they were always very good to us. I learned later that Uncle Art had loaned or given money to my dad on a number of occasions when he couldn't make ends meet.

I felt terrible for my dad one time when he and Uncle Art came along on a Boy Scout campout with young Art and me. There was a general store near the campground, and one afternoon Uncle Art peeled off a couple of bills, gave them to Art and told him to take the whole troop to the store for treats. My dad just stood there. I knew he would have liked to have treated the kids, too, but he didn't have the money.

Yet despite my family's relative poverty, things weren't all bleak. In the summer of 1945, when I was 10, I set off on a three-week vacation—a week each at three summer cottages. The first was at my grandparents' place on Pewaukee Lake. Then I went to the Finks' place on Silver Lake and, finally, to the Gehrs cottage on Cedar Lake.

Every Fourth of July, the family had a big celebration at Pewaukee Lake. There were three cottages in a row on the north shore of the lower lake. One belonged to my grandfather and grandmother, Frank X. and Katherine (Toennessen) Aukofer. Next door was my grandmother's sister, Mary Manning, and her husband, Joe, whose name originally had been Machesky, and the third cottage belonged to my grandmother's niece, Lena Stransky, and her husband, Elmer. Lena was about the same age as my grandmother, and all three families had kids and grandkids. The Fourth of July was my grandfather's birthday and the wedding anniversary of Joe and Mary Manning.

Each cottage had a basement bar, with a quarter- or half-barrel of beer tapped in, and plenty of soda pop and snacks for the kids. Everybody would party all day, with the older kids shooting firecrackers, blowing tin cans sky-high. On several July 4 holidays, my teen-age cousins set up booths down at the lake, where we played carnival-style games for prizes. At night, my grandfather put on a fireworks show, complete with rockets and dazzling pinwheels nailed to the hickory trees.

The carousing was so complete that sometimes we kids would wake up the next morning and find our fathers passed out and snoring on the front lawn. We were always forced to go to bed early, but we would lie awake in the hot attic bedrooms and listen to the loud conversation and singing as our parents partied well into the early morning hours. My grandfather, however, always went to bed promptly at 10 p.m., no matter what.

So I was comfortable at Pewaukee Lake, where my grandmother fed me favorites like apple kuchen and home-canned pears. I tried to stay clear of Uncle Frank, my dad's bachelor older brother, whose irascible disposition came from a lifelong handicap. As a boy, he developed a disease that twisted his bones. Instead of amputating a leg, the doctors crossed them, and he lived his life as a short man with crossed legs. But he had powerful arms and upper body strength, a lot of it from rowing a boat on the lake, and if he caught you misbehaving, there was no mercy. Fortunately, the younger kids could outrun him most of the time. Because of Uncle Frank, nobody in my family was ever allowed to use the word "cripple." Also living with my grandparents was another of my dad's bachelor brothers, Uncle Ray, who was a kindly, laid-back man with a thick shock of hair and a face creased by laugh wrinkles.

The problem at Pewaukee Lake was a shortage of kids my age, so I was excited when I left to spend the second week at the Finks' cottage on Silver Lake. That was a kid's dream. There was a pier and a raft, and my cousins and their friends and I swam every day until our fingers shriveled. We'd go for boat rides and walk to a near-by resort for ice cream. On Aug. 15, 1945, we all gathered around the radio to listen to the reports of the Japanese surrender and the end of World War II. I was only six in 1941, but could remember the solemn announcement of the attack on Pearl Harbor when my mother turned on the kitchen radio. It was a confusing and frightening time.

After the great week at the Finks' place, the week at Uncle Warren and Aunt Ann's was a disappointment. They were nice people, but all of their kids—my cousins—were older than me except for the youngest, Michael. I didn't know him very well and didn't particularly like him. I was miserable. I started having headaches every day and, despite the fact that Uncle Warren owned a drug store, they had no aspirin. I spent the whole week lying in a hammock, my head pounding.

The following October, I was excited when my dad asked if I wanted to go back to the Finks' cottage on Silver Lake to board it up for the winter. With my brother John bedridden from his auto accident, there were four of us to handle the chore—Pop, Uncle Art, my cousin Art and me.

When the four of us arrived at the Silver Lake cottage, it was a sunny but cold fall day. My dad put two bottles of Grandpa's homemade wine on top of the kitchen stove, where they'd be handy for a nip against the chill. Then he and Uncle Art went to work winterizing the cottage. Art and I occasionally helped, but we mostly ran around and played. The wine level in one bottle steadily dropped until there was about an inch left in the bottom. Chilly, I asked my dad if I could have a sip to warm up.

Except for the fact that it was wine, this was not an unusual request. We kids often took sips of beer at the Pewaukee Lake gatherings, and I think some of my teenage cousins imbibed even more. With Pop's OK, I went to the kitchen for a sip. It tasted great, warm and wonderful going down, and before I knew it, I had finished off the bottle. Throughout the afternoon, I returned for more nips at the second bottle, careful not to cross paths with either Uncle Art or Pop, who also were taking pulls at the bottle.

By late afternoon, I was getting dizzy. When I told my cousin Art what I had done, he was disdainful. He thought I was pretending to be drunk over a couple of mouthfuls of wine.

On the way home in Uncle Art's green 1940 Ford two-door sedan, I got increasingly queasy when Pop and Uncle Art stopped for beers at a Cedarburg tavern. To keep us happy, they bought us ice cream cones. I got out of the car, took a couple of licks of the ice cream and the whole town started spinning. To counter the effect, I grabbed onto a metal sign pole and started spinning around it—in the opposite direction. I fell flat on my face and threw up. I lay there covered in ice cream and red vomit, too sick to move.

Pop and Uncle Art stood there and laughed. When we got home, I was still so sick that my dad had to carry me up the steps. My mother, thinking I had been an accident victim like my brother the day before, must have been close to a heart attack.

I escaped punishment because was I sick all night and the next morning. When I finally got up, my mother ordered me to get dressed. I was going to school in the afternoon and, no, she would not write me an excuse for the missed morning. I would have to deal with that myself. That was my punishment.

When I finally dragged myself into my fourth-grade classroom, the nun asked the inevitable question of where I had been that morning, and where was my written excuse. "'Ster," I said, "I was hung over because I got drunk yesterday." She was not amused, and I wound up with one of those punishments where I had to write a sentence a hundred times. But the word got around the classroom, and I became something of a celebrity.

THE CORD AND THE PEDOPHILE

It wasn't usually that way. I was never among the elite in any of my grade school classes. Low down in the social order, I got into occasional fights with the class bullies, who would sometimes make fun of my name: Ow-fugger and hookafart were two of the printable pronunciations. My close friends were mostly older guys not in my grade.

In the 1940s, kids were mostly left on their own during their free time, and especially in summer. We roamed the neighborhood freely on foot and on our used balloon-tire Schwinn bikes. Sometimes we sneaked up behind the horse-drawn garbage and trash wagons to catch a tow. In the summer, we went on what we called raiding parties. After dark, we rode up and down the alleys, plucking fruit from the trees that almost everyone had in their back yards. It was theft and it was grand.

A lot of people had victory gardens. We usually didn't bother with them because they were mostly vegetables, but one time we sneaked into a backyard field of sweet corn. It was the small, white variety and we sat between the stalks in the gathering dark shucking ear after ear of the corn and eating it raw. It was so sweet and tasty that one night I ate so much I became as sick as I had been with my grandfather's wine. It was years before I could eat white sweet corn, cooked or raw, and of course I was well into adulthood before I ever tried sweet red wine again.

The freedom we enjoyed was as exhilarating as it was taken for granted. On Saturdays, we'd bike or walk a couple of miles to a movie theater for the cartoons, double feature and, of course, the serial. The Phantom or Flash Gordon would get into a pickle every week, so we'd have to return the next week to see how he got out of it. Admission was a nickel, and later a dime.

One summer afternoon, I went by myself to the movies and, in the dusk on the way home, encountered the only homosexual pedophile I've ever met in my life. I was a kid of 11 or 12, lackadaisically walking east on Burleigh St., when a Cord convertible, top down, intersected my path at the stop sign. I stopped dead, staring. The driver looked at me and grinned. "That's a Cord," I said. "Yes," he replied.

I'd never seen a Cord in anything but photographs. And this was a convertible, a 1936 model 812. The hubcaps gleamed. The flexible tubes snaked out of the coffin-shaped hood. I thought I was dreaming.

"Would you like a ride?" Would I? He opened the right door. I climbed in, marveling at the engine-turned dash, the electric shifter sticking out of the steering column. My host casually flicked the shift lever, no bigger than my little finger, and slowly took off. We hadn't gone more than a half block when I felt his hand on my thigh, groping toward my groin.

Gripped by fear, I recoiled, and he took his hand away. I didn't know much if anything about homosexuals or pedophiles, but I had heard enough from my friends—and warnings about strangers from my parents and the nuns—to know I was in trouble. He obviously knew he had overplayed his hand, and he started telling me about the car. I didn't hear a word. I was looking for an escape, so I told him to turn off Burleigh onto a side street maybe five blocks from my home. As soon as we had gone about half a block onto the dark street, I pointed to a house and told him that was mine. He pulled over to the curb, and I grabbed the door handle, jumped out of the car and started running. Temples pounding, I ran between houses, down alleys and across streets all the way home, looking behind me the whole time.

FIRST LOVES

I fell in love twice in grade school. First was Betty Caspary, and it happened in the second grade. She had blond hair and Shirley Temple curls, and reminded me of the way I imagined Becky Thatcher, Tom Sawyer's girlfriend. I was an early fan of Tom, Huckleberry Finn and Tom Swift, when I wasn't reading comic books.

My infatuation lasted through several grades, and I mostly admired her from a distance. However, one winter, when I was in about the fourth or fifth grade, all the kids went to the Sherman Park outdoor rink on a Friday evening to go ice skating. Betty was there, and so was my cousin Art. They both had their own skates. Even if I had known how to skate, I couldn't have because I didn't own any.

But I was determined to make my mark with Betty. My opportunity came when she and Art were holding hands and skating, I grabbed her other hand, and ran around on the ice while they skated, oblivious to how ridiculous I must have looked. We both walked her home later.

In the sixth grade I got interested in opera. A radio station in Chicago had a program called the "Saturday Night Theater of the Air," which presented operas. I knew nothing about the music, but loved some of it. My favorite was "Carmen," especially the Habanera and Toreador songs.

My infatuation with Betty waned when I got interested in Joanne Lobotzke, partly because she was developing faster than Betty. Plus Joanne lived only a half a block away. As I had with Betty, I mostly admired Joanne from afar. But that summer, in a batch of old clothes she had gotten somewhere, my mother found a navy blue cape with a red lining. Though it was designed for a woman, I thought it was dramatic and even operatic. Nobody else wanted it, so it became my favorite prop. With the cape, I was the swashbuckling Zorro, or Batman or Superman.

One warm and dark evening, strains of "Carmen" coursing through my brain, I sneaked down the block and stationed myself behind a large elm tree across the street from Joanne's house. I didn't know if she was home, or if the windows were open, but I stood behind the tree in my cape and serenaded her with the refrain from the Toreador song. I finally skulked away, sheepish but flushed and feeling powerful. I had no idea whether she or anyone else had heard me.

WE GET OUR NEW HOUSE

By that time, we were living in a proper home. My parents somehow scraped up enough money to fix up our old barn. A contractor arrived one day and dug a big hole in the front of our lot. Workers poured a concrete floor and built a basement of concrete blocks and a steel I-beam.

Most spectacular were the house movers. They came with jacks and big logs, and they raised the house at the back of the lot, turned it perpendicular to the alley, rolled it forward and lowered it onto the new basement. It was the biggest attraction in the neighborhood. But a huge problem developed. Because the house was originally built over a hole, nobody had paid any attention to whether it was true. It was leveled over the hole, but when it was turned and dropped onto the new foundation, it was about four inches higher in the front than the back.

Supporting the front of the house was a large wooden beam, maybe three or four by twelve inches, and my dad figured he could level the house by cutting about four inches off the beam. He persuaded the house movers to leave a couple of the jacks. Then he jacked up the front of the house and attacked the beam with a simple hand saw. For weeks every night after work, my dad climbed on a ladder and, sweating and covered with dirty sawdust, sawed away at that beam, until he had cut four inches off it all the way across the front of the house—maybe 30 feet or more. When he finally cranked the jacks down, the house settled level onto the new basement walls. To a boy, it was an amazing feat of determination and stamina, and I was in awe of him.

With only the help of his cousin, Ralph Mauch, a carpenter, Pop turned that unpromising structure into a promising house. We now had a living room, dining room, kitchen, half bath and one bedroom on the first floor. On the second, they built four bedrooms and a bathroom. Later they built us a two-car garage out back where the house had been.

THE BOY ON THE BAR STOOL

I spent a lot of time on bar stools as a boy. Whenever I went out with my dad, there was always a stop at a tavern. Pop would have a beer or two, or a brandy and beer, and I'd sip an orange soda. Occasionally, we'd each have a hard-boiled egg, with salt and pepper, or a tin of anchovies wrapped around capers, which we would eat with salted crackers. Most of the taverns also had hot beef for sandwiches in a slow cooker on the back bar.

Though I didn't realize it at the time, those stops were a cause of friction and sometimes rage in our house. Pop ran up bar bills at the taverns he frequented, and on payday he stopped to pay them off. Whatever was left he gave to my mother to buy food and pay the bills. By the time I was a teenager, Pop was working two jobs—second shift as a pressman at Wisconsin Cuneo Press and days in the small print shop he bought in the Plankinton Arcade building in downtown Milwaukee. But he still made his rounds.

Pop loved to kid around and tell jokes, which made him a popular guy in a bar. Because he was the youngest child in his family, he was close in age and outlook to his older nieces and nephews, and they gravitated to him at family gatherings. There was always trouble when he got together with his brother, Elmer. They would disappear for the whole day, sometimes longer, and return with what was then kindly called a snoot full.

Still, he was funny. He always said that he knew his limit; his problem was he got drunk before he reached it. There were other jokes, some of which I didn't understand at a tender age. Looking at a woman in a tavern, he once told me: "There's something I like about her; I just can't quite put my finger on it." Or, "I don't get along too well with that woman. All she wants to do is talk, and all I want to do is jabber."

Pop's single mindedness when it came to entertainment—sitting on a bar stool—was a cross for my mother. She wanted to go dancing, or to movies, anything else. But she usually ended up on the stool next to Pop. In later years, when I was a teenager, that and the chronic lack of money led to monumental arguments, with both of them yelling through an alcoholic haze. Often Pop would simply go to bed, leaving my mother brooding over her beer, and I would sometimes become her target arriving home late after a date or a night out. She'd accuse me of anything that came into her mind, from drinking to illicit sex, taking out on me her anger at Pop. It was gut-churning for me, but I came to realize that they somehow still managed to take care of us kids.

I don't think my mother had ever even kissed a boy before she met my dad. Neither ever had sex with anybody else, and their relations started only after they were married. That's why it was so funny in later years, after Pop died, to hear one of my mother's favorite lines: "Men are all alike. All they want to do is sneak a feel." Of course, she was talking about Pop.

The characteristic I remember most vividly about my dad was his visceral hatred of "big shots," which he defined as anyone who lorded it over someone lower on the totem pole. I think it reflected his experience as the youngest child in a middle-class family who, because of the Great Depression, wound up worse off financially than his father and siblings. He had the demeaning experience of having to borrow money from friends and relatives because the family considered it a disgrace to accept welfare. To this day, I carry his attitude with me. There's nothing that outrages me more than hearing people chewing out or putting down someone they regard as a lesser human being.

SCHAUM TORT AND COMIC BOOKS

My favorite activity in grade school was to visit my Aunt Leona and Uncle Dick Powell. Aunt Leona was my mother's older sister and, like all of my relatives on my mother's side, she lived on the South Side and spoke with a Polish accent. She and Uncle Dick were childless and took a liking to me. Their home was a small, second-floor apartment over a store, and they always fussed over me when I came to visit. They lived way across the city, so it took a streetcar and a couple of buses to get there, which in those days was no big deal for a nine- or ten-year old. Uncle Dick was a great kidder, and Aunt Leona always made my favorite desserts—strawberries with juice over schaum tort, which was made from egg whites, and cheesecake embedded with pineapple chunks or green maraschino cherries.

But I came mostly for the comic books. Aunt Leona and Uncle Dick were consummate comic book fans. I think they bought every new comic book that came out, and there were stacks of them all over the apartment. On my periodic visits, I sat for hours reading the exploits of Billy Batson and (Shazam!) Captain Marvel, Bruce Wayne and Batman, Clark Kent and Lois Lane and Superman, Plastic Man, the Phantom, Wonder Woman, and all the other comic book heroes of the era. On many days, I read so many I'd get a pounding headache and be forced to quit. The beautiful thing was there were always more comic books to read next time. I don't think I ever read them all.

At home, the radio was the main entertainment, and my hero— from the broadcasts and comic books—was the Lone Ranger. He never killed anybody; he always shot the gun out of the bad guy's hand, and no crook could ever stand up to him in a fist fight. He had a brave and steadfast sidekick, Tonto, and he always left without waiting for the people he helped to thank him, shouting "Hi yo, Silver, away." There was nobody I wanted to emulate more than the Lone Ranger.

But of course I liked the other radio broadcasts, too, especially "The Land of the Lost" on Saturday mornings. The program purported to find things kids had lost, and I believed in it totally—until I tried it myself. I lost a small penlight, so I wrote a letter to the show describing what had happened. A couple of weeks later, a package arrived in the mail. It contained a beautiful, high-quality flashlight. But it was a full-size one, nothing like the one I had lost. I thought it was wonderful, but I had learned a lesson about fantasy and reality.

I believed in Santa Claus until I was about 12 years old. I had the best argument for his existence: My parents could not afford all those presents we found under the tree. I was right.

GRADUATION GIGGLES AND A DEAD FRIEND

I was afraid I would never make it to high school. The 8th grade graduation at St. John de Nepomuc was, as usual in a Catholic school, done in church, complete with Mass, and Billy Verbaten and I got the giggles. He was a close friend, and something about the ceremony got the better of us. It was one of those situations where probably even a death threat could not have stopped us. There were repeated stern warnings from our eighth-grade nun, who was also the principal, but after a few moments of silence we'd start giggling again.

She was furious, and refused to sign our diplomas. The pastor had signed them all earlier, but I was terrified when I saw the blank space where the principal's signature was supposed to be. I thought I would not be accepted into high school, but my mother checked with the pastor, who told her the principal's signature was not required. She never did relent; I still have the diploma with the blank spot.

I was in grade school when I saw my first corpse, and I can still feel how it terrified me. Two of my best friends in the neighborhood were Dennis Bieser and Pinky Schwinn, even though, at 15, they were a couple of years older than me. One day they went out shooting with their .22 caliber rifles, and Dennis killed Pinky. It was ruled an accident; they got separated and Dennis said he had shot at a tree branch. The shot ricocheted, and it hit Pinky in the eye.

The wake was in the evening at a funeral home about two miles from my house. It was daylight when I got on my bike and rode down there. When I saw Pinky lying in the coffin, I barely recognized him. He was as pasty and scary as anything I'd seen in horror movies.

By the time I walked out of the funeral home, it was dark. I rode my bike home as fast as I could, trembling and looking over my shoulder the whole time, as frightened as Ichabod Crane had been in *The Legend of Sleepy Hollow*. When I got home, I was still so spooked that I crawled in bed with my mother. I was 13 years old.

THE YOUNG NEWSPAPERMAN

I had a Milwaukee Sentinel paper route at the time. What I really wanted was a Journal route because The Milwaukee Journal was the biggest and most popular paper in town. But everybody wanted a Journal route, and there were none available. The Sentinel, a Hearst newspaper, was a poor also-ran. Because The Journal had such saturation coverage, you could have a profitable route with 60 or 70 customers in just a couple of square blocks, whereas a Sentinel route with 40 spread-out customers might force you to cover several miles. Besides, The Journal was an afternoon paper, which meant you could deliver the papers after school.

With the Sentinel, you had to get up very early in the morning, mostly in the dark. I had a particularly long route to serve my meager 35 or 40 customers, mainly because I gave up a shortcut I had used next to Pinky Schwinn's house. After he was killed, I rode my bike an extra two or three blocks to avoid coming anywhere near where he had lived. Even then, I was terrified when I came within even a half a block of his house in the morning darkness.

I was a business failure as a paper boy, but it wasn't entirely my fault. In those days, carriers had to collect from the customers once a week. It was a chore because you'd have to go back when people weren't home, and sometimes people would tell you to come back because they didn't have the money. Worst of all was the fact that the Hearst Corporation sold insurance policies and magazine subscriptions to the Sentinel's subscribers, and the carriers had to collect for them. The magazine subscriptions were a nickel a week and the insurance was seven cents.

My distributor's numbers of insurance and subscription customers were always higher than the number of people from whom I collected. I had a list of maybe 15 or 20 such customers, divided among only insurance, only magazine, or both. My numbers never jibed with those of my distributor. His were always higher, and so I was paying for the difference out of my own profits. At the end of each week, I'd wind up with take-home pay of only a few dollars, most of which I spent on candy and ice cream.

My parents figured out that I never seemed to make any money on my paper route. When they investigated, they found out about the discrepancies on the magazine and insurance collections, and made me quit. I didn't mind. It meant I never had to go near Pinky's house in the dark.

HIGH SCHOOL DAYS

There was never any thought of a public high school. My cousin Art was destined for Marquette University High School, which was all boys and run by the Jesuits. I had my eye on Messmer High School, which also was Catholic but had both boys and girls. There was one problem: Messmer was a three-year high school, sophomore through senior, fed by Catholic grade schools that went from the first through the ninth grades. I could have gone to ninth grade at one of those—St. Elizabeth's or St. Catherine's—but I chose Pius XI instead. It was a four-year Catholic high school on the southwest side of town, which for me was a bus and a streetcar ride, or two bus rides, depending on how I went, and an eight-block walk from there to the school.

Pius had Franciscan nuns, as well as some lay teachers, and the teachers there were much easier than the tough Notre Dame nuns I'd had at St. John's. So my freshman year at Pius was a breeze. It was a good thing because I spent three or four hours a day just getting to and from school. I rarely took books home and never did homework.

I had little interest in and no talent for sports, having managed to avoid any gym or physical education classes. The closest I had ever come to that sort of activity was in grade school when my dad signed me up with the Turners, or Turnverein, a gymnastics organization. But I didn't last long. There were reports that the group, founded by German-Americans, was sympathetic to the Nazis, and my dad pulled me out. I didn't like the classes anyway.

But I went out for football at Pius. There were two programs—the varsity and the B team for everybody who couldn't make the varsity, which obviously included me. I was a nonentity. When the coach asked what position I wanted to play, I blithely told him quarterback.

It didn't matter because he knew I was destined to be a non-participant, a tackling dummy in the practice drills. I think I was fourth or fifth on the quarterback depth chart—if the coach even had one.

I didn't like the practices, where I often got run down and hurt trying to tackle bigger guys, and I didn't like the stink in the locker room, or the stupid bantering among the jocks. But I did enjoy the bus rides to away games, when we'd laugh and sing songs as loud as we could. A favorite was "That Lucky Old Sun," which was a popular recording by Frankie Laine.

I never played in a game. Mostly I didn't care. I'd put in my time walking the sidelines, then get back on the bus for the trip back to Pius. One time, however, I longed to get in for at least one play. The game was at a school near my home, and my dad came out to watch. It was the only time he ever came. Usually, he was unable to get away on a week night because he worked the second shift. It was as dismal a night as I had ever experienced. It was cold, and a steady drizzle fell as the two teams battled back and forth in the mud. I stood with my dad near-by, fists clenched and praying hard that the coach would put me in, even for a minute or so, so Pop could see his boy play. It didn't happen, and neither Pop nor I ever mentioned it afterward.

But I did get a letter because everybody on the team got one. I never did sew it on a sweater or jacket because I wasn't that proud of it. Besides, I was going to Messmer the next year.

Messmer was on the northeast side of Milwaukee, the opposite from Pius, on the southwest. It was still two bus rides for me, but without the extra eight-block walk, so I considered it quite convenient. In my mind, it was also a cut above Pius. I was back with the tougher Notre Dame nuns.

It was 1950, with Harry S. Truman in the White House. The Cold War and Korea had not yet intruded into our consciousness. The president, however, had marked a big change in my life. As a kid, there were two constants: Franklin Roosevelt was always the president, and Pius XII was always the pope. When Roosevelt died in 1945, some of my friends and I made a lot of money hawking The Milwaukee Journal's extra editions on the streets.

"President croaks," we shouted when we didn't see anybody around. "Roosevelt keels over." We were more respectful and subdued only when customers showed up. We were kids.

At Messmer, as always, I was somewhere in the middle, not among the athletes and other hotshots, nor with the high-grade achievers, and not with the grungy low-lifes, who were grungy only in their attitudes. Some of them dressed better than I had in my entire life, in drape pants and expensive suits. They modeled their attitudes on the rebellious characters in movies like "Blackboard Jungle" and "Rebel without a Cause." I had a few friends from all of those groups, but mostly I hung out with guys like myself from working families.

In three years at Messmer, I don't believe I ever took a book home or did any homework. If there was any to be done, I'd work it out in a study hall or otherwise finesse it. Math was my nemesis. I managed barely to make it through algebra and geometry but I flunked trigonometry and biology. I had to re-take biology in my senior year because, without it, I would never get into college. But for my folks' insistence, I would never have bothered. I had no notion of ever going to college.

English classes were all right, though I didn't excel there either, and I didn't get involved in any extracurricular journalism activities like the school newspaper or yearbook. Most days I had to hustle out of school at the end of the day because I had a job working in Uncle Art's drug store.

From the time I was 14 years old, I worked. In the summer, I carried golf clubs as a caddy at the Milwaukee Country Club, where I envied the rich guys who drove up in their beautiful Cadillacs. When things were slow, we sometimes played hooky from the caddy shack and went skinny dipping in the Milwaukee River.

THE MIGRANT WORKER

One time I heard you could make good money doing field work. All you had to do was show up at the intersection of Green Bay Avenue and Capitol Drive. I decided to give it a try.

A ton-and-a-half stake truck picked up a group of us and drove us, standing up in the back, out into the countryside, where we were loosed on a field of radishes baking in the bright summer sun. It was all piecework. We pulled the radishes and made them into bunches, held by rubber bands. We were not paid by the bunch, but by the flat. Each flat held 24 bunches, and for that we received a nickel or a dime. We had 15 minute breaks in the morning and afternoon, and another 15 minutes for lunch.

The work was hot and hard, and gave me a lifelong appreciation for the travails of migrant workers. I lasted three days, each day earning only a few dollars. Still, I had no notion of going to college.

Later, as a soda jerk and clerk in Uncle Art's drug store, working after school and on Saturdays, I planned to follow my father and grandfather into the printing trade. Some of my friends scoffed at me. They went to work in the Nash automobile plant, where they earned upwards of $1.50 an hour. After high school graduation in 1953, my dad got me a job at Wisconsin Cuneo Press, where he worked, running a proof press in the composing room. The pay was $1.01 an hour, a penny more than I had made at the drug store.

But I already had my eye on an apprenticeship. I knew that would lead to journeyman status as a compositor, and I knew compositors made a lot more money—with strong union protection—than anybody in a factory.

High school social life wasn't much. I occasionally dated, but never had much feeling for any of the girls. Mostly, I enjoyed my small circle of friends. On Friday nights, we hung out at the Pig 'n' Whistle, a drive-in restaurant and frozen custard stand near Messmer. And later we took to hanging out at Joe's, a pool hall, where I honed my skills with a cue. As usual, I was somewhere in the middle—neither the best nor the worst.

The pool hall was in a basement catty-corner from my Uncle Warren's drug store. I played a lot with my best friend, Dick Neimon, because we were evenly matched. Dick had a steady girl friend, Margo Gasper, whom he eventually married and later divorced. Like me, he expected to get a trade, and he did—as an electrician. Later he rose to become the head of the Milwaukee electricians' union.

We spent many a Friday night at Joe's, "playing for time." It meant that, if you lost, you paid the 60 cents for the hour on the pool table. Our game was straight pool, 14-1, with each ball worth a point and the first to get 50 points was the winner. The better players would spot the less skilled 10, maybe 20 points and still beat them. Don Czech was the best in the joint, rarely losing to anyone. He was an absolute master with a cue, able to play position and run 10 or 15 balls easily, and he giggled constantly in a way that reminded me of Richard Widmark as the sadistic Tommy Udo in the movie, "Kiss of Death." Don regularly beat me, even when he'd spot me 20 balls. My proudest moment came when, angry at his superior attitude, I told him I'd shoot him straight, with no spot. I beat him by one or two balls. He'd had a bad game and I'd had a great one.

Cars had only AM radios and we listened to a disc jockey named Joe Dorsey, who mostly played the big band music of Artie Shaw, Tommy and Jimmy Dorsey, Glenn Miller, Benny Goodman and the other greats of the era. Our favorite singers were the Mills Brothers, Bing Crosby, Frank Sinatra, Ella Fitzgerald, Frankie Laine, Dinah Shore, Doris Day, Rosemary Clooney, Patti Page, Jo Stafford and Vaughn Monroe.

I never had a car, nor did any of my friends. My dad had mostly junkers, which I could occasionally borrow. One was a balky 1941 Hudson with a smashed right-front fender, which on a good day could reach an astonishing top speed of about 35 miles an hour. Dick Neimon's dad had a '47 Chevy, which was in much better shape. Sometimes my parents would let me drive the old Hud to school, so I didn't have to take the bus, and I'd occasionally get to drive it to the Pig on a Friday night.

I didn't participate much in extracurricular activities. I don't think I ever attended a Messmer football or basketball game, and the only thing I did outside of class was to take a bit part in our senior class play, a comedy called "The Mummy Steps Out."

2

TRANSITION

After high school, I left my uncle's drug store to take a job at Wisconsin Cuneo Press, where my dad worked as a pressman. I was hired as a proof boy, which meant I ran a hand-fed cylinder press to produce page proofs for the proofreaders. I was aiming for an apprenticeship. The mantra in our family was that a trade was something you could always fall back on.

My dad wouldn't let me apply in the pressroom. Too hot and dirty, he said, and he was right. He died of cancer at the age of 52, and it likely was caused not only by the unfiltered Camel cigarettes he smoked but by all the spray and solvents that were in the air in the gigantic pressroom where he worked, with its 74-inch flatbed cylinder presses that could print 32 pages of a magazine on one side of a sheet of paper.

Instead, I went to the composing room, where skilled tradesmen ran typesetting machines—Linotype, Intertype and Ludlow—and made up the pages and forms for the presses. It was as high-tech as anything, and I loved it, but not until I got my apprenticeship with the International Typographical Union. I hated running the hand-fed proof press. It was dull and boring: put the galley onto the press, run off the proofs, use type-wash solvent, a brass brush and a rag to scrub the ink off the type, put it away and grab another galley.

As an apprentice, I actually got to handle the type, make corrections, and follow layouts and fit engravings and type into ads and pages. It had a creative side, and I soon learned to insinuate myself into the affections of the best veterans in the shop so they would teach me the tricks of the trade. One older guy, Eddie, was an absolute master at crafting mathematical equations. He'd take a full galley of 150 or more metal lines of type, 30 picas (five inches) wide, and reduce them to a single equation maybe an inch or two in size, cutting pieces on the power saw as small as four or six points square (a 12th of an inch or less) and fitting them into the equation. The finished product had to "lift"—meaning that it had to be assembled so tightly that none of the pieces would come out when it was being hammered on a big printing press. Amazingly, Eddie could do that. And he taught me how to do it.

But I was most fascinated by the Linotype and Intertype machines, which clattered merrily away as the brass matrixes and space bands dropped into place, obedient to the fingers of the operator, who had to master a keyboard of 90 keys. It took a light touch and an understanding of how the machine worked because the operator often had to make simple repairs himself. If something got crooked, or the line wasn't full, sometimes you got a squirt, which meant the melted lead that was molded into lines of type got loose and shot into areas where it didn't belong—sometimes burned onto the operator. Then you had to take it all apart and clean it up. Or the matrixes would jam as a long arm returned them to the magazine on top of the machine.

I was so enamored of the Linotype that once I learned the basics, I volunteered to work on it at every opportunity. When I became proficient, I spent many nights doing my entire shift at the keyboard. Sometimes I'd set type for pulp magazines—science fiction and detective stories, or astrology. I didn't read the stuff unless it was really interesting because that slowed me down. Mostly, I delighted in "hanging the elevator," which meant keeping the machine running as fast as it was capable, and setting clean, error-free type.

In those Cold War days, the United States and the Soviet Union had made a few half-hearted attempts to keep communications going, despite the animosity that infected the relationship. Part of the effort involved two slick and colorful magazines that contained upbeat propaganda: Amerika, published by the U.S. in the Soviet Union in Russian, and Soviet Life, published by the Soviets in the U.S. in English. Cuneo had the printing contract for Soviet Life, and we set the type and made up the pages. The magazine was printed in the pressroom downstairs.

A makeup editor came in once a month to supervise the final pages and make any last-minute changes. The Soviets sent a man named Valeri Yuryev, and I got to know him slightly when I made corrections in the galleys. At the time, I also was a budding journalist at Marquette University, which had a student-produced quarterly literary magazine, the Marquette Journal. Though I mostly worked for the semiweekly newspaper, the Marquette Tribune, I queried the Journal editors to see if they wanted a story.

The result was my first published magazine article, "My Communist Boss," which ran in the Journal. It was a first-person account of working with Yuryev. Suspicious of anything Communist, I had not told Yuryev that I was doing a story. But he found out and kidded me because I had misspelled his first name. I was mortified.

It was a valuable journalistic lesson. Throughout my subsequent years as a reporter, I never again blind-sided a source. The first thing I customarily told a new congressman in Washington was that I would never write something said in an off-handed way in a casual conversation at a reception or fund-raiser. But I reserved the right to pursue it later if it was a possible story. The principle stood me in good stead. I learned many more things than I would have if people had thought of me as an open microphone.

MILITARY SERVICE, SORT OF

As a 17-year-old junior at Messmer, I had joined the Air Force Reserve. I learned about it from classmates who were doing the same. It was 1952, there was fighting in Korea, and there was the draft. Along with most of my friends, including my best friend, Dick Neimon, the goal was to get out of high school, get a job and buy a car. But we also expected to get drafted and sent to Korea.

The Reserve looked cool, despite the fact that it didn't get you an exemption from the draft. You got a bunch of dress and fatigue uniforms, complete with shoes, socks and gloves, and a neat dark blue raincoat without any insignia that you could wear with your civilian clothes, though that was not an approved use. And it paid you double what a regular airman earned on the one weekend a month you spent training at Gen. Mitchell Field, the Milwaukee airport where the 438th Fighter-Bomber Wing was based.

In the summer of 1953, after barely squeezing out enough credits to graduate from Messmer, I took my first airplane ride, went to my first Air Force Reserve two-week summer camp and saw my first nude women. They flew us in C-119 Flying Boxcars to Atterbury Air Force Base, near Columbus, Ind., a town that was distinguished by its claim that it had more churches per capita than any city in the country, and also by the fact that the American Legion post sponsored weekend stripteases and nude dancing in a tent connected to a stage that flipped down from the side of a semi-trailer truck. Of course we went.

I started out as an Airman Basic, a mechanic in the motor pool. (The 438th's mission later was changed and it became the 440th Troop Carrier Wing, flying the C-119s). I knew nothing about servicing cars or trucks, so I transferred to become a driver. That was boring, so I became a personnel clerk in the motor pool.

My boredom tempted me to quit. But then President Dwight D. Eisenhower signed a decree that granted draft exemptions to reservists like us. It meant that all we had to do to avoid slogging around as Army grunts in Korea was to fulfill our military obligation, which was to stick it out for eight years.

I was flipping through a manual of Air Force regulations on a training weekend when I came across a section on publications. The 440th had a crude, mimeographed newsletter for the troops, usually taken up by a column called "Commander's Call," which was booster stuff from the colonel in charge of the Wing.

The regulations said that an Air Force unit, active or reserve, could publish an "unofficial" newspaper. All you had to do was find a publisher who would print the paper without charge and, in return, would get 50% of the space to sell advertising. Revenue from the ads would go to the publisher.

By then, I was studying journalism at Marquette and had put in a summer working for the weekly South Milwaukee Voice-Journal, where I honed my journalism skills in 60-hour weeks, at the astounding salary of $45 a week, under Gordon Lewis, a quiet, principled but practical newsman, among the best I've ever known. He could be tough and uncompromising, but he also taught me that sometimes it was better to back off. I learned that one day when I was planning to relegate a public relations photo from Bucyrus-Erie to an inside page.

Bucyrus-Erie, a manufacturer of gigantic machinery for mining, earth-moving and other chores, was the biggest employer in South Milwaukee and a big advertiser in the Voice-Journal. So Lewis overruled me and the picture wound up on page one, as did most of the stuff from the big company. But I had no doubt that if it had been a story about malfeasance of a Bucyrus-Erie executive, it also would have gone on page one. Lewis was a pragmatist who made distinctions between what was transitory and what was important.

At the Voice-Journal, I did about everything you can do on a small newspaper. I reported and wrote stories, took pictures, pasted photographs on brown craft paper so they could be copied for engravings, rewrote the society news, which was submitted in longhand by our correspondent, edited stories, laid out the paper and, on Thursday afternoons, went in back to sub sections of the paper together before they went to the Post Office. Once when we were shorthanded and on deadline (and in violation of all that was holy in the International Typographical Union), I even sat down in that non-union shop and set some type on the Linotype machine. It was all exciting and fun.

Gen. Mitchell Field is only a few miles from South Milwaukee, so I figured the Voice-Journal would make a great publisher. I contacted Lewis, and the Flying Badger was born as a monthly newspaper. It ran anywhere from four to twelve tabloid-sized pages, with me producing the editorial content and the Voice-Journal filling up the ad space.

So now I was a military journalist. But I would not have lasted except for another benefactor, Leonard (Sam) Dereszynski. He was a plumber from the South Side of Milwaukee who was a pilot, a lieutenant colonel in the reserves and the deputy commander of the 440th. More importantly, despite his shortage of skills in that area, he had worked himself into a civil service job as the civilian public affairs officer of the 440th. He was interested in me and learning more about journalism.

My problem was that I had a martinet of a first lieutenant (later captain) who was in charge of the public affairs office on reserve training weekends. He was a public relations man for Allis-Chalmers, but mostly he was a jerk who wanted the only enlisted man under his command to be a soldier who saluted, wore a spiffy uniform and worked regular hours to the minute. When it came to journalism—even the elementary form I practiced on the Flying Badger—he was totally clueless.

I suffered under his glare for a time, figuring I'd eventually just quit the reserves and take my chances with the draft. But in a casual conversation with Sam, I mentioned my problem, and that was the end of it. As the deputy commander, Sam outranked my inept boss. I never knew what Sam said to him, but I was soon left to my own devices, not even required to wear my uniform on training weekends. I had one job: Get the Flying Badger out every month, which I did joyfully.

Sam became a lifelong friend. After I moved to The Journal's Washington bureau in 1970, he came out to visit. Happily, the visit coincided with one of the many problems we were having in the house we had bought in Annandale, Va. The kitchen sink stopped up and Sam reverted to the trade of his youth and fixed it for us.

THE MOVE TO JOURNALISM

My journalism career started with a vague notion and a lovely woman named Joy Steinel. I was 19 and she was several years older than I. I fell for her, but her interest in me was, alas, somewhat maternal. Joy knew the great Jeremiah L. O'Sullivan, the dean of the Marquette University College of Journalism, and she was kind enough to open doors for me there.

I already knew that I wanted to do something beyond the printing trade. I was almost two years into my apprenticeship, learning rapidly and full of the expectation that I could complete my six-year apprenticeship early (I did, in four and one-half years). Journalism intrigued me because it was directly related to printing. I also knew there might be some bucks in it. My dad's cousin, Joe Manning, was an advertising man who was doing very well.

Through the dean's secretary, Evarista (Evie) Hamilton, Joy set up an appointment for me with Dean O'Sullivan. I put on a jacket and tie and went to see him in his office at Copus Hall, which had been converted from an early 20th-century turreted mansion. I sat there nervously and told my story: I was an apprentice compositor with a terrible high school record, but realized that my journeyman's card would be as far as I could go. I wanted to go to college, and I wanted to study journalism.

O'Sullivan rarely spoke. He mostly growled his words, and had a booming laugh that sounded something like a Model T Ford cranking up on a cold day. "You're just the kind of people we need here," he rasped. "Come back tomorrow with $200."

Walking out, I thought I was done for. All the cash I had was a few dollars, and I couldn't go to my parents, who never were able to pay all the bills. But I did have my five-year-old 1949 Mercury coupe, which I had purchased for $500 and paid off. So I went to a finance company near my home and, sure enough, the guy there loaned me $200, with my Mercury as collateral. There was nothing like a credit check. He knew I lived in the neighborhood, and maybe he liked my story about wanting to go to college. I paid back the loan in small installments.

The next day, the dean put me on as an "adult special student," saying that if my grades were decent in my first semester I would be pro-

moted to regular freshman status. He did need a transcript of my high
school grades and credits, which I provided. But they were so dismal,
he told me, that he needed a waiver. So I traipsed out to Messmer
High School and told my story to the principal, Father Louis E. Rie-
del. He wrote a letter saying that despite my poor high school record,
he believed I could make it in college. I hand-carried it to the dean and
became a university student.

I never had to battle the registration lines to get the classes I wanted.
O'Sullivan simply decreed my schedule. In my first semester, I carried
four classes for 10 credits, bunched daily between 8 and 10 a.m. I'd get
off work at 6:30 a.m., drive home, change clothes, eat something and
head down to Marquette for classes. I usually studied in the morning
and afternoon, and went to bed around suppertime. The dean even got
me parking passes. One semester, he also invented a job for me.

As remarkable as that was, it wasn't the first time people had gone
out of their way to help me. At Cuneo Press, the International Typographical Union rules specified that, throughout the six-year apprenticeship, an apprentice was to alternate shifts every six months—days,
then second shift (4 p.m. to midnight) and the lobster shift (midnight
to 6:30 a.m.).

After I started at Marquette, the composing room foreman and the
chapel chairman (the ITU's name for the shop steward), allowed me
to stay on the lobster shift for almost the entire duration of my college
years. I did wind up working days and second shift in the summer,
but then it was back on the midnight to 6:30 a.m. shift for the school
year.

It meant that, with O'Sullivan's cooperation and the acquiescence
of my professors, I could schedule all my classes in the morning and
have afternoons and evenings for study and sleep. Still, I did manage
to abuse the schedule—and myself. I was required to take apprenticeship classes in such matters as layout and design at the Milwaukee Vocational School. They came on Monday afternoons and Friday nights,
and I was given time off from work for one, but not both.

I was still a member of the Air Force Reserve and had to spend one
weekend in training each month. And I had read about Jacques Cous-
teau and his invention of the Aqua Lung, and wanted to learn scuba
diving. So with my brother John and a friend, I signed up for scuba
diving lessons on Thursday nights at the Jewish Community Center.

My schedule went something like this: Midnight to 6:30 a.m. Monday through Friday at Cuneo, with half time off on Monday because of the apprentice class that day; five mornings a week at Marquette journalism; Monday afternoon and Friday evening at the Vocational School; Thursday night at the Jewish Community Center, and, once a month, all day Saturday and Sunday with the Air Force Reserve at Gen. Mitchell Field.

Needless to say, there were many times when I needed some slack. And it seemed as if everybody was ready to help and cooperate. My co-workers in the composing room at Cuneo, including the bosses, looked the other way when I'd snooze a little too long on a stone (a steel table where forms of type were assembled). Nobody was ever resentful, and I think they were proud of the fact that I was a college student.

BROTHER AND SISTERS

My sisters (there were five in all, aged 6 to 15), kept me from being fired. With devilish glee, they'd wake me up about 11 p.m., laughing and ducking when I threw things at them. But sometimes they'd come at me with a back massage or a head scratch, which turned me into a purring mass of blubber. But it got me to work on time.

While I was in college, my dad—looking for a way to augment his income—scraped up enough money to buy the Century Printing Co., a small business in downtown Milwaukee. Although Pop was a superb pressman, he was not much of a businessman, so it was never very profitable. There were cases of handset type, a 10x15-inch hand-fed platen press, which was good for printing envelopes and business cards, and a 12x18 Kluge platen press with an automatic feeder, which my dad used to produce beautiful four-color printing jobs, including labels for wine bottles. He was such an expert, especially on makeup—making colors register and impressions print uniformly—that even other printers didn't believe his work had been done on a platen press, which printed by banging two plates together, instead of on a cylinder press, which rolled over the type. The cylinder press was more precise and the overwhelmingly preferred method for color work.

Dad worked in the shop during the day, then closed down to go to work on the second shift at Cuneo Press. My brother, John, and I both worked in the shop, setting type and running the presses. We got very skilled on the hand-fed platen press. Because the shop had only monotype and foundry type, it had to be tediously hand-set. But sometimes I would take the copy to work at Cuneo Press and either set the type myself on a Linotype or Ludlow, or get someone else to do it. It was a common practice, called a "government job," among the compositors and pressmen—and even some supervisors—who had outside work. Still, I felt guilty about it, even though it helped my dad, and I swore that someday I would repay the company for all our "government" typesetting.

As my college load increased, I gradually drifted away from working in Pop's shop. Curiously, the business came with almost the same name as the Century Press, which my grandfather, Frank X., had owned with several partners many years before. It was a much larger enterprise, but my grandfather lost everything when his partners decided to move the business to Philadelphia. It all had been done with handshakes and, when Grandpa decided he didn't want to move, they went without him, with no compensation given. It soured the entire family on any sort of business for many years. Establishing a business was the one thing my grandparents would not loan money to my parents to do.

I felt bad for my brother John because my dad often excused me while insisting that John help out at the shop. I know Pop was proud of the fact that I was going to college, and I always felt that he favored me over John. But I didn't object or offer to ease the load on him. So John was one in a string of friends and family who propped me up.

THE PROFESSORS

In addition to my family, I had a lot of help at Marquette. All of my instructors and professors knew of my circumstances—tipped off by O'Sullivan or others, or briefed by me. I was never shy about sharing my situation, figuring it might make a difference, which it did. There were times when I missed a deadline on a paper, or had to reschedule an examination, and I usually got by without a penalty. At the end of my first semester, I had earned B grades in all four courses, and my status changed to that of a regular freshman.

A few professors stood out. The first was Robert Dufour, a good-humored but relentless young man who taught the journalism college's version of freshman English. It was a pure writing course, and Dufour pushed us to write, write, write—articles, short fiction, news features, rhetoric. I sweated over them, but developed a love for putting words on paper. I was terrible at the rules of grammar, but fortunately Dufour didn't care and didn't bother to put us through the misery of learning them. I didn't know a gerund from a toilet seat, but I had a feel for what was correct and what flowed, and I never had a problem with spelling. At a minimum, I learned the journalist's craft of stringing together declarative sentences to make ideas understandable.

In my second year, it was Donald K. Ross and second-semester sophomore reporting. Ross had a dry, impish sense of humor that he kept well hidden behind a dour and uncompromising demeanor, which most of us discerned early on. First-semester reporting consisted of classroom exercises in learning how to construct a news story—writing leads (ledes in journalism jargon), putting the important elements in the inverted-pyramid style of writing, getting names with proper titles or other identification, and, most of all, writing tightly. But the second semester was the real stuff. It consisted of a one-hour lecture and a four-hour lab each week, which Ross operated as if he were the city editor and we were reporters chasing stories on a p.m. newspaper. We received assignments at 8 a.m. and had to go out, get the story, return and write it before the noon deadline. It was close to reality because The Milwaukee Journal, only a few miles away, was a p.m. and Ross patterned his class after it.

Ross was more than a teacher. Like Dufour, he went out of his way to challenge any student he thought was worth the effort. That meant he worked them harder than the rest, and I was fortunate to be among them. Where some of the budding reporters were going out and struggling to get short stories in on time, a few of us were cruising. So he just kept giving us more difficult assignments, and finally assigned a small group of us to do a series of stories on Milwaukee's Negro community and the problems of its people. So not only did we learn how to write stories on deadline, we also learned how to do interviews, and research and write comprehensively on more complex subjects.

Another professor, James Robb, was not in journalism but philosophy. At Marquette, although journalism had its own college, the subject basically was treated as a major in liberal arts, much like history or political science. Moreover, because it was a Jesuit institution, everybody in journalism or liberal arts had to take a minimum of 15 credit hours of philosophy. All it took was one extra course to get 18 credits, which gave you a minor. So it was only natural that most journalism majors also pursued minors in philosophy.

Robb was tall, amiable and laid-back, a perfect stereotype of the rumpled, pipe-smoking, absent-minded professor, except that he was anything but absent-minded. He had one of the finest minds I've ever seen, and an ability to gently nudge ideas around until they clicked into place in our young minds. The only course I ever took from him was Philosophy of Man, which emphasized Aristotle and Thomas Aquinas. Robb was a most open-minded man—always receptive to other disciplines and never condemnatory of any school of thought. Though he led us through—and I intellectually accepted—a philosophic proof for the existence of a First Cause in the universe, I also learned tolerance for ideas and principles other than my own—even those that were at odds with my own beliefs. My years as a reporter only reinforced those insights.

Many years later, two of my children—Becky and Joe—attended Marquette, and both took courses from Robb. In fact, though I had only taken the one Robb course, they each took several. He was still teaching the Philosophy of Man, which I was eager to discuss with them, thinking that they could refresh my memory on what I had learned decades earlier. But in typical Robb fashion, he had moved on, and the course was nothing like the one I remembered. I was not surprised, and was sure the ones he had taught my kids, several years apart, would not be the same either.

I never took a course from O'Sullivan, which I always regretted. I would have liked to know him better, but his courses never fit my schedule. It probably was for the better. Taking a course from him might have diminished my awe of the man. But he was always in the background, keeping tabs, though I was not conscious of it. It was said that he carried scholarships in his hip pocket for deserving students, and that he was the only lay dean in the university who could stand up to the Jesuit leadership. He had been a bureau chief in Kansas City for the United Press before quitting with a telegram to the New York headquarters that said, "Hours too long, pay too short. I quit." At Marquette, he ran a journalism college that some derided as a trade school. But he turned out a lot of solid reporters, editors and even public relations and advertising practitioners whose principles were rooted in honesty, fairness, accuracy and a determination to do what was right regardless of politics or pressure.

After finishing second-semester sophomore reporting with Don Ross, I was hooked. I lost all desire to pursue advertising. I was going to be a reporter, so I started writing stories for the Marquette Tribune, the semi-weekly published by the journalism college. Later I became the city editor and, in my senior year (actually, my fifth year because it took me that long to accumulate enough credits to graduate), I became co-editor along with Walt Gray, a promising fellow student whose great ambition was to get a journalism job away from his native Hawaii, which he said was a stifling place to live.

The job paid a half-tuition scholarship, so I didn't have that much money to make up, and by then I was making good wages as a journeyman compositor and Linotype operator, working mainly in the composing room at The Milwaukee Journal. Earlier, however, I had overextended myself and gotten into financial difficulty. I got rid of my old '49 Mercury with the busted driver's seat and bought a brand-new car—a 1957 Ford Custom two-door, as bare bones a conveyance as you could find, with a six-cylinder engine, AM radio and three-on-the-tree manual shifter. It was gray with a gray interior and grayer prospects, and cost $2,350. I came to hate it when the rattles started. Moreover, the payments shorted me, partly because I always paid room and board to my parents.

Thus overextended, I poured out my plight to O'Sullivan. I could increase my hours at the printing trade, but it would interfere with my work on the Tribune. O'Sullivan simply created a job for me. For one semester, I became the advertising director of the Marquette Press. It had its own composing room, non-union because of its university ownership, so I couldn't work there as a compositor. Mainly, its purpose was to publish books and papers, train students in typography, and print the Marquette Journalism College publications: the Tribune; The Journal, which was the quarterly magazine, and the Hilltop, the yearbook.

My hours totaled about 20 a week, tailored to my class and editor's schedules, and O'Sullivan decreed that I would be paid the same amount of money as I would make running a Linotype machine at The Journal. It amounted to about $60 a week—a princely sum even for full-time work at the time. The job was simplicity itself. All I had to do was lay out the ad pages for the different publications, something I could easily do in less than 20 hours a week. So I hung out, and even helped teach parts of the typography courses, showing young journalism students how to hold a stick to set hand type, and how to read it upside-down, left-to-right and bottom to top.

COLLEGE FRIENDS, LOVE AND A JOB

Though my social life during the Marquette years was almost nonexistent, I met three of my best friends there, fell in love with a journalism coed, got dumped and met and pursued my future wife, Sharlene. The first friend was Ray L. Enderle, an amiable and instantly likable Texan who was at Marquette for only a year to get his journalism credits. He had quit the Redemptorist order before being ordained a priest and later served in the Navy, working as a shipboard journalist. Both he and John P. Doyle, a dour but funny Air Force veteran from Menomonie, Mich., were older than me, and we hit it off instantly as the old-timers' cadre among all the young journalism students.

John and I remained close after college, when I went to work at The Milwaukee Journal and he became a reporter at the Green Bay Press-Gazette. In later years, after his marriage collapsed, we drifted apart. He died of Alzheimer's disease in 2005.

Ray and I continued as lifelong best friends and colleagues. He worked as a reporter at the New Bedford (Mass.) Standard-Times, the Wall Street Journal in San Francisco and the Philadelphia Bulletin before leaving daily journalism to become a public relations manager at Sun Oil Co.

The coed was Bernadette (Bernie) Wolf, from the Iron Range city of Hibbing in Minnesota. I believed she was as unreasonably in love with me as I was with her, but she ultimately lost interest and briefly dated another journalism student before marrying William Janz, who went to work for the Milwaukee Sentinel—and later the Milwaukee Journal Sentinel—and morphed from reporter into the sort of empathetic, people-oriented columnist for which any newspaper editor would sell his first-born.

In those days in the 1950s, some of the male journalism students, all white, lived in an upper flat on Walnut St. in Milwaukee's black community, not far from the downtown Marquette campus. We called it "the Walnut Arms" and often went there to party on weekends. One of them was Bob Harlan, who was a few class years ahead of me, though about my age. A sports nut, he eventually went on to become president of the Green Bay Packers.

Another Walnut Arms denizen was one of my best friends at Marquette, Jim Cotter, who was from Connecticut and later was a grooms-man at my wedding. Cotter was an indifferent student, a horrible self-abuser—at one point, he was hospitalized for malnutrition because he'd been living on pizza and chocolate milk—one of the few true wits I've ever met, and a steadfast friend who would not hesitate to sacrifice himself for anyone he regarded highly.

Near the Walnut Arms was a tavern called the White Rose Inn, where we occasionally went to party and argue about the state of Marquette and the world. Though the drinking age was 21, the owner seldom checked IDs. The bar had a hall upstairs, which the Marquette chapter of Sigma Delta Chi rented for informal initiations of new members.

The fraternity, now called the Society of Professional Journalists, was classified as professional, which meant no hi-jinks. But that didn't stop the guys from informally inducting the new recruits. Cotter and I were taken in at the same time. We didn't know the routine, but I learned it first because my name started with A and I was first in line.

We had to write a song and then sing it in the darkened upstairs room, lighted only by candles. As I sang, someone set the piece of paper on fire with a candle and, as it burned in my hands, someone else doused it with beer. Then I was told by a voice in the room that because I was going to become a journalist, I had to come up with an original thought in five seconds or suffer the consequences.

I did not, and part of a pitcher of beer was poured over my head. I was then told to stand off to the side to witness the humiliation of the other pledges. Soon Cotter came in, sang his song, had the song sheet set on fire and doused with beer, and was told to come up with an original thought in five seconds. To my knowledge, he's the only one who ever passed the test.

He thought for a second, then said: "Quote from Franklin Delano Roosevelt: 'I've been in peace. I've been in war. I've been in Eleanor. I'll take war.'"

Cotter went on to become a television newsman and an international development specialist. Iconoclastic, profane and self-indulgent, he nevertheless spent most of his working life trying to improve the lot of the poor and dispossessed. Late in life, he became a teacher and said that he always preferred teaching juvenile delinquents to the well-behaved middle-class kids.

THE NEWSPAPER REPORTER

In the spring of 1960, the pressure was on. My duties as the Tribune's co-editor were winding down and I was into final exam time before graduation. I was working weekends and occasional weekdays running a Linotype at The Journal. But I didn't have a newspaper job, and I was determined not to be working in the printing trade after graduation.

The conventional wisdom was that an ambitious young journalism grad should go to work at a medium-sized daily to get a couple years of experience before moving to a paper like The Journal. The problem was that they didn't pay much—maybe $65 to $80 a week. I had a notion that I shouldn't get less than $100 a week as a reporter. After all, the weekly wage for a journeyman compositor, which I could make anywhere, was then $130 a week. So I set my sights on The Journal, which I knew was a step up and obviously could pay more.

I got an appointment with the managing editor, Arville Schaleben, and went in to sell myself. His first reaction was that I had no experience. The Journal, he said, only hired reporters who had earned their spurs at smaller newspapers. I countered that I had some experience—one summer at the South Milwaukee Voice-Journal, under the editor Gordon Lewis, and my work on the Flying Badger. That counted for something. Schaleben knew Lewis and his reputation as a stalwart and skilled newsman. But it was only one summer on a weekly.

Then I played my trump card. I told Schaleben I had been working weekends in The Journal's composing room with Leon Hughes and Bob Stoke. Hughes was a great reporter as well as an editor, who covered both labor and politics. Stoke was a crusty copy editor who related as much to the back shop guys as he did to reporters and editors. They alternated Sunday afternoons as makeup editors for the Monday WUP edition. The WUP, which stood for "Wisconsin-Upper Peninsula," was a morning paper in northern Wisconsin and the Upper Peninsula of Michigan. On every day but Monday, it was mostly a re-plate of the final afternoon edition of the day before, but for Monday it had to be fresh because the whole state got the Sunday morning paper.

The Monday WUP was the smallest paper of the week, and it was entirely put together by either Hughes or Stoke from the wire services, stories from stringers and standing type. When I worked Sundays, I often was on the head-letter Linotype, the one on which smaller headlines were set. Larger headlines were set on the Ludlow, which I also could handle. But because the WUP was my only responsibility, there was a lot of dead time, which I used to pester Hughes and Stoke to let me help out. I proofread corrections and helped rewrite headlines that didn't fit.

My argument to Schaleben was simple: Maybe I didn't have daily newspaper experience, but I knew the system at The Journal. I knew the stylebook, I knew the headline counts and I could write headlines, I knew how copy flowed from the newsroom to the composing room, I knew how to make tear sheets and corrections, I could proofread the galley proofs and, thanks to my Marquette and Voice-Journal training, I knew how to report and write a news story—in short, nobody would have to train me to do anything. Experience would come with time.

Schaleben didn't seem particularly impressed, but he didn't close the door. He asked me how much money I wanted. I said I thought $100 a week was reasonable. He said he'd let me know. I asked if I could check in with him from time to time. He said okay.

Over the next two or three weeks, whenever I had a break from working in the fifth-floor composing room, I ran down the stairs to the fourth-floor newsroom and poked my head in Schaleben's office. "Anything yet?" Usually he'd just shake his head, sometimes with a smile on his face, so I wasn't put off.

Graduation, on June 5, was looming. The last week in May, I stuck my head in Schaleben's office once more with my usual question. This time, he said, "How much did you say you wanted?" I almost peed in my pants. "$100," I said. "How about $95?" he replied.

I worked my final night in The Journal's composing room on Saturday, June 4, 1960, setting classified ads—not news copy—on a Linotype. The next day, Sunday, I went through the Marquette graduation ceremony in my cap and gown, at age 25. On Monday morning, June 6, I reported to work on the fourth floor at The Journal.

I was, by God, a reporter—at $35 a week less than I'd been making as a compositor. I never looked back.

3

THE JOURNAL NEWSROOM

The Journal newsroom in that summer of 1960 should have been an intimidating place. It had a reputation among outsiders as an aloof and arrogant place, which it had every right to be given its status as one of the best newspapers in the country. But I never felt that. On the contrary, only a few people ignored the new kid. Most of them went out of their way to help.

One standout episode happened only a few days after I had started when Wade Mosby came over to introduce himself. He was the city hall reporter, and by reputation one of the best reporters and writers in the room. He handed me a box with file cards inside. It contained the names and phone numbers of all the sources he had gathered in his years at The Journal, and he said I was welcome to copy them. It was a mother lode for a Milwaukee reporter, and I eagerly copied everything onto my own cards.

Rod Van Every was another influence. A rewrite man, he was lightning fast with a story on deadline, and he reminded me of some of the printers I had worked with over the years—men who were superb at what they did and disdained promotions. They were like the storied, tough sergeants who hated even the idea of becoming officers. Van Every had a gruff, iconoclastic manner and had turned down promotions, saying he didn't want to be an editor. If he had taken the promotions when first offered, he likely would have wound up running the newsroom. In later years, he relented, and ultimately became the city editor—one of the best ever, though he was in superb company.

In time, Van Every reminded me of Don Ross at Marquette. But in the beginning, he drove me nuts. In addition to doing obits, one of my jobs was as a swing reporter, filling in for the beat reporters on their days off. Early on, I was not trusted with anything as lofty as city hall, so I often ended up on the news-starved Federal Building beat. At the time, it was considered near the bottom of the ladder, only half a rung above obits, mainly because not much ever happened there. The court cases often were civil matters without much general interest, the U.S. marshals basically guarded the building and served subpoenas, and the U.S. attorney's office, when it had a story, usually was tight-lipped, especially to a substitute reporter who didn't know anybody personally.

Jim Wieghart, who ultimately became editor of the New York Daily News, was the only reporter who managed to make something of the beat, mainly because of his skill at cultivating confidential sources and his near-evangelistic fervor for chasing only big stories. But whenever I substituted on the federal beat, I usually wound up visiting every office and coming up empty-handed, except for Dyer Act stories.

It seems strange now, but The Journal actually ran stories on Dyer Act violations—a federal offense for taking a stolen car across a state line. Almost universally, they were one-paragraph fillers in the paper, and sometimes they didn't run at all. But I was required to pick them up and phone them in to Van Every, who usually was the late rewrite man.

In the beginning, I'd pull together just enough information for the one-paragraph story. But that was never enough for Van Every. He asked me more questions than I even thought existed about those simple stories, sending me back time after time until he was satisfied. It ticked me off, as it did other young reporters who had the misfortune to phone information to Van Every. We used to gripe that if he were writing a story on the crucifixion of Christ, he'd want to know the penny size of the nails.

But it gradually dawned on me that Van Every was doing to me just what Don Ross had done at Marquette. Without letting on that he was doing anything except trying to understand the facts, he was running his own training school for young reporters. After that, it became a game. I'd scoop up every fact, and plug every hole I could think of in any story I had to phone into Van Every. I got good at it, too. He'd ask a far-out question, and I'd have the answer. It taught me a valuable lesson in how to tackle a story. When he decided I didn't need the harassment any more, he'd quietly give me other tips. One was to always carry a pencil and some dimes; the pencil in case a ballpoint pen froze or ran out of ink, and dimes for the pay phone. Both came in handy when I had to cover a five-alarm fire in below-zero weather.

The other was something that stood me in good stead throughout 40 years of reporting. The Van Every school of journalism taught that once you had all the reporting done on a story and you were ready to write it, you'd pause, think about it some more and then make one extra phone call, or do one more interview, or seek out one additional fact. There were countless times over the years when that one bit of advice made a mediocre story good, or a good story great, or saved my butt from making a big mistake.

Van Every was forever railing, usually with sarcastic comments, against young reporters becoming emotionally or otherwise involved in stories they covered—especially on volatile issues like civil rights. More than once, he'd mutter under his breath as he read a story I had written—not because there was anything wrong with the story, but simply to keep me aware that he was watching for any sign of editorializing on my part.

After I started covering the civil rights beat, and Van Every was spending increasing amounts of time as an assistant city editor, he came to me one day and said I was ignoring a great civil rights story— the plight of American Indians in Wisconsin. I could not disagree, so he put me on "special" for a few days, which meant that I would have no duties other than to background myself on Indian issues, mainly by reading clips in the library. He also arranged for me to take a trip to some of the reservations in northern Wisconsin to meet tribal leaders.

SWEET REVENGE

In the course of reading the clips, I came across a yellowed, one-paragraph item from years before. It said that Rod Van Every, the Indian affairs reporter for The Milwaukee Journal, had been made a blood brother in the Consolidated Tribes of American Indians for his comprehensive and understanding coverage of Indian issues.

Gotcha! I almost laughed out loud. Here was this guy ragging me about getting involved in the civil rights stories I covered, and he had been guilty of the same thing himself.

I made a copy of the clip and stashed it in a drawer in my desk. Months later, after covering a night civil rights meeting, I came in early the next morning to write the story. I was on rewrite and Van Every was the city editor that day. I wrote the first take and flipped it into the wooden box on his desk. He picked it up, started reading and started muttering under his breath about young reporters getting emotionally involved in their stories. I knew I had written a straight story, and he was just kidding me, but it was my chance. I reached into the drawer, grabbed the copy of the clipping and flipped it into the box.

Van Every picked it up, read for a moment and then, without looking up, said: "Okay, Auk, you son of a bitch. You got me."

He never again, kidding or otherwise, accused me of getting involved in a story. But he had made his point, and I never forgot it.

Van Every usually called me "Auk." It was the abbreviation I used for my name at the top of the page when I wrote a story. But it became more than that when Van Every found a book that had been discarded from the Milwaukee Public Library and gave it to me. It was a novel, titled *The Great Auk*, by Allan W. Eckert. It told the dramatic and sad story of a flightless penguin-like bird that migrated 3,000 miles each year from Eldey Island in the North Atlantic to the Carolinas. The great auk, which was monogamous, was hunted into extinction in the early 1840s. I embraced the nickname, mostly tongue-in-check because of the "great" part.

Richard S. Davis still worked in the newsroom when I started as a reporter in 1960. He was the most renowned of all The Journal reporters, with a writing style that could meld fact, emotion and rhetoric in stories that were worth reading for their own sake, regardless of the subject or any time element. Several times, The Journal published book collections of his stories. I knew him only as a gruff old man at a desk in the front of the newsroom, with eyeglasses so thick they looked like the bottoms of Coke bottles and who, despite that, had to hold the newspaper about an inch from his glasses to read it. His acolyte and ardent admirer was Alicia Armstrong, a liberal-leaning reporter who backed up David Runge as the religion editor and, as a consummate animal lover, eventually became the beat reporter for and chief promoter of the Milwaukee County Zoo. Both Davis and Armstrong were staunch supporters of John F. Kennedy, then battling Hubert H. Humphrey for the Democratic presidential nomination.

Kindly and knowledgeable, with a demeanor that would suit an archbishop, Runge belied that with no-nonsense reporting, and was regarded as one of the finest religion writers in the world. One time, both he and Armstrong were both away at the same time, and for two weeks after some Runge tutoring I was the replacement, putting out the Saturday church pages and covering whatever spot stories came along. I was fascinated. Suddenly I was back in the world of philosophy and ideas I had enjoyed at Marquette, especially in Robb's philosophy course. I did a big takeout on the Church of Jesus Christ of Latter-Day Saints, a religion I knew nothing about until then.

On another occasion, again during vacation time, I spent two weeks as the garden editor, mostly filling the pages with standing type and wire copy because I didn't know anything about flowers and vegetables, and couldn't fake it as I had as an 18-year-old working in a nursery. When finally forced to write something on my own, I turned to something I did know a little about, and wrote a piece on how to maintain a lawn mower engine.

I was an eager beaver in the newsroom. In the afternoons, when there wasn't much going on, I volunteered to do feature stories, which led to personal-participation stories on automobiles, motorcycles, scuba and skin diving, and even spelunking. On Saturday nights, which were often dull when nothing happened, I'd go over to the local copy desk and offer to edit copy and write headlines to reduce the usual pile of "time copy"—stories that weren't imminent and could be used as filler any time.

As I had as an apprentice compositor, I sought out the veteran reporters and tried to learn the skills and shortcuts of the craft. To a man and woman, they were uniformly helpful—even those who had reputations as crotchety curmudgeons. I managed to get along with everybody, but I couldn't always charm the assistant city editor, Bob Wills, who handled assignments and schedules. I even missed a wedding reception one time because he wouldn't let me off the Saturday night shift. Wills went on to become the editor of the Milwaukee Sentinel and the publisher of the Milwaukee Journal Sentinel.

In the 1960s, my contemporaries on The Journal staff were a talented young crew, and I counted myself fortunate to be among them. They included Paul Salsini, who had been a couple of years ahead of me at Marquette, and Dick Vonier, a funny, great reporter and writer who moved to Arizona, where he became a magazine editor and eventually succumbed to alcoholism.

Among the others: Dave Mitchell, a profane iconoclast and police rewrite man who went to Tucson about the same time as Vonier and eventually left the news business for other ventures; Bruce Brugmann, a talented arts reporter and muckraker who moved west and founded the San Francisco Bay Guardian; Dave Behrendt, a serious, knowledgeable and productive education reporter who later became The Journal's editorial page editor; his successor on education, Dave Bednarek; Chuck Buelow, a sharp police reporter who went on to university public relations; Paul Hayes, a brilliant and sometimes arrogant environment and science reporter; Charles Morgan, a buttoned-down reporter who became an editor at the Readers Digest; Pat Graham, a sarcastic, tough and talented city hall reporter who went on to become city editor and political coordinator; Jim McCulla, my deskmate for years, who covered economics while I covered civil rights, had eight kids and eventually became Sen. Gaylord Nelson's press secretary and then deputy public affairs director of the National Aeronautics and Space Administration, and my best friend at The Journal, Chris Lecos, a principled and skeptical reporter who did hard-hitting stories for the Home Section and, later, led one of our investigative teams.

A Greek-American, Chris left The Journal to join his brothers in the restaurant business in Maryland and Virginia. It went belly-up in the high-interest Jimmy Carter years and Chris later became a press spokesman for the Food and Drug Administration in Washington. A heavy smoker who refused to quit even though he knew it was killing him, he died of lung cancer.

The young reporters were surrounded in the newsroom by some of the best and brightest veterans anywhere: Alex Dobish, a dogged reporter who could dig a front-page story out of almost anything, including obits; exacting science and space reporter Harry Pease, who became furious if an editor dared to so much as change a comma in his copy; humorist and classicist Gerald Kloss, who could quote Shakespeare out of his head and would put together columns such as "Shakespeare on Mowing the Lawn"; David Runge, the kindly religion reporter; Wade Mosby, the knowledgeable and fearless government reporter who later became editor of the Green Sheet, The Journal's daily entertainment section; pipe-smoking Bob Wells, feature writer extraordinaire, who likely made more money free-lancing outside than his Journal salary; Walter Monfried, a distracted egghead reviewer of classical music; Avery Wittenberger, who knew more about county government than anybody in the government and whose stories were as complete as they were dull, and many others.

The Journal had the finest photo-journalism staff in the country, with great shooters like Jim Stanfield, who went on to become the all-time top photographer at the National Geographic. Others included George P. (Sam) Koshollek, John Ahlhauser, Hank Larson, Jim Meyers, Sherman Gessert, Fred Tonne, Dick Bauer, Allan Y. Scott and Irv Gephardt. They were consummate professionals all, and no young reporter like me was ever allowed to tell them how to take pictures when we were on assignments together. In later years in Washington, I occasionally had to hire free-lance photographers and always became disgusted when they'd whine and ask for detailed instructions on how to take their pictures. I had been spoiled.

We also had incredibly well-educated and well-read copy editors who could smell out errors and inconsistencies with bloodhound-like persistence They included acerbic Eddie Caplan, the local copy desk chief; gentle Tom Barber; harsh Howard Fibich on the news desk; Stuart Hoyt, who knew about eight languages, and Leonard Scheller, a bachelor graduate of Marquette University who collected Rouault prints and donated them to the university.

TWO COLUMN "POPE PRAY"

Scheller, a devout Catholic, often served as the makeup editor in the composing room for The Journal's nod to old-fashioned tabloid journalism. It was called the Peach Sheet, a single newspaper page, printed on both sides, with late stock market quotations, sports scores and late-breaking tabloid-style stories. Pale peach in color, it was wrapped around the final edition of the day's Journal as a spur to street sales. It featured large, provocative headlines and even an occasional pinup photograph.

But not when Scheller was upstairs on makeup. Any time he had a hint that a scantily-clad female might wind up in the Peach, he axed it in favor of some dull engraving of a file photograph languishing in a dark galley somewhere. But somebody on the Picture Desk figured out that Scheller never got to actually see the photographs that were dummied in the Peach, and was going by the slugs. In those days, stories carried one-word slugs ("fire" or "shoot") while pictures had size designations with two-word slugs, such as "lake boats."

So naturally, knowing Scheller, when the picture desk had a particularly enticing shot of a young starlet, the dummy would go to the composing room with a slug of "two-column pope pray" or some other comforting designation.

In those days we were proud of our newspaper and were among its toughest critics. We all knew we worked for one of the top papers in the country. In various surveys, The Journal almost always ranked in the top 10; in one, the paper came up in the top five. But though I think we were all secretly puffed up about our paper's stature, we'd scoff at the surveys and how they were conducted, and we constantly criticized the editors for perceived shortcomings. Unlike some of the attitudes I saw in the newsroom many years later, when the operating attitude was the mighty Me, our major concerns had to do with whether we thought somebody was doing something to diminish The Journal's quality, independence or fearlessness.

At one point, a few of us set up after-hours bull sessions in The Journal cafeteria. We persuaded Mrs. Foster, the cafeteria manager, to cater a fixed-menu dinner for $1 apiece, and we invited everyone in a position of power. Our first guest was none other than Irwin Maier, the chairman of the board. He paid his dollar, ate his meal and answered questions, some fairly hostile, for more than an hour. In other sessions, our guests included top editors. The sessions eventually died out, but they reduced the rumors and gripes in the newsroom.

4

LOVE AND MARRIAGE

Okay, so I stalked Sharlene.

The saddest time of my 24 years was a bleak day in October, 1959, when I was still a journalism student at Marquette and working part-time as a journeyman compositor at The Milwaukee Journal.

I was setting news copy on a Linotype machine in The Journal's composing room. But I was anguished, in a numb fog, because it was the day that the woman who dumped me, Bernadette Wolf, married Bill Janz. We three had been fellow journalism students at Marquette. Many years later, we are distant friends with our own children and grandchildren, and I can testify that it was all for the best—one of those unanswered prayers.

Weeks later, still in an inconsolable haze over the loss of Bernie, I noticed a cute, dark-haired girl in The Journal cafeteria. She wore short skirts, high heels and had great legs—gams, as we used to say then. It was at least a distraction from my emotional woes, at best maybe something more. I was determined to figure out a way to meet her.

I used the reporter's training I had learned at Marquette. The first step was The Journal's library and back issues of The Little Journal, the newspaper's house organ. I knew that it always ran half-column head shots of new employees, so I simply flipped through the pages of the back issues until I found Sharlene's photograph, with her first initial and last name. That's all there was. It was confusing because it listed her first initial as "D." because her first name is Deanna. She always used her middle name.

Thus armed, I went to the telephone directory, but found no listing. So I surreptitiously followed her after she left for the day along with the other ad takers from the classified ad department (I already had followed her to learn where she worked in the building).

I saw that she caught a southbound bus on 3rd St. at the corner of State St. Determined to offer her a ride, I got into my '57 Ford one day and timed it so I was at the stoplight on 3rd St. while she stood on the island waiting for her bus. I was no more than two feet away from her, window wound down and heart thumping, but I chickened out and did not speak to her.

So I followed the bus, leapfrogging it as it made its stops. She finally got off at Mineral St and walked west. I circled the block, but she never crossed 4th St., so I deduced that she lived somewhere on Mineral between 3rd and 4th.

Thus armed, I went back to The Journal newsroom and, using the city directory and the street-address telephone directory, learned that she "roomed" in an upper flat with someone named Spasoff. It turned out to be the current married name of her mother, Ethel.

On a Sunday afternoon, I telephoned her and blurted out the whole story of how I had stalked and researched her. She said later that she was ironing at the time—not a chore she particularly enjoyed—so she agreed to go out with me. I arrived a few hours later.

It was still daylight, so we played miniature golf. Then we went to a German beer hall for sandwiches and a beer. I remember thinking, because of her olive complexion, that she might be part Negro. But it was her Greek heritage. I didn't care. She was pretty and fun to be around, and we started dating steadily.

In 1959 and 1960, it was my last of five years at Marquette, and a busy time. I worked part-time as a Linotype operator at The Milwaukee Journal, and was the co-editor of the semiweekly Marquette Tribune, in addition to attending the classes I needed to graduate. Often, on Monday or Wednesday evenings, when we put the Tribune to bed, I would slip out early, telling everyone I had to go "study a little Greek."

Sharlene then was working as a sales clerk in a dress shop on Wisconsin Ave., only a few minutes from Copus Hall, the MU journalism headquarters. So I'd drive down to pick her up for a few hours of cuddling.

We soon became serious, but I had nagging doubts, probably because not enough time had passed since Bernie's marriage. Sharlene and I talked obliquely about possibly getting married, but I said I wasn't sure. She made it clear that she didn't want to continue indefinitely in limbo.

At the time, Marquette University required all of its Catholic students to attend an annual religious retreat. The university sponsored a general retreat, but students also could attend retreats sponsored by approved organizations. I decided to attend the retreat for MU members of Sigma Delta Chi, the Journalism fraternity. It was held at a monastery outside Milwaukee, and I spent the weekend fervently praying about a whole bunch of things, including getting married.

By Sunday afternoon, I had made up my mind. I knew where Sharlene would be: in the office of a young priest in Marquette's Johnston Hall, where she was taking instructions in Catholicism. I had nothing to do with that. Raised in the Greek Orthodox Church, she had become disillusioned with its attitude toward women, including not allowing them to receive communion when they were menstruating, because they were considered "unclean."

It was like something out of a romance movie. I walked into the main corridor on the first floor of Johnston Hall just as she was leaving the priest's office. We ran toward each other, met, hugged and kissed, and I led her into the chapel, where we knelt down and I proposed.

We were married in Gesu Catholic Church, next door to Johnston Hall, on Aug. 6, 1960, two months after I left Marquette and the printing trade, and started as a newspaper reporter. My brother, John, was the best man, and my college friends, John Doyle and Jim Cotter, were the groomsmen. Ray Enderle would have been there as well, but he was getting ready to marry Denise Cormier the following Saturday, Aug. 13, in New Bedford, Mass., where he was working as a reporter on the Standard-Times.

I was the best man. Sharlene and I combined our honeymoon with the Enderle/Cormier wedding. We drove our little Saab 93 to Cape Cod for the honeymoon at Mrs. Cavanaugh's bed and breakfast in Brewster, Mass., and returned to New Bedford for the wedding.

On the honeymoon, I decided to test the power of the press. The Kingston Trio, one of the most popular musical groups in the country, appeared at Storyville, a venue on Cape Cod. We got tickets and, at the intermission, I went to the backstage door and showed my press pass. Sharlene and I were immediately invited in and we had a nice chat with Dave Guard, Nick Reynolds and Bob Shane. They invited us to stay backstage, which actually was upstairs, over the stage. We watched the second half of the concert through a hole in the floor, looking down on the performers. Later we decided it wasn't such a good idea because we couldn't hear very well. But it was exciting nonetheless.

We spent all the money we had received as wedding gifts—first on paying off the wedding reception, and then on our honeymoon. When we finally returned to Milwaukee, the gas tank was almost empty and we had 63 cents between us.

WE BUY A HOUSE

At The Journal, one of the newsroom icons was affable, pipe-smoking Robert W. Wells, the most prolific writer in the room. It was said that he earned more money free-lancing than he did as a Journal reporter and feature writer. He was the sort of reporter who could be sent anywhere to cover anything and was guaranteed to come back with a story—on deadline or not—that read as well as a good novel. He wrote a number of books, including one in 1970 titled, "This Is Milwaukee: A Colorful Portrait of the City that Made Beer Famous."

It had an opening paragraph that I always thought captured him and the town perfectly:

"It is not true that Milwaukee is exactly like every other American city, only more so. It has a distinctive personality, although not one that is as immediately apparent as San Francisco's foggy cosmopolitanism or Chicago's hopeful cynicism. Milwaukee is a place that grows on you gradually, like a beer belly."

By late 1964, Sharlene and I had three kids—Juliann, Matthew and Becky—and we were fed up with our lower flat on the west side and dealing with our chintzy landlord, a Milwaukee police detective. We talked about buying a house, but we had no money. In fact, we still owed a couple of hundred dollars we had borrowed from my sister, Cici. So I went to talk to Wells about it.

Puffing his pipe and lolling back in his chair as he usually did when there was nothing going on—I always admired Wells because he never pretended to be working; he'd simply sit there and read the paper or a book when he had no assignment—Wells took out his pipe and told me, with a straight face, that becoming a homeowner would transform me in two important ways: I would become a home handyman and a Republican. At first, good ol' gullible Frank took him seriously; then I got the gag.

The big hurdle, of course, was money. Well, Wells said, there's a way around that. Like virtually every other person in the newsroom, I had joined The Journal Credit Union. Wells pointed out that I could borrow $500 on my signature, and an additional $300 for every person

I could get to co-sign the loan. But he said I'd have to be careful because some people in the newsroom had been burned co-signing other loans.

Salvation was at hand. I ran down to the credit union, got the forms and, over the next couple of weeks, solicited everybody I thought might help—friends as well as acquaintances. As Wells had predicted, some said they had been burned before and would not sign, but it wasn't long before I had 20 signatures on my loan application—enough with my signature for a $6,500 loan. Sharlene and I settled on building a brand-new home in Cedarburg, about 20 miles north of Milwaukee.

We moved into the house in the summer of 1965. It had four bedrooms, one and one-half baths, a kitchen, dinette, family room with fireplace, living room, dining room, full basement and a two-car attached garage. The price was $25,000, without extras. We kept some of the money for incidentals and plunked the rest down as a down payment on a conventional mortgage at five and one-half percent interest. I worried about a credit check showing that I had borrowed the down payment. It would show that I did not have enough income to make the house payments and pay off the down payment. So I went to see Joe Kopp, the jovial, rotund head of the credit union, who made it a practice to send a card to every member on his or her birthday.

Kopp's answer was quick and final. "What they don't know," he said, "won't hurt them."

Over the next five years, we struggled financially, but we seemed to have guardian angels with dollar signs instead of halos hovering over us. I was constantly on the lookout for overtime and free-lance opportunities, which always seemed to arrive in the nick of time. I became a stringer for McGraw-Hill World News and Newsweek Magazine, and sold stories to the New York Herald-Tribune and Washington Star, on subjects as diverse as civil rights and automobiles. In addition, we had a friend in a vice-president at the Cedarburg State Bank, who could always be counted on for a short-term signature loan at a low interest rate. Before we moved to Washington in 1970, we had paid off the loan at the credit union.

I bought my first shares of Journal stock in 1963, having served the mandatory three years to participate in the employee ownership plan. I continued to buy the stock, always heavily leveraged, every time it was offered, which was a source of irritation with Sharlene. She'd argue that we didn't have money to buy shoes for the kids, and I kept buying the stock. But I had grown up with stories about how The Journal took care of its own, and was always a good place to work. Eventually, the stock—through periodic loans—put all four of our kids through college, paid for our two daughters' wedding receptions and settled us into a more-than comfortable retirement.

THE AUKOFER DYNASTY

Our first child, Juliann, was born April 26, 1961, about two weeks before our nine-month wedding anniversary. The gag then was that if you were rich people, you had a premature child. If you were ordinary folks like us, you had to get married. I wrote a news story about Juli's birth, and had it set in type and printed as a birth announcement. It was a "government job" at The Journal, but forgivable I think.

We started our married life in a one-room apartment on N. Cass St., on Milwaukee's east side. It had a small kitchenette, a small closet-like alcove off the bathroom, and a living room with a sofa bed.

But with Juli's arrival at St. Francis Hospital, we needed a bigger place, so we moved to an upper flat, also on Milwaukee's east side, on N. Newhall St. It had two bedrooms, a dining room, living room and kitchen. Our eighties-something landlord and landlady, crotchety Mr. and Mrs. Gunther, lived downstairs. We shared a garage on the alley out back. Later, we moved to 57th St. and then to Cedarburg.

When I went to The Journal's Washington bureau in 1970, we moved to Annandale, in Northern Virginia. Juli was 9 and our youngest, Joe, was 3. Juli attended Annandale Elementary School and Annandale High School, as did all three of our other children. After the turn of the millennium, all three of Juli's daughters also attended Annandale High.

We experienced financial and culture shock with our move to Washington. When we sold our house in Cedarburg to move to Washington, we were delighted to get $35,000. But we were slapped down by the high price of housing in the Washington area. Eventually, we paid $38,000 for the Annandale house, about 10 miles west of downtown Washington, which was not even a pale shadow of what we had left. It was a split foyer design—essentially a jacked-up ranch house with a mostly-finished basement—with four bedrooms, three baths, an L-shaped living and dining room, a small kitchen, a family room and a small utility room. There was no garage; just a cracked concrete slab out front.

We could have gotten a better house by moving out farther. But we had determined that to save money we would be a one-car family and I would take the bus to work. It also was within easy walking distance to Annandale Elementary School.

The house had been rented and was not in good condition. On the day the movers came, we spent part of the day at the house with Juli, ripping out the carpeting in the living room and dining room because it—and, as it turned out, the wood floor underneath—was soaked with stinking dog urine.

In the weeks following, as we battled plumbing and other problems, there were times when we sat on the floor and wept. Soon I had to go to work, so Sharlene was left at home to cope, which she did courageously but not without anger and tears. At least she had the car—our big 1970 Chevrolet Kingswood Estate station wagon, though the one-car idea didn't last too long because I came to passionately hate taking the bus to work. I also hated the smell of the boxwoods that flanked our front door, which were alien to a Wisconsin nose.

THE DOGS OF COMMUTING

It was a three-block walk to the bus stop, part of it down an unpaved lane inhabited by attack dogs that ran yapping out of yards whenever I walked past. Heart pounding, I often had to beat them off with my briefcase or a newspaper. Then the bus wended its way slowly down Columbia Pike to 14th St. and Constitution Ave., where I had another three-block walk to The Milwaukee Journal office in the National Press Building. Overall, the trip took about an hour and 15 minutes. On the way home, I had another long walk to the bus stop at 12th and Constitution. If I caught the 6:08 bus I could sometimes be home by 7:30. If I missed it, I did not arrive home until an hour later.

Juli was married on Apr. 5, 1986, to Enrique José Navarrete, who was born in Havana, Cuba, on May 17, 1964, and came to the United States with his parents in 1966 in the Fidel Castro-inspired exodus. They produced our first three grandchildren: identical twins Alyssa Ann and Rachel Elizabeth, born Nov. 4, 1988, and Hanna Sharlene, who arrived on June 29, 1991.

Matthew Patrick was born on New Year's Day, 1963. We had hoped for a December birth so we could claim him as a tax deduction. Sharlene and I sat home on New Year's Eve, playing gin rummy. When she woke me early in the morning for the run to St. Mary's hospital, I donned a red shirt. In those days, the only way you could look at your newborn was through a window at the nursery, and I wanted Matt to be able to spot me.

Matt turned it into a tradition. He married Jill Catherine Buikema (b. June 8, 1965) on June 9, 2002, and he wore red shirts for the birth of his son, Seth Patrick, on Apr. 14, 2004, and his daughter, Kyra Catherine, on Feb. 6, 2007.

I wrote and printed another "news" story about Matt's birth, complaining in it that he had cost us $130, which was the amount of the extra federal tax refund we would have received if he had been born on Dec. 31.

Becky's real name is Mary Elizabeth. She was born at St. Joseph's Hospital on Sept. 18, 1964, when we lived in the lower flat on N. 57th St., on Milwaukee's west side, that was owned by the penny-pinching Milwaukee police detective.

By then, fathers were allowed to witness their child's birth. So I watched Becky's birth, as I did later for Joe at the same hospital. When her first child, Zoe, was born, Becky asked Sharlene and me to attend. I spent most of the time looking out the window.

Sharlene had decreed that no matter what name we chose, Becky would be called Becky, after Sharlene's half sister, Adrianne. In the Greek Orthodox Church, in the old days, babies were named by their godparents, but sometimes were not baptized until they were a year old. The Greek name for an un-baptized girl is "babaka," so Sharlene's sister was known as "Becky" for the first year of her life.

Becky married Nicholas Joseph Hawryluk (b. March 9, 1964), from Lebanon, Pa., on May 26, 1990. Zoe Deanna was born Oct. 27, 1996, and Cole Andrew arrived on June 19, 1999. We did not attend Cole's birth.

Our fourth and last child, Joseph John, was born at St. Joseph's Hospital on Jan. 20, 1967, at a particularly wrenching time. The other three kids all had caught chicken pox, as did Sharlene. The doctors, who couldn't check Joe's condition inside the womb, didn't know whether he had it, too.

Sharlene developed a pox-induced kidney infection in the hospital just before Joe's birth, so the doctors refused to give her any painkillers until I threatened mayhem. And poor Joe, after he was born, was set off by himself in an isolation ward. He didn't develop chicken pox, but looked so forlorn there we cried.

Joe married his Annandale high-school sweetheart, Joanne Lynn Gaines (b. Oct. 12, 1966), on July 29, 1995. They lost their first child before birth and we had a full funeral, with 11 cars in the procession. I wrote an article about it, which was published in The Journal, intending it as an anti-abortion statement as much as an expression of grief. Had the child been born, it likely would have been handicapped. Yet there never was a question of terminating Joanne's pregnancy by anyone in either family. After that, Joe and Joanne brought us Aliya Lane on Jan. 19, 2000; Lucas Alexander on Apr. 5, 2002, and Anna-Lyn Elizabeth on May 15, 2005.

Sharlene and I ended up with 10 grandchildren—seven girls and three boys. As grandparents, we now experience "the most exalted state in life"—a description I first heard from my friend, the late Richard Schmidt, who was a longtime lawyer for many journalism organizations.

5

NEVER A SLOW DAY

Iused to tell everyone—not expecting them to believe it—that I'd never had a slow day in 40 years as a newspaper reporter.

It was true, though. Sure, I had days when I basically loafed, but even those were enjoyable. When I was working it was always interesting, sometimes dramatic, glamorous or exciting, occasionally frightening, but never boring. Not a day went by when I didn't learn something—even if all I did was sit around and read the newspapers.

That's one of the great things about the job. Where else can you sit with your feet on the desk reading the newspapers and not get yelled at by the boss?

But having fun at work can be a bummer when you're a dad. I always tried to get home for dinner and, when the kids were younger, to give them their baths before they went to bed. I'd walk in the house, wearing a coat and tie, and somebody would ask what kind of a day I'd had and I'd say it was great.

You get no respect. Your wife has been slaving away all day with household chores and kids, and you've been out having a good time playing newspaper reporter. I always thought the kids would be more impressed if I'd been, say, a construction worker or a miner. I'd come in dirty, sweaty and exhausted, and collapse into a chair and everybody would sympathize with me, comfort me and wait on me.

But a reporter who says he's had fun at work? Forget it.

The other downside is you don't get excited about the same things that other people do. When you're a reporter—at least a general assignment guy like I was—you get to see a lot of different stuff like Playboy Bunnies and protest demonstrators and wars and presidential impeachments, and you usually get a front-row seat. So when somebody suggests going out for a good time, you're lukewarm because you've already had a good time working.

The upside, of course, is that it's exhilarating to go to work, especially when you don't have a clue about what you're going to be doing that day. There were days when I walked down the sidewalk ready to break into song as I headed toward something interesting and exciting, amazed that they paid me for having so much fun.

As a young reporter on The Milwaukee Journal in 1960, I got to dress up in a tuxedo and go to debutante parties—on overtime. The Women's department (this was before anybody got upset about having women's and men's sections in newspapers) had gotten a tip that there was a lot of drinking going on at coming-out parties for debutantes, the daughters of wealthy and socially-prominent families.

Although I was 25—fresh out of the Marquette University College of Journalism—Sandra Cota and Barbara Schmoll, who covered social events for the Women's Section, said I was the youngest-looking male reporter on the staff. So I got the assignment to pretend I was a rich amusement for the pretty debs in their strapless gowns and armored bodices. (Schmoll later married E. Michael McCann, for many years the Milwaukee County district attorney).

Crashing the parties was simplicity itself. Dress in a rented tux and walk right in. Nobody figured there'd be an undercover news guy among all the budding polo players. When people asked who I was, I just let my imagination run.

I was whoever and whatever popped into my head at the time. It was a lot of fun being an imposter and we did get an exposé of sorts. I reported that there was drinking going on at the deb balls, but I couldn't work up much outrage over it. Nor could anybody else, apparently, because other than a couple of snotty letters to the editor about how The Journal was doing its usual best to intrude into people's private lives, there wasn't much in the way of reaction.

A few years later, I was again telling lies in the course of my reportorial duties, but this time to my editors and a couple of strippers in the Downtowner, a notorious joint a few blocks from The Journal. It was owned by Frank Balistrieri, the mob boss in Milwaukee.

The Journal had been trying to nail him for years, without much success other than to publicize the fact that he had been identified by the law and on the floor of the House of Representatives as the Milwaukee mafia godfather.

Eddie Kerstein, one of our gumshoe reporters, had done a big Sunday investigative takeout bringing our readers up to date on the deeds of the Balistrieri family. So anxious were we about the story that the city desk assigned me to go hang out at the Downtowner that Sunday night to see if there was any talk among the bartenders and patrons about Kerstein's story.

THE STRIPPERS

It was a naïve undertaking. For one thing, the Downtowner did hardly any business on a Sunday, and in retrospect I doubted whether anybody there even read the newspaper. But I went. In those days, a young reporter would never have the temerity to beg off on an assignment, especially one that looked at least mildly interesting.

I didn't have much stomach for it, however. So for backup, and on my own, I asked Owen King, another reporter, to go with me. King was single and readily agreed. So we went off to the Downtowner about 8:30 or 9 that night, sat down in a booth and ordered drinks. The place was almost deserted—just us, a couple of bartenders, maybe one or two other customers, and two strip-tease dancers.

To a couple of inexperienced 20-somethings, the strippers were more than intriguing. They were young and good-looking, though of two different types. One was named Scorch. She was, as we said in those days, extremely well built, with long black hair, cleavage, net stockings and a dark complexion. The other, who called herself April Storm, was slim, blonde and looked like a college coed.

Almost before we realized it, the two women, still in their costumes, were sitting in the booth and being ogled by us. We pretended to be traveling salesmen and, as best we could, tried to find out whether they or anybody else had read The Journal story about Frankie Bal. They, of course, said they had never heard of Frankie.

We probably should have quit right there. I was running out of my advanced expense money, and Owen had long since spent his meager pocket cash. But we didn't want to quit, so on the pretense of going back to my hotel room to get more cash, I hotfooted it over to the to the Milwaukee Sentinel newsroom. The Journal had bought the Sentinel in 1962, and I had worked there for six weeks during the transition, so I knew there were people in the newsroom on a Sunday night.

I was able to borrow 20 bucks with a promise to pay it back the next day after I submitted my expense voucher. I had to confess what I was doing, but it didn't matter anyway because Kerstein's story was already out and the Sentinel wasn't interested in reaction to a Journal story in any case.

So Owen and I got to spend a little more time with Scorch and April Storm. He was really warming up to April and thought he had an arrangement take her home. He asked me to keep them entertained while he went to get his car. While he was gone, my conscience—and alcohol—got the better of me. I blearily blurted out the whole story about how we were really reporters looking for reaction to the big Journal story.

If I expected any sympathy, I didn't get it. The two strippers simply got up and walked away. They were sitting at the bar when Owen returned. He went up to April and spoke to her. She pointedly ignored him. When I told him what I had done, I thought he was going to kill me. He didn't, but he yelled and cussed at me outside as I walked away.

The next day, I had to write a memo to the desk about the failed assignment, which was what we always had to do. If we didn't get a story, we had to write a memo. Investigative guys like our old police rewrite man, J. Paul O'Brien, spent most of their time writing memos, many of which wound up in locked filing cabinets. Of course, my memo didn't get into any of the details about Scorch and April Storm, though I was sure that my expense voucher for $40 would be rejected. But nobody said a word. So I got out of that one with a hangover and a vast feeling of relief.

I did almost get fired one other time, and that one wasn't even my fault, so I figured that eventually things evened out. At that time, I worked a lot as a swing man, a reporter who filled in on the beats of other reporters on their days off. It was a lousy assignment because a swing man, unless he'd been around for a lot of years, didn't know anybody, had no sources, barely knew where the building was, and was basically there to get his finger in the dike if something big happened. It was not unlike what is expected these days of a pool reporter on Air Force One.

I drew the county and circuit courts on a Friday. There were a dozen or more of these civil courts in the Milwaukee County Courthouse, and Friday was motion day, a busy time when lawyers were filing, and judges hearing, motions on various cases before them. They produced almost nothing in the way of stories, but the reporter was expected to keep track of them nevertheless.

THE PUTZIE BOX

It was a frantic day. When I checked into the office in the morning, Waldon Porterfield, sitting in as the assignment editor, handed me a sheaf of legal-looking papers to check out. On my way to the Courthouse, I scanned them and saw that the writer was complaining about his treatment at the hands of different judges in Milwaukee and Brown (Green Bay) counties, accusing the judges of everything from misconduct to criminal actions. The treatise was not signed, but paper-clipped to it was a small piece of note paper that said further information could be had from Walter Block. It gave a phone number.

One of those mentioned was Circuit Judge Myron Gordon, who was scheduled to hear a motion by Block that morning. I walked into Gordon's courtroom and Block, who was representing himself, introduced himself. I said, "Oh yeah, we got your letter." I pulled it out and Block started pointing out different passages, but I waved him off, saying I had other courts to check and would be back later.

I spent the whole day rushing from one court to another without scaring up even a single story worth reporting. I didn't return to Gordon's courtroom until the end of the day, and by then Block was long gone. As was the custom, I simply walked back into the judge's chambers to find out what had happened. The judge was alone. I asked a few questions and Gordon asked how I knew so much about the case. I took the papers out of my pocket and said, "Well, we got this letter."

The judge grabbed it out of my hand and started reading, muttering occasionally to himself. He handed it back without a word and said he had denied Block's motion for a change of venue. I didn't think it was a story and didn't plan to write one.

That night, there was a knock at the door of our one-room apartment on N. Cass St. It was a deputy sheriff with a summons ordering me to Gordon's court at 9 the following morning with the letter. I had no idea what was going on, but I was scared. I went in early Saturday morning and told the whole episode to Harry Hill, the deputy city editor.

He exploded. What in the hell was I doing, showing a judge a letter that had been sent to The Journal? My protest that the judge had snatched it out of my hand was no excuse. Hill told me to honor the subpoena and assigned another reporter to cover the hearing.

It was bizarre. It was Block, Judge Gordon, a bailiff, a court reporter, The Journal reporter and me. Gordon acted as both prosecutor and judge. He put me on the stand and basically had me recount how I had gotten the letter.

I learned later that Block had been in and out of courts in both Brown and Milwaukee counties. His wife had sued him for divorce and he had filed a counterclaim, accusing her of prostitution. He said she had "putzie box" on the dresser in their home, and when he wanted to have sex with her, he had to put $20 in the "putzie box." Judges had uniformly ruled against him and he had just as routinely accused them of prejudice, criminal conduct and whatever else he could think of.

Unknown to me, Gordon had told Block at an earlier encounter that if he ever vilified another judge he would be held in criminal contempt of court. After listening to my testimony, Gordon said from the bench that he was convinced Block had written the letter to The Journal, in direct violation of his warning. He found Block guilty of contempt and sentenced him to six months in jail.

I thought for certain that I would be fired on my return to the office. But Hill simply chewed me out once more and told me to never, ever give a news source any communication a reader might send to the paper. We carried a short story in the Sunday paper about Gordon sending Block to the slammer, but that was it. I never heard another thing about either him or the "putzie box."

The incident, however, did earn me the enmity of Porterfield, a tall, matinee-idol type with wavy hair who was a good reporter, a superb writer and an ardent admirer of Ernest Hemingway. At the time, he was working as an assistant city editor, which meant he handled assignments and occasionally sat in the slot as city editor. In many respects, Porterfield was a strange duck. He drove a Morgan Plus 4, a British sports car with a design that hadn't changed in decades. It was largely hand-built, with a wood frame and wood seats covered by pneumatic cushions. It was notoriously unreliable and, even with two batteries, often refused to start in the cold of Milwaukee winters, when Porterfield would sometimes drive around with the top down. It was all part of his macho self-image.

After the Block incident, I could always predict when I would be on obituaries the next day: If Porterfield was on assignments, I got obits. But he wasn't alone in putting me there. As a rookie reporter on what was then one of the country's best newspapers, I spent a lot of time writing obits, the entry-level job for newcomers. I even once wrote an obit on a horse.

HOTSHOT REWRITE MAN

The Porterfield pendulum swung in a single day about a year later. We were short-handed during summer vacation time, and the assistant city editor assigned me to rewrite. We usually had three people on rewrite—one to write stories from the reporters covering police, police courts, fires and other disasters, and two others handling anything else. When I showed up in the morning, I saw to my horror that Porterfield was the city editor for the day, which meant that I was right under the gun. He would be the first one to look at any copy I turned in. But I was good and I was fast, and I knew it. We had a flood of stories that day, right on deadline, and I was writing stories in takes— meaning a couple of paragraphs at a time—and flipping them into Porterfield's inbox. After the final deadline passed, I was flabbergasted when he said, "Nice job." With Porterfield there were no grays. I was suddenly one of his boys. He never again assigned me to obits.

No matter if you were among the lowest reporters doing obits, everybody had beats to cover. Every day you'd get a half sheet of copy paper in your pigeon hole in the newsroom. It listed your hours, your days off, your regular beats and what you were supposed to do that day. My regular beats were Boy Scouts, traffic safety and veterans' affairs. It meant that I was responsible for making sure that if there were any stories in any of those areas, they landed first on the city desk of The Journal. Woe to the reporter if a story on one of his beats first appeared in Willie Hearst's Milwaukee Sentinel.

We never worried about radio or TV because all the stations simply followed or copied The Journal. We wrote our stories on manual typewriters, on "books" of copy paper, four sheets of blank newsprint with three sheets of carbon paper. The original went to the desk and one copy went on a spike for the Associated Press—the AP was entitled to anything in The Journal, which was a member newspaper. Another went on a spike for WTMJ radio and television, and the last carbon was for the reporter's files. (WTMJ stands for "Watch The Milwaukee Journal" and it was owned by the employee-owned Journal).

Of course, no reporter who had a good exclusive story would ever spike carbons for the AP or WTMJ until after the story had appeared in The Journal. In fact, although the official line was that we were supposed to spike those carbons immediately, editors threatened us with lifelong obits if we ever did.

One day in July, about six weeks after I'd started as a reporter on The Journal, I went to the downtown railroad station to see off a group of Milwaukee Boy Scouts who were on their way to the big national Jamboree. The Journal's editors had not seen fit to send me along with the group, so this farewell would have to do as the feature story on their participation in the big do.

It was about 1:30 in the afternoon and I was almost alone in the newsroom, trying to peck out something interesting about the Scouts, when Ray McBride, a rewrite man who had "late lunch"—meaning he minded the city desk while everybody was out eating—came running over and told me to grab some notebooks and pencils and get out the door to meet Hank Larson, one of the photographers.

McBride said a department store had blown up in Merrill, up north, and I had to cover it. There was no way any editor would have picked a rookie like me to cover a big story like that, but there was nobody else around and we reacted to big stories instantly.

I grabbed my stuff and headed for the fourth-floor elevator. The door opened and there was Larson. He didn't know me, although I knew who he was. In those days, The Journal had the finest corps of news photographers and photo editors of any newspaper in the country. Many, like Bob Gilka and Jim Stanfield, went on to fame with the National Geographic, Life, the Smithsonian Magazine and other picture-oriented publications.

(When Stanfield, with whom I had worked a number of times in the 1960s, retired from the Geographic in Washington many years later, I covered the farewell party. Gilbert Grosvenor, chairman of the National Geographic Society and the main speaker, said that because the magazine had so many great photographers, he had never commented publicly on their abilities. But he said he was violating his own principle of 44 years to say, "Jim Stanfield is the greatest photographer we've ever had at National Geographic Magazine.")

Larson, like all of The Journal's photographers, had a two-way-radio-equipped company car. We sped to Timmerman Field, a small airport about 20 minutes away on the northwest side of town. When we arrived, a twin-engine propeller plane was already warming up. When we landed in Merrill, a couple of Journal circulation guys were waiting for us with their cars and their intimate knowledge of the community.

COVERING THE BIG STORY

It was a devastating scene. The one-story J. C. Penney department store's sides had been blown out, the roof had been blown straight up and came crashing down on what was left. We learned later that it had been a gas explosion, and ten people had been killed.

Even though I had little experience and this was the biggest story I'd seen in my life, I knew enough to find the highest-ranking fireman available. I got to him and he gave me a quick fix: Big explosion, didn't know what but suspected gas, eight people dead, unknown number injured. I headed for the nearest pay telephone.

It was close to 4:30 p.m., our WUP deadline. WUP stood for Wisconsin-Upper Peninsula, an edition The Journal sent to Northern Wisconsin and Upper Michigan. Dick Leonard, who eventually became editor, used to joke that the WUP went to remote areas where, if you increased your circulation, you could go broke because it cost so much to deliver the papers. But The Journal was proud of its reach. And we were proud of The Journal.

Leonard was the state editor that day, and I gave him enough information over the phone from Merrill for him to put together a story that led the WUP the next morning.

I went back to work. I interviewed everybody I could find at the scene who had seen or heard anything. I went to the hospital and talked to as many survivors as the doctors would allow. I went to the temporary morgue, set up in the National Guard Armory, and looked at the charred remains of the victims, noting the smells as well as the sights and sounds. (Lindsay Hoben, then the editor of The Journal, was famous for, among other things, saying that a good reporter had to get close enough to the story to smell it).

Larson and I stayed until about 10 p.m., flew back to Milwaukee and worked through the night to meet the morning deadline.

The Met Edition, the first of the day, carried an eight-column banner headline, with my byline over the Merrill dateline. To a newsman, it doesn't get better than that. I was so pumped I didn't even go home right away when they told me to take off early.

Next morning, I floated in, chest out and grinning. I checked my pigeon hole for the day's assignments. I was on obits.

That was The Journal's way. It told you that the paper was important, not the individual. I was shocked in later years to see colleagues on other newspapers start their stories with their bylines. Except for a very few veteran specialists or reviewers, no reporter on The Journal was ever allowed to put his byline on a story. That was the editor's prerogative, and to this day you can search the files and read beautifully reported and written Journal stories with no bylines.

It was some summer. Soon after the big story in Merrill, I was assigned to cover an evening meeting of an organization called the Advisory Council to the Mayor. It was a private citizens' organization and had nothing to do with the mayor or city government, although it was driving the mayor nuts.

The mayor was Henry W. Maier, a Democrat newly elected in a nonpartisan election in 1960. He succeeded Frank P. Zeidler, the last Socialist mayor of any big city in the country. Maier would become the bane of The Journal, or The Journal would become the bane of Maier, in a battle that ultimately lasted throughout his political career as mayor, which spanned 24 years.

I could have wound up on either side. The Advisory Council to the Mayor, which I covered that summer evening, had endorsed a state sales tax. Maier regarded it as political suicide, even though he had almost four years left in office, and wanted in no way to be even remotely associated with the advisory council or its views. I was not aware of any of that.

The next morning, as I arrived early to write the story from the previous night's meeting, I had a telephone call from Arthur Else, the top aide to the mayor, saying Maier wanted to talk to me. Before I could react, the mayor was on the telephone, seeking to make certain that whatever story I wrote would make it clear that the advisory council had no connection to him or the office of the mayor.

I was flattered and a bit surprised because I had done what all Journal reporters did—I had gotten clips out of the library (or morgue, as some newspapers called it) of previous stories on the Advisory Council to the Mayor. They all had made the point that the council was an independent entity, and I had planned to simply repeat that background information in my story.

THE MAYOR OFFERS A JOB

But remembering one of my journalism principles from Marquette—that no news source should ever dictate what a reporter writes—I politely demurred and told the mayor that I would have to write the story as it happened. He, just as politely, didn't press the point. Of course, when I wrote the story I included the obligatory line that the council was a private organization with no connection to the mayor. Else called back that same afternoon to say Maier was pleased with the story.

Not many days later, I received another telephone call from Else, who said the mayor wanted to see me at his home on Sunday afternoon.

I went to the mayor's East Side home and was shown into his study. He got right to the point. I was an upstanding, principled and promising young reporter, he said, and he needed a press secretary. Would I take the job? I asked how much. He said $9,400 a year.

I was making $95 a week at The Journal, so this would almost double my pay. I was only weeks away from getting married. It could mean the difference between penny-pinching and relative comfort. I asked if I could think it over for a few days, and he agreed.

In all the discussions I'd had with my fellow journalism students at Marquette, money had never come up. We all knew that journalism paid starvation wages. It was an accepted fact of life. Starting jobs on mid-size dailies ran $65 to $75 a week. I had worked one summer at the South Milwaukee Voice-Journal, 60 or more hours a week, for $45, to learn journalism from Editor Gordon Lewis, a great newsman. I had taken a $35 a week pay cut from my $130 a week wage as a journeyman compositor when I started as a reporter. It was always about doing something useful, fun and fame, not money.

But here I was being offered a bunch of it, plus the prestige and excitement of being the spokesman for the mayor. At the same time, I really liked being a reporter. I agonized over the offer. I talked to Sharlene, my fiancée. I talked to my colleagues at The Journal, especially the veterans I respected—people like city hall reporter Wade Mosby, who had given me his entire telephone list of sources. I talked to my professors at Marquette, most particularly Don Ross, who had taught me more about reporting in one semester than I learned before or since.

I was still agonizing on my way to the mayor's office in City Hall to tell him my decision. Almost without thinking, I told Maier that I was sorry but I had to decline his offer. The reason, I said, was that I'd only been on The Journal staff only a few months, and if I bailed out now I would never know if I could make it as a newspaper reporter, which had been my goal. It was an honest statement and he accepted it gracefully.

Several years later I bumped into him once at the Milwaukee Press Club, where he greeted me warmly and, only half-kidding, I thought, asked me when I would accept his offer to be his press secretary. I passed it off with a laugh

Despite that, it wasn't long before I made Maier's enemies list. Our relationship deteriorated mainly because I started to cover the civil rights movement in Milwaukee, which was anathema to the mayor. He regarded the activists as, variously, outside agitators, pawns of the iron ring of lily-white suburbs around Milwaukee, and simply people out to get him. They were, in short, the enemy—and I became part of the enemy camp because I was covering them and writing stories about their activities. Fortunately, I didn't have much contact with hizzoner, who was well covered by other reporters on the staff.

However, matters came to a head on several occasions. In the summer of 1967, along with reporter Ken Field, I was sent to cover the riots in Detroit. In those days, we always did Sunday stories to amplify and provide background on the events we had covered during the week. I wrote a story, the thrust of which was that Detroit apparently had been doing a better job on race relations than Milwaukee. It was well documented with interviews of key people in both cities.

That night, Milwaukee had its own riot. I heard via the grapevine that the mayor, if he didn't exactly blame me for starting the riot, at least was convinced that my story contributed to it.

Then came Crying Sunday. After the riot, when the NAACP Youth Council and its adviser, Father James E. Groppi, resumed daily marches for open housing, Maier banned night marches and demonstrations. The following Sunday, The Journal carried three prominent stories in which Maier had a direct interest. Our courts reporter, Bruce Thorp, wrote a story that questioned the constitutionality of the mayor's proclamation because it appeared to be directed only at one group; I wrote a story quoting white liberals and leaders of the black community who were questioning Maier's wisdom and supposed liberal credentials, and the city hall reporter, Larry Lohmann, had a profile of Maier's top aide that raised doubts about the aide's effectiveness.

The mayor telephoned Lohmann in the early Sunday morning hours after the first edition came out, broke down in tears and threatened to resign. Lohmann, knowing his subject well, told the editors but didn't write a story. As he expected, it all had vanished by Monday and the mayor resumed his attacks on The Journal.

NATIONAL TRAVELING SQUAD OF DISSENTERS

Later, I was a key player in a notorious press conference in which Maier blamed the city's woes on what he called "the local chapter of the national traveling squad of dissenters." It was at a time of high friction between The Journal and the mayor. With Maier accusing The Journal of distorting everything he did, The Journal's editors decided to run complete texts of virtually everything he uttered, including transcripts of his press conferences.

I rarely had anything to do with city hall or the mayor, but that day was assigned to cover the press conference, most of which was also televised live by one of the local Milwaukee TV channels. When Maier launched into his diatribe about the "traveling squad of dissenters," I went after him, demanding that he be specific about who or what he was talking about.

As he stammered his non-response, his press secretary, Dick Budelman—who had been a Journal reporter and a friend of mine—interrupted loudly and asked me why, as a civil rights reporter, I had not requested an interview with the city's No. 1 civil rights figure. And who might that be? I asked innocently. Why, the mayor, of course, he replied. Then Ray Taylor, the editor of the Milwaukee Labor Press and a Maier toady, jumped in to accuse me of attacking the mayor. The interruptions changed the subject and allowed the mayor to recover and end the press conference.

We had fun with it. The Journal gleefully printed the transcript of the press conference, with emphasis on the "national traveling squad." Of course, we were all convinced that it demonstrated conclusively that the mayor was crazy, or a demagogue, or both. And just as surely, most of our readers read it as yet another dastardly attack by The Journal on the city's beloved chief executive.

Beloved, that is, by the majority white community. I once interviewed Mrs. Ardie Halyard, a classy and quietly conservative leader in the Negro community. She and her husband, Wilbur, ran a savings and loan association in the inner city and were anything but civil rights activists, though in their own way they helped many people to buy homes and get out of debt. I asked her opinion of Maier. She replied quietly that her view was that Maier believed "those people"—meaning her people—did not support him or vote for him, so he didn't feel he owed them anything. He represented the majority white community.

Mrs. Halyard was right, although Maier did manage, on several occasions, to muster at least a public showing of support from Negro preachers who had no connection to the budding civil rights movement in the city. He did it to discredit the activists like Father James E. Groppi and the Milwaukee NAACP Youth Council.

I loved covering the kids of the youth council. They were pre-teens and teens, and some may have participated in the marches and protest demonstrations for the fun of it, but they were always totally dedicated to Groppi, who was a charismatic leader.

The kids had a great time making up their own songs and chants to help make their point. My all-time favorite was the words they put to the old labor and civil rights song, "Which Side Are You On, Boy?"

Their version:

"They say that Mayor Maier

"Has gone and lost his mind.

"He went and got some Coppertone

"To join our picket line.

"Hey, which side are you on, boy . . ."

I only occasionally had contact with the mayor over the following years, but I continued at the top of his enemies list. Once I covered a speech he delivered at the Milwaukee Vocational School. He spotted me sitting in the front row and, departing from his text, informed his audience through gritted teeth that one of the most serious problems a big-city mayor had to deal with in those perilous times was "young reporters who don't know the difference between liberals and the new left." It was an obvious reference to the "Crying Sunday" story I had done.

Years later, after I had been assigned to Washington, Maier traveled there to deliver a speech at American University. I went to cover it and once again sat in the front row. Sure enough, he spotted me and repeated those same words about young reporters and liberals and the new left. Students around me, baffled by the reference, exchanged incredulous glances. I laughed out loud.

THE GOOD AND THE GREAT

In the sixties, even the bad assignments were good, and the good ones were great. By turns, they were emotional, sobering and serious, dramatic and exciting, and sometimes downright hilarious. Subjects were as varied as the Beatles, the saga of Hertogas McParpson, my last full day with my dying father, President Lyndon B. Johnson and the Playboy Club.

My assignment was to travel to Lake Geneva, Wis., for the groundbreaking of the new Lake Geneva Playboy Club. It took a lot of imagination. There was nothing there except for a couple of large white tents on a low hill facing a very large cornfield. One of the tents was reserved for the press and the other for the Playboy organization.

The event obviously had been dreamed up by a hyper-imaginative publicist. At the appointed moment, all the reporters and TV cameramen were herded into a group and lo! Suddenly out of the skies flew a giant black helicopter, two large rotors whup-whupping, with a white Playboy bunny painted on the side. Roaring magnificently and blowing away hats and notebooks, the chopper settled to the ground in front of the group. The door opened, steps dropped down and out of the door trooped a bevy of giggling Playboy bunnies, all in their clubwear high-thigh-cut costumes with bunny tails, pushup bras and net stockings, spike heels and bunny ears bouncing from their hair bows.

Then Hugh Hefner stepped out, resplendent in his black silk "outdoors" pajamas, smoking his pipe. The bunnies squealed, wiggled a few times and ran off to the Playboy tent. They emerged a few minutes later, changed into their outdoors costumes of tight T-shirts, short shorts and sneakers. The newsmen were astonished at the transformation. Where a few minutes ago we had seen these sexy women of the evening, we now were looking at a group of wholesome-looking girls of the sort you could see at any summer picnic.

The press conference was all the usual stuff: What the club would look like, how much it would cost, the amenities that it would offer, how important its contributions would be to the local economy and Playboy, and so on. But the best part was the demonstration.

Out there in the cornfield in front of us, "Hef" and his cohort planned to dig a lake. To give the assemblage some idea of what it would look like, there were three guys out in the cornfield, each holding a sailboat mainsail on a pole stuck in one of those belt sockets that flag bearers use. At a signal from one of the Playboy people, those unfortunate souls were forced to run around in the cornfield so we could see how the sailboats would look once the mighty Playboy Club and its attendant lake were built.

Most of the newsmen could not stifle their laughter. At that moment, as at many other times over the years, I was grateful to be a newspaper reporter and not somebody who had to do something ludicrous to earn a living.

Many years later, in early 1979, I encountered "Hef" again. By then I was president of the National Press Club and he, along with his daughter, Christie, Playboy's vice-president, spoke at one of the club's newsmaker lunches to mark Playboy's 25th anniversary.

I introduced him as "the Mao Tse-Tung of the sexual revolution— or, as one columnist put it, a man whose chief claim to fame is that he put staples in the navels of naked ladies."

POP, THE BEATLES AND THE PRESIDENT

One memorable assignment came in the summer of 1962, when the desk assigned me to do a story directing Fourth of July holiday travelers away from the freeways and on to byways. In those days, Wisconsin's county trunk roads were better than the state highways in many areas of the country, and they wound their way through towns and countryside that were as interesting as they were scenic.

Nobody knew the back roads of southeastern Wisconsin better than my dad, so I asked him to come along and be my navigator. He had been diagnosed with cancer the previous April (he died in September), and was in some pain and discomfort. But we spent a wonderful day together, with him directing me to roads I had never traveled. We frequently stopped at taverns in little towns, and it seemed that Pop knew every bartender around. The story made page one.

In September of 1964, the Beatles visited Milwaukee to star in a concert at the Milwaukee Arena, across the street from The Journal building. I was part of a team of reporters assigned to cover the fabulous four, then at the height of their popularity. It was amazing. The Arena was jammed with screaming fans. Not a note of the concert could be heard. The only sound was a constant scream that simply rose, fell and changed pitch.

Earlier, I had done a big Green Sheet feature story on a popular folk music group—Peter, Paul and Mary. They were surprisingly easygoing and unaffected by their new-found fame, and I loved their way with a song. Four decades later, I still enjoy listening to Peter Yarrow, Paul Stookey and Mary Travers.

In October, 1964, I covered a campaign visit to Milwaukee by President Lyndon B. Johnson. I was on a press bus half a dozen cars behind the presidential limousine and, having learned of Johnson's penchant for unscheduled stops, I stood in front and asked the bus driver to pop the door open any time the limousine stopped. Sure enough, Johnson stopped at a tiny grocery store on the South Side, the driver opened the door and I was off running. I breezed right past the protective detail and wound up alone in the store with Johnson, the store owner and his wife, and a couple of Secret Service agents. Johnson borrowed money from an agent, and bought peppermint candy and bologna sausage, and I had an exclusive story. Johnson even wrote a note to my wife, Sharlene, and gave me a little LBJ pin and a pass to the presidential gallery in the House of Representatives.

Later I also covered some of the campaign appearances of Johnson's opponent, Sen. Barry Goldwater of Arizona. One of his campaign workers was David Keene, who years later became chairman of the American Conservative Union. We both wound up with fellowships at the Freedom Forum First Amendment Center in Nashville in 1994-'95, with side-by-side offices. I always enjoyed David. He was a certified conservative with an impish sense of humor and a lot of liberal friends.

HERTOGAS LIVES AND DIES

Hertogas McParpson was born and died on the same day, between editions of The Milwaukee Journal. It happened in a train wreck, a disaster for the railroad and the people who were injured—nobody died—but a great story for me and The Journal because it happened on our time and I was the rewrite man on the story. In those days, reporters and editors mostly started work at 7, 7:30 or 8 in the morning. Word of the train wreck on the northwest side came in just as the whole complement was assembling, sleepily sipping coffee and munching rolls and doughnuts from the cafeteria.

There was never any hesitation on a big story. The editors and photo department managers scrambled as many bodies as they thought they needed—at least six reporters and I don't know how many shooters, but enough. I got the nod to write the main story, and the adrenaline started pumping.

Taking notes phoned in by the reporters on the scene, I wrote a long story for the metro edition, then made a paste-up after the edition came out and tore the story apart and re-did it for the next two editions. Everything I did was under the gun. I killed earlier versions and wrote new ledes, inserts and adds, banging them out on the old Underwood typewriter a paragraph at a time, with copy boys picking up the takes and running them over to the city editor.

I put some names of the injured in the main story, but to make certain everybody was covered, another rewrite man—Paul Salsini, who had been a couple of years ahead of me at Marquette, worked up a sidebar listing the names of the injured, their ages and home towns and what their conditions were at what hospitals.

One of the reporters who had been sent to one of the hospitals was Dick Vonier, a marvelously talented and funny, but ultimately fatally flawed, friend and colleague. He was being kept out of the hospital, so he got his information from the ambulance drivers as they brought in the injured.

Salsini put together a list for the second edition of about a dozen injured. One of them was Hertogas McParpson, of Derse, Wis. The usual practice was to check a state directory to make certain of the spelling of small town names, or whether they even existed. But there was no time, so the list was published with Hertogas, just as Vonier had telephoned it in. By the time the edition came off the presses and copies showed up at the rewrite desk, Vonier was phoning in with updated information. One of the names was Hortense McPherson, of De Pere, Wis.

Could it be? It was. Hertogas was really Hortense. The poor fellow died between editions, never to be heard from again. Another fellow named Gregorio Kuipers also succumbed. We never found out who he really was.

6

CIVIL RIGHTS

Notwithstanding 9/11, the Vietnam War and presidential impeachments, any reporter who covered the civil rights movement in the 1960s will tell you those were the best of times. I didn't cover 9/11, though it was the biggest story I had ever seen as an adult. By the time the airliners crashed into the World Trade Center and the Pentagon in 2001, I was retired. Carl Schwartz, the Journal Sentinel's national editor, asked me to come back to work, but I declined.

I was a year and a half into retirement and at some distance from the sources I had cultivated over the years, especially those in the Pentagon. So I would have had to go into that story cold, like a rookie reporter. Besides, the story was so big that any given reporter would get only a small piece of it. Con Eklund, The Milwaukee Journal bureau chief whose retirement brought me to Washington, once said he was ready to let the young reporters with the strong legs take over. I felt the same way.

I'd had more than my share. I covered two of the country's three presidential impeachment proceedings—the 1974 House Judiciary Committee hearings and votes to impeach Richard M. Nixon, as well as Nixon's resignation, and the impeachment and Senate trial of William J. Clinton. In between, there was the Persian Gulf War, stories in Central and Latin America, and a dozen national political conventions.

But the civil rights movement was the best. A big part of the reason, of course, was that it was the biggest story in the country at the time, though the spotlight frequently shifted from city to city: Watts, Birmingham, Selma, Newark, Detroit, Milwaukee and Memphis. But covering a part of the story, even for a white newspaper, was like being part of the movement.

The issue was clear-cut, right against wrong, black and white if you will. It was a struggle for humanity and equal rights on the part of a substantial segment of the American citizenry. There were few nuances, at least as far as the reporters I knew were concerned. We all knew we were covering epic stories that we would someday tell our grandchildren about, which I'm doing here.

But the beauty of the situation was that a reporter could feel as if he were part of the movement simply by reporting what was going on, without compromising journalistic principles. I never had to step over the line to point out to the reader, for example, that the president of the school board was talking like a raving bigot. All I had to do was report the story and quote him or her accurately. Despite the latter-day criticisms of the insensitivity of the "white press" to minority concerns, which was true enough, the white press did make the entire country aware of the legitimate grievances of the nation's Negro minority, simply by covering the marches, sit-ins and other movement events.

KU KLUX KLAN VISITED

In 1965, I traveled to South Carolina to spend two weeks as an exchange reporter on the Spartanburg Herald. The exchange was the idea of the Herald's managing editor, Tom Fleming, who was from Wisconsin and wanted to show people back in his home state that the South wasn't totally populated by redneck bigots and Klansmen. The Herald sent its top reporter, Fred Rigsbee, to spend two weeks on The Journal. He was a disappointment. Though he was a big fish in Spartanburg, he never would have made it on The Journal. For his stories, he mostly interviewed the black reporters in our newsroom. And he was a terrible writer.

Eventually, I wrote a series of stories for The Journal. But I also did a few stories for the Herald in my two weeks in Spartanburg. The most interesting was an interview with one Robert Scoggin, who had the mouth-filling title of Grand Dragon of the Realm of South Carolina of the United Klans of America, Inc., Knights of the Ku Klux Klan. I got directions to his place out in the country and drove out in my rental car.

It was like something out of a horror movie. The unpaved road to his cabin was dark, under a canopy of trees that blocked out the sunlight. The yard was littered with abandoned old cars and appliances. Inside, the house was even darker, with no electricity, running water or indoor plumbing.

Scoggin was unkempt and unwashed, with rotting teeth and scraggly hair. I listened to this pathetic creature tell me how he and his ilk were superior to millions of Americans who happened to have darker complexions than they. As I said, I didn't have to compromise journalistic principles. I simply described the situation and wrote a straight story, making, I hope, a small contribution to the civil rights movement right there in Spartanburg.

SYNAGOGUE WORK

I didn't start out with any particular sensitivity toward minority groups, though I had no antipathy either. I grew up in a blue-collar neighborhood in Milwaukee that was white and mostly Catholic and Lutheran. I attended Catholic schools and didn't know very many Protestants, much less minorities or non-Christians.

My horizon expanded at age 15 when I went to work for my uncle, Arthur H. Fink Sr., who owned a drugstore in what was then a Jewish neighborhood on the fringes of the small but tightly packed and sharply circumscribed Negro community in Milwaukee. (In those days, African-Americans and other black people were referred to as colored, Negroes or the N-word).

Despite the fact that he was a Catholic of German extraction, my Uncle Art's name gave him a degree of credibility in the community. Most of his customers thought he was Jewish and he, being a good businessman, did nothing to alter their perceptions.

One of my customers was a young rabbi, stationed at an orthodox synagogue a few blocks away. I was 16, he was probably somewhere in his late 20s or early 30s, and we talked a lot when I wasn't busy. I was eager to learn more about his religion. One day he came to me with a proposition: Would I be willing to come to his synagogue on Yom Kippur and do a small chore for $5? He explained that on Yom Kippur, the Day of Atonement, Orthodox Jews were forbidden to do any work—not even writing, driving a car or flipping a light switch.

I was then making $1 an hour, so the idea of picking up some easy money for a little work over a couple of hours was appealing. Besides, I was curious to see the services and the inside of a synagogue. But I told him I couldn't do it unless I cleared it with my parish priest. When I asked one of the assistant pastors, he said it would be okay as long as I didn't participate in the services, which I couldn't do anyway because I had no clue about what went on and didn't speak the language.

On the appointed day, I went to the synagogue and was issued a yarmulke, which I promptly popped on the top of my head, figuring that wasn't participation. With that little beanie, I was just one of the guys.

I sat on a straight bench along one side, next to a man who was introduced as the treasurer of the congregation. Most of the first hour or so was taken up with a lot of chanting and bowing and praying in a language I didn't understand. But I loved the singing. One man, who the treasurer told me was the cantor, had a beautiful singing voice—not at all like the screeching old voices that sang Latin in the choir at my church. This guy sounded like a professional.

Part of the service was set aside for members of the congregation to stand up and pledge money to the United Jewish Appeal, with the money going to charities and Israel. I think maybe 20 people eventually pledged, but the most interesting part were the comments that the treasurer whispered in my right ear as I sat expressionless, dutifully writing.

Somebody would stand up, say his name and announce his pledge. The treasurer would lean into my ear and say the name, then spell it. But he also added editorial comments, such as, "He's good for it." Or, "If some of it comes in at all, we won't see it for six months." Or, "I don't think we'll ever see that."

I was so serious about my task that it didn't occur to me to laugh, and I even started to write down his comments, until he told me that I should record only names and amounts. But I got my $5 and my introduction to the Jewish faith and Jewish humor.

AIR FORCE AND BLACK FOLKS

I was 18 when I first met a Negro. It was at my first Air Force Reserve summer camp in 1953, at Atterbury Air Force Base near Columbus, Indiana,

They had an airman's club, which was reserved exclusively for anybody below a staff sergeant. I was an airman basic, the lowest of the low. The club consisted of picnic tables in a tent, and the only beverage you could buy, other than soda pop, was Oertel's 92 or some other local beer. In those days, 18 was the age for drinking beer; it was 21 for anything harder.

I met Jim Durrah, a Negro enlisted man. He was in his twenties, which gave him an aura of maturity that we lacked. A group of us spent hours talking to him, mainly because there wasn't anything else to do, other than drink beer out of long-necked bottles.

Durrah opened our eyes. In a quiet way, without any bitterness that I could detect, he calmly told us stories about how Negroes couldn't eat in most restaurants or stay in hotels, especially in the South, or if they could, there were separate places and entrances for them. There were even separate public bathrooms and bubblers—the Milwaukee word for drinking fountains. He said Negroes in the South couldn't vote in most places, and were ridiculed and victims of prejudice even in Milwaukee.

We were honestly shocked. If we didn't know anything about colored people, which was absolutely the case, we certainly had no idea they were subjected to horrendous humiliation, discrimination and even lynching. We'd grown up in our families, our neighborhoods, our schools and churches, and never had given much thought to "those people" who lived in their own neighborhood downtown. But then, I knew nothing about Jews, either. I don't think I learned about the Holocaust until after I was out of college and working as a newspaper reporter. As a kid, World War II meant shortages, rationing, saving string and tinfoil, and watching cartoons at the movies that ridiculed Adolf Hitler and the Japanese emperor Hirohito.

As uniformed and uninformed 18-year-olds, our unanimous and angry reaction to Durrah's stories—given the number of beers we usually managed to consume—was, "It isn't fair." But it wasn't something we felt personally obligated to do anything about except to express our moral outrage. I never saw Durrah again, but I thought about him periodically for the rest of my life.

My outrage had its roots in the teaching of the Notre Dame nuns in grade school that every human being was a child of God. We also learned that anyone with sincere beliefs who had not been exposed to the true church could also go to heaven. We saved our pennies and nickels to "buy pagan babies." We were told that for $5, a baby in Africa could be ransomed, cared for and taught about Jesus and the Catholic Church, making it easier for that baby to eventually get to heaven. But I was never taught that heaven was closed to anyone, except grievous sinners and those who knew the truth and rejected it.

So despite the occasional derogatory reference or joke, I didn't grow up in an overtly racist environment. On the contrary, I had a firm belief that every human being had a soul that was destined to be united with God, except for people who screwed up and went to hell. At the same time, we didn't give race much thought because we had no contact with anyone of color or, for that matter, anybody who wasn't pretty much like us—white and Catholic, of low to middle-class income.

REPORTING ON RACE

Though it had nothing to do with race, I learned about another minority group when I was an apprentice compositor. The printing trade attracted many deaf people because you didn't need to be able to hear to set type. At Wisconsin Cuneo Press, where my dad and I both worked, there were a number of deaf compositors and pressmen, and my dad had even learned rudimentary sign language. He taught me the alphabet, so I could sign words by spelling them out.

In the composing room, where I worked, we had several deaf Linotype operators. They were teased mercilessly by some of their coworkers, who sometimes would play practical jokes on them. One particularly gross trick was to empty the guy's lunch box and substitute a dead mouse buried in sawdust. I hated the hazing, but did not have the courage to speak out.

I had my second encounter with race in my second year at Marquette. In the first semester, I had taken a basic course in how to write news stories. In the second semester, we got to actually play at being reporters. The course, called sophomore reporting, consisted of a one-hour lecture and a four-hour lab each week. The idea was to work as a reporter would on an afternoon paper like The Milwaukee Journal. The professor, Don Ross, gave us assignments when we showed up at 8 a.m., we'd go out and cover the event and come back to write the story before the noon deadline.

It was fun, and soon Ross noticed that a few of us, including my friend, Jim Cotter, were getting out too early for his tastes. We'd rush out, get back and write the story in a couple of hours. So he decided to give us something to use up the time. He assigned a group of us to do a series of stories on the problems faced by Negroes in Milwaukee. It was 1957, and Ross obviously had an awareness of the indignities and discrimination suffered by black people, though we blithely did not, despite my earlier acquaintance with Jim Durrah.

We attacked the assignment as a lark. We researched background materials in the library, but mostly got our information on the street. We went into the Negro community, visited storefront businesses and did man-on-the-street interviews. We had no fear of going into predominantly Negro neighborhoods. For me, the experience brought back and reinforced the things I'd learned from Durrah.

The assignment also taught me how much fun it was to be a reporter, poking my nose into other people's business. Everywhere we went, we were well treated, and I'm sure some of the stuff we were told was either sugar-coated or exaggerated. We'd get so tied up in our interviewing that sometimes we wouldn't make it back to class. One time, we sent a telegram to Ross, telling him we wouldn't be back that day because we were out reporting. We signed it, "The Ross Task Force."

We managed to write a four-part series on the plight of the Negro in Milwaukee, and Ross gave it an A. There was even some talk of offering it to The Milwaukee Journal. But nothing ever came of it, and I have no idea what ever happened to the copy. I'm certain by later lights it looked naïve and amateurish.

THE CIVIL RIGHTS BEAT

In 1964, with four years of experience as a general assignment reporter and rewrite man at The Journal behind me, the civil rights beat came open. Like most of the secondary beats at the time, it was part-time, and I eagerly went after it. The civil rights movement was heating up in Milwaukee, particularly over de facto school segregation, and I wanted to get in on the story. I was always what I later called a grass-is-greener reporter. If I was doing one thing and there was a better story somewhere else, that's where I wanted to be. Anybody with half a brain could see that civil rights was on its way to becoming one of the biggest and most exciting stories in the country.

The Rev. Martin Luther King Jr. had delivered his historic "I have a dream" speech at the Lincoln Memorial in Washington in 1963, with the biggest turnout for any civil rights demonstration in the nation's history. Everywhere, aspirations were stirring in the Negro community. Sometimes in the years after, they took the form of nonviolent protest demonstrations; at other times, it was civil disobedience. And in places like Watts, Newark, Detroit and even staid old Milwaukee, there were riots.

I got the beat, and set out to learn the issues and meet the people. In retrospect, I was as fresh-faced and uninformed as I had been in college when, as editors and reporters on the Marquette Tribune, my classmates and I had decided to be the Paper of Record for the

Marquette community and campus, and mostly ignored the outside world.

The Milwaukee Journal was one of the best papers in the country, and a good part of its strength lay in its vacuum-cleaner local news coverage. I fit right into the philosophy, but as a result didn't know much about what was going on anywhere else, especially in Washington. I could cover school segregation or open housing issues in Milwaukee, but was only vaguely aware of what the federal government was doing about any of those matters.

But nobody cared, because my job was to cover the local story. Eventually I moved onto the national story as well, but only in specific instances. I covered the aftermath of the Detroit riots in 1967, I went to Alabama for the historic Selma to Montgomery march for voting rights in 1965, and I spent my 33rd birthday in Memphis, trying to make some sense out of King's assassination on Apr. 4, 1968.

Those were memorable times with memorable people: King; his second-in-command, the Rev. Ralph David Abernathy; the Rev. Andrew Young, who went on to become ambassador to the United Nations; the dignified Rev. C. T. Vivian; the volatile James Forman; Milwaukee's Father James E. Groppi, called "the white nigger" by the bigots; hearty Brother Booker T. Ashe; saintly Father Matthew Gottschalk; cerebral Atty. Lloyd Barbee; zealous Marilyn Morheuser; intellectual John H. Givens Jr. and emotional Alderwoman Vel Phillips. I got to cover the national figures; the locals I also eventually chronicled in a book, *City with a Chance*, a history of the civil rights movement in Milwaukee.

I didn't contribute much to the King assassination story, though it scared the hell out of me—as well as the rest of the country. Despite the fact that King's influence was waning in the face of the black power movement, some of whose adherents derided King as "de Lawd," the assassination traumatized people everywhere. Negroes rioted in the cities and whites shivered in fear that the riots would spread into their comfortable lives.

THE KING ASSASSINATION

The Journal's editors sent me to Memphis on Apr. 5, the day after King was shot. I knew nothing about the city; only a little about what had brought King there—a strike by sanitation workers—and obviously I had no sources whatever. I did, however, know the names of the local newspapers—the morning Press-Scimitar and the afternoon Commercial Appeal. I even had a nodding acquaintance with the former because I had used it as my model newspaper in an editing class at Marquette. I picked it because I liked the name.

So I did what I have often done in 40 years as a newspaperman. I leaned on my colleagues. I went to the Commercial Appeal newsroom and introduced myself. I was immediately given a desk and a telephone to use—something that was not uncommon in journalism then. You could always count on being welcomed into a newspaper newsroom anywhere. In Milwaukee, we often played host to out-of-town reporters. The Christian Science Monitor's Godfrey (Budge) Sperling, who I met after I moved to Washington, spoke many times of the professional courtesies he had received at The Journal while covering Wisconsin politics.

But I had few tools to cover such a momentous story. I read the accounts of the assassination in the Press-Scimitar and Commercial Appeal, and reporters there shared telephone numbers with me. I made a few calls to the authorities, and then decided I had to see the crime scene at the Lorraine Motel.

The area around the motel, as well as the tenement across the street where it was believed the assassin had fired, was deserted. With more than a little apprehension, I approached the Lorraine Motel from the front, divining from the photographs I had seen where King had been standing. I climbed a staircase to the outside concrete walkway on the second floor and walked to the door to King's room, where a bloodstain had soaked into the concrete. I was numb, didn't have the nerve to knock on the door to the room, and quickly left.

I crossed the street to the tenement where, on the back side, I found an open door leading to a dark staircase. Sweating and shaking, I made my way up the stairs into the hallway littered with broken glass and debris. Not knowing whether any of the apartments were occupied, I didn't have the courage to try any of the closed doors. I worked my way down the hallway, stepping into each open room, trying to see where the shooter had been.

In the entire time I was there, I did not see a single living thing, which was an eerie feeling. The neighborhood was deserted. Today, a crime scene of anywhere near that magnitude would be teeming with investigators and cordoned off for many days.

That night, a Friday, there were riots in downtown Memphis, so I went out to take another look. The riots were confined to about a square block area, which was ringed by police and National Guard soldiers. I was struck by the fact that I could stand across the street behind them in relative safety and look into the riot area. Yet if you watched the coverage on television, it looked as if the entire city of Memphis was going up in flames. It was a lesson about the impact of television, which can convey false impressions because it focuses on only a few square feet of an event.

I wrote a lame story for the Saturday afternoon editions, filed some additional material for Sunday, and went home depressed because I knew I had not gotten a handle on the story. Our Sunday story was mostly compiled wire service reports, though some of my file made it into the story as well.

SELMA

But it was not the first time I'd been frustrated by not being able to do the big story. Three years earlier, in March of 1965, The Journal sent me to cover the voting rights campaign in Selma, Ala. King's Southern Christian Leadership Conference was leading daily demonstrations on behalf of a federal law to guarantee the right to vote—a right that was widely denied to Negroes in the South by poll taxes and other subterfuges. A group of 500 marchers had been attacked and beaten by police, sheriff's deputies and vicious posse men when they tried to march across the Edmund Pettis Bridge in Selma on March 7. "Bloody Sunday," as it became known later in the civil rights movement, was front-page news everywhere.

Then one of the demonstrators, a Unitarian minister from Boston, the Rev. James J. Reeb, was beaten to death by a gang of whites on a Selma street. Predictably, civil rights activists and sympathizers from all over the country immediately traveled to Selma to demonstrate solidarity with the SCLC and its supporters. Among them were Father James E. Groppi, the volatile Catholic priest who later would emerge as a civil rights leader in Milwaukee, and Father Matthew Gottschalk—a Capuchin friar and Groppi's confessor—who had led the first civil rights march by clergy in Milwaukee. In 1964, he had led a group of seminarians in protesting an appearance at Marquette University by segregationist Gov. George Corley Wallace of Alabama.

Years later, I would come to regard Gottschalk as the man I most admired. But then he was one of a group of priests, nuns and ministers from Milwaukee who descended on Selma to participate in the demonstrations.

My job was to cover the local angle—to bird-dog the Milwaukee contingent. But with my usual hubris, I decided that I could cover the whole story by myself, and that's what I set out to do the first day. I soon realized that I was up against cohorts of pros from the wire services and great newspapers like the New York Herald Tribune, The New York Times and the Atlanta Constitution.

Jim Cattey, who later went to The New York Times, was working the national desk when I filed my first story, which was feeble—and he told me so—compared to the comprehensive pieces produced by teams of reporters that were coming across the wires. Try as I might, I simply couldn't cover a story that was being reported from sources all over the place.

Chagrined, I went back to covering the local angle, dogging the paths of my Milwaukee forces. I did a feature story one day about a 47-year-old nun from Milwaukee who stood in the hot sun with other protesters, facing the combined might of law officers, deputies and posse men from Selma, Dallas County and the state of Alabama. Dressed in a traditional habit, with her face and hands exposed to the blistering sun, Sister Mary Jeanine of Milwaukee's Cardinal Stritch College, suffered from severe sunburn and heat exhaustion. She later limped her way through a march to the Dallas County courthouse and was rewarded with a handshake from King.

Selma was not a big city, and the few motels already had been taken by the television networks, wire services and the big papers. So the demonstration leaders from the Rev. King's Southern Christian Leadership Conference had made arrangements to house some of the northern demonstrators, including some of my priests and ministers, with people who lived in the George Washington Carver Housing Project, which straddled Sylvan St. and was at the center of the voting rights protest.

"WE SHALL OVERCOME"

I had no place to stay and did not consider it right to ask for lodging for myself. I was a spectator, not a participant. So I planned to sleep in my rented Plymouth station wagon. Meanwhile, however, I had to find a telephone to dictate my story. I asked a woman in an apartment in the project if I could use her phone. She ended up offering me a place to stay as well, which I gratefully accepted.

Regrettably, though I wrote a story listing the names of housing project residents who played host to the priests and ministers, I had my hostess's name only in my notebook, which has been lost. But I will never forget her. She was a widow, probably in her forties (I was 29 at the time), who lived in first-floor apartment with her brother, a World War II veteran who suffered from what today would be called post-traumatic stress disorder. Back then, he was considered shell-shocked and feeble-minded. The woman's daughter, a single mother with a baby, lived in another apartment near-by.

The widow gave me her daughter's old room, which was bright and pretty and had a small desk where I could sit and write on my Journal-issue Olivetti portable typewriter. At night, when I was writing, she brought me food—wonderful southern stuff like ham with red-eyed gravy, fried okra and hush puppies. It was an oasis in the midst of a fearful situation. The troopers, cops and posse ringed the housing project day and night, and not even news people like me felt comfortable crossing the lines.

While I was there, President Lyndon B. Johnson delivered his famed nationally televised speech in which he promised passage in Congress of what became the Voting Rights Act of 1965. It was remarkable for the fact that he adopted the anthem of the civil rights movement. Throughout his speech, Johnson repeated, "We shall overcome."

I will never forget the scene in the living room of the widow's apartment. She and her brother and I sat in the dark, watching Johnson on a black and white console TV set. Her brother sat on a hassock right in front of the screen, punctuating Johnson's speech with comments and praises, much as he might have done in church on Sunday during the sermon. "That's right," he'd say. "Yes, sir" and "You tell it."

I had the chair behind him but to the left of the screen. My hostess sat in another upholstered chair to my right. She held her left hand up to the side of her face. After glancing over there a few times, I finally realized that she didn't want me to see that she was crying.

CAN'T LET THE WORDS GET WET

One day, word circulated among the demonstrators in Selma that a group of posse men on horseback had attacked a group of civil rights workers in Montgomery. Groppi, displaying the impulsiveness that would later characterize his civil rights leadership in Milwaukee, got in his Dodge station wagon and left immediately with Gottschalk, three other priests and a Methodist minister from Worcester, Mass. I followed in my rental car. None had a clue about what they would do in Montgomery; they simply felt they had to be there.

Along with a half dozen other priests they met there, they wound up at a rally that evening at the Beulah Baptist Church, where King was scheduled to speak. The church was packed with local citizens and demonstrators. I had long since learned that I needed good vantage points to watch the action, so I climbed up and sat on a ledge beneath one of the tall, stained-glass windows, where I could look down at the throng.

Pumped up by King's aides in the sanctuary, the crowd was in an excited, festive mood. They loudly sang hymns and civil rights anthems, their raised hands moving sinuously in the air. In between, speakers kept them fired up for the cause.

As was his custom, King arrived late. He always moved around in secrecy and with erratic stops for his own safety. Aides would announce a press conference at a hall or some other location and King would show up someplace else—perhaps on the back porch of the house of a supporter. Trusted reporters would be tipped off.

This time, King was exactly an hour late, and when he stepped into the Beulah Baptist Church the crowd almost blew the roof off with its cheering. Beaming, King said, "It's a marvelous thing," referring to "the white brothers and sisters" who had traveled to Alabama to participate in the voting rights campaign, and who looked like salt in the pepper of Negro faces in the church.

As always, there were other speakers in addition to King. One of them, in bib overalls, was James Forman, head of the Student Nonviolent Coordinating Committee, a youthful and more militant group than King's SCLC. Like most of the protest leaders, he delivered a loud, impassioned speech that had the crowd cheering. Caught up in his own rhetoric near the end, he shouted, "If they ain't going to let us sit at the table with them, we're going to knock the fucking legs out from under it!"

The entire church went dead silent. Hardly anybody used the f-word in public in those days anywhere, much less in a church. The silence lasted only a few seconds because the Rev. Ralph David Abernathy,

King's top aide, leaned into the microphone and said something to the effect that "the boy" had gotten himself a little excited and could be forgiven. The crowd erupted in laughter and Forman, looking sheepish, sat down. Many years later, in the mid-1990s, I met Forman, then a prominent mainstream citizen in Washington, and reminded him of the story. He laughed uproariously.

After King's speech, the priests and ministers went in a group of about 35 to conduct a prayer vigil on the steps of the gleaming white state capitol. They wound up in a tugging match with Maj. John W. Cloud of the Alabama state police, who said they could say one prayer but only on the sidewalk. The clergymen held out for praying on the steps, and sat down on the sidewalk. Finally, Cloud escorted them up the steps for their prayer. Victories then were won in modest increments.

Even though most of the clergy were Catholic priests, they recited the Our Father in the Protestant King James version. It takes longer, several said. When it was over, a flushed Groppi said to Gottschalk, "That's something I've always wanted to do—sit down in the heart of the segregationist south with a group of priests and ministers in an ecumenical protest."

"You just have a martyr complex, that's all," Gottschalk kidded him. As later events in Milwaukee would prove, it was a prophetic remark.

The next day, King led a march to the county courthouse in Montgomery to protest the violence against the demonstrators. I tagged along with the four priests and the minister from Milwaukee, and decided—stupidly, as it turned out—to write a piece about what it was like to actually participate in a protest demonstration.

The march, only about a mile from a Baptist Church, was uneventful. After our arrival, we stood outside the courthouse when King and several aides went inside to negotiate. We had been there just 46 minutes, according to the story I wrote later, when the skies opened up. It rained heavily for the next three hours as we stood there. Except for one priest in a windbreaker, all of us northerners wore suits. It took exactly 20 minutes for the rain to soak through to my skin.

I had the nearly impossible task of trying to shield my notebook from the rain. At one point, a Negro youth, maybe 14 years old, noticed my plight and asked, "Are you a reporter?" I said yes.

"Can't let the words get wet," he said. He took off his cap and held it over my notebook for almost the entire three hours we stood there.

He saved the notes, written in pencil and ballpoint ink, which already had started running.

RESOURCEFUL PRIESTS

After King reappeared, the demonstration broke up and our soggy little band retreated to St. John the Baptist, a Catholic mission parish in the middle of a poor black neighborhood with unpaved streets near downtown Montgomery. There were about a dozen of us, including other clergymen who had been in the march.

We all trooped into the rectory, where we were welcomed by the Irish-American pastor. Despite the warmth of the day, we were all wet and shivering. The pastor handed out bed sheets, which we wore like togas, and we all struggled out of our wet clothes. Nuns appeared at the rectory door and hauled the clothing away for drying. Incredibly, the pastor not only had a bottle of Irish whiskey available for those of us who needed a shot of warmth, but a big pot of Irish stew as well.

At one point, the harried pastor came up to me and asked if I could go into the church to take over that evening's Lenten devotions. I sheepishly confessed that I was not a priest, merely a journalistic hanger-on. One of the other priests quickly accepted and slipped into one of the pastor's vestments to lead the devotions.

Eventually, the nuns returned our clothes, which they had apparently simply stuffed into the convent's clothes dryers. I had been wearing a dark blue wool suit, and when I got dressed it had shrunk by about three or four sizes. The jacket, with sleeves three inches short, pinched my back, and my trousers were in a similar state—about four inches short at the ankles. I couldn't zip the fly up all the way.

But I also had learned a lesson. If you're a reporter in strange and hostile territory, and you have an opportunity to hook up with a bunch of Catholic priests, do it. The guys I was following around never lacked for lodging or food. No matter how dicey or unexpected the circumstances, it seemed they could always find a place to stay, as I would learn again during the 50-mile march from Selma to Montgomery.

All of the people I was covering participated in the historic march, and I tried to cover it as best as I could. I played leapfrog, driving my rental car ahead along highway 80, then walking back to join the marchers, walking with them a ways, then repeating the process.

King showed up from time to time to march up front. Though I had interviewed him by telephone for a profile I wrote back in June, 1964,

I didn't try to talk to him on the march. At that point, having learned that I couldn't do it all, I was doing the local angle and color stories, leaving the big picture to the wires.

BONANZA, THE POSSE AND THE COFFINS

About 20 miles east of Selma, the marchers stopped for the night in an open field, where the SCLC had set up a big circus tent. It had rained most of the day and the field was a vast expanse of mud the consistency of peanut butter. The tent housed a small aid station, where volunteer doctors and nurses treated blisters and other ailments. The marchers tried to get some sleep on blankets and sleeping bags lain on plastic sheeting. But the mud kept oozing through. Women slept in another tent.

Wandering around, soaking up the scene, I ran into a young man sitting alone on a space heater, tending a generator. He was Pernell Roberts, 36, then a big star as Adam Cartwright on the popular "Bonanza" television show. He told me he was there with his wife, Judy, 30, to support the voting rights effort. They planned to spend the night in the mud with the other marchers.

As a rookie reporter years earlier, I had learned to be as precise as I could. I counted marchers and people in crowds instead of estimating them. By my count, it was exactly 496 steps from the campsite to highway 80, along a narrow, rutted farm road.

Late that night, after I'd finished interviewing people and roaming the campsite, I headed back along that road to the highway, where I had parked my rental car. The only light came from the highway and the lights behind me at the tents. As I walked slowly along, a squad of Alabama National Guardsmen marched toward me, in double file and route step. The Guard had been federalized by President Johnson to protect the marchers, and most of them were not happy about it. The soldiers, all white, carried carbines at the ready, diagonally across their chests. I squeezed as far to the right as I could to let them by.

I don't know what triggered it, but as they marched past me, one of the men in the middle of the line whacked me in the shoulder with his elbow—or maybe his rifle butt—sending me tumbling into the ditch. Fortunately, I caught my balance just before I would have sprawled face down in the mud, so I ended up with mud only up over my ankles and forearms. Heart pounding and scared stiff, I bolted to my car.

The next night, before the final march up to the Alabama Capitol, the SCLC staged a huge rally on the outskirts of Montgomery at the City of St. Jude, a 40-acre Catholic mission that contained a church, a rectory, two convents, elementary and high schools, two hospitals and a gymnasium.

In a field behind the rectory, rally organizers had set up a makeshift stage—a platform resting on metal coffins and packing crates borrowed from a local Negro undertaker. Many of those who attended came to participate in the voting rights march, but many others simply came to be entertained by more than 30 personalities led by King and Ralph Bunche, the United Nations undersecretary for special political affairs who, like King, was a Nobel Peace Prize winner.

The stars included Harry Belafonte, who served as the master of ceremonies; singer Tony Bennett, actress Shelley Winters, composer and conductor Leonard Bernstein, folk singers Peter, Paul and Mary, actor Tony Perkins, and entertainer Sammy Davis Jr.

Along with most of the crowd, I arrived early and managed to stake out a few square feet of space on a corner of the stage, where I could look at the crowd and the performers. For more than seven hours, until 1 o'clock the next morning, anywhere from 10,000 to 30,000 people—this was a crowd I couldn't count—stood jammed together like crayons in a box. Some women fainted and were passed over the heads of the crowd. I almost got into a fist fight with a late-arriving TV cameraman who was determined to take over my little spot on the stage. He finally backed off.

After the show, I connected once again with my little band of clergymen, who led me off to one of the St. Jude buildings, where we were greeted by three FBI priests. They were the three assistant pastors there. The FBI stood for "foreign born Irish."

We were all exhausted. Without a clue about my location, I was led into a dark room with a bed. I couldn't believe my good fortune. Here was a bed with clean sheets, and a bathroom nearby. I got out of my clothes and fell asleep as soon as my head hit the pillow.

I awoke the next morning to laughter and the sounds of children playing. Raising my head, I looked at the doorway, where a couple of little Negro kids were peeking in and grinning at me. I found out later that the bed the priests had found for me was in the children's ward of one of the St. Jude hospitals. I even had access to a desk and a telephone in an office to dictate my story back to Milwaukee.

Before the final march to the Capitol, I managed to get myself quoted in Newsweek magazine. By then I had gotten to know some of the other reporters who were covering the Selma-Montgomery story. Enjoying the camaraderie that often results with reporters on the same story, we gathered in a hotel room in downtown Montgomery to sample some of the local hooch. You couldn't get name brand liquor in Alabama. The state controlled everything, and it decided what brands would be sold.

As we sat around and swapped stories, the Newsweek guy came into the room and said one of his editors was looking for a snappy comeback to a criticism Gov. Wallace had made about the press covering the voting rights campaign. I was feeling important, in the company of some of big-name reporters for newspapers like The New York Times and The Herald-Tribune, so I blurted out, "If he'd been here, he couldn't say that." The quote wound up in Newsweek's press section the next week. I felt the flush of fleeting fame.

INVISIBLE VIETNAM

For me, Vietnam was almost a blank. Wrapped up in the civil rights movement, I paid little attention to the war, and even less to the protests against it. Like others, I was privately critical when King, in a famed speech at the Riverside Church in New York in April, 1967, denounced the war as the enemy of the poor. I thought it was a mistake for him to dilute his message. As later events proved, he was prophetic.

When I started covering civil rights in 1964, the beat still was part-time, and Laurie Van Dyke was covering civil rights for the Milwaukee Sentinel. She had been a superb reporter for The Journal and, when The Journal bought the Sentinel in 1962, she was among the four Journal reporters sent over to help get the Sentinel up and running. I was one of the others, along with Jim Wieghart and Paul Hayes.

After a few months, Hayes and I returned to The Journal. Harry Sonneborn, the Sentinel's managing editor, who had been my city editor at The Journal, offered me a job. But I didn't want to work on the city's No. 2 paper, and I didn't want to work on a paper without a Sunday edition. (The company had abolished the Sunday Sentinel. We used to ridicule the Sentinel's old Hearst motto that it was the only major Milwaukee paper that was published 365 days a year. We said it was the same under Journal ownership, published 365 days a year "except Sundays.") Also, Sonneborn said he couldn't guarantee me a day job, and with one small child and another on the way, I didn't want to work nights.

Hayes went on to become The Journal's premier environment and science reporter. Wieghart later became the Sentinel's one-man bureau in Washington. He jumped to the New York Daily News, where he ended up as the editor in New York. Van Dyke became the Sentinel's day city editor.

When I started covering civil rights, Van Dyke terrified me. She seemed to know everybody and everything about civil rights in Milwaukee. But a lot of my fear was self-imposed. I don't think I got beat too badly—mostly because we were both covering the same things and the time of day determined whose paper got the story first.

THE PORTOMOBILE

One of the first things I covered was as much a political as a civil rights story. Alabama's Gov. George C. Wallace came to Milwaukee in February of 1964, ostensibly to recruit Milwaukee industries to locate in Alabama. But he also was readying a campaign for the presidency, and spent a good deal of his time denouncing the Civil Rights Act of 1964, which guaranteed access to public accommodations.

I tagged along after Wallace and his entourage. One stop was for a television interview at WTMJ, The Milwaukee Journal station. I stood in the wings as Wallace was interviewed, and was puzzled by his frequent references to a "portomobile." With his thick southern accent, half the time I couldn't understand Wallace anyway, and I couldn't imagine what a "portomobile" was—maybe some sort of baby buggy? He pronounced it "poht-a-mo-beel."

So after the interview, I stopped Wallace's press secretary, Bill Jones, and asked him, "What the heck is this 'poht-a-mo-beel' he keeps talking about?"

Not enamored of this upstart young Yankee reporter, Jones replied through clenched teeth, "The governor is referring to the Port ... of ... Mobile."

Oh.

Pickets from the Milwaukee chapter of the Congress of Racial Equality (CORE) dogged Wallace's tracks, carrying signs saying, "Racist Not Welcome," "Police Dogs Must Go," "Fire Hoses Must Go" and "Gov. Wallace, White People Are Ashamed of You," among others.

Wallace replied, correctly, that Milwaukee also had segregation. The only difference, he said, was, "Yours here is a subterfuge; in Alabama it is above board." However, he also said, falsely, that he could prove that anywhere racial violence broke out, Communists were responsible.

During his Wisconsin tour, Wallace also spoke at the University of Wisconsin in Madison and at Marquette in Milwaukee. Outside as he spoke at the Marquette Dental School were a group of pickets— sandal-clad and robed Catholic seminarians led by Father Matthew Gottschalk, a Capuchin priest. As far as I knew, it was the first time in the history of the state that Catholic clergy had participated in a civil rights protest.

Over the following years, I would come to regard Gottschalk as a living saint and the man I most admired in the world. He never sought headlines as Groppi did, preferring to work quietly in the background for civil rights and the poor, the mentally ill and other outcasts in Milwaukee society. He served as an assistant and pastor at inner city parishes, and founded the House of Peace in 1968 with Booker T. Ashe, a rotund and jovial man who was a Capuchin lay brother. The House of Peace, supported by private donations, takes care of the poor and dispossessed in one of the toughest neighborhoods in Milwaukee.

THE MOVEMENT MOVES

It was in those neighborhoods that the city's civil rights movement had its start. In July, 1963, a month before King's famed speech at the Washington Monument, a small group of blacks and whites formed a local chapter of the Congress of Racial Equality (CORE), which professed nonviolence and had conducted sit-ins and freedom rides to protest segregated transportation and public accommodations in the South. The head of the new chapter was young John H. Givens Jr., who as a soldier in France in 1961 had developed so strong a friendship with the residents of a small town in Normandy called Pont L'Eveque that they petitioned President John F. Kennedy to let him stay there after he was ordered back to the United States.

Givens was a friendly man who could put anybody at ease, and was non-threatening to most whites. He was handsome, educated and erudite, and bore no resemblance to the stereotypical Negro feared by many white Milwaukeeans. Over the years, we got to be friends—or at least as friendly as a reporter gets with a news source. Years later, he even went to work for Mayor Henry W. Maier.

But the young Givens soon became a threat. It pained him to witness inequality in Milwaukee after he had basically been adopted by the French citizens of Pont L'Eveque. He and members of the CORE chapter found an issue that summer in Fred E. Lins, a sausage maker who had been appointed as a Milwaukee County representative on the city's new Community Social Development Commission, which had been proposed in 1962 by Mayor Maier to work on problems of juvenile delinquency, the aged and Negroes in the inner city.

Lins likely was picked because he had experience in the inner city, where he was president and treasurer of his sausage manufacturing company. But he soon put his foot in his mouth and alienated the city's nascent civil rights movement. In a newspaper interview, Lins said some way had to be found to keep the ignorant poor from moving to Milwaukee. The new arrivals, he said, took advantage of people who already lived there.

But it was comments near the end of the story that, not surprisingly, prompted CORE to conduct sit-ins against his appointment to the commission. He was quoted as saying, "The Negroes look so much alike that you can't identify the ones that committed the crime." He also said, "An awful mess of them have an IQ of nothing."

CORE conducted three weeks of picketing and sit-ins—at Lins's company, the county courthouse and even in Mayor Maier's office, after Maier refused to repudiate Lins. As was not uncommon in those early days of the civil rights movement, most Milwaukeeans reacted to the city's first major demonstrations by focusing on the demonstrations, not the issue.

The protests did prompt the establishment of a keep-the-lid-on organization called the Committee of We—Milwaukeeans, which was a composite of wealthy members of the city's white power structure and a group of Negro community leaders, including educators, clergy, attorneys, physicians and other professionals. It never did very much except keep the lines of communication open between the leaders of the white and black communities.

One of the leaders of We—Milwaukeeans was none other than Irwin Maier (no relation to the mayor), who was the chairman of The Journal Company and publisher of The Milwaukee Journal and Milwaukee Sentinel.

THE POWER STRUCTURE MOVES

The committee, of course, was news. But it never announced its meetings, which were intended to be closed to the public and press. To his credit, when I found out about a meeting and showed up to cover it, Maier never kicked me out. But I'm certain the meetings I did cover were sanitized for my benefit. My inside source, who tipped me off to the goings-on among the members of the white power structure, was Ben Barkin, the city's leading public relations man.

Barkin was a pillar of the Jewish community, as well as the business community, whose biggest account was the Schlitz Brewing Co. and, with it, the Uihlein family, which owned the brewery. With help from circus impresario Chappie Fox and gentle persuasion of Robert Uihlein, then the head of the brewery, Barkin invented the Great Milwaukee Circus Parade, which for many years was sponsored by Schlitz.

A man of many interests and passions, Barkin was a part-owner of Jake's, a Jewish delicatessen in the heart of the city's Negro area, and he was passionate about civil rights. (Another owner was a local Ford dealer, Bud Selig, who years later became commissioner of baseball). Barkin seemed to know everyone everywhere, and he was a shameless name-dropper. He also had an invalid wife who required 24-hour nursing care, but fortunately he was wealthy enough to handle the expenses. Nevertheless, he took his wife along on his many travels to Israel and elsewhere in the world.

I admired his commitment to his wife. Once I sympathized with him about the burden of taking care of her. His response was typical: "It's not happening to me," he said. "It's happening to her." His commitment to civil rights was equally steadfast, which I also admired. Of course, I loved the fact that he kept me informed—on a non-attribution basis, of course—of whatever he knew about the goings-on among the city's movers and shakers.

In the years between 1964 and 1966, I covered civil rights on a part-time basis. As a practical matter, it meant that I covered protest demonstrations and did the occasional roundup. The issues—mainly de facto segregation in the schools and the reactions of public officials to Milwaukee's nascent civil rights movement—were covered by the other beat reporters, at city hall, the school board and the county government building.

I didn't mind. I liked the action, and I developed a rapport with the people. I think it mainly was because I never tried to be anything other than myself. I didn't try to adopt the mannerisms or speech patterns of the young people in the inner city. I always wore a sport coat and tie, and I did my best to cover the beat fairly and courteously, with understanding, and, after I became more familiar with the people and issues, a certain amount of affection as well.

After Father James E. Groppi organized the NAACP Youth Council Commandoes, I had a graphic illustration of the correctness of my instinctive approach. A young white guy, dedicated to the cause, asked to join the commandoes, a loosely-organized group of young black men in their teens and twenties. They were basically young ghetto toughs, some with physical disabilities and others who were poorly educated. A few had been in and out of jail. Groppi saw a need to give them a sense of purpose and belonging. Their job was to function as marshals during marches and other protest demonstrations, to protect the kids—most of them pre-teens—who made up the bulk of the protesters.

Though there was some suspicion and hesitation among the commandoes when the white guy asked to join, they accepted him. They could hardly have done otherwise, given their stated dedication to equal rights and integration. To reject him would have been to adopt the racist attitude of the white majority.

Soon the young man was wearing a commando sweat shirt and hanging out with the mostly ghetto youths who constituted the core of the group. He meant well, but I soon began to think he was a bit emotionally disturbed. He certainly was emotional. His ardor for the cause was almost too much, and he did his best to be one of the guys, adopting their culture, language and mannerisms, and the way they related to each other.

As an outsider, I saw it as a pathetic attempt—something like the class wimp trying to be accepted by the clique of the popular kids. I think some of the commandoes saw his puppy-dog efforts to please as phony, or at a minimum sycophantic, and it turned them off. It was only a matter of weeks, and the white kid stopped showing up, mainly because he was being politely shunned.

I never knew what happened to him. I felt sorry for him, and hoped that his experience had not turned him against the cause and its people.

HYPOCRITES AND HELPERS

In that 1964-'66 period, my experiences as a reporter constituted an education in reactionary versus progressive attitudes—in human relations and politics. I frankly came to be appalled at the resistance and, for want of a better word, the unwonted anger and cowardice of Milwaukee's majority white community and its elected and appointed officials.

Though many members of the city's power structure were maddeningly tentative in dealing with the issues, too many, including Mayor Maier, were downright callous in ignoring and downplaying the problems of black Milwaukee.

As a reporter, I could not—and would not—express my opinions in print on such matters, though there were times I itched to do so. I believed in the ideal of the fair reporter who tried to be as non-judgmental as possible. I tried to empathize with both sides, believing that if I just told the story accurately, everything would work out and right might even prevail.

I could relate to the politician, businessman or industrialist who was trying to move matters forward without causing even more resistance and with the civil rights advocates who operated quietly behind the scenes and seldom laid their bodies on the line.

The ones I could not stand were the hypocrites and obstructionists—people like District Court Judge Christ T. Seraphim and Lorraine Radtke, the Milwaukee School Board president, who seemingly did everything they could to stymie civil rights. Seraphim was a flamboyant judge, popular among many whites partly because he made it a practice to humiliate defendants, especially Negroes, who appeared before him. Nevertheless, I tried always to give even the dinosaurs a fair shake by quoting them accurately and doing my best to correctly represent their positions, figuring they would hoist themselves on their own racist petards.

I still believe that was the right approach. When history judges such people, it will be by their own words and actions—not a young reporter's opinions. That is why I never had much use for the so-called "new journalism," with its emphasis on the journalist's own evaluations of events. In the history books, some kid commentator's view of what happened will have far less credibility than the actions of the actors themselves.

Radtke and her ilk resisted any integration of the schools by enshrining as an unbending principle the preservation of Milwaukee's neighborhood school system. That, of course, meant that segregation would continue unabated, including the practice of busing classes of Negro children from overcrowded schools to schools in white neighborhoods, where they were kept segregated.

Operating against that power structure was the Milwaukee United School Integration Committee (MUSIC), which was founded by an erudite and cultured black lawyer, Lloyd A. Barbee, and a white former Catholic nun, Marilyn J. Morheuser. Together, they revved up resistance against de facto segregation and led two boycotts of the Milwaukee public schools, in May, 1964, and October, 1965. I covered some of the action—mainly picketing and sit-ins at schools, including Groppi's first civil rights arrest in June of 1965, when he and other protesters linked arms and sat down in front of a school bus at an elementary school.

As always, the larger community focused on the protests and boycotts, not on the issue, until Barbee finally took the issue to the federal courts, charging Milwaukee with operating a segregated school system. It dragged on for many years, to no real solution. Eventually, after the turn of the millennium, choice programs and charter schools operated to improve the educations of children in neighborhoods that were still predominantly black.

Even back then, I was amazed at the caveman attitudes of many supposedly educated and sophisticated whites, especially prosperous businessmen. On one occasion, Wesley Scott, the director of the Milwaukee Urban League, brought in the national director, Whitney M. Young, Jr., to speak to a group of Milwaukee area entrepreneurs. The Urban League was always the quiet, respectable and non-threatening arm of the civil rights movement which worked to improve employment opportunities for minorities.

At the end of Young's speech, the floor was opened to questions. As always at such events, someone asked the age-old racist question of whether the real reason for integration and equality of opportunity was so Negro men could marry white women. Young seemed to almost relish the question.

"Well," he said impishly, "it has been my observation that at least 50% of people seeking such relationships are white."

OFF ON A FELLOWSHIP

In the fall of 1966, Dick Leonard, who by then was The Journal's managing editor, called me into his office and made me an offer. Northwestern University's Medill graduate school of journalism had come into some Ford Foundation money and was offering fellowships. One of them was for a full academic year—nine months—to study civil rights and civil liberties.

Leonard was aware of how big a story civil rights had become. He wanted to send me on the fellowship, and promised that when I returned I would be full-time on the civil rights beat. Though it proved to be hard on my young family, especially my wife, Sharlene, it was too good an opportunity pass up. I never considered turning it down.

During the first semester, I took a course on freedom of speech in the university's speech school, a graduate seminar on the workings of the United States Supreme Court, and a seminar in the Law School on constitutional rights, with an emphasis on civil liberties. The last was my introduction to the legal profession. As part of the course, students were split up into teams to argue both sides of an issue—as if they were constitutional lawyers arguing before the Supreme Court.

Students had to do their own research, so I wound up spending hours in the law library, researching cases to use in my arguments. The Law School was in Chicago, while back on the Evanston campus I learned another side of the Supreme Court, which was more interesting to me because it was taught by the Washington Post's Supreme Court reporter, Robert Clayton. With all that Ford Foundation money, Dean Ira W. Cole simply paid to fly Clayton in from Washington once a week to lecture at the seminar. I was fascinated because the course provided a newsman's perspective. I also was amazed that Cole could spend money that way.

Along the way, I learned a great deal about—and developed enormous respect for—the Supreme Court and, especially, the First Amendment. I was particularly impressed by one of the books I read: *Toward a General Theory of the First Amendment*, by Thomas I. Emerson. It opened my mind to the importance of the Constitution and Bill of Rights, and the Supreme Court's role in developing those rights.

I also was looking for a project to do in my second semester at Medill, when I had no formal classes scheduled. Rooting through the index cards in the library one day, I was struck by the fact that there were drawers full of titles on freedom of speech, press and religion. But there were only a few books on the First Amendment right of assembly, which guarantees citizens the right to gather in protest demonstrations and to petition the government for redress of grievances.

Because the assembly books were all academic studies, I decided to write a popular book to tell people—mainly those with grievances—what their rights were to assemble and protest. I focused strictly on Supreme Court decisions, which over time had provided a basic outline of the right. My research taught me a great deal about how a constitutional right evolves over time.

Years later, talking to young journalists or interns, I used the analogy of a child's dot-to-dot coloring book. A Supreme Court decision on one aspect of the right of assembly—say, whether a state could prohibit picketing a courthouse—would connect a couple of the dots. Then another decision, in another area of the picture, would connect a different set of dots, and so on until a vague outline of the right began to emerge.

THE LONG, HOT SUMMER

The analogy works with all constitutional rights, and it demonstrates that the Constitution, as interpreted by the high court, is a living document that is always evolving. All of the rights are incomplete and subject to change. I did quite a bit of work on the assembly book. But it, too, was incomplete by the time I finished my fellowship, and I abandoned it after a few half-hearted efforts to find a publisher. I even had to cut my research short by two weeks—at Leonard's request—because we were entering the "long, hot summer" of 1967, and I was needed back in Milwaukee.

The summer was mostly a blur. Father Groppi and the NAACP Youth Council turned their attention to the fact that the Milwaukee Common Council had voted four times against an open housing law proposed by Mrs. Vel R. Phillips, who was the only woman and the only Negro on the council. They decided to confront the aldermen in their homes, starting with Martin E. Schreiber, the Common Council president. The kids, with their commando escorts, picketed the homes of Schreiber and other members of the council, rang their doorbells and demanded to know why they had voted so overwhelmingly against the proposed ordinance. Each time, Mrs. Phillips had cast the only "aye" vote.

Usually, the reply was that Wisconsin already had an open housing law, which pre-empted local communities. The state law, however,
covered only about a third of the housing in Milwaukee and generally
was considered ineffective.

In July, the Detroit riot exploded, and The Journal sent me there
with Kenneth C. Field, a Negro colleague who had recently covered riots in Newark, N.J. We made no attempt to cover the riot itself, which
was well-chronicled by the wire services and the local newspapers. My
job was to see if I could learn something about what caused the riot,
in which 43 persons were killed and 2,000 injured. The entire city was
locked down with a curfew and bands of police and National Guard
troops patrolled the streets.

Field and I had a couple of harrowing experiences poking around
the riot areas. In one, we came across a battered old Chrysler that had
stalled on a street near what was considered the riot area. Inside were
two middle-aged Negro men and a young woman with a sick, crying
child about 16 months old. She was crying, too, because she had been
trying to get her baby to a hospital when she got caught in the curfew.
The men had given her a ride, but then the car conked out.

They got out of the car, obviously scared silly, and pleaded with us
to help. As I reached around to unlock the back door of the big Ford
I was driving, Field started yelling, "Press! Press!" He was hunched
down in the right front seat, waving his press pass out the window.

I looked in the rearview mirror. Behind us were two police cruisers
and maybe 15 policemen on foot, armed with rifles and shotguns at
the ready. I started yelling, too, and stepped out of the car. Half a doz-
en cops dropped on one knee, their weapons pointed at us. Trembling,
I walked toward the group, looking for somebody in charge. There
wasn't anyone, so I talked to the nearest officer and told him what had
happened. Eventually satisfied, he told me to back the car out because
there were snipers up ahead.

When I started backing up, three of the cops—obviously angry and
scared—brought their rifles up to their shoulders and screamed at us
to get the hell out of there. I shifted into drive and peeled rubber. Later, we drove slowly around the riot area, looking for a way to get our
passengers to safety. We finally got about half a block from the home
of one of the men, who offered to put the other man and the woman
with the baby up for the night. After we dropped them off, the older of
the two men came around to my side of the car, told me his name and

address, and thanked us. "If you ever need anything—anything at all," he said, "you come on over. You saved our lives."

Field and I worked out of the city room of the Detroit News— common professional courtesy in those days—and split up as we pursued our sidebars. I had gotten the name of a leader in the black power movement in Detroit, Kenneth V. Cockrel, and set up an interview with him at his home in one of the city's housing projects.

It was like a fortress, with steel doors and bars on the windows. Cockrel let me into his apartment, and we talked sitting at his kitchen table. I occasionally glanced down a hallway, where I caught glimpses of a woman, likely his wife, and a small boy about 2 years old. Sitting on the table between us was a large brown envelope with the open side toward Cockrel.

I must have been asking the right questions because Cockrel, initially wary and suspicious, became increasingly expansive in his answers. At the end of about an hour, most of our mutual reserve had disappeared. Just before I left, Cockrel showed me what was in the envelope. It was a .45-caliber automatic pistol, pointed at me. He explained, somewhat sheepishly, that he had not wanted to take any chances.

My story, including some of what Cockrel had to say, ran on The Journal's front page on July 30, 1967. The thrust of it was that Detroit had been "the best in the nation" in its efforts to deal with race relations and the problems of the poor. The lede on the story said, "If there is a lesson for Milwaukee from the riots here last week, it is that the best is not good enough." Weeks later, I also expanded the Cockrel interview into a Sunday piece about black power. The boy, Ken Cockrel Jr., grew up to become the mayor of Detroit.

THE MILWAUKEE RIOT

That Sunday night, Milwaukee had its own riot. I was unaware of it because Sharlene and I had taken the four kids to a drive-in movie. We did not get home until about 1 a.m. Monday. About an hour later, the phone rang and, through a sleepy fog, I learned that the riot was under way.

I never covered any of it. The assistant city editor, Bob Barewald, called just to tell me what had happened. He already had deployed reporters all over the riot area on Milwaukee's North 3rd St., later renamed for the Rev. Martin Luther King Jr. The riot lasted only about five hours on Sunday night and Monday morning. Two people were killed and six police officers were wounded. Mayor Maier declared a state of emergency, Gov. Warren P. Knowles mobilized the Wisconsin National Guard, and the mayor imposed a curfew that lasted for nine days.

During the state of emergency one of my contacts, Joseph P. Fagan, got in hot water with the mayor. Fagan, a Republican who was conservative on everything but civil rights, was the chairman of the Wisconsin Department of Industry, Labor and Human Relations. He was the sort of source every reporter dreams about—candid in his answers to questions but a man who never asked to have any of his comments taken off-the-record or even on background.

In one conversation in a bar, Fagan was harshly critical of his boss, Gov. Knowles, who managed to escape questioning or criticism on civil rights issues largely because Fagan took the heat. I said, "Joe, this is explosive stuff. It's a great story, but if this gets out, you could be in trouble." He replied, simply, that he regarded me as a professional who would know what and what not to report.

Of course, I didn't do the story. It would have been a short-term gain—a rocket burst—but also would have shot down one of my best sources. I operated the same way throughout my years as a reporter, foregoing sensational quickie stories in favor of nurturing long-term sources—always more tortoise than hare.

During the state of emergency after the riot, Fagan issued letters to Father Groppi and other civil rights leaders to help them get through police lines. The letters had no official standing, but Fagan thought they might help the leaders move around and help calm the situation. Mayor Maier, as soon as he learned about it, called Fagan a "curbstone commissar," and asked the state attorney general whether legal action could be taken against him. But it was a one-day story and nothing came of it.

Fagan was a fascinating character. He developed a close personal relationship with Helen Barnhill, a Negro single mother of seven children who was one of the city's civil rights leaders. She had worked her way to a position as the head of the state's Equal Employment Opportunity Office in Milwaukee. Fagan later went on to become the executive director of the federal Equal Employment Opportunity Commission in Washington, a job that chafed at him because he had no say in policy. He left the job to become the chief executive of a contractors' association in Connecticut, then abruptly vanished, leaving his wife and children without a word of explanation. He later turned up selling souvenirs in the Hampton Roads area of Virginia, and still later ended up living with Barnhill in Washington.

After the state of emergency ended, Groppi and the Youth Council infuriated the mayor and many of Milwaukee's whites by jumping right back into their campaign for an open housing law. For me, it meant a lot of overtime covering the night marches and demonstrations, most of which were uneventful.

THE SOUTH SIDE REACTS

Things changed when Groppi decided to march to the South Side, which was separated by viaducts over the Menomonee River Valley from the city's North Side, where most black people lived. On several of those forays, the Youth Council marchers were harassed and eventually attacked by groups of young whites. At one point, the whites rioted, throwing eggs, bricks and other debris at the marchers, and rocking a squad car.

The policemen guarding the marchers reacted by firing shotguns into the air as fast as they could pump new shells into the chambers. They also shot and tossed tear gas canisters into the crowd. It was the first time I had ever tasted tear gas, and would not be the last.

I was now into a big national story. Platoons of reporters from newspapers and broadcasters around the country parachuted into Milwaukee to cover the story, and I had a lot of company on the marches and demonstrations. Comedian and civil rights activist Dick Gregory appeared to lend his support and his body to the cause, and white Milwaukeeans held their collective breath.

Curiously, while Milwaukee resisted, one community in the area passed an open housing law. It was tiny Bayside, a wealthy North Shore bedroom community. Jerris Leonard, a conservative Republican (and Marquette graduate) who represented the area in the state Senate, talked the village's leaders into passing the ordinance. Though scoffers in Milwaukee's city hall said it was hypocritical and made no difference because Negroes could not afford to buy homes in Bayside, it was a small victory for Groppi and the Youth Council. Leonard went on to become President Nixon's assistant attorney general for civil rights and, later, administrator of the Law Enforcement Assistance Administration. After leaving government, he became a respected lobbyist in Washington, with ties—and contributions—to both Republicans and

Democrats. In later years before he died, we often had lunch together at the Monocle, a restaurant on the Senate side of the Capitol, where we mostly reminisced and discussed Wisconsin politics.

By the spring of 1968, 12 other suburban communities had passed open housing laws. Milwaukee passed one, too, in December, 1967, but it exactly duplicated the state law, except for local enforcement. Groppi denounced it as too weak. "Tokenism and crumbs," he called it.

SMOKING AND THE POOR PEOPLE'S CAMPAIGN

About that time, I had started writing a book on the history of Milwaukee's civil rights movement, called *City with a Chance*. Working evenings, weekends and through a two-week vacation, I delivered the manuscript on Apr. 1, 1968, Sharlene's 30th birthday, and it was published that fall.

By then, my days as a civil rights reporter were numbered. Black power and separatism had become the predominant new movement in Milwaukee, and it did not welcome a paleface reporter. So The Journal put me to work mainly as a backup assistant city editor. My job every day was to make the assignments for the staff on the following day. I enjoyed it for awhile; it had aspects of creativity when I was able to match a good story with a good reporter, and then see the story on page one. But I soon tired of it.

There was one fortunate aspect. I was on the desk most of the time that I worked on the book. It meant I didn't have to do any writing during the day, so I was never written out when I worked on the book in the evenings.

My last big civil rights story was the Poor People's campaign in Washington, organized after King's assassination by the Rev. Ralph David Abernathy, King's number one in the Southern Christian Leadership Conference. I spent two weeks covering the story, and went on to cover the national NAACP convention in Atlantic City.

I took the occasion to quit smoking cigarettes. After starting smoking at the age of 15, I had worked my way up to more than three packs a day, but resolved to finally quit after several earlier failures because I wanted my kids to have a father when they became teenagers. I smoked my last cigarette before I got on the plane in Milwaukee on June 18, 1968.

There were a few other civil rights stories in the year and a half before The Journal sent me to the Washington bureau in June, 1970. I covered the NAACP convention in Jackson, Miss., in June of 1969, and the inauguration of Charles Evers, the brother of the slain civil rights leader Medgar Evers, as mayor of Fayette, Miss., in July, 1969. Evers was the first black mayor in Mississippi since Reconstruction.

With four children and the low pay of a newspaper reporter, I did all the free-lancing I could find. At different points, I was the Milwaukee stringer for McGraw-Hill World News and Newsweek Magazine. I also sold stories at different times to the New York Herald Tribune and The Washington Star. Newsweek was fairly lucrative during the civil rights years because the magazine was always seeking information for national roundups about whether riots were expected in cities around the country.

Newsweek paid by the word, and I knew that most of what I submitted would never get used, so I didn't take the job too seriously. What I did was to get all the information I could about whatever the subject was, and to sit down and empty my notebook. It was ridiculously easy because I never had to figure out what was important—never had to get involved in the old query, "Do you have time to write it short?"

It also taught me something about news magazines, and convinced me that I did not want to work for one. In November of 1969, a group of demonstrators on behalf of the poor occupied the old United States Disciplinary Barracks on Milwaukee's North Side. The barracks had been used to house prisoners of war in World War II and later had become part of a base for the U.S. Army Reserve.

Newsweek wanted to cover it. I filed a total of more than 4,000 words, and got paid for every one of them, and the story ran a column and a half in the magazine—a big story for Newsweek. But I was appalled. I barely recognized it. The information was mine, but it had been distilled and rewritten as to be nearly unrecognizable. Later, when an editor at Newsweek asked me if I would be interested in moving to Chicago as the magazine's deputy bureau chief, I declined.

But I was getting restless. My big national story was gone, and at various times I had covered almost every beat on The Journal. I had filled in on most of the building beats, covered politics and protests in Madison, worked rewrite, substituted as the religion editor, put out the garden pages, did features for the Green Sheet and Sunday sections, and wrote fairly regular stories about automobiles. I was running out of things to do.

At one point, Sharlene and I concocted an exciting adventure. We would sell the house and furniture, pack up the kids and move to London, England. Reading the papers had convinced me that Great Britain had an incipient civil rights problem of its own, mainly with the commonwealth immigrants who were flooding into the country. I figured I could go to Fleet Street and sell my civil rights reporting expertise to one of the newspapers. We would live in the U.K. for a few years, give the kids a cultural experience, get our adventure out of our systems and move back to the United States.

It never got beyond the talking stage. In December, 1969, Dick Leonard, the managing editor, called me into his office and told me that the Washington bureau chief, Laurence C. (Con) Eklund, would retire the following June. His sidekick, John W. Kole, would be the new bureau chief. Leonard asked if I wanted to go to Washington to join Kole. Spasms of excitement shot up my spine. This was no time to consult or temporize.

Would I?

Addendum: The civil rights story came nearly full circle for me on Jan. 20, 2009, when I sat in the second row of the press section up front at the inauguration of President Barack Obama. With me was my 17-year-old grandaughter, Hanna Navarrete, who now also will be able to tell her grandchildren about witnessing history.

7

THE PROFESSIONAL CREAM SKIMMER

There's an old cliché that says you make your own breaks. But I think there's a lot of serendipity involved, too. In my 40-plus years as a newspaperman, it was serendipity and Dick Leonard.

Leonard was the editor of The Milwaukee Journal from 1967 to 1985—the longest tenure of any editor except The Journal's founder, Lucius W. Nieman—who after his retirement became something of a Jimmy Carter of journalism, donating countless hours to helping young people, often underprivileged, develop an interest and skills in reporting and writing.

Leonard had a hand in just about everything good that happened to me at The Journal—and it started even before I ever thought of going to work there. In 1958, the Milwaukee professional chapter of Sigma Delta Chi, the Journalism fraternity, established its first scholarship. Leonard, then the state editor of The Journal, was half of a committee of two, along with George Wolpert, a local public relations man, who chose me for the award. It was a few hundred dollars, but it gave me a boost when I needed it.

Later, as state editor, Leonard bought a free-lance story from me—the first I ever had published in The Journal. After he became managing editor, he put me on the civil rights beat, and sent me off on a nine-month fellowship to Northwestern University in 1966 to study civil rights and civil liberties. It was Leonard who moved me to the Washington bureau in 1970.

As editor, he wholeheartedly supported my extra-curricular professional activities. Not only was I elected to the Standing Committee of Correspondents and the presidency of the National Press Club, I went on to serve 26 years on the board of the National Press Foundation. When the Defense Department established its National Media Pool, he designated me as The Journal's representative, which eventually led to my being in the first group of journalists to go Saudi Arabia for Desert Shield in 1990. That indirectly resulted in another fellowship, at the Freedom Forum First Amendment Center in Nashville, where I co-authored a book on military-media relations.

In the 1960s, Leonard was often criticized in the newsroom, where he was regarded as an absentee editor who left the daily operations of the paper to Joseph W. Shoquist, the tough-minded managing editor. However, Leonard spent a lot of time working in journalism organizations, national and international, which served to polish The Journal's profile in professional circles. I am convinced his activities played a big part in maintaining the professional reputation of The Journal. His successor, Sig Gissler, eschewed such associations to concentrate on mismanagement, and the paper slid steadily into non-entity status.

My first Journal story came about because of Lance Herdegen, who was a friend and fellow Marquette journalism graduate with a great first name for a guy who was—and is—a Civil War historian and author. Lance worked for UPI for many years before going to Carroll College in Waukesha, Wis., where he started a Civil War history department. But back in those days he was mostly a hobbyist.

He had organized an outfit patterned after a Confederate unit, the 15th Virginia Cavalry. Such groups dressed in authentic uniforms and participated in skirmishes, where they engaged in marksmanship competitions, firing muzzle-loading .58-caliber Springfield rifle-muskets against units from all over the country. Lance had achieved a degree of fame by being featured in a Sunday magazine picture story in The Journal. The cover showed him in a Confederate cavalry uniform, riding at a gallop on horseback, saber drawn and leading a charge.

He and his unit were recruited to stage a mock battle at Fort Dells in Wisconsin Dells, and he invited me to come along. It was the summer of 1959 and I was dating Sharlene, my future wife. Lance got us outfitted in Civil War era costumes—me as a Union soldier and Sharlene as a young Yankee belle in a hoop skirt.

Lance had a cannon, a scaled-down replica of a 12-pounder that could fire cement-filled frozen orange juice cans propelled by black powder. For the mock battle, of course, it only fired blanks. The two sides in the battle were duly organized, and with much yelling and smoke from our percussion-cap revolvers, carbines and muskets, we staged a grand engagement. At one point, I spun around, mortally wounded, and collapsed in a twisted heap on the ground.

Of course, the rebels won. They had the cannon. But it was too much for one of the spectators, who loudly protested to anyone who would listen. She identified herself as the head of the Wisconsin chapter of the Daughters of the American Revolution, and pronounced herself morally outraged because the Confederates had won the battle over Wisconsin's loyal Union boys.

I smelled a story. I got some paper and a pencil and interviewed the lady, then interviewed Lance and the guy who was in charge at Fort Dells that day. I telephoned Dick Leonard on the state desk. He liked the story, ran it the next day and paid me 10 bucks, the standard fee for stringers. Of course, this being The Milwaukee Journal, I didn't get a byline. The story had a Wisconsin Dells dateline with a line above it that said, "Special to The Journal." It was the first story I ever got in the paper.

DRIVE ALIVE

So Leonard had now gotten me a scholarship and a story in The Journal. But his involvement in my journalistic life didn't end there. At almost every turn, he was there. I was covering traffic safety when he and others decided that The Journal would embark on a campaign to cut down on motor vehicle accidents and deaths. It was called "Drive Alive in '65." Some of it was embarrassing, but we also had some fun. And it led indirectly to my transfer five years later to the Washington bureau.

For one of the events, I enlisted the Wisconsin State Patrol, Milwaukee County Stadium and two of my fellow reporters to demonstrate the effects of drunken driving. At the time, the state's standard for a presumption of driving under the influence was .10% blood alcohol content. (Years later, most jurisdictions dropped it to .08%).

The state troopers set up an autocross course in the County Stadium parking lot and we had the two reporters—David Mitchell and Charles Morgan—drive the course. Then we proceeded to get them drunk on Chivas Regal Scotch and Jack Daniels Tennessee whiskey.

They were quite a pair. Dave was a profane iconoclast who kept in trim by smoking cigarettes, running five miles a day, and skipping breakfast and lunch to keep his weight down. He later left The Journal to become a managing editor in the southwest and northwest, and even ran a used sports equipment business for a time. Charlie was a quiet, buttoned-down type who wore conservative Brooks Brothers suits and would never utter some of the words with which Dave punctuated his every sentence. He later became an associate editor at the Readers' Digest.

But a curious thing happened. As they became drunker and drunker, their personalities reversed. The loud and profane Mitchell became quiet and polite, and the mannered and subdued Morgan became increasingly boisterous and profane. Of course, they both flunked the driving course once their blood alcohol level reached .10%. They, of course, could not have cared less.

I won a national award for the story, $500 and a trip to Washington with Sharlene, from the American Trucking Associations [sic] (in those days, but not later, The Journal allowed reporters to accept awards from interest groups). Morgan and Mitchell got the left-over booze and ragged me mercilessly for not splitting the prize money with them.

HOOKED ON WASHINGTON

The trip to Washington for the award was an eye-opener. The Journal's Washington bureau chief, Laurence Conrad Eklund, took us under his wing and showed us around. Con seemed to know everybody. We went to the National Press Club and a fancy Capitol Hill reception where we met Melvin R. Laird, then a congressman from Wisconsin and later defense secretary and White House counselor in the Nixon administration.

I was hooked. I was sure that working in a small bureau in Washington for a paper of The Journal's quality and stature had to be one of the best jobs in journalism. Besides, The Journal's Washington bureau had status among the editors and was one of the most sought-after jobs in the newsroom. Eklund had started the bureau in 1947 and had worked alone until The Journal gave him a No. 1 in 1961, when Ira Kapenstein, a talented young politics reporter, was sent to join him. Kapenstein didn't last long, however. He took a job with the Wall Street Journal; then learned that he was suffering from cancer.

The Journal magnanimously took him back so his health insurance would remain in force. But by that time, the editors had replaced him with John W. Kole, who had covered city hall and politics in Milwaukee, so Kapenstein went back to Milwaukee and a desk job. He left The Journal again in 1963 and returned to Washington, where he died of cancer at the age of 35.

When I returned to Milwaukee from that Washington trip, I wrote a one-line memo to Dick Leonard, who by then was The Journal's managing editor. "If there is ever an opening in the Washington bureau, I would like to be considered," it said.

We moved to Washington in 1970. At first, we hated it. But what a wonderful place it turned out to be, especially for a young newspaper reporter, though it took years for us to become comfortable.

It brought me stories and experiences I could never have had in Milwaukee. I covered impeachment proceedings against two presidents, the resignation of one and the acquittal at trial of the other. I covered a war and the buildup to the war. I traveled through Cuba, Colombia, Central America and Texas. I flew on the first commercial flight of the Concorde supersonic transport. There were exciting national political conventions every four years, occasional forays to the White House, and regular coverage of Congress and the U.S. Supreme Court

I reported on some of the best and most notorious politicians and public servants of the age, including Presidents Richard M. Nixon, Gerald Ford, Jimmy Carter, Ronald Reagan, George H.W. Bush and Bill Clinton, as well as Vice Presidents Hubert H. Humphrey, Nelson Rockefeller and Walter Mondale; Sens. Bob Dole and George McGovern, and Reps. Henry Hyde, John Conyers Jr., John Dingell and Walter Fauntroy. Wisconsin politicos included Sens. Gaylord Nelson and William Proxmire, Melvin R. Laird, Tommy Thompson, Patrick Lucey, Lee S. Dreyfus, David R. Obey, F. James Sensenbrenner Jr., Clement J. Zablocki, Henry S. Reuss, Robert W. Kastenmeier, Les Aspin, William Steiger, Gerald Kleczka, Harold Froehlich, Tom Barrett and Father Robert Cornell.

I came to respect and like most of the home-state people, without regard to their political principles or parties. Much of it I credited to the Wisconsin way of politics, as I understood it. It meant integrity, hard work, a lack of personal animus and a willingness to compromise whenever the end result would contribute to the public good. I even liked Alvin O'Konski, a sly curmudgeon, because he was fun and a good story. Some were merely mediocre, though likeable, like Glenn Davis. A few prompted disillusionment and distaste: Toby Roth and Bob Kasten.

Though a reporter's dream is to cover the big national stories, I soon learned that a regional reporter for a good newspaper, as I was for The Journal, was the best of all worlds. Except for a few columnists and political writers, the reporters for the marquee papers like The New York Times and The Washington Post were stuck on beats. Some were great beats, like covering Congress or the Supreme Court, but they were still circumscribed. The reporters had their own turf, but didn't venture much away from it. I, on the other hand, was all over the place, though there were times I felt as if I were barely hanging on.

Almost from the beginning, I had a White House press pass, as well as press passes for Congress, the Pentagon and the State Department. One of the perks was invitations to the press parties at the White House—usually one in the summertime and another during the Christmas holidays. Sharlene loved the Christmas parties because we were allowed to roam around the White House to ogle the beautiful decorations.

At one of the parties, Jimmy and Rosalyn Carter joined in the dancing after the buffet dinner, and I danced with Mrs. Carter. I told Sharlene she should dance with the president, but she said, "If you tap him on the shoulder, you're dancing with him." Some members of the press corps were not happy with the Carters because they banned hard liquor at the parties; only beer and wine was available.

A TIE AND A HEADDRESS

We went to most of the parties for many years, except during the administration of President George H.W. Bush, when for some unknown reason we were dropped from the invitation list. At the parties, there invariably was a receiving line with the president and first lady. A White House photographer would shoot pictures, which the guests later received in the mail. At one Christmas party, I was wearing one of the neckties I customarily bought from the Korean sidewalk merchants on K Street. The ties sold at three for $10.

President Bill Clinton had a reputation as a tie aficionado, and when Sharlene and I went through the receiving line, he complimented me on my tie.

"Three bucks on K Street, Mr. President," I said. He threw back his head and laughed loudly.

A local angle for me was Supreme Court Justice—later Chief Justice—William H. Rehnquist, who had grown up in the Milwaukee suburb of Shorewood. I pestered him for years for an interview so I could do a profile for The Journal's Sunday magazine. He told me that if he ever decided to co-operate in a profile, I would get the nod. It never happened.

I did not get to know Rehnquist much beyond seeing him in court and at occasional receptions, but he was well-liked by the regulars who covered the Supreme Court. It was said that he sometimes went out for cheeseburgers with the reporters, with all the conversation off the record, of course.

Two incidents stand out. In his early years on the court as an associate justice, Rehnquist drove a BMW two-door—a 1600 or 2002—with one fender that was a different color from the rest of the car, and he customarily dressed in chinos, a tweed sport coat and dirty buck shoes. After the 1971 bombing of the U.S. Capitol, the Supreme Court installed magnetometers and security protocols. I went to the court on the first day of the new system and watched as tourists and other visitors went through the magnetometers and had their purses and bags searched by a court police officer.

Rehnquist showed up, in his usual duds and carrying a brief case. He stood in line. The harried police officer didn't notice him at first. When he did, he got flustered and said, "Oh, my God, Mr. Justice Rehnquist. You don't have to stand in line."

"Oh, okay," Rehnquist offhandedly replied as the officer led him around the magnetometer.

After Rehnquist became chief justice, the court's press corps occasionally sponsored informal, off-the-record receptions in the law library so the reporters could meet, booze and schmooze with the justices. Though I didn't cover the court full time, I was there often enough so that I was included, and I chipped in—on The Journal expense account, of course.

At one of the receptions, the justices all showed up in formal wear because they were on their way to a dinner or some other event. Toni House, the Supreme Court's press officer, had set up a small lectern so the chief justice could deliver a few remarks.

Rehnquist stood at the lectern, welcomed everyone and then, deadpan seriously, said it had come to his attention that some reporters had referred to him in stories as "Justice Rehnquist." That was not accurate, he said, and he resented it.

"As you well know, it's Chief Justice Rehnquist," he said.

At that, he reached under the lectern, pulled out a full-feathered Indian headdress and put it on, to howls of laughter from the assemblage.

Rehnquist enjoyed spoofs and satire. He told me one time that he wished the Supreme Court press corps would put together a show, similar to the annual Gridiron Dinner, which would feature parodies of the court and its members.

CUTTING OFF THE CANDIDATES

The only member of the court I ever interviewed was Justice Antonin Scalia, and that was on background. I was doing a profile on Abner Mikva, a Milwaukeean who was elected to the House from a district in Illinois and later served on the U.S. Court of Appeals with Scalia. Despite being polar opposites politically, Scalia and Mikva were friends. Scalia had only good words about Mikva, except for pointedly saying that he abhorred liberal Mikva's political philosophy.

In 1990, I did a profile on Supreme Court nominee David Souter. I traveled to Weare, N.H., and peeked into the windows of the weathered farmhouse where the bachelor nominee had lived, noting that it looked "brooding and sinister."

Souter, who had been nominated by President George H.W. Bush, was identified as a conservative, though not archly so. But I had a fascinating interview with Steve McAuliffe, a New Hampshire attorney who had been the husband of teacher Christa McAuliffe, the astronaut who was killed in the Challenger disaster in 1986.

McAuliffe, as well as several other lawyers in his circle who knew Souter well, said ideology would not play a role in his Supreme Court decisions. "If you ask Judge Souter what he thinks about abortion," McAuliffe said, "it's irrelevant to what Justice Souter might do." It was prophetic. Souter, appointed with conservative credentials, became a linchpin of the liberal wing of the high court.

For a profile of nominee Clarence Thomas in 1991, I traveled to Pin Point, the tiny Georgia town near Savannah where the he had grown up. It was a throwback to times long ago, a sleepy black enclave with unpaved streets. I also covered the Thomas confirmation hearings, with the explosive charges by Anita Hill of his alleged sexual advances and harassment. I started with an open mind, giving Thomas the benefit of the doubt. But by the time he was confirmed, I had become convinced that the U.S. Senate was placing a criminal perjurer on the Supreme Court.

In the 1992 presidential campaign, I covered two events that could not have been more dissimilar. One was an old-fashioned whistle-stop train ride with President George H.W. Bush, from Atlanta through South and North Carolina. It was all very organized, punctual and comfortable, with plenty of food and drink, and time for filing stories.

A few weeks later, I was on a similar trip in the same general territory with the campaign of challenger Bill Clinton, except it was by bus in a motorcade, and it was disorganized and fatiguing. Clinton and his running mate, Al Gore, could not keep to a schedule, and ran hours behind.

At one stop at a fairground late at night in the middle of nowhere, a group of reporters stood around the parked buses as Clinton and Gore went off to press the flesh with people who had been waiting for hours. We were soon joined by Hillary Rodham Clinton and Tipper Gore, and we stood around bantering. Several of us complained that we had no food or drink on the press bus, and opined that things had to be a lot better on the candidates' bus.

Not so, the women said. In fact, one said, "If we don't get something to eat pretty soon, we told them we were cutting them off."

I don't remember which one said it, but our laughter broke the tedium of the day, which did not end until early the next morning.

IRAN-CONTRA AND HEALTH CARE

Though they both ultimately failed, Hillary Clinton and Oliver North were the two most impressive witnesses I ever covered on Capitol Hill—Clinton when she testified on behalf of the administration's universal health care initiative, and North when he was called on the carpet to explain his involvement in the Reagan administration's clandestine support for the Nicaraguan contra rebels. Clinton, testifying without notes, was amazingly well-prepared, right down to knowing intimate personal details about the House and Senate committee members before whom she appeared. But the Clinton initiative overreached and was defeated.

North, testifying before the joint Senate-House Iran-Contra committee, was ramrod straight and handsome in his U.S. Marine Corps uniform, impressing everybody with his seemingly principled actions as a White House aide in supporting the contra rebels against the Sandinista regime in Nicaragua.

But the committee chairmen, Sen. Daniel K. Inouye and Rep. Lee H. Hamilton, were not fooled and dismantled North at the end of the hearings. Inouye, a World War II veteran who had lost an arm in attacking a German machine-gun nest in Italy in 1945, said he could not believe that North had "embraced one of the most important tenets of communism and Marxism—that the end justifies the means."

Hamilton was even more forceful and eloquent, telling North that he could not agree "that the threat in Central America was so great that we had to do something even if it meant disregarding constitutional processes, and deceiving the Congress and the American people. The means employed were a profound threat to the American process. We've weakened our country, not strengthened it."

Over the years, I covered many presidential inaugurations and State of the Union Addresses. For the latter, a low-ranking cabinet member was always spirited away somewhere by the Secret Service to guarantee presidential succession. If by some unimaginable disaster, the president, vice president, Speaker of the House, President Pro Tem of the Senate and others in line to become president were killed, there would be someone to constitutionally become president.

In 1992, the designated cabinet member was Edward Derwinski, secretary of Veterans Affairs. He was a former Illinois congressman, and I had gotten to know him because he was a friend of Rep. Clement J. Zablocki of Milwaukee. I interviewed Derwinski about his experience.

He told me he had visions of being whisked away to a bunker somewhere out in the countryside, or perhaps flying high in one of the presidential aircraft. Not so, he said. The Secret Service, Derwinski said, had sequestered him in the basement of an Arlington pizza parlor.

I had always been a generalist, a professional cream-skimmer as I came to call it, and as a regional reporter in a two-man bureau I had my pick of stories, as long as I could plug in a local angle. That was easy. Wisconsin senators and representatives had responsibilities all over the congressional map: Proxmire on banking and economics; Nelson on environment, poverty and small business; Zablocki on foreign affairs; Reuss on conservation and urban affairs; Aspin on military affairs; Kastenmeier on patents, copyright, prisons and parole; Steiger and Jerry Kleczka on taxes; Obey on appropriations, foreign operations and ethics; Alvin Baldus and Steve Gunderson on dairy and agriculture, and Sensenbrenner, Kastenmeier, Tom Barrett and Harold Froehlich on judiciary and presidential impeachments.

In addition, there were always visiting firemen. Governors Pat Lucey, Lee S. Dreyfus and Tommy Thompson came to town to lobby the feds, as did Milwaukee Mayors Henry W. Maier and John Norquist. So I could be writing one day about housing legislation related to Milwaukee, dairy price supports for Wisconsin farmers the next, or the stimulating—though often hard to get in the paper—issues of copyright and intellectual property.

Dreyfus was one of my favorites, and it had nothing to do with his politics, but with his expansive sense of humor and his skill with coming up with snappy quotes. I could question him on anything, and almost always come away with a story that was well marbled with pithy and sometimes funny comments. That was in stark contrast to Lucey, who spoke as if he were reading a technical manual, sprinkled with turgid initials and acronyms that had to be translated and explained.

However, Lucey became one of my better stories when, in 1980, he abandoned his Democratic colleagues to become the running mate of Republican maverick John Anderson of Illinois, who mounted a third-party candidacy for the presidency.

LUCEY BOLTS THE PARTY

The story percolated at the 1980 Democratic convention in New York City, and I had a delightful time—and solid stories—about Lucey and the bitterness toward him expressed by his old allies in the party. Lucey came to the convention as deputy campaign manager for Sen. Edward M. Kennedy of Massachusetts, who challenged President Jimmy Carter for the nomination. Kennedy failed, and Lucey said he could not support Carter. "The guy is a disaster," he said. He resigned as Kennedy's deputy chairman and later became Anderson's running mate.

Lucey's political free fall started with his resignation as Wisconsin's governor in July, 1977, to accept an appointment from Carter as ambassador to Mexico. Then he resigned that post and subsequently joined the Kennedy presidential campaign. All that turbulence became one of the best side stories in a national convention that I had ever covered.

Lucey inadvertently steered me into one of the more bizarre—and memorable—evenings in my years as a reporter. After he had been in

Mexico City about two years, the Wall Street Journal carried a story that said, among other things, that he had been a disaster as ambassador. The Milwaukee Journal assigned me to travel there to check out whether the story was true. As I learned from many interviews, he had been doing all right, although there was some minor criticism of the fact that he did not speak Spanish.

I had never been to Mexico City before, but I had become acquainted with Jeannette Becerra Acosta, the Washington correspondent for Uno Mas Uno, a leftist daily newspaper in Mexico City. She was interested in the Lucey story from the Mexican perspective. As it happened, she planned to be in Mexico City at the same time I would be there.

Not knowing any Spanish myself, I welcomed her help. I called her on a Saturday evening after I arrived. She picked me up at my hotel, not far from the U.S. Embassy. As I stood waiting, a two-door Volkswagen Brasilia came roaring around the circle and screeched to a stop in front of me. Jeannette was driving; in the front seat was Wendy, a gorgeous young Mexican of Italian extraction. I squeezed past her into the back and we roared off into the night.

Some time later, we stopped at a loading dock and went into the back door of a building. This was the headquarters of Uno Mas Uno, and Jeannette said Wendy would give me a tour while she went off to conduct some business with her brother, who was the newspaper's editor. Wendy spoke no English and I spoke no Spanish, so the tour consisted mostly of walking around and pointing. I didn't care. I could have simply sat and looked at Wendy.

Presently, Jeannette re-appeared, we returned to the car and once again roared off into the darkened Mexico City streets. This time the VW stopped in a residential neighborhood and we went into the house. It was a strange scene. The living room was dominated by a roped-off section, in which stood an old television camera on a wood tripod. There were three people seated there, drinking brandy—a handsome man with a plunging neckline and lots of gold chains (a movie actor, I was later told), and two women. One was Antoinette, a beautiful redhead and, it turned out, Jeannette's mother. The other was a good-looking blonde named Julie, who unbelievably was from Wauwatosa, a suburb of Milwaukee. Silently moving around in the background were two servants: deaf-mute Indian women. Besides serving drinks, they obviously were caring for a little boy, about 2 years old, who ran in and out of the room.

"THE REAL MEXICO"

In a few minutes, the actor finished his brandy and left. I had barely started my drink when Jeannette announced, "Now we will show you the real Mexico."

We went outside and climbed into Antoinette's two-door hardtop Plymouth Duster, with a three-speed stick shift on the steering column. Antoinette drove and I was pushed into the middle up front, with Julie on my other side and Jeannette and Wendy in back. Again we roared off into the darkened Mexico City streets, eventually arriving at Garibaldi Place—"the real Mexico."

It was an amazing sight. The plaza was filled with mariachi bands. My hostesses told me that they gathered there in the hope of being hired for parties, or simply to sing a song to a young couple. They were auditioning everywhere. After taking in the scene for a few minutes, my hostesses led me into the Tlaquepaque, one of the cantinas that ringed the plaza.

For the next several hours, we drank tequila and beer, and snacked on Mexican delicacies. Antoinette, who spoke good English, obviously had taken a liking to me, and sat next to me. As the alcohol lubricated our good fellowship, she became increasingly expansive in response to my questions.

In a nutshell, here's her story: the television camera in the living room honored her late husband, who had been a pioneer in Mexican TV. She and her friend Julie were "number twos," meaning they were secondary mistresses of wealthy men who had wives and "number ones." The men maintained their mistresses in houses and paid all their expenses. Wendy and Jeannette were lesbian partners and lovers. The little boy at the house was her grandson, the son of her son— Jeannette's brother—and Wendy. They had made a deal after he could not have children with his wife.

This, I guessed, was part of "the real Mexico." Nevertheless, despite my astonishment, I had a great time that night and, many months later, Sharlene and I even invited Jeannette and Antoinette out to the house for an evening when Antoinette visited Washington.

POLITICIANS AND COUNTRY MUSIC

Wisconsin Gov. Tommy Thompson—later secretary of Health and Human Services in the George W. Bush administration—was the best natural politician I ever covered, even better than Bill Clinton. One example serves to illustrate. In 1992, at the Republican national convention in Houston, I was assigned to do a "day at the convention with the governor" story. Thompson was indefatigable, on the run from early morning until late at night. Like Clinton, Thompson seemed to draw energy from political activities, mainly meeting people. His aides and I could barely keep up as we went from interviews to meetings to speeches and simply pressing the flesh.

Around lunch time, we persuaded Thompson to take a break for something to eat. I doubt if he would have thought of it on his own. We headed for a sky suite in the Astrodome, where the Republican Governors' Conference had a hospitality area exclusively for governors and their guests.

On the way to the escalator, we bumped into four men and women from central Wisconsin. They were all alternate delegates to the convention, and were dressed casually in blue jeans and jackets. Of course, they were delighted to meet the governor, and Thompson of course stopped to talk.

While the governor's entourage shifted from foot to foot, the chit-chat went on for 10 minutes or so, at which time Thompson could simply have politely taken his leave. But he did not. He invited all four of the delegates to accompany his party to the governors' hospitality suite. Minutes later, they sat in stuffed chairs, so delighted they were almost open-mouthed, attended by waiters in black ties and white waistcoats.

Thompson didn't stick around long. He wolfed a sandwich and we were all off to his next appointment. We left the alternate delegates there to enjoy the largesse, and I thought to myself: he's got their loyalty for life.

Charley Pride came into my life at a reception in Washington. I don't remember the occasion, but I was introduced to the only black man who was a popular country music star. We hit it off as soon as he learned I worked for The Milwaukee Journal. He was a huge baseball fan and had worked out in spring training with the Milwaukee Brewers. It was an obvious story, so I set up an interview with him.

We met in the coffee shop at the Madison Hotel for what I expected to be a short interview and a brief feature story. We connected so thoroughly that the interview and conversation went on for more than three hours. The story became a Sunday magazine piece, and Charley and I became friends of a sort. Coincidentally, he later performed at Milwaukee's Summerfest when Sharlene and I and the kids happened to be there. He shook hands with the kids and dedicated a couple of songs to them.

When Arthur Bremer shot Alabama Gov. George C. Wallace in 1972 at a shopping center in Laurel, Md., Charley telephoned me in the Senate Press Gallery to commiserate about what a terrible thing it was, notwithstanding Wallace's history of racism and advocacy of segregation.

Because of his unique status in country music, I thought Charley should do a book, and I proposed doing it. He was enthusiastic at first, but later became caught up in his career, and I was reduced to trying to deal with his protective secretary in Dallas, his home town. Charley and I lost contact, and the project fizzled.

More than a quarter of a century later, when I was ready to retire and Charley's career had faded, he telephoned me out of the blue and invited me to meet with him and his wife at his suite in the Four Seasons Hotel in Alexandria, Va.. We had a nice visit, and Charley asked if I'd be willing to take up the book project we had once discussed. He told me he had done a book with a paid writer, but never was satisfied with it. However, it soon became apparent that the bond we had once shared had dissipated, and I was at a stage in my life where I wanted to write my own stuff, not somebody else's. We parted cordially.

I enjoyed doing the original magazine article on Pride because Washington was all about politics and legislation, and what I missed the most were people stories. I did get a few other opportunities, however. One was when Sharlene and I went to see "Phantom of the Opera" at the Kennedy Center for the Performing Arts, and noted that one of the backup singers was Sarah Pfisterer, from Greenfield, a suburb of Milwaukee. I contacted her and wrote a profile. Later she returned in the lead role as Christine Daae. We took our granddaughters, Alyssa and Rachel, and Sarah gave them a backstage tour.

Another time I did a profile of news co-anchors at a Washington television station. One was Patrick McGrath, a Marquette journalism graduate who had been a reporter for the Milwaukee Sentinel.

The other was Maureen Bunyan, who had attended the University of Wisconsin—Milwaukee and worked for The Milwaukee Journal.

THE SST

An early big story in Washington was the supersonic transport, or SST. It was special because both of Wisconsin's senators, Nelson and Proxmire, opposed it, and the two Washington state senators, Warren Magnuson and Henry (Scoop) Jackson were ardent supporters because the plane would have been built by Boeing in their home state. Sharlene and I had become friends with William Prochnau and his wife, Lani, who lived near us and had three young daughters. He was the Washington correspondent for the Seattle Times and one of the finest newspaper writers I ever read. He covered Magnuson and Jackson (and later co-authored a book with on Jackson with Seattle Times political reporter Dick Larson, became a Washington Post reporter and wrote several novels). I covered Nelson and Proxmire. Between us, we reported the SST story until Congress finally killed the plane in 1971, leaving the commercial supersonic transport field open to Aerospatiale, a British-French consortium that ultimately produced the Concorde SSTs that flew around the world from 1976 to 2004, when they were retired.

In 1976, I promoted myself into an assignment to cover the inaugural flight of the Concorde from Charles de Gaulle Airport in France to Washington Dulles International Airport. It was not the sort of story that The Journal would have routinely covered, but I worked an angle. By then, Sharlene was a reservations agent for United Airlines, a job she had gotten in 1972 to ease our financial peril in Washington.

In those days of government regulation of airlines, employee passes for almost-free travel were extremely valuable because you could actually get on most flights as a stand-by. When deregulation and competition made the airlines more accessible to the hoi polloi, it became difficult and sometimes impossible as the planes filled up.

I told The Journal's editors that I could get to Paris on my own, so the paper would only have to foot the bill for some minimal expenses and a ticket on the inaugural flight. They went for it, and Sharlene and I flew off to Paris for a brief vacation.

On the return trip, Sharlene left Charles de Gaulle Airport at noon on a Boeing 747 for Boston and a plane change there for Washington. The Concorde left at 1 p.m. and I was back at noon, Washington time.

She did not return home until 8 p.m. Such was the romance of super-sonic travel. You could arrive before you left.

The inaugural flight, though exciting, was an ordeal. About half of the passengers were news media representatives and the other half Aerospatiale executives and potential customers. After we leveled off at more than three times the speed of sound, the cabin resembled a bee hive, with people crawling over each other to get up to the cockpit for brief rides with the pilots. That included TV cameramen with their giant cameras on their shoulders.

The plane was so small that the poor flight attendants could barely get down the aisles to serve drinks and food. In the lavatory, a man had to lean backwards to take a pee, and the passenger seats were about the size and comfort of those on the regional jets that proliferated in the early 2000s. Virtually everything disappeared into pockets and purses as the passengers grabbed souvenirs—plates and silverware, and anything else not bolted down.

My seatmate was the North American distributor for Courvoisier cognac, and we watched the goings-on with some amusement. Weeks later, several bottles of the best Courvoisier appeared at my office in the National Press Building.

Congress eventually shot down the American SST, but not before Prochnau and I had a lot of fun and page one stories in our newspapers. Many of the stories were about the maneuvering in the Senate over the legislation.

During one of the debates, Nelson was railing away to a Senate chamber empty except for Magnuson and the presiding officer. He claimed that the White House was hiding a report on the SST's detrimental effect on the environment. Just as he reached the pinnacle of his dudgeon, demanding to know where the report was, his time expired and he was gaveled down.

He sat down immediately and Magnuson, his hands folded on his ample girth, commented loudly enough that visitors in the galleries could hear: "Now we'll never know."

Later, Prochnau and I asked Magnuson about the remark and he said Nelson's comment had reminded him of an old story about two drunken cockneys in an underground air raid shelter in London in World War II. One of the cockneys, spying a tall man standing against a wall, said to the other, "I say, isn't that the archbishop of Canterbury?" The other replied, "I don't know. Why don't you go ask him?"

So the drunk lurched over to the man and, getting in his face, asked, "I say, aren't you the archbishop of Canterbury?" The man replied, "None of your goddamn business!"

The drunk staggered back to his compatriot, shrugged his shoulders and said, "Now we'll never know."

GETTING THINGS DONE

That was a characteristic of politics on Capitol Hill in the 1970s. Opponents on legislation could argue bitterly all day long in the Senate or House, but it did not detract from good humor and friendship. As far as I knew, Nelson and Magnuson were, if not buddies, at least amicable colleagues who were simply representing the interests of their home states.

But they were principled as well, as I learned from the late Sen. John Stennis, Democrat of Mississippi. When I first encountered him in the early 1970s, I was prepared to be disgusted. I had covered the civil rights movement in the 1960s, and Stennis was one of those evil old segregationist Senator Claghorn types, or so I thought. I was unprepared for his integrity.

One day in the early 1970s I covered him as he managed a defense bill on the Senate floor. He was already an old man, yet he waged a mighty battle against an amendment to cut the military budget. In the end, after 12 hours on his feet during the debate over that and other provisions of the bill, he lost. The amendment passed despite his best efforts.

Afterward, a few reporters gathered with Stennis in an anteroom off the Senate floor. One of them asked him, in light of his bitter defeat on the amendment, what he planned to do. The question appeared to puzzle him.

"Why I will of course go to the conference committee to fight for the Senate bill," he said.

Obviously tired, he then leaned back in his chair, looked up at the reporters gathered around him, and changed the subject.

"You know," he said in that languorous Mississippi drawl, "I have come to understand that you members of the press really are the fourth branch of the government, the fourth estate. You are essential to our democracy."

Where did that come from? In an instant, I changed my mind about Stennis. Here was this Old South senator, whom I believed was anathema to all the convictions I had developed as a reporter covering civil rights, providing validation for my job and demonstrating an integrity that surprised me. Over 40 years as a newspaper reporter, there would be many such revelations and surprises.

In many respects, the comity among lawmakers of different philosophies reflected the atmosphere that pervaded the Wisconsin legislature in an earlier era. Nelson and Republican Melvin R. Laird, ideological and political opposites, had served together in the Wisconsin Senate in the 1940s and early 1950s, before Laird went on to become a Wisconsin congressman and secretary of defense in the Nixon administration. At the time, Republicans controlled the State Senate and Nelson was part of a minority of four Democrats. But it took five members to raise their hands to force a recorded vote on a bill or amendment. Nelson recalled that Laird often provided the fifth vote. He said that at first he thought that was generous, but then concluded that Laird loved to humiliate the Democrats with lopsided votes against them.

Nevertheless, Nelson and Laird became lifelong friends. After legislative sessions, Laird would often go home with Nelson for a supper cooked by Nelson's wife, Carrie Lee. Many years later, when Nelson was in the Senate and Laird was defense secretary, the two were having drinks together at a reception when Nelson asked about the supersecret "war room" in the bowels of the Pentagon, which contained the triggers for military action. Though it was late at night, Laird called for his car and driver, and took Nelson to the Pentagon for a personal tour.

Over the years, Nelson became one of the two men I most admired. The other, as is told elsewhere, was Father Matthew Gottschalk, a Capuchin priest who worked with the poor and outcasts in Milwaukee. I don't quite understand fully myself why two such disparate characters should have made an impression on me, but much of it has to do with their selfless dedication to their vocations, as well as their unfettered optimism and good humor.

Nelson and Wisconsin's other Democratic senator, Proxmire, were compatible in their politics, which was mostly Wisconsin progressive. But their personalities and methods were starkly different. Proxmire was intense and uncompromising, a maverick with few friends. Nelson was laid-back and good-humored, with friends everywhere. One survey of senators rated him as the most popular member of the Senate.

A couple of personal notes illustrate the difference between the two men. Proxmire was famous for his rigid diet and physical fitness regimen, along with more than a little vanity. The whole country knew about his hair transplants. He was willing to go through the embarrassment of sitting in Senate hearings with big bandages on his head to get a few more hairs growing out of his bald pate.

He once told me that his favorite food in the whole world was peanut butter. But he said he never ate it because it was not part of his strict diet, to which he was dedicated to maintain the same weight—about 145 pounds—as when he was in college.

His hundreds of daily pushups, long-distance running and other exercise, along with the low-calorie diet, sometimes gave him a cadaverous look. Interviewing him one time, and noting that he looked particularly grave, I asked if he were feeling well. He asked why I had asked, and I said I thought he looked a bit peaked. He exploded in anger.

"Why is it," he shouted at me, "that in this country you're not considered healthy unless you have fat cheeks?"

Proxmire likely shook more hands than any politician in Wisconsin history, especially at the Wisconsin State Fair. He'd stand outside for hours, his right hand bandaged to protect it, shaking hands with everyone who walked into the flower show building. One year I was at the fair, on vacation with my family. Just for the heck of it, I got in line and shook hands with Prox. He greeted me, smiled, shook my hand—and showed not one sliver of recognition, even though I had been covering him and interviewing him regularly for years in Washington.

Nelson never was a Proxmire-style glad-hander. The walls of his office were bereft of any of those photographs showing the politician pictured with or shaking hands with the famous, though he had many such pictures on the walls at his home in Kensington, Md. But he had many friends and was fun to be with, sometimes to the exasperation of his staff. In the 1970s, I used to treat the congressional offices much the same as a building beat like city hall or the courthouse in Milwaukee. I'd make the rounds of all the offices, schmoozing with the staff and even the secretaries and interns. I called them my pheasant hunting expeditions, except I was trying to scare up stories, not birds. I always asked to see the congressman or senator, if available.

DRINKING BUDDIES

Nelson often had a line of staff people waiting outside his office door to see him. I was always shown to the head of the line, but after I got to know him a bit, I never had to run that gauntlet. I could simply open his private door to the hallway of the Russell Senate Office Building and poke my head in. If he was with someone, I'd simply back out, unless he waved me in. If he was alone, I'd go in to shoot the breeze and see if there were any stories brewing.

Sometimes, if it was late in the afternoon, Nelson would invite me to have a drink. We'd slip out through his private door—often with some of his staff still waiting outside the other door—and walk down the hallway and across the street to the Carroll Arms, an apartment building—later torn down—that had a nice bar. We'd sip scotch whiskey, swap stories and jokes, and he'd give me the inside information about what he was doing.

Because he was so well liked in the Senate, Nelson could get things done quietly and quickly in a way that was never possible for Proxmire. He was a member of an informal group of Democratic senators who met frequently for drinks, usually in the late afternoon, in the office of Stan Kimmitt, the secretary of the Senate who ultimately became a close Nelson friend. Kimmitt, like Nelson a World War II veteran, was a conservative Democrat who delighted in ribbing Nelson as a "tree hugger." Nelson, in turn, often called Kimmitt a "tool of the military-industrial complex" after Kimmitt had left the Senate and started lobbying for a defense contractor.

The group consisted only of Kimmitt and the senators—no staff, and only an occasional guest like Spencer Rich, the trusted Senate reporter for The Washington Post. Though the gatherings were mostly social, it was not unusual for senators to cut legislative deals. For example, one of the members was Sen. Russell Long of Louisiana, the chairman of the Senate Finance Committee and a friend of Nelson's. They'd simply put their heads together on something like a revenue-sharing bill and Nelson would get Long to include a "tax effort" component in the formula. That was a way to make sure that Wisconsin, which was a high "tax effort" state, to be favored in the legislation—or at least not to get screwed. Of course, such back-room deals were not the stuff of page one stories, or even stories at all unless Jack Kole, my Washington bureau colleague, or I found out about them. Nelson wasn't hiding anything, but he didn't volunteer anything either. I don't know how many deals Nelson cut in those sessions, but I'm certain it's more than we ever wrote about.

KILLING A JUDGESHIP

A famous result of one of those meetings was the denial of a federal judgeship to a Wisconsin Republican congressman, Glenn Davis, who was from the Waukesha area. Davis was a rock-ribbed conservative and a founder—with then-Rep. Richard M. Nixon—of the Chowder and Marching Society, an informal group of conservative House Republicans.

After Nixon became president, he signaled his intention to nominate Davis for a federal judgeship. Nelson publicly opposed the nomination, but did not want to formally object. In the Senate, a formal objection from a senator of the nominee's home state was enough to kill the nomination. Nelson believed he would be pilloried politically if he single-handedly killed the nomination of a fellow member of the Wisconsin delegation.

So at one of the social hours in Kimmitt's office, he approached Sen. James Eastland of Mississippi, a segregationist Democrat who was every bit as far to the right as Davis. Because of seniority, he was the powerful chairman of the Senate Judiciary Committee, through which all judgeship nominations had to pass. Nelson told Eastland he hated to ask for favors, but was making an exception.

As Kimmitt recalled the scene, Eastland asked Nelson what the problem was. Nelson replied that interest groups regarded Davis as anti-labor, against civil rights and the environment, and anti-Semitic.

Removing his ever-present cigar from his mouth, Eastland drawled, "Why, Gaylord, you've just told me all the reasons I should be for that boy."

In that situation, as in others, friendship meant more than ideology. Davis's nomination never made it out of the White House.

I liked Davis personally, though he seldom made much news. He was friendly and affable, usually chewing on an unlit cigar with the cellophane still on. In those days, he was mainly a conservative naysayer who voted against almost anything that involved spending. I did not get to know him well because he was around only a couple of years after I arrived in Washington.

Many years later, after Davis died, I covered a memorial service for him in the Rayburn Room off the House floor. Delivering the memorials to him was an array of Republican notables, including former President Gerald Ford and former Defense Secretary Melvin R. Laird, who had been colleagues of Davis in the GOP House caucus and in the Chowder and Marching Society.

I wrote a straight story about the memorial service, but I remember being appalled at the tributes to Davis. There was virtually nothing about his work in Congress, whether he had gotten any significant legislation passed, or whether he had ever done anything directly or indirectly to help people or contribute to the common good. Almost all of the expressed memories had to do with the fact that Glenn Davis had been a hail-fellow-well-met. The top tribute to him was that he was great at organizing gin rummy games in the clubhouse at the Burning Tree Country Club, an all-male hangout in Maryland for power brokers.

GOOD GUYS

I soon developed favorites among the elected officials I covered, and it had nothing to do with their politics. Rep. William A. Steiger was a delight. A young, boyishly handsome Republican from central Wisconsin, he died at age 40 of a heart attack brought on by diabetes in December, 1978, after 12 years in the House. His wife, Janet, an exceptionally bright Lawrence University graduate, went on to become chairman of the Postal Rate Commission and chairman of the Federal Trade Commission. They had a son, Billy, who was pictured as a toddler sitting with his father at hearings of the House Ways and Means Committee, where Bill Steiger was a member.

Steiger loved gossip, and had an impish sense of humor. Whenever I visited his office, which was often, he'd grin as he filled me in on the latest overheard political and personal peccadilloes of members of the Wisconsin delegation—or their wives. We had an understanding. He knew I would pursue the story, but he would never be connected with it. As often as not, the tidbit turned out to be just that, but occasionally it led to a story, or part of a story. None of them were ever big disclosures because we didn't have any crooks or true miscreants in the Wisconsin delegation.

Though I liked and respected both Bill and Janet Steiger—they even invited Sharlene and me occasionally to social occasions with their family—my upbringing left me with reservations. They were so perfect and wonderful, so moral and upstanding—so Republican— that I sometimes worried that they didn't have a handle on the world. I had that same feeling many times about upstanding Republicans and conservatives—that they were as about as good as it gets in their personal lives and dedication to service for their country, but that they had no fundamental understanding of people in society who are alienated and sometime screwed by the system.

There were others who fit into that category, people like Melvin Laird and Jerris Leonard, Republicans who basically did well by doing good. It was almost as if there was a threshold—that as a public servant you had to make certain that you were first comfortable and taken care of, and then you could turn your attention to the less fortunate. Though I admired and even envied the Steigers and Lairds of the world, I preferred the more selfless approach of people like my heroes, Father Matthew Gottschalk and Senator Gaylord Nelson.

I liked Laird as well, though he never struck me as particularly selfless. Yet his ethics were as strong as anyone I covered. After serving as Nixon's secretary of defense for one term, he left the office—as he had promised. Later, when Nixon came under siege in the Watergate scandal, he recalled Laird to the White House to be his domestic policy adviser. It was to Laird's credit that he served the president honorably, but was never even slightly tainted by the Watergate cover-up.

Laird was always accessible and straightforward, though I didn't try to cover him much while he was defense secretary. That would have been a full-time job in itself. But I caught up to him occasionally with stories bringing The Journal's readers up-to-date on what he was doing. One was a long profile for Wisconsin, The Journal's Sunday magazine. It was overwhelmingly favorable, but that was where the story took me. However, it did point out that Laird was an inveterate name-dropper.

In one interview, I told Laird that he had a reputation in Washington as a "mover and shaker." He affected an aw-shucks demeanor and said he disagreed.

"I'm not a mover and shaker," he said. "I like people in politics. Like this week I've had dinner with the president (Reagan) and his wife."

Case closed.

ZABLOCKI AND REUSS

Another of my favorites was Milwaukee Rep. Henry S. Reuss, who was farther to the left than Steiger was to the right. In fact, he was a near Socialist—but in the good sense of Milwaukee Socialism, which cared for people but was fiscally conservative. I remember a gathering on Capitol Hill of old Socialists in Washington, attended by Reuss and a friend of mine, Hobart Rowen, whose politics belied his occupation as a business reporter for The Washington Post. I was impressed by the sight of all these aging people from a nearly forgotten movement, still gripped by an idealism that sought to better the lives of the poor and downtrodden. And I always loved the folk singers, like Pete Seeger and the Weavers, who sang their anthems and those of the labor and civil rights movements.

Reuss had an almost bipolar personality. In Washington, he was a dignified committee chairman—he served as chairman of the House Committee on Banking, Housing and Urban Affairs—who wore pinstriped suits like an international banker, traveled in their circles, and spoke in formal, stentorian tones. Back home, he'd don a seersucker suit, bow tie, white socks and a straw hat to march at the head of a doll buggy parade on the Fourth of July. Both he and his wife, Margaret, were avid outdoors people, and Reuss championed the Ice Age hiking trail in Wisconsin.

Reuss's Milwaukee counterpart was Rep. Clement J. Zablocki, another Democrat whom I came to admire and almost love. He was of Polish extraction, from Milwaukee's South Side, the same as my mother's side of our family. Short and squat with a mustache, Zablocki had almost a cartoonish look about him. He was Catholic, conservative and a graduate of Marquette University. It was said in later years that the only way to get a job on his staff was to be Catholic and a Marquette grad, which was nearly true.

Zablocki rose to become chairman of the House Foreign Affairs Committee, a position that some initially thought was above his abilities. In those days, I did what I called "performance profiles" of people I covered. The stories were detailed snapshots, describing how the people were performing in their jobs. To do them, I did background research and typically interviewed 20 to 25 people, on the record and on background. I compared those interviews to tumblers falling in a lock. If 19 of 20 people said the subject was an egotist and a tyrant, I could write that the subject was "widely regarded" as an egotist and a tyrant, without quoting any of the individuals.

Those descriptions, however, never fit Zablocki. Though he was comfortable with prime ministers, presidents and kings, he was humble and self-effacing, usually saying his main talent was finding good people to work on his staff and make him look good. Every year, on Jan. 6—the day of the Three Kings' visit to the infant Jesus—Zablocki threw a party at his northwest Washington home for members of his staff, friends and even a few select reporters like myself, with their spouses. He and his wife, Blanche, did most of the cooking, and a featured dish always was the fresh and succulent Polish sausage Zablocki himself made—using only the finest and most expensive ingredients.

In 1977, when it came time for Zablocki to ascend, through seniority, to the chairmanship of the House Foreign Affairs Committee, there was an undercurrent of opposition from some members who worried that he wasn't up to the job. One of them was a fellow Democrat, Benjamin Rosenthal of New York, who said he did not believe Zablocki should become chairman, and expressed pro forma opposition to him in the Caucus of House Democrats. The seniority system ruled in those days, and Rosenthal deduced correctly that any real effort would simply backfire.

After Zablocki had held the chairmanship for about a year, I did one of my "performance profiles" to tell Wisconsin readers how he had been doing. The first person I interviewed was Rosenthal. Sitting across his desk from him, I explained what I was doing and kidded him, saying that if he gave Zablocki good marks, it was all over. I wouldn't be able to find anybody critical of his performance.

To my surprise, Rosenthal said flatly that he had been wrong, and he launched into a paean of praise for Zablocki's stewardship of the committee. My offhand remark turned out to be true. Try as I might, I was not able to find anyone willing to criticize Zablocki, even off the record. There were those who disagreed with him on issues or political philosophy. But everyone praised his evenhanded, competent and fair leadership. I inserted a disclaimer into the story I wrote, saying that none of my interviews had produced substantive criticisms of Zablocki's performance. Zablocki and his people, of course, loved the story, and I was embarrassed when a constituent later had a bronze copy of the story made and affixed to a plaque, which he gave to Zablocki.

Zablocki was largely responsible for the War Powers Act, which requires the president to report to Congress whenever he puts American troops in harm's way. His staff, including George Berdes, another Marquette product, wrote the legislation and Zablocki shepherded it through the House. Later it also passed the Senate, where it was dubbed the Javits-Zablocki Act, for Republican Sen. Jacob Javits of New York. But Zablocki and his Marquette mafia had done all the work.

For the most part, the Wisconsin members were so ethically strait-laced that they cooperated even on the stories that were not expected to be favorable. Democrat Les Aspin, whose district was in southeastern Wisconsin, came to Washington shortly after I did, and quickly set out to make his mark.

THE PRESS RELEASE KING

He had worked for Proxmire and believed in the efficacy of using the press to get his message across. His office soon became a press release mill, to the point where the press releases themselves became a story. I did several, noting the scores of releases that flew out of his office on a regular basis.

It was almost impossible to keep up with them all, so for one story I simply asked Aspin's staff for a copy of every press release they had issued over a period of several months. They could have stiffed me, saying that if I wanted all those back copies, I should have saved them. But, reflecting Aspin's attitude toward the press, they complied.

There were more than 90 of them, which I arbitrarily sorted into routine announcements for small publications and stories about Aspin's activities, including legislation he was working on. Others were accusations of impropriety and misfeasance, usually against the Defense Department because Aspin was a member of the House Armed Services Committee. He often sent out a press release about some perceived Pentagon boondoggle on a Friday afternoon, knowing the story likely would make the papers on the weekend but the Pentagon would not be able to respond.

I compared it to a kid with a .22 rifle or BB gun taking potshots at an elephant. Even when I tried, the Pentagon almost never was able to respond to an Aspin charge in a timely fashion. One time, I waited three weeks for a response. Another time, I never did get a response.

Aspin, who went on to serve just one year as President Clinton's first secretary of defense before the president fired him, never lied to me, as far as I could tell. If he didn't want to talk about something, he simply became unavailable. When I'd catch him in a hallway, he'd grin and say, "Stay tuned."

But he also could be an open book. On one occasion, I did one of those "day in the life of" stories and Aspin gave me total access. I trailed him from morning to night, and sat in on his private staff meetings and sessions with visitors. Never once did he ask me to disregard something or put anything off the record. Basically, he trusted me to use my own discretion on what to include in the story. There were no revelations anyway, but I did get a feel for the flavor of the daily life of a congressman.

In 1975, Aspin and Reuss made history. Bucking the seniority system in the Democrats' caucus, Reuss, 62, and his allies ousted 81-year-old Wright Patman of Texas and Reuss took over as chairman of the House Banking Committee. Aspin, working behind the scenes, orchestrated the ouster of the pork-barrel-prone chairman of the House Armed Services Committee, F. Edward Hebert, 73, of Louisiana. Rep. Melvin Price of Illinois became the chairman, but years later Aspin engineered Price's demise in the caucus as well and became the Armed Services chairman. When he shoved Hebert aside, Aspin was a 36-year-old upstart, aided by a bright staffer, Bill Broydrick, who went on to become a prominent lobbyist in Wisconsin.

A FUN CURMUDGEON

I liked people for different reasons. Alvin E. O'Konski, a Republican whose district was in northern Wisconsin, was the antithesis of Zablocki. He was wily, not overly burdened by ethical considerations, and a good politician with a sense of humor. As soon as he learned that my mother's maiden name was Kaminski, I was one of his boys—though that didn't prevent him from lying to me.

O'Konski owned a television station in Rhinelander, and some of the people who worked there also were on his congressional office payroll. His wife, Bonnie, served as his administrative assistant, and most observers said she was the best thing about his office—capable, straightforward and charming.

I enjoyed O'Konski's company, and visited him fairly frequently. We had a joshing relationship, with a lot of kidding back and forth. There wasn't much news because O'Konski didn't do a lot. One unconfirmed story was that he had switched committees because he was in line to become chairman and didn't want the responsibility.

His name had once surfaced in an investigative news story about prostitutes who had visited members of Congress in their offices. Not only did O'Konski not deny the allegation, he reveled in it, saying the story put the lie to the contention by his political enemies that he was too old for the job. It was said that he even volunteered the information at a campaign stop in northern Wisconsin, and gleefully credited his press secretary with getting him named in the story.

I received a tip from a Democrat that O'Konski had been admitted to the Bethesda Naval Hospital, suffering from hepatitis. It would not have been much of a story—maybe a few paragraphs—except for the fact that everybody I contacted on his staff stonewalled and lied to me. There were denials all around—first that he had been hospitalized, then what the ailment had been. Eventually I wrote a long, page one Sunday story about his illness and the fact that he and his staff had worked mightily to cover it up.

Years later, just before he left office, I interviewed O'Konski for nearly four hours with a tape recorder running. I did that several times over the years to do farewell stories when Wisconsin members left office, but also for posterity. I donated the tapes to the State Historical Society of Wisconsin.

I asked O'Konski about the hepatitis story. "Ah, Aukofer," he said, "you had that one right." But why, I asked, had he gone to such lengths to cover it up when it could have been just a few paragraphs in the paper?

"You don't understand," he said. "My constituents don't know the difference between hepatitis and cirrhosis of the liver. They'd have thought I had a drinking problem."

I asked O'Konski what he looked forward to in retirement. He said he planned to walk down the main street in one of the small towns in his district. Invariably, he said, someone would walk up, get in his face and say, "I bet you don't remember my name."

When that happened, he said, "I'm going to look him in the eye and say, 'You're right, and I don't give a shit.'"

THE SHORTEST FUSE

After redistricting combined much of northern Wisconsin, O'Konski's territory was taken over by Democrat David R. Obey, who had succeeded Melvin R. Laird when Laird left to become defense secretary in the Nixon administration. Obey was not as likable as the curmudgeonly O'Konski, but he was a breath of ethical fresh air and possessed a passion for his personal mission of representing and helping the working people of his district and the nation.

A Wisconsin progressive who was correctly labeled as a liberal in Congress, Obey was a tough partisan who nevertheless learned to work with his opposite colleagues on the Republican side of the aisle—a skill he credited to the fact that he was a member of the House Appropriations Committee. Appropriators, who control the money, have to compromise or government can shut down, which it actually did on occasion. Obey, regularly and easily re-elected, rose to become the Appropriations Committee chairman.

I always liked and respected Obey, a disciple of Gaylord Nelson, despite the fact that he had a fiery temper and the shortest fuse among anybody I covered. As a reporter, I could often judge a member of Congress by his or her staff. I won the confidence of many staff members and learned a great deal from them about the people I covered. Though some Obey staff members were cowed by their boss's tough and abrupt demeanor, and the fact that he worked them hard and relentlessly, they never bad-mouthed him. On the contrary, they acted more like acolytes on a mission.

Obey's top aide was Lyle Stitt, a onetime radio newsman in Wisconsin who loved his boss but sometimes quaked in his presence. On one of my routine forays to congressional offices in the 1970s, I stopped by Obey's office in the Cannon House Office Building, walked into Stitt's office and asked what was going on.

Nervously, Stitt said, "I'm sorry, Frank, but I can't talk to you."

I thought he was kidding and said so. No, he replied, Obey had instructed the entire staff that they were no longer to speak to anyone from The Milwaukee Journal. He couldn't even talk to me to explain why.

Puzzled but amused, knowing of Obey's volatile personality, I walked out of the office and down the hall, and ran smack into Obey walking in the opposite direction.

With mock anger, I said, "What's this business about not talking to The Journal?"

"You really want to know?" he barked, and motioned me to follow him into his office, where he violated his own rule and launched into an angry tirade about a cartoon by The Journal's editorial cartoonist, Bill Sanders. In those days, the cartoons ran on page one, which only enhanced Obey's anger.

I patiently explained that Sanders was mostly autonomous, and Obey should direct his anger there. But I also said I would relay his complaint to Sanders and the editors. As was his wont, Obey quickly settled down and rescinded the do-not-talk order.

Years later, I was doing one of our periodic stories on the question of pay raises for members of Congress—a subject that was always guaranteed to light Obey's short fuse—as well as everyone else's. In an opinion column in 1977, I wrote: "No other issue produces as much backbiting, backing and filling, irritated responses and demagoguery. Even in the Wisconsin congressional delegation, generally regarded as one of the most able in Washington, the silly putty rises to the top."

The pay raise vote was coming up, and as usual I was interviewing the Wisconsin House members on how they would vote. As an afternoon paper, we always tried to get ahead of the news.

But Obey was unreachable because he had checked into the Bethesda Naval Hospital with one of his periodic back problems. Rather than bother him at the hospital, I decided to look up what he had said in a previous story about pay raises. I wrote in the story that he could not be reached; then quoted his earlier remarks.

On the day of the pay raise vote, I went to the Speakers' Lobby off the House floor, where reporters were allowed to hang out and summon members from the chamber for interviews. I asked one of the doorkeepers to ask Obey to come out. He returned, red-faced, and said, "I don't know how to tell you this, but Mr. Obey told me to tell you to go to hell."

I laughed because I knew instantly that he was unhappy with the story I had written. But I didn't know exactly why.

Obey voted against the pay raise—as did many others on the volatile issue. But then he and a New York congressman, Democrat Major Owens, scheduled a "special order" session of the House. Such sessions, after the House had adjourned for the day, allowed members to speak out—usually to an empty chamber—on issues of their choice, and have the comments printed in the Congressional Record. Obey and Owens spent about an hour talking about the pay raise and why it was justified, despite the fact that they had voted against it.

I sat through the exercise in the gallery; then waited outside the chamber for Obey to emerge. He greeted me cheerily, as if nothing had happened.

"Why are you telling me to go to hell?" I demanded.

"You really want to know?" he replied in a reprise of our encounter years earlier.

What ensued was a loud argument between the two of us over his contention that reporters didn't understand the political consequences of their stories, and my counter that reporters had a duty to pin down members on their stands on issues.

We argued in the hallway, down the Capitol elevator to the sub-basement, on the subway car from the Capitol to the Rayburn House office building, up the elevator there to Obey's fourth floor office, and into his office where, behind closed doors, we finally exhausted the subject.

Once again, with the matter off both of our chests, we both calmed down and parted amicably. For a long time after that, Obey was friendly and always available when I called. That was his way. Though he could explode quickly, he got over it almost as quickly and never held a grudge.

My Washington bureau partner, Jack Kole, who went to work as a press aide for Obey after his untimely departure from The Journal, said on many occasions that what amazed him most about Obey was how he was able to keep his edge over the years, with an intense passion for his principles, when most people would burn out and become passive.

On the other side of the aisle, Republican Rep. Henry Hyde of Illinois had that same sort of passion, but on abortion, the most divisive of all issues. Hyde was the most eloquent spokesman on behalf of the unborn that I ever heard, and he also had a warm personality and a great sense of humor. I got to know him and he was always available, despite the fact that, as far as I knew, no Milwaukee Journals ever made it into his congressional district.

Henry loved to swap jokes. One day, while I was standing in the Speakers' lobby, he walked up behind me, leaned over and whispered in my ear:"You know, I told my wife I like black underwear. She hasn't washed my shorts in six months."

JIMMY HOFFA IN PRISON

A political polar opposite of Hyde was Democrat John Conyers Jr. of Michigan, a liberal from Michigan, a leading member of the Congressional Black Caucus and ultimately the chairman of the House Judiciary Committee. He became a good source for me mainly because of Jimmy Hoffa.

Hoffa, the notorious former head of the Teamsters Union, was serving a prison term in 1971 in the federal penitentiary at Lewisburg, Pa. One of my Wisconsin congressmen, Democrat Robert W. Kastenmeier, was chairman of a House Judiciary subcommittee that, among other things, had jurisdiction over federal prisons and parole. Conyers was a subcommittee member.

The subcommittee traveled on a fact-finding tour to Lewisburg. I tagged along. When we arrived, the warden greeted us and had arranged a tour of the facility. But Conyers wanted to see Hoffa, who was his constituent. Guards soon produced him and, as the other subcommittee members left on their tour, Conyers stayed to talk with Hoffa. I figured Hoffa was a better story than the tour, so I stayed, too.

It was an amazing encounter. Conyers greeted Hoffa like a long-lost buddy, but all Hoffa wanted to talk about was the treatment he was getting at Lewisburg, which then was considered something of a country club in the federal prison system. He even produced a handwritten list of demands, which he and Conyers relayed to the warden. When the session was over, I asked Hoffa if I could have the list, and he gave it to me. Years later, I turned it over to the State Historical Society of Wisconsin.

As I had anticipated, it was a good story, and not only for The Journal. I also sold it to the Washington Post. And over the years to come, whenever I needed a quote or information from Conyers, who didn't always remember me or The Journal, all I had to do was remind him of our encounter with Hoffa.

Another Capitol Hill powerhouse with whom I developed a casual relationship was Democrat John Dingell of Michigan, who was chairman of the Commerce Committee and a renowned defender of and advocate for the nation's domestic automobile industry.

For a couple of years, I went deer hunting in southwestern Virginia with a group of guys from the National Press Club. One year, Dingell showed up as a member of the group, completely outfitted with new calf-high lace-up boots, jodhpurs and enough guns and other equipment to go on a safari. He was a passionate hunter.

But in deer camp, he also was a pussycat. Though widely feared on the Hill, especially by anyone who became a target of his investigating subcommittee, Dingell was meek and mild-mannered. He never raised his voice, and volunteered every day to do dishes or wash the pots and pans, explaining that he didn't know how to cook. On the few occasions when I needed information or a quote from Dingell, who sometimes was inaccessible to other reporters, all I had to do was remind him that we'd once gone deer hunting together.

Kastenmeier was another Wisconsin politician I came to admire. A traditional liberal whose district included the state capital, Madison, and the University of Wisconsin, he was soft-spoken, avuncular, and possessed of an integrity that kept him to his principles but also allowed him to respect the principles of people who disagreed with him. His House Judiciary Subcommittee on Courts, Civil Liberties and the Administration of Justice operated in an atmosphere of good will.

The subcommittee dealt with a lot of complex issues that I found fascinating, particularly on patents, trademarks, copyrights and other intellectual property matters. Because the subject matter tended to lean toward the dense side, I often had trouble getting stories in the paper—so much so that I once led a story with an invented anecdote with sexual content to use as an example. The story got in.

Kastenmeier never ascended to the chairmanship of the Judiciary Committee, though he came close. During the committee's hearings into the impeachment of President Richard M. Nixon, he sat to the right of the chairman, Rep. Peter W. Rodino Jr. of New York.

He also was a member of the House Intelligence Committee, which I initially thought would make me privy to some interesting inside stories. But to my chagrin, and to his credit, Kastenmeier never leaked anything to me—and I didn't expect him to. The Wisconsin members I covered, regardless of party, did not engage in that conduct. Kastenmeier even said on several occasions that he and the other Intelligence Committee members learned more from CNN than they did from their classified briefings by the CIA and other intelligence agencies.

KOTEX AND POLITICS

Though Kastenmeier never ran the Judiciary Committee, another Wisconsin member eventually did. Rep. F. James Sensenbrenner Jr., a Republican who represented Milwaukee suburbs, became the chairman after I retired. Politically, he was 180 degrees away from Kastenmeier, yet when I covered him he possessed the same sort of stiff-necked integrity that characterized other members of the Wisconsin delegation.

Sensenbrenner was loud, sometimes bombastic and without much of a sense of humor. It was said that when he was in college he read the Congressional Record in bed. But he was a reporter's delight because he always was extremely well-informed, and quotable, on any issue—even those for which he had no direct responsibility.

A lot of people said the best thing about Sensenbrenner was his wife, Cheryl, whom he had married after she was severely injured in an automobile accident that forced her to wear leg braces. She was as charming and friendly as Sensenbrenner was brusque.

Sensenbrenner, a member of the family that had founded the Kimberly-Clark paper company, was independently wealthy. His great-grandfather had invented the sanitary napkin, which was named Kotex. It was said that, in a rare burst of humor, Sensenbrenner once had said it was a good thing great-granddaddy had not put the family name on the product or he would never have had a career in politics. I never did check out whether the story was true because I didn't want to take a chance on ruining it.

Though wealthy, Sensenbrenner was a tightwad. That was graphically illustrated once when Sharlene and I met Cheryl Sensenbrenner in the Cleveland airport. Sharlene was then working for United Airlines, and we often flew back to Milwaukee on her employee passes to visit relatives. But the only way to get there on United was to change planes in Cleveland.

On our way back home on Easter Monday one year, Sharlene and I were waiting at the gate in Cleveland when Cheryl showed up. She had her two young boys, Jimmy and Bobby, with her, and she also was schlepping a stroller and a couple of large, cellophane-wrapped Easter baskets. She had been visiting her parents. Her dad was Federal Judge Robert W. Warren.

Sharlene and I jumped up to help out. For the next hour until we boarded the plane, we helped baby-sit, playing with the boys, and we carried some of Cheryl's stuff when we boarded the plane.

At one point I asked why, in view of all of the things she had to carry, her wealthy husband had not put her on a nonstop flight between Milwaukee and Washington.

"Well," she said, "Jim had these coupons . . ."

Later, Kimberly-Clark founded an airline, Midwest Express, so that its executives could travel more easily between the headquarters in Appleton, Wis., and major cities around the country. But despite the fact that it had some of the best service in the skies, especially between Milwaukee and Washington, Sensenbrenner refused to fly on the airline. He had Kimberly-Clark stock and regarded it as a conflict of interest.

OTHER GUYS

That sort of integrity did not extend to one of Sensenbrenner's colleagues, Toby Roth. A Marquette graduate (to my shame), he represented northeastern Wisconsin and, as far as I could tell from years of covering him, was mainly interested in perpetuating himself in office. He had gotten there by emulating Sen. William Proxmire, shaking as many hands as possible.

We had a cordial relationship until I started one of my "performance profiles" on him. I learned that his home office was subscribing to scores of weekly newspapers throughout his congressional district, with the subscriptions paid for by the taxpayers. His staff members pored through the papers, looking for personal items—for example, a photograph of a deer hunter who had shot an eight-point buck, somebody who caught a fish or who had received some sort of an award. Then they signed Roth's name to a personal, handwritten note of congratulations, and mailed it to the constituent—with the congressman's frank to avoid paying postage. More than 1,500 such notes were sent out over a two-month period.

At best, it was a questionable expenditure of taxpayer dollars for what essentially was a campaign effort. The efforts disgusted members of Roth's staff as much as they did the readers of my story, and they told me so—though not for attribution.

In 1973, I started a campaign to elicit full financial disclosure from members of the Wisconsin congressional delegation. The Senate and

House required the members to annually disclose their earnings, assets and debts, but the forms required them to only list items by broad categories, which only provided a fuzzy outline, such as a holding that was worth between $10,000 and $50,000.

I wrote letters to each member, using what I hoped was the moral suasion of Wisconsin's reputation for clean and open government, as well as the fact that several members already provided full disclosure. I requested complete net worth statements as well as copies of the member's federal income tax returns.

To my surprise, I received some cooperation from every member. Sen. William Proxmire already published his tax returns and net worth statement each year in the Congressional Record. Sensenbrenner published his net worth statement, but not his tax returns, in the Record. Rep. Henry S. Reuss of Milwaukee, responding to my request, provided full disclosure for the first time. Other members, even Roth, provided varying amounts of information. But after several stories about Roth's campaign efforts, he stopped disclosing, and would only provide the amounts he had paid in state and federal taxes.

Republican Thomas E. Petri of Fond du Lac, another solid officeholder in the Wisconsin tradition, who had succeeded Bill Steiger, customarily wrote his net worth statement in longhand on a yellow legal pad. Each year, he placed it in a plain envelope and mailed it directly to me, bypassing his staff. He knew that, because I was doing a roundup story on the finances of the entire Wisconsin delegation, there was not much chance that I could get into great detail about his finances. And I did not. Except for the story, we kept all of the financial information in confidence. But our story was always far more complete, with real numbers, than any based on the official reports that were done by other newspapers or the wire services.

Like his predecessor, Petri was a principled moderate Republican who was always open and available to reporters. He wasn't as much of a gossip as Steiger had been, but he had a sense of humor and the patience to spend a lot of time with me, explaining some arcane legislative provision. Petri always had a soft spot for anything that would provide financial relief to poor people.

Next to Roth, the only other member of the Wisconsin delegation who lost my respect was Sen. Robert W. Kasten Jr. A Republican, he had defeated Sen. Gaylord Nelson in a close election in 1980. The contrast was immediate, and not only because of their disparate politics.

Kasten was another of those members who seemed mainly interested in himself, though he occasionally did stellar work, largely because of his staff.

One of those was when he battled against a proposal to impose withholding taxes on income from dividends and interest. Kasten showed some grit because he bucked not only the GOP leadership in the Senate, headed by Sen. Bob Dole, but President Ronald Reagan as well. He had two young female staffers, both in their 20s, who became expert on the legislation and Senate procedures, and tied the legislation's proponents in knots. Backed by senior citizens and the AARP, Kasten killed the legislation in 1983.

A BEER CAN AND GAY BASHING

Despite my admiration for that effort, I regarded Kasten as a phony who nevertheless had a good instinct for politics. I wrote many stories about the withholding issue, as well as other favorable stories. But when I wrote a story about a junket he took to Africa, with his wife and members of his staff, he refused to talk to me for about a year. All the positive stories were forgotten.

My distaste only increased when, driving home from the Capitol one day, Kasten passed me on the Southwest Freeway. He was driving his car, with a young aide in the right front seat. Clearly visible in Kasten's left hand was a can of beer. I had done that myself in my younger years, and few people would give a second thought to seeing someone holding a beer can while driving a pickup truck in rural Wisconsin. But he was a United States senator, practically in the shadow of the Capitol.

In Wisconsin in December, 1985, Kasten paid a $50 fine for running a red light and $75 for driving on the wrong side of the road. He entered alcohol counseling.

One of Roth's legislative staff members was Steve Gunderson, who went on to become a congressman. A moderate Republican who represented the western Wisconsin district that was the biggest producer of dairy products of any district in the country, Gunderson served on the Agriculture Committee and soon became one of the top experts in Congress on dairy-related issues. I always marveled at his ability to patiently explain, clearly so a newspaper reporter could understand it, the complexities of the government's dairy price support programs.

Almost from the time he came to Congress, rumors circulated that Gunderson was homosexual. Though I heard the gossip, and despite my personal distaste for that lifestyle, I paid little attention to it. The guiding principle in the press corps in those days, and my personal conviction as well, was that a member's personal life was off limits unless it intruded on his official duties. If a senator had a drinking or womanizing problem, it was not something to be reported unless he came to the Senate floor drunk or with a floozy on his arm.

We did nothing about the Gunderson gossip for years, until an alternative newspaper in Milwaukee carried a story by a man who identified himself as a member of Queer Nation, a fringe gay group, and claimed that he had confronted Gunderson in a gay bar in Washington to "out" him.

When the national desk contacted me about the Shepherd Express story, I checked it out. Though the story said the police had been called, there was no official report and therefore no way to verify what had happened. All we had was the word of the guy who said he had done the deed. I said there was no story and, as a matter of principle, it was none of our business anyway. What Gunderson did on his own time was not a story unless it was illegal.

Despite my objections, including a memo I wrote to the desk, The Journal carried a story. But it was totally phony. It was based wholly on the Shepherd Express story, but it changed the facts to say that Gunderson had been confronted by an AIDS activist who complained that he had voted against funding for AIDS research. That was totally made up, apparently because The Journal didn't want to accuse Gunderson of being gay.

I was furious. I wrote a lengthy memo to Sig Gissler, The Journal's editor, saying that the story we carried was bogus. Besides, I said, since when does a great newspaper like The Journal deal with such a subject with a wink and a nod? If we were going to carry a story, we should have had one that was fully reported and accurate. To his credit, Gissler agreed and subsequently established a policy saying that The Journal would not get involved in the sexual orientation of public officials unless it directly affected their jobs.

I did not regard what I did as a defense of gay rights, or even of Gunderson. It was simply a matter of journalistic integrity.

Zablocki and Reuss rose to positions of power in the House. Their successors—Jim Moody, Tom Barrett and Jerry Kleczka—never reached those heights. But they followed the Wisconsin model of integrity and open government.

In some ways, Kleczka was a clone of Zablocki. A fellow Polish American, his politics were more liberal than Zablocki's, but he had an instinctive sense of where his constituents in the 4th congressional district stood on matters of national importance. He shared with Zablocki a pride in his home and a do-it-yourself commitment. They both reveled in their yards and gardens, and had the best trimmed lawns in the neighborhood. Kleczka did almost everything around the house, and had a shop full of power tools in his basement.

He was also tough and smart, but not sophisticated. In a profile, I mentioned that he had the feistiness of a Jimmy Hoffa, and would be someone you'd want on your side in a bar brawl. He liked the story, but appeared a bit hurt about a comment that his syntax was more like a man of the street than a man of the House.

THE PRIEST OF THE HOUSE

Father Robert Cornell was a short-timer in the House, unfortunately defeated by Roth. He was a Norbertine priest from St. Norbert's College in De Pere, a suburb of Green Bay. Affable and always eager to please, he was a staunch liberal and so detail oriented he sat in his office until the wee hours answering all of his correspondence himself. In some respects, Cornell was almost too nice to be a member of Congress, and he was dismayed when Roth beat him.

With Kasten as the Republican interlude, the eventual replacements for Nelson and Proxmire were Sens. Herb Kohl and Russ Feingold, both Democrats. In January, 1989, when Kohl was sworn in, one of the guests at the reception was his mother, Mary, 81. I sought her out and asked her what she thought of her son, the senator. "I'm sure Herbie (she pronounced it 'Hoibie') will do all right," she said. "Kohls always do all right."

There was no question about that. At the time, Kohl was estimated to be worth in excess of $200 million. Interestingly, we were both about the same age and had grown up in adjacent neighborhoods—Kohl in the Jewish neighborhood west of N. Sherman Blvd. in Milwaukee, and me in the working and middle class area east of that street. But there was a tremendous divergence from there. When I was a kid, Kohl's father owned a supermarket not far from his home, which eventually became a chain of supermarkets and department stores. Kohl was a bachelor and businessman, and the owner of the Milwaukee Bucks basketball team; I was a way less than wealthy newspaper reporter with four kids and two new grandchildren.

Nevertheless, I liked Kohl. He was the antithesis of the big shots my father hated when I was a kid. Kohl was unfailingly polite and interested in everybody and anybody he encountered. He often ate with the regulars at George Webb's hamburger parlors in Milwaukee, and in Washington he could be seen frequently in one of the Senate cafeterias dining with the employees. Politically, Kohl was liberal and progressive and, from a reporter's standpoint, was upstanding, honest and usually available.

Feingold, also a liberal, was not nearly as likeable. Though straightforward for the most part, he came across to me as more calculating and protective of himself. He was seldom without an aide in tow, there to see to whatever needs he may have had. He patterned himself as a maverick in the Proxmire tradition, to the point of allying himself with a prominent conservative Republican, Sen. John McCain of Arizona, on campaign finance reform.

WOMEN'S AND CIVIL RIGHTS

Because of my background of covering civil rights back in Milwaukee, I retained a keen interest in anything in Washington that smacked of a civil rights story. Shortly after I arrived in June, 1970, I started covering the movement in Congress to pass the Equal Rights Amendment to the Constitution, which was intended to guarantee civil rights to women.

An unusual aspect of the story was that some senators and representatives who might have been expected to vote for the amendment did not. They opposed it because, they said, it could wipe out laws, such as those that regulate wages and hours, which were intended to benefit women. But in the Wisconsin delegation, only two members—Republicans John W. Byrne of Green Bay and Glenn Davis of Waukesha—voted against the amendment. They wound up on the winning side when Congress eventually killed it.

Though I never told anybody, I considered myself to be a feminist. In 1983, when the White House invited members of the press corps and their families to watch the fireworks from the South Lawn, I was struck on the way home at the length of the line to the women's rest room on the Washington Monument grounds. Because of it, some women were barging into the men's room. Impressed, I wrote an op-ed opinion column arguing that equal treatment demanded that women get at least twice as many toilets as men.

I expected the women's movement to pounce on and embrace the arguments. The reaction was zip, zilch, nothing. When I mentioned the issue in conversations with women I considered enlightened, the usual response was that too many women took too much time puttering in the ladies' room. I never did figure that one out.

As the bicentennial year of 1976 approached, a statue of the Rev. Martin Luther King Jr. appeared in the Capitol. It was temporarily installed in the Rotunda, on a pedestal with the words: "The Rev. Martin Luther King Jr. Humanitarian."

I was offended by the characterization. All around were statues of the nation's historical figures, which were engraved only with their last names: "Washington," "Jefferson," and so on, because they were so revered that they needed no identification. It was analogous to the standard introduction of the president, which traditionally does not use the person's name. The introduction says simply, "The president of the United States," because the office is what is important and needs no embellishment. The identification of "humanitarian," I felt, could be attached to many thousands—perhaps millions—of Americans, where King was unique.

One of the members I had interviewed several times for civil rights stories was the Rev. Walter Fauntroy, who was the elected nonvoting delegate for the District of Columbia. I told him of my annoyance over the identification on King's statue. He saw my point and said he would relay my concern to Coretta Scott King, the civil rights leader's widow.

Later, when the statue was installed in its permanent location in the Capitol Rotunda, the "Humanitarian" designation had disappeared. Like other national leaders, the statue was identified only with King's name. I was proud of my small role.

8

THE WAR CORRESPONDENT, MILITARY
AND THE MEDIA

After we moved to Washington in June of 1970, it was years
before serendipity reared up again. It happened after the 1983
invasion of Grenada, ordered by President Ronald Reagan to
rescue American medical students from Cuban troops who were supposedly threatening them.

Except for reading about the invasion in the newspapers, I was unaware of all of the turmoil that surrounded the Reagan administration's decision to sequester American reporters to prevent them from
covering the action on Grenada. But I was destined to become involved.

It was Dick Leonard and serendipity again. The journalism community raised hell with the Pentagon and the Reagan administration
over the Grenada debacle. It led to the formation of a special commission headed by an Army general, Winant Sidle. The commission did
a study of the military-media relationship, which had been poisoned
over the Vietnam War and came to fresh woe in Grenada.

The Sidle Commission recommended the establishment of the Department of Defense National Media Pool, which evolved into a system in which reporters for major news organizations were on stand-by
constantly, ready to be flown to whatever military action was under-
taken by the United States.

Originally, the pool consisted of the wire services—AP, UPI and
Reuters; the four television networks—NBC, CBS, ABC and CNN;
seven radio networks, including National Public Radio; three news
magazines—Time, Newsweek and U.S. News & World Report, and
26 newspapers selected by the American Society of Newspaper Editors.

The Milwaukee Journal was one of them. Leonard, by then the editor, decided that I should be The Journal's representative in the Pentagon press pool.

As pool members, we had to be prepared to go into a combat zone on a moment's notice. A stand-by period lasted three months, after which the pool rotated to a different group. In each period, the pool consisted of the wire services, one TV network, one radio network, one news magazine, two newspapers and assorted still photographers.

Because there were 26 newspapers, The Journal's turn only came up about every two years, whereas it was about once a year for each of the TV networks. Occasionally, the Pentagon would activate the pool for a practice exercise. That happened to me the first time I went on stand-by.

I had bought about $800 worth of equipment with The Journal's money: Hiking boots, a poncho, a portable manual typewriter, a sophisticated backpack with a blowup mattress and a goose-down sleeping bag, and different jackets and other clothing for different climates. The military was committed to supplying such items as flak jackets and extreme cold-weather gear.

It was okay, the military folks said, if we wound up marching down the Champs Elysee in Paris in our grubbies, carrying backpacks. But it would not do to be wearing jackets and ties and carrying American Tourister luggage in a Nicaraguan jungle.

The purpose of the pool was to land independent observers—U.S. journalists—at the scene of military action so they could provide dispassionate dispatches at the outset of hostilities. They would be on the ground when the announcement came from the White House or the Pentagon. By definition, a pool shares its reporting with all news organizations, and that is what we were supposed to do. But the ideal was to end the pool reporting as soon as possible and provide for open coverage by any news organization that wanted to send reporters.

During my first pool rotation, the Pentagon activated the pool for an exercise. I was called late at night and ordered to Andrews Air Force Base at 5 o'clock the next morning. After a briefing, the pool participants were hustled onto a windowless KC-135 aircraft—a type of plane usually used as a tanker but outfitted for passengers. This particular KC-135 had been used before, by flying a high curve, to give astronauts brief moments of weightlessness.

We were flown in secret to the El Toro Marine Air Station in California, where we were transferred to Sea Stallion helicopters for a ride out to a helicopter landing ship that was the flagship for what was to be a mock invasion by U.S. Marines of San Clemente Island off the

California coast. On the ship, we were given choices of where to witness the exercise.

Some of the guys went off to the island to watch the Marines charge ashore. Elliott Brenner, a UPI reporter, and I decided to go over to a landing ship that was designed to disgorge armored amphibious vehicles carrying about 20 Marines apiece.

The skipper, a Navy commander, was a real Dudley Do-Right type. He reminded me of the actor Tony Curtis in the movie, "The Great Race." He was handsome, with white teeth that glinted in the sunlight, and ran a tight, though informal, ship. Members of the ship's crew who were not on duty at the moment, including kitchen personnel in their white chef's outfits, were allowed up on deck to watch the invasion.

FILING A POOL REPORT

I went down into the hold to check out the ship's invasion force and immediately got whacked with an appreciation of what soldiers and Marines sometimes must endure. There were scores of the AAVs in the hold, each with about 20 Marines locked inside its armored belly, and they were waiting to go into action, diesel engines roaring away.

The exhaust fumes were overpowering. I was instantly dizzy and thought all the Marines inside those metal monsters must have already succumbed. They sat that way for hours, their eardrums and lungs assaulted by noise and noxious gases.

Back on deck, Brenner and I watched as the skipper maneuvered his ship in as close as he could to the beach. Then he did a 180, turning the stern to the island, and the AAVs popped out the back and chugged toward the beach, bobbing in the waves. So now the forlorn Marines inside had to cope with seasickness as well.

The pool system worked. After the exercise, the "pencils"—the newsprint reporters—put together a couple of pool reports, which were dutifully filed back to the Pentagon via the flagship's communications system. Then helicopters took us back to El Toro, where we filed independent reports back to our organizations. It was only an exercise, so I didn't bother—I wrote an account later—but obviously would have filed my own story if it had been the real thing.

Over the following years, I attended periodic pool meetings at the Pentagon, first as a participating reporter, then as a bureau chief. There was apparent good will on both sides of the military-media relationship, and we believed we had worked out most of the kinks. The exercises worked reasonably well, but when the real thing happened, the system simply broke down. When the U.S. invaded Panama in 1989, pool reporters were once again kept away from the action, causing a new round of complaints and promises of corrective action.

Serendipity popped up again in 1990, when I happened to be on stand-by in the pool when Iraq's Saddam Hussein invaded Kuwait and the U.S. responded by fortifying Saudi Arabia against a possible invasion. The buildup of forces was called Desert Shield, but the operation was largely invisible at first because the Saudis refused to allow American reporters into the country.

There was an outcry in the U.S. journalism community over the news blackout. Secretary of Defense Richard Cheney and Gen. Colin Powell, chairman of the Joint Chiefs of Staff, eventually persuaded the Saudi leaders to at least allow the Pentagon pool into the country.

When the Defense Department finally activated the pool, it became a public event. As expected, I received a telephone call at home late at night and was told to report early the next morning to Andrews Air Force Base for transport to Saudi Arabia.

We were a groggy bunch that morning. Few of us knew each other; I didn't know anybody. We had a lot of time to kill—the military was true to its "hurry up and wait" tradition—so I went around with my notebook and introduced myself to each of the pool members, and wrote down their names and affiliations.

They were reporter John King of the Associated Press (later a correspondent and anchor for CNN); reporter Jim Adams of Reuters; Peter Copeland, a reporter (and later Washington editor) for Scripps Howard News Service; Jay Peterzell, a Time Magazine reporter; Michael Ross, a reporter for the Los Angeles Times; Scott Applewhite, a photographer for the AP; Dennis Brack, a Time Magazine photographer; John Ydstie, a reporter for National Public Radio; Martin Jeong, a UPI photographer, and Carl Rochelle, a correspondent for CNN. Rochelle brought a crew with him: Producer Chris Turner, along with video and satellite technicians Tom Mote, Bob Torpey, Mike Green, Frank O'Connor and Al Levin.

Our escort officers were Army Lt. Col. Larry Icenogle and two Navy lieutenant commanders, Gregg Hartung and William D. (Dave) Barron.

After what seemed an interminable wait, we piled onto a C-141 cargo plane and took off for MacDill Air Force Base in Florida, the headquarters of the U.S. Central Command, which was in charge of Desert Shield and, later, the warfare of Desert Storm.

A bus took us from the plane to the CentCom headquarters building. As we stepped off the bus, blinking in the bright sunshine, we were met by local television reporters and crews, seeking on-camera interviews. We declined; we didn't have anything to tell them. But they were pleased just to be "live" from the scene. So much for Pentagon pool secrecy.

We sat through a briefing and met the CentCom commander, H. Norman Schwarzkopf, or "Stormin' Norman" as he came to be known. After the briefing, the six "pencils" in the pool looked over John King's shoulders as he tapped out a pool report on his Tandy 102 laptop computer. It was excruciating.

A few words about such pool reports: They're necessary but mostly useless. Pool reporters always accompany the president on Air Force One. They're there mainly to be witnesses in case something dire happens. Usually nothing does, so the reports tend to be listless—and often illiterate—recitations of non-happenings and mundane descriptions of what people are eating and wearing. There occasionally are exceptions, when a talented reporter produces something readable and interesting, but the public never sees it.

STORIES REPLACE THE POOL REPORTS

After going through that similar silly exercise at MacDill, we talked it over on the plane ride to Saudi Arabia and resolved to divvy up the story. We decided that the wire guys—King and Adams—would chase the "hard leads," or breaking news. Copeland and I would work the feature stuff, the Ernie Pyle sorts of stories where we talked to the grunts in the ranks. Peterzell had some military experience, so he was to work the "command and control" stories. And Ross, who had been the LA Times's Cairo bureau chief, would work diplomatic sources and refugee stories.

We also decided to write real stories instead of pool reports. The stories would be shared with everybody, and thus function as pool reports. It worked. In the first three days, the six writers filed 23 stories; in the two weeks that the pool lasted, the total climbed to about 75. After open coverage started, it was months before anybody came up with a story we hadn't already done. Meanwhile, the still shooters, Rochelle's TV guys and radio reporter Ydstie were doing their thing, gathering photos, film and actualities that were shared with all the print media, networks and stations.

There was a real feeling of glee in our group. We were on the inside, with access to anything and everything our military escort officers could cook up, while the rest of the world journalism community was outside, their noses pressed to the glass, waiting for the word on open coverage. One day, we sat in the hotel lobby, cackling as Tom Brokaw of NBC news reported from outside the fence of the Dhahran air base, saying little more than how hot it was. We'd already been inside the Saudi F-15 bunkers on the base, had watched them scramble, and had written stories about them.

When we first arrived in Saudi Arabia after our long flight from MacDill, we had no clue where we were. We stumbled out of the C-141 and were taken to a small building, where we met with our U.S. military escorts, along with Saudi diplomats and military officers.

Despite having tried to get some sleep in the canvas sling seats on the plane, where the top half of your body cooked in the heat and your feet froze, we were dog-tired. I think most of us expected to wind up in a nasty tent somewhere in the Saudi desert.

Instead, the little mini-bus that transported us and our backpacks pulled up in front of the Dhahran International Hotel, with bright lights and splashing fountains in the lobby. We were ushered into de-cently-furnished and appointed rooms on the first floor. Some grubby war.

It was great. The Saudis love buffets, so there were buffets for break-fast, lunch and dinner. No pork or bacon, but lamb and crispy spiced meat that tasted somewhat like bacon. And you could even order a cheeseburger and fries off the menu. I gorged myself on the hummus and black olives, which—like tortillas in Mexico—were a fixture at every meal.

We worked hard, sometimes all together and sometimes split into groups. On the go from early morning until late at night, we tried to cram in everything the military escorts could schedule. The JIB, or Joint Information Bureau, was headed by a Navy captain, Mike Sher-man, and one of the main handlers was one of our original escorts, the Army tank guy, Lt. Col. Larry Icenogle.

The helicopter rides were the most exciting—and grueling. We flew in Black Hawks, with the doors removed. On most days in that Au-gust of 1990, the temperature in eastern Saudi Arabia climbed to 110 or 115, with high humidity brought from the Arabian Gulf. To top it off, a constant hot wind blew from the northeast.

It was so windy on a helicopter ride that you could do little but cross your arms and curl up into as near a fetal position as you could manage with your seatbelt on. The wind tore off eyeglasses and ripped pages out of notebooks if you tried to write something down. Flying over the desert felt like standing behind a roaring jet engine on a hot day. It was relentless. I thought of what my father used to say when I was a kid about a hangover: you think you're going to die, and you're afraid you won't.

One day we were scheduled to fly by helicopter to some troops who were camped in the desert. But there was a misunderstanding with the Saudis and we were forced to land at a Saudi naval base, incongruously also in the desert. We sat in the helicopters in the heat for an hour or so with no resolution until the Saudis took pity and invited us inside the headquarters.

We were ushered into a huge, air-conditioned room with a giant oval carpet in the middle, colored light beige. Arrayed around the carpet were large padded chairs upholstered in white leather. Giant gold-framed photographs of King Fahd and the crown prince dominated one wall. It apparently was a room used for important high-level meetings. Waiters in white waistcoats bustled around, serving us tiny cups of sweet tea and Arabian coffee from silver trays.

A HAM SANDWICH TO DIE FOR

But there was nothing to eat, and we were hungry. So our military escorts returned to the choppers and grabbed boxes of MREs, or Meals, Ready to Eat—the standard fare for troops in the field. They broke open the boxes and passed them out.

I opened my MRE and found, to my shock, that it contained as the main course a big slab of ham. By then, I knew that it was a prison offense, or worse, to eat any form of pork in Wahhabi Muslim Saudi Arabia. But nobody seemed to be paying much attention, so I slapped it between two crackers and munched happily.

I later learned that there was a great deal of circumventing going on in Saudi Arabia. One day, four of us pencils—King, Peterzell, Copeland and I—decided to escape our captors at the Dhahran International to go see the city. We grabbed a cab right outside of the lobby and Peterzell, who had a Woody Allen aura about him, decided to practice his Arabic. He sat in the front seat with the driver and, in his best-accented Arabic, said, "Take us to the souk!"—the main market place.

The driver looked at him and said, "Huh?" Peterzell repeated his order and the driver repeated his "Huh?" After a few rounds of this back-and-forth, the driver finally said, in almost perfect English, "Sir, where is it you would like to go?" In the back seat, we dissolved in laughter.

We'd learned another lesson about Saudi society, where there was so much oil money that most Saudis did not do menial chores. They hired foreigners—Pakistanis, Bangladeshis, Filipinos and others. Their common language was not Arabic, but English. Our cab driver was from Pakistan. From that time on, Peterzell's nickname was, "The Interpreter."

In the local Saudi newspapers, King Fahd was always referred to as "the keeper of the two holy mosques." We joked that the lede on the main story in the a.m. editions was "King Fahd, keeper of the two holy mosques" and the p.m. lede was "Keeper of the two holy mosques, King Fahd." So we adopted our own nicknames. I became "the keeper of the holy inverted pyramid," Copeland was called "the yuppie," and King, because he was wire-service fast with a story, became "top gun."

Shortly after the cabbie dropped us in downtown Dhahran, we had another Saudi moment. We were walking along, ogling the surroundings, when a young woman stopped me and said, with a Queen's English accent, "You look like you're looking for a pub." She had a black veil on her head and was covered by the long black cloak, called an abaya, which all women were required to wear in public in Saudi Arabia.

She was British, an administrator at the Dossary military hospital. Smiling and friendly, she was obviously delighted to run into a bunch of Yanks. So, of course, she told us where we could get a drink—in a pub, no less. King was the most interested, and got directions. So that night, we took a cab to the walled compound where British Aerospace employees lived, and King talked us past the guard at the gate. Inside, there were rows of identical bungalows, all dark with the curtains and shades drawn, arrayed along straight and well-maintained streets.

We stopped at the appointed address, which looked uninhabited, with no lights showing. King knocked on the door and, sure enough, we were admitted into an amazing facsimile of a British pub, complete with a bar, glasses hanging from overhead racks, and chairs and tables off to the side. All the alcoholic beverages—there were only three—were homemade. There was a sort of bitter, or beer, that didn't taste very good, and two types of siddiki—clear and brown. The clear was a white lightning you drank with tonic water and the brown was a substitute for whiskey, to be mixed with Coke or ginger ale. It was fairly potent stuff. The bartender explained that siddiki was Arabic for "my friend," so that if someone had a party and asked you to bring your friend, you knew what it meant.

After the pool disbanded and we were free to do our own stories, I did a local angle piece on a Wisconsin school teacher who was vice principal of a school for employees of Aramco, the Arab-American Oil Co. He lived in Abqaiq, a walled compound built and maintained by Aramco. It was as if the little community had been plucked out of a suburb in the United States. The American-designed houses were on curving, tree-lined streets that could have been anywhere in Arizona or California. Inside, they had U.S. furniture and appliances.

I noticed one oddity. All the houses seemed to have what looked like small mud rooms or storage areas in back. But they were made of concrete block, while the rest of the house was of frame construction. My hosts explained that many of the residents ran stills to make their own booze, and that sometimes the stills exploded, so the Aramco authorities had decreed that the stills be located in secure bunkers. In addition, they explained, the explosions had been considerably reduced after Aramco decided to help the residents build better-designed and safer stills.

But while the press pool was still functioning—it lasted about two weeks before it disbanded and the military welcomed open coverage—we had about as much fun as you can have as a reporter. We talked to troops in the desert, climbed on tanks, visited ships, flew in helicopters and even were feted at lavish receptions and dinners thrown by Saudi princes and businessmen. And in the process, we convinced our military handlers that we were as patriotic and supportive of the troops as they were.

THE MORALE BOOSTERS

The first time came on the day we were treated to an extravagant buffet lunch at a wedding palace in Riyadh. Earlier, we had been given a tour of the 552nd AWACS (Airborne Warning and Control Wing), a spy plane outfit which was stationed at the Riyadh air base. Late in the afternoon after the lunch, we were all on an air-conditioned bus riding out on the tarmac to the Saudi C-130 that would take us back to Dhahran. One of our escort officers pointed to one of the hangars, where a crowd of uniformed men and women from the wing were lined up, waiting to be interviewed and photographed by the home country press.

It wasn't a story, and we all knew it. We were tired and grubby, and just wanted to get back to Dhahran and our nice hotel rooms. But it was clear that this was a morale situation. We couldn't just arrogantly blow off all these people, though nobody actually said that. I suggested that we get out and at least talk to the troops. We gathered our notebooks, cameras and tape recorders, trooped out of the bus and spent the next hour doing interviews. We left to smiles and waves. I don't think any of it was ever published or broadcast.

As we were boarding the C-130 for the flight back to Dhahran, a young blonde woman, who was an Air Force captain and a public affairs officer, handed us each a folder that contained a press kit about the 552nd. On the flight back, the LA Times's Michael Ross was idly flipping through the pages when he shouted, "Holy shit! Look at this!" The press kit contained a locator sheet, detailing all the motels and other buildings in Riyadh where members of the wing had been assigned to living quarters. It was complete with maps, bus routes, telephone numbers and lists of individuals and their billets.

"Wouldn't a terrorist love to get one of these?" Ross asked rhetorically. We didn't even give it much thought. We simply went around and collected all the offending documents and turned them over to an astonished escort officer.

Another time, we were on a cargo ship in the port of Jubail, being briefed by a rear admiral who was in charge of unloading operations at the port. We had been strictly admonished that we were not allowed to disclose locations as a matter of operational security. But when the admiral stood up in front of the cameras, he beamed and announced, "Here we are in the beautiful port of Jubail." CNN's Carl Rochelle ordered the cameras shut down and gently reminded the red-faced admiral of the security prohibition.

I returned to the AWACs wing in Riyadh later to do a story on what it was like to fly on a 15-hour surveillance mission. It included two air-to-air refuelings, which I watched from the cockpit. The mission crew commander, Lt. Col. Laszlo (Skosh) Bakonyi, also allowed me to sit at the command console, where I ordered refueling for a couple of Canadian jets flying cover for us. I saw classified information on the computer screen, but I had agreed in advance not to disclose any secrets. My brief commander's role came to a halt when a couple of Iraqi jets streaked toward the Saudi border, and I quickly handed the headphones back to Bakonyi.

Unfortunately, I had to go back to cover the Gulf War, called Desert Storm. I'd been there under the best of circumstances, and didn't want to go back. But The Journal wanted it covered, so I flew back to Dhahran on British Airways in time for the start of the air war on Jan. 15, 1991. The Journal also sent another reporter from Milwaukee, Dave Hendrickson.

With only a few exceptions, it was a miserable time. I was now in the Carlton al-Moaibed Hotel, some miles away from the Dhahran International, and despite the fact that I had good contacts among the military people running the JIB, I was shut out of the action along with the vast majority of my colleagues. That was because the JIB, in concert with the networks and the other big organizations that had the money to keep correspondents in Saudi Arabia between Desert Shield in August, 1990, and Desert Storm in January, 1991, had established several score of combat pools.

The Pentagon, fearing that its forces would be overrun with journalists, foreign and domestic, had decreed that the only access to the action would be by pools. No independent coverage would be allowed. The pools were formed in the no-news months of September through December, 1990. There were 13 newspapers involved, but not The Milwaukee Journal because we didn't have anybody in the country. As always, the networks and wires were included, along with the news magazines.

I'm not a conspiracy theorist, so I'm not inclined to believe that the combat pool system was intended as a way to control access by the press, but it certainly worked that way. If the generals and other commanders did not want reporters covering their operations during the Gulf War, they didn't get any. As Lt. Col. Bill Mulvey, the JIB commander, put it, "I know how to salute."

The system frustrated even the military public affairs officers. Lt. Col. Larry Icenogle, who was Mulvey's No. 1 at the time, envisioned what he believed would be great public relations back home. There were two old battleships in the war—the Wisconsin and Missouri—that were equipped with cruise missiles in addition to their giant 16-inch guns. The Missouri was the same ship on which officers of the Japanese high command had signed their country's surrender in World War II.

Icenogle said he could imagine a split-screen TV shot, with file footage of the surrender on one half and the Missouri firing cruise missiles at Iraq on the other side. There was only one problem: The skipper of the Missouri didn't want any reporters—and he didn't get any.

The sheer silliness of the situation came home to me when I learned that the Coast Guard outfit handling security for the port of Dhahran was none other than a reserve unit from Milwaukee. It was the first reserve unit ever activated for combat duty in the Coast Guard's history, and about 90% of the personnel were from Wisconsin, northern Illinois and northern Indiana. If there were ever the sort of home town feature story that military public affairs people and hometown editors salivated over, this was it. Moreover, the unit's headquarters was only a few miles from my hotel.

But when I went to Mulvey and Icenogle to ask if I could go there to do the feature story, they apologized and said orders dictated no exceptions to the rule that access to any military units or operations was permitted only through the combat pool system.

MARDI GRAS IN THE DESERT

I was angrily griping about the situation to some of my colleagues when somebody mentioned that a USA TODAY reporter, Marilyn Greene, had done a story about the Coast Guard reservists a few days before the pool system had gone into effect. I sought her out and she graciously handed me her laptop computer with the story. I took extensive notes from it and wrote my own story for The Journal, prominently citing her story as the source.

But Bruce Alpert of the New Orleans Times-Picayune did not fare as well. He was in Saudi Arabia for one reason and one reason only: The local story. He spent virtually all of his time stopping everybody in uniform to ask them if they knew of any Louisiana soldiers or units.

One day he struck pay dirt. He learned that a National Guard unit from Baton Rouge was camped out in the desert not far away. He called the lieutenant colonel in charge, who was happy to hear from him and invited him out. Not only that, the officer told Alpert that, with Lent coming on in a few days, the unit would be having a mardi gras party.

Talk about another great hometown feature. Alpert lined up a photographer and planned a trip to the unit to do a story on the desert
mardi gras. But it never happened. He was turned away at the gate by
a public affairs officer who told him the same thing Mulvey and Icenogle had told me: Nobody goes anywhere unless he is part of a pool.

So we were truly hotel warriors, which became the title of a memorable book by John Fialka of The Wall Street Journal. It was frustrating.
Though I filed stories on a daily basis, virtually all of the information
came from the pool reports that cascaded into the JIB on a daily basis.
What we didn't realize at the time was what we were missing. Many
of the pool reports filed by reporters in the field simply never got back
or didn't get back in a timely fashion. The hotel warriors spent a lot of
time watching CNN.

About the only excitement we had came when Iraq started firing
the notoriously inaccurate scud missiles at the Dhahran area. In the
first attack, we dutifully trooped into the basement of the Dhahran
International Hotel, where we all sat disconsolately listening to our
battery radios tuned to a station in Bahrain that always announced
the beginnings and ends of air raids with musical tones. The military
people were all in their chemical warfare (MOPP) suits and most of
the journalists had gas masks. Mine was an East German model that I
had bought for $20, and didn't think it would work anyway.

That was the first and last time I went to a shelter during a scud
raid. After that, I would go outside to watch, or sometimes go up on
the roof with the photographers who were there waiting for a shot. If I
was in bed at my hotel, I sometimes got up to peer out the window for
any tell-tale signs. Usually I just rolled over and went back to sleep. We
all knew the scuds weren't accurate, and I took a fatalistic approach. I
figured if one was going to hit me, it already would have done so by the
time the air raid sirens went off. (A scud did hit a barracks in Dhahran
later, in February, 1991, killing 28 American troops and injuring 98).

If you happened to be in one of the hotels when the air raid sirens
went off, you were treated to a comic scene. Men and women in uniform, obviously under orders, trooped dutifully down the stairs to the
basement "shelter" areas, pulling on their MOPP suits on their way.
Photographers and reporters elbowed past them, going up the stairs
to the roof for a better view of the attack.

I did try to do as many enterprise stories as I could dream up, but
unlike some other reporters, I didn't push the system much. In other

words, I didn't get in my rental car to go looking for the war in violation of the agreement we had all signed to get our press cards. Some others did and got good stories. But they were mostly from the AP, the networks and other news organizations with lots of backup and an imperative to get whatever they could. And they also had reporters in the pools. A few journalists were captured by the Iraqis.

My constant carping at the JIB finally got me a pool slot. The Baltimore Sun dropped out of one of the ship pools and I was assigned as the replacement. But I didn't get the word until shortly before the pool was to depart. Of all things, it was headed to the battleship Wisconsin first and then perhaps some other ships. When I tried to join the group, I was told I couldn't go along because nobody could find my MOPP suit and flak jacket. The Baltimore Sun guy had turned it in, but the supply sergeant who took it had neglected to tell anybody.

I was bitterly disappointed, but it turned out to be a blessing. That pool was gone a couple of weeks and didn't get much in the way of the news, so I would have been wasting my time.

Meanwhile, I passed up one good story out of patriotism and got one great one because of my earlier involvement in the first pool that had gone into Saudi Arabia.

One day, out of sheer boredom, I headed out the front door of the Dhahran International Hotel to catch one of the periodic tours around the area organized by the JIB to mollify the hordes of journalists who came in from all over the world. These forays, which came to be known collectively as "the Sluggo tour," usually went down to the flight line at the air base, where photographers could shoot incoming cargo and troop planes.

As I headed to the bus, one of the Saudis, who had been with us on the original tour and now was working with the JIB, stopped me and told me to take a minibus off to the side instead. There were only a few of us on the bus, which took us out to the F-15 bunkers on the air base, where we were introduced to a Saudi pilot who had just shot down two Iraqi warplanes.

It was a great story, one of the few I got to report first-hand. And with the time difference between Milwaukee and Saudi Arabia, I was able to make that day's paper, even though The Journal was an afternoon paper. The story ran on the top of page one and a photograph of the impromptu news conference with the Saudi pilot in the bunker ran in newspapers and news magazines all over the country. There I was, prominently in the picture next to the pilot, taking notes.

SKIPPING A STORY

The story I passed up was one that, in retrospect, I maybe shouldn't have. The Carlton al-Moaiebed Hotel, where I was staying, had pigeon holes behind the reception desk where they put our messages and mail. One day, riffling through my mail, I came across a faxed memorandum addressed to a civilian also staying in the hotel—an engineer, it appeared.

The memo, from somebody at the Chrysler Corp. in Detroit, discussed a problem with the armored Bradley Fighting Vehicles that had been deployed to Saudi Arabia. It seems there was a transmission problem that sometimes prevented them from backing up.

I debated with myself over whether to take down the information and chase the story. But I decided it would not be ethical, and I returned the memo to the embarrassed desk clerk, who promised to get it to its rightful owner.

Besides the ethics, I was concerned about the security aspects of the story. I recalled doing an innocuous feature story during the Desert Shield pool the previous August. I had interviewed some soldiers sitting in the shade of their Humvee, asking if they had experienced any problems. After complaining about cold french fries and warm Pepsi—the only early food available from Saudi sources for the troops—one said, "Yeah, the sun is frying the radios." I asked what they did about it and he replied, "Easy, we just replace them."

I put the quotes in the story and, as we all had agreed, allowed one of our military escort officers to read it. The deal was that we were to submit all of our stories to the escorts to check for security problems, but they were not allowed to order us to remove anything. If there was a dispute, it had to be referred to the public affairs office in the Pentagon, headed by Pete Williams, which would then negotiate any changes with editors back in Washington. (Williams went on to a career as an NBC News correspondent covering the Supreme Court and the Justice Department).

The escort officer had no problem with anything in the story—even the part about the sun frying the radios. But he said it would violate operational security to include what the troops were doing about the problem. I argued journalistically, saying that you could not state the problem and then not answer the question about what was being done to solve it. But he was adamant. In the end, I excised the quote about replacing the radios, sure in the knowledge that editors everywhere would be firing off queries to get the answer. They did not.

Back home months later, I read a story about the backing-up problems of the Bradley Fighting Vehicles. But it was short and didn't get much play, so although I was miffed with myself for passing it up, I figured I hadn't lost much. On the other hand, I was sure that it would have been a bigger story during the military offensive in the Gulf War.

Increasingly frustrated by the lack of access, and concerned about getting behind at home on my weekly automobile review column, I finally talked The Journal into letting me head back less than three weeks after I had arrived in Saudi Arabia. Hendrickson stayed, but I managed to get out on a giant C-5 transport plane that was evacuating Americans and their dependents to Frankfurt.

A military plane crashed that day, and unknown to me it turned out to be a gut-wrenching time for my wife, Sharlene. She heard about the plane crash on CNN and frantically contacted the Pentagon to find out if it was the one I was on. It wasn't, and Pete Williams himself called to reassure her, while one of my daughters, Becky, who was acquainted with one of the daughters of Gen. Colin Powell, chairman of the Joint Chiefs of Staff, tried that avenue.

A few years later, my experiences in Saudi Arabia stood me in good stead in another of those serendipitous happenings that altered the course of my newspaper career. In early 1994, I was now The Journal's bureau chief, and in that capacity I received invitations to a lot of receptions by one interest group or another. One day, an invitation arrived from The Freedom Forum in Arlington. I had only minimal knowledge of it; only that it was a journalism-oriented foundation somehow connected with the Gannett news empire.

The invitation said The Freedom Forum would have a groundbreaking of sorts for an institution called the Newseum, a museum of journalism and its practitioners. It was scheduled for the Newseum site in Rosslyn, in downtown Arlington, and Alan Neuharth, the flamboyant chairman of the Freedom Forum, would initiate the project by whacking some plaster board with a sledge hammer.

Ordinarily, I would have passed up such an event. But that day I had already filed my story, the Newseum was practically on my way home, the invitation included free parking, food and drink, and I didn't have to be home for dinner. So I stopped by.

As always with The Freedom Forum, it was a nice reception with plenty to eat and an open bar (I later learned that its clandestine nickname was "the feed 'em forum") and I ran into a number of people I knew. One of them introduced me to Paul McMasters, the executive director of The Freedom Forum's First Amendment Center at Vanderbilt University in Nashville. We had met briefly earlier when he was national president of the Society of Professional Journalists. I had won the organization's Sigma Delta Chi medal for Washington correspondence, and received the award at the 1993 SPJ convention in Miami Beach.

OFF TO NASHVILLE

In the course of exchanging pleasantries with McMasters, he suddenly said, "Maybe you can help us out." He explained that the First Amendment Center had established fellowships to do a study of media-military relations and had lined up a retired admiral to do the military side. A working journalist was needed to work with him. I asked what it entailed, and he said it would cover an academic year in Nashville, with a stipend to cover the journalist's salary. An apartment and expenses would be provided for the journalist and his spouse. There would be secretarial and research help, as well as air fare back home once a month for both the journalist and spouse.

"Do you know anybody who might fit the bill?" McMasters asked. My mind was racing. "How about me?" I said. He was momentarily taken aback, but I quickly outlined my experiences with the DOD national media pool and my two trips to Saudi Arabia for the Gulf War. He was clearly interested and asked me to put together some biographical and other materials for consideration by the First Amendment Center board. I explained that I obviously would have to get approval from my editor.

I had some hope of success because we had a new editor, Mary Jo Meisner, who had been recruited from the Fort Worth Star-Telegram. (Ironically, I had been one of her competitors when I sought the editor's job myself). She was flamboyant and controversial, a tall woman in her forties, not pretty but with a good body who was fond of wearing micro-miniskirts. The first time I met her was when she visited the Washington bureau after she was named editor but before she had started in the job. She was wearing one of the miniskirts, and sat directly opposite me and Richard Foster, our Washington-based editorial writer. Her chair was higher than the sofa where we sat, so I was at eye level with her waist. I decided I'd best maintain eye contact and not let my eyes wander.

The meeting was cordial and, although Meisner later did some shaking up back in Milwaukee, we got along fine—mostly because we had little contact. I always thought one of the main advantages of the Washington bureau was being 800 miles away from the editors.

Under earlier Journal regimes, my request for a nine-month leave likely would have been summarily rejected—the argument being that it would not be easy to replace the Washington bureau chief. I sent a memo and called Meisner personally, emphasizing the prestige of the fellowship and how it would reflect on The Journal, and also how it would enhance our relationship with sources in the military. There also was some urgency because of the time frame, so a decision had to be made quickly.

By then I also had a talented sidekick in the bureau, Patrick Jasperse, who already had proven that he could handle the coverage when I was away for the Gulf War. Moreover, the military-media fellowship, in 1994-'95, fell between presidential election years, so that pressure was not present. Meisner barely hesitated before she gave her approval.

On The Freedom Forum side, I also had a powerful inside advocate, though I didn't realize its full importance at the time. Charles Overby was The Freedom Forum president, Neuharth's No. 1. We had known each other casually back in the 1970s as regional reporters on Capitol Hill. Overby worked for the Nashville Banner then and remembered me.

McMasters had mentioned the name of the admiral who would be my counterpart. At the time, it meant nothing. But I soon learned that I would be working side-by-side with an American hero, retired Vice Admiral William P. Lawrence. A Nashville native and a graduate of the U.S. Naval Academy, he was in the same class as Astronaut Alan Shepard and was close to being an astronaut himself. A slight heart murmur scotched that chance and Lawrence became a fighter pilot and squadron leader.

His F-4 Phantom was shot down over Hanoi during the Vietnam War and Lawrence was imprisoned in the infamous French-built Hoa Lo prison, nicknamed the "Hanoi Hilton" by the prisoners. He was the senior officer there, ranking over such later-to-be-famous prisoners as future Sen. John McCain and future vice-presidential candidate Admiral James Stockdale, who was on the third-party ticket with H. Ross Perot. Coincidentally, Perot was an old classmate and friend of Lawrence's from their Naval Academy days. After his release from the prison camp, Lawrence went on to become commander of the Third Fleet, superintendent of the Naval Academy and, at his retirement in 1986, was chief of Naval Personnel, the second-ranking job in the Navy.

I was in awe of Lawrence, thinking that I was not even in the same league with him. But we soon became friends, consulted daily—our offices were across the hall from each other—and had long conversations when we took airplane and car trips to do interviews for our book.

Lawrence spoke slowly and had a disconcerting manner of not making eye contact. In a one-on-one conversation, he mostly looked down, with occasional glances at the other person's face—a manner I soon attributed to his six years as a prisoner of war, when making eye contact likely would prompt a beating or worse. We talked a little about his POW days, but not much. He told me that when he was released, he learned that his wife had divorced him, the result of an affair with an Episcopal priest with whom she had been counseling. But he was happily remarried to Diane, a physical therapist who had treated McCain after his release. McCain called her his "physical terrorist." He had introduced her to Lawrence.

Lawrence opened doors that likely would have been closed to me. He knew practically everybody in the military establishment and made it a practice to arrive at his office at the First Amendment Center early in the morning, when he telephoned friends in the Pentagon. He explained that he needed to catch people before they went into meetings, and Nashville was on central time while the Pentagon was on eastern time.

With his clout, we interviewed virtually everybody from Defense Secretary Richard Cheney on down. I soon learned that there was a ritual when high-ranking military officers met. I'd sit there, anxious to get on with the interview, while Lawrence and the general or admiral would reminisce and get caught up on what had happened to mutual friends. Lawrence joked one time that he was at the stage where "we reminisce about things that never happened." I knew it was necessary, but I chafed at the practice because it seemed to waste about half our interview time. Lawrence, with a deep understanding of his military colleagues, seldom let an interview run more than a half hour before he'd say, "Well, we know you're busy and we'll get out of your way."

THE ODD COUPLE

Lawrence surprised me. I had expected a crusty, set-in-his-ways right-wing conservative. He was anything but. Like me, he made his political judgments based on his view of the issues and the people, though with a preference for people he knew and admired, McCain among them. He was also sensitive to women's rights—he had that reputation when he was superintendent at the Naval Academy at a time his daughter, Wendy, was a midshipman there—and he was savvy about the news media. (Wendy later became a Navy captain and an astronaut who flew on the space shuttle and logged more than 1,200 hours in space). Lawrence understood the press and believed when there was bad news the best course was to get the story out and get it over with. He said he had offered just such advice to the Naval Academy superintendent at the time a woman midshipman was chained to a urinal in a prank by her male classmates. Sadly, he said, the superintendent did not follow his advice and the news media made much of what they saw as a cover-up.

During our nine months together, Lawrence and I became friends. When we dealt with the issues that arose in our study of the military and the media, we talked them through and invariably came to a meeting of the minds. Though we disagreed occasionally, there was never any rancor. Lawrence had done some writing, but his style was formal and military, and he slaved over it. So he took over several sections while I wound up writing most of the book. The title, *America's Team: The Odd Couple,* was mine. It was a combination of what the Dallas Cowboys liked to call themselves and the "Odd Couple" play and movie. I thought the title aptly summed up the importance of and differences between the military and the news media.

Natilee Duning was the editor, and she was a delight to work with, mostly giving us free rein but injecting enough questions and comments to cause course corrections here and there. She completed her work, along with the layout and other graphics, in the summer of 1995. I enlisted my cartoonist friend, Bill Rechin, who draws the "Crock" comic strip, to do the book's cover. It was both funny and appropriate.

We also lightened up the mostly serious content, including results of a poll we had commissioned, with a sprinkling of cartoons. I am a huge fan of both strip and editorial cartoons, which I think can convey more meaning and truth with a few strokes of a pen than a writer can with thousands of words. So I picked out all the cartoons for the book.

I was determined that our book would never be the subject of criticism other than disagreement with some of our conclusions or recommendations. So we had all of our taped interviews transcribed and I edited them to take out redundancies and extraneous vocalization. Then we shipped the edited transcripts to the subjects and gave them the opportunity, as members of Congress always have, to "revise and extend" their remarks. Most shipped them back without changes.

In one case, an interview with Gen. John Shalikashvili, then the chairman of the Joint Chiefs of Staff, I basically had to rewrite the entire interview. Shalikashvili, though an accomplished military officer, was anything but erudite, so I simply corrected his mangled syntax without, I hoped, changing any of the meaning. I sent the text off to my Gulf War contact, Col. Larry Icenogle, who by then was the chairman's public relations chief. He called back and said, "The general couldn't have said it better himself."

While I was away on the fellowship, the powers in Milwaukee decided to axe The Journal and the Sentinel, and create the new Milwaukee Journal Sentinel. I was miffed when I was required to re-apply for my job as Washington bureau chief. I almost didn't do it, but then decided that prudence was better than pride. It turned out to be a formality.

After I returned to work in Washington for the new Journal Sentinel that summer, Natilee sent me the page proofs for proofreading. I went over them very carefully because I didn't want any of those little "erratum" pieces of paper stuck into our final product. I didn't want any typographical errors, either, not even so much as a badly divided word. Natilee and I even went around and around on how to divide the word "standard," until we learned that it could be either "stan-dard" or "stand-ard."

I was proud of the final product, and even got into a good-natured bet with Charles Overby, who became The Freedom Forum chairman after Al Neuharth retired. I told him he'd get five bucks for every typo he found, and I'd get fifty bucks if he didn't find any. I think he forgot about the bet almost as quickly as I did. In any case, nobody ever found a typo because there weren't any.

The Freedom Forum did the "rollout" of *America's Team: The Odd Couple* in September in San Antonio, with a good turnout of the military leadership, headed by Sheila Widnall, the secretary of the Air Force. Lawrence and I were poised to take the show on the road, introducing the book to news and military organizations. But it was not to be.

In October, 1995, Lawrence went into the Bethesda Naval Hospital to have a heart valve replaced—the same one that had produced the murmur that kept him out of the astronaut corps. A blood clot developed while he was on the operating table. It reached his brain and caused a massive stroke. But for heroic efforts by the doctors, he likely would have died.

Sadly, the stroke left him partially paralyzed. In the years following, his wife, Diane, kept him on a strict regimen of physical therapy and he gradually recovered some use of his muscles. But his days of playing tennis and driving an automobile were over. Bill also suffered from clinical depression, which didn't help. It wasn't fair. Here was this strong and gentle man, this hero, who had endured more in a Vietnamese prison camp than anyone could imagine, and after all these years of recovery, was in a prison of a different sort. I was angry and frustrated.

The practical result was that I became a solo act for the speeches, symposiums and panel discussions that covered issues discussed in our book. Over the next several years, I was the main speaker, panel moderator, panel member or seminar leader for a variety of programs sponsored by the military services and their education arms. Usually they went under the rubric of a media day of some sort. The military leadership was beginning to develop a new appreciation of the need to more effectively work with and through the news media.

Military folks are great at after-action analysis—"lessons learned," they call it. One of the lessons of the Gulf War was that press coverage could be a good thing. It brought public recognition. The Gulf War's U.S. Marine commander, Gen. Walt Boomer, understood that well. He was the Marines' former public affairs chief, and he issued an open invitation to reporters—especially former Marines—to visit Marine units. His biggest coup was to host Molly Moore, a reporter for The

Washington Post, who did an extensive series of stories about Marine operations.

At the same time, a number of Army commanders involved in the famed "left hook" operation that brought Iraqi forces to their knees, had refused to host reporters or otherwise thwarted press coverage.

WHO WON THE WAR?

The end result was a public perception that the Marines had won the Gulf War—or certainly had a major hand in it. The truth was otherwise, but that didn't matter. The value of news media coverage began to dawn on the Army's leadership.

It all came to fruition in 2003, when the United States invaded Iraq to finally oust the dictator Saddam Hussein. Recommendations Lawrence and I had made in *The Odd Couple* became Pentagon policy—most notably the decision to "embed" reporters with military units. It resulted in dramatic coverage of a sort never before seen, and the public received unprecedented insights into military operations. Overall, operational security was not threatened.

Inevitably, however, there was carping. Some critics groused that embedding reporters with the troops brought them too close to the subjects they were covering, and therefore they could not be objective and critical. Of course, getting the reporters close to the troops, and understanding them and their problems, was precisely the point. You're damned if you do and damned if you don't.

Meanwhile, in the years following publication of *The Odd Couple* in 1995, I had a great time participating in "media days" sponsored by the various services, including the National Guard, Army, Navy, Air Force, Marine Corps and Coast Guard. I went into it with some trepidation, harboring the old stereotype that most military people were right-wing zealots. There was some of that, of course, such as having lunch in a crowded military-base cafeteria with Rush Limbaugh holding forth on a giant screen, with loudspeakers placed so you couldn't avoid hearing his pretentious babbling.

But for the most part, I learned that most military officers, gung ho or no, were highly educated, thoughtful people. It bore out one of the results of the surveys we had done for *America's Team: The Odd Couple*. That was that, as a group, military officers were more highly educated than journalists. Much of the higher education, it is true, was of a technical nature, but there were certainly more degrees attached to military names than those of reporters.

I was even surprised a few times. When I was invited to be the main speaker at a military-media program for captains and majors at the Marine Corps University at Quantico, Va., acquaintances warned me that I'd be "eaten alive" by that bunch of anti-media jarheads. They related tales of other journalists who had spoken there and figuratively had their heads bitten off.

But if I may say so, they were pussycats, listening respectfully and hitting me with only a couple of tough questions. There was no hostility. Maybe it was the aura that surrounded me because Bill Lawrence was the co-author of the study. I usually started every speech or introductory remarks with a brief description of Bill, his career and his troubles, and pointed out that every conclusion and recommendation in our study was the result of a meeting of our minds.

I also used the R.T. Kingman description of the media's watchdog function to warm up audiences. R.T. made his mark as a lobbyist and public relations man, but he was an unreconstructed newsman who had once worked for the Kansas City Kansan. We got to know each other when both of us served on the board of directors of the National Press Foundation. Before his death, when he ran the Washington office for General Motors Corp., he helped put together a national advertising campaign to celebrate the 200th anniversary of the U.S. Constitution.

THE WATCHDOG

Somewhere in the course of that task, R.T. developed his own definition of the watchdog function of the news media. It went something like this:

Any security professional will tell you that the best way to protect your home is with a watchdog. The dog is superior to any sort of electronic surveillance or alarm system you can devise. But if you decide on a watchdog, you have to put up with a few things.

First, unnecessary barking. That's because the watchdog will go nuts and bark at everybody who shows up, not just the bad guys.

Second, hair on the furniture and carpet.

Third, occasional barfing, peeing and crapping on the floor.

R.T. said that was a pretty good approximation of the way the news media functions: lots of unnecessary barking over trivial matters (See

Michael and Janet Jackson, Anna Nicole Smith and Paris Hilton). Certainly, mistakes and inaccuracies like hair on the furniture (See Enron before the fall). And, finally, those big dumps on the floor when someone in the media screws up monumentally, as happens far too often but less than we sometimes think (See Janet Cooke, Jayson Blair and Jack Kelley).

I've used that description hundreds of times to disarm potentially hostile audiences. I make the point that news men and women are anything but perfect, and that our First Amendment-protected craft is as open to error, misjudgment, meanness, deception and plain silliness as any other human endeavor. It is analogous to what Winston Churchill said about democracy: It is the worst possible way to do it—except for all the others.

Nevertheless, I was startled when I was the main speaker at the end of a media program at the U.S. Coast Guard Academy. After I arrived, I was taken to the "green room" at the main auditorium with the academy's top cadet. We waited until the appointed time, and then the two of us walked out onto the stage.

I knew I was to be the main speaker, but I didn't realize the extent of the audience. The entire academy was there, from the commandant through the faculty to the lowest member of the student body. They probably had the gardeners and kitchen workers there as well.

As I walked across the stage, somebody shouted, "Hooh!" and the entire assembly leaped to attention.

I was visibly startled, then grinned and sat down. Then they all sat down. After the introduction, I told everybody that I had been taken aback because my military career had consisted of eight years as an Air Force reservist, with my highest rank at three stripes: an airman first class. Nobody had ever stood at attention for me before.

The speech and the questions went well, and then my escort presented me with a beautiful gold foil replica of the Coast Guard's training ship Eagle, a renovated sailing ship captured from Germany in World War II. I opened the gift-wrapped package right there at the lectern and thanked everyone profusely.

As I walked off the stage, there was another shouted, "Hooh!" and I flinched involuntarily again. But I was grinning, too.

I had one gimmick that I used often on the military audiences. At the start of a speech or a moderator's introduction, I usually asked for a show of hands from members of the audience who believed, in their

heart of hearts, that reporters promoted political agendas in their stories. Invariably, half to two-thirds of the hands would go up.

Then I'd launch into my "I can't prove it to you, but . . ." message. I
never tried to speak for my broadcast or magazine colleagues, saying
that I had quit reading news magazines many years ago because they
came at stories with a point of view and a lot of opinion. I pointed out
the different areas of a newspaper that held opinions—the editorial
page, signed columnists and the sports pages. I also noted that newspapers, like people, had personalities that contributed to perceptions
that they were liberal, conservative or something in between.

But I tried using common sense to disabuse them of the notion that
reporters and editors tried to slant stories politically, by first pointing
out that the vast majority of stories didn't have political content. Sec-
ondly, reporters and editors, busy with the daily basket of stories to
cover and millions of words of news every day, simply didn't have time
to shape a political slant to every story, even if they were so inclined—
although I conceded that there likely were individual instances where
that happened. Finally, I'd point out that a reporter who consistently
slanted stories one way or the other likely would cut off at least half
of his or her news sources. In a craft where sources are everything, I
asked, why would anybody do that?

I'm sure I didn't convince everybody, but enough people came up to
me after the programs for further discussion that I believe I at least
started some of them thinking. I usually made the point that the Rush
Limbaughs and Bill O'Reillys of the world got their news from the
newspapers like everybody else, and would be completely dumbstruck
without them. I'd also note the nonpolitical potpourri of information
in newspapers: disasters and weather, entertainment and sports, fash-
ions and popular culture, cooking and consumer help, churches and
religion, business and economics, and local, national and international
happenings.

Although the military leaders were eager to learn lessons from the
Gulf War experience and our book, news organizations were a disappointment. If there was any reaction at all from publications, broadcasters or their professional associations, it wasn't apparent. Lawrence
and I had made a number of recommendations for ways to avoid the
military-media pitfalls and clashes of the past, and many of the military people took them to heart. The news people, as far as we knew,
ignored the subject.

Obviously, some of that can be traced to the autonomy of individual news organizations. But I would have thought that the Associated Press Managing Editors Association, the National Association of Broadcasters or the American Society of Newspaper Editors would have at least broached the subject to their members. The only exception was when the executive editor of the Baton Rouge (La.) Advocate, Linda Lightfoot, asked me to write several articles for the newsletter of the American Society of Newspaper Editors.

The question of access to military operations did become the subject of congressional hearings, where I had the privilege of testifying along with some of my colleagues, including the nation's "most trusted man," Walter Cronkite.

Though I disagreed with Cronkite on some of his analysis of the military-media relationship, he did make one telling point when he said most responsible journalists, though they didn't like it, could live with censorship. In World War II, correspondents wore uniforms and traveled with the troops—"embedded" in today's terminology—and were required to submit all their stories to military censors before filing them.

But they had the most important thing—access to the story. It meant that even if reporters could not tell the entire story immediately because of security concerns, they still covered it and could tell the story eventually. On the other hand, if reporters are denied access to the story—as many were in Desert Storm—the story can never be told by an independent observer. The only accounts come from parties who had an interest in the outcome.

The *Odd Couple* was a success, with many thousands of copies delivered by The Freedom Forum to military academies, war colleges and units. Even years later, when it was no longer up-to-date, it was still being used as a text in military public affairs courses.

Bill Lawrence died in December, 2006, while Sharlene and I were away on a trip around the world. The Navy gave him a hero's funeral at the Naval Academy in Annapolis and I wrote a tribute to him that ran in the Milwaukee Journal Sentinel and the Tennessean in his home town of Nashville.

9

CUBA AND COLOMBIA

Reporters rarely get to participate in Codels, but I managed to get on one. Codel is short for Congressional Delegation, and it is used to describe a group of congressmen who travel together—usually overseas. The rationale for the trips is always fact-finding, to help the senators and congressmen better understand the issues they face as lawmakers.

Sometimes, however, the trips are little more than thinly-disguised vacation and shopping jaunts. Sometimes they also are grinding work trips. And sometimes they are a combination of the two.

The Codel I went on, in 1978, was organized by Rep. Henry S. Reuss, the Milwaukee Democrat who was the chairman of the House Banking Committee. As chairman, it was his prerogative to choose the participants. I had just been elected president of the National Press Club and was pleased when he agreed to add me to the roster.

The committee was scheduled to visit Cuba, followed by a number of other Latin American countries. At each stop, the Banking Committee members met with their counterparts in the banking and financial communities. Reuss was interested only in Cuba and Colombia, where the country director of the U.S. Agency for International Development was James Megellas, an old Democratic colleague of Reuss's who had once been mayor of Fond du Lac, Wis.

Cuba was the first stop. We flew on a plush Air Force jet, a Boeing 737, outfitted for VIPs, out of Andrews Air Force base and landed in Havana. Then, as now, the U.S. maintained a trade embargo against Cuba and the two countries did not have direct diplomatic relations. Our man in Cuba was Wayne Smith, who headed the "U.S. Interests Section" in Havana.

Despite our estranged relationship, the Cubans rolled out the red carpet. The Codel was ushered into what may have been the only luxury hotel in Havana. It formerly had been the famed Riviera, owned by Meyer Lansky in pre-Fidel Castro days.

The committee members, staff, escorts and this one lone reporter toured the island by bus. We went to Santiago de Cuba and saw the house from which Castro launched his revolution against the Batista regime. We visited schools and factories, and were treated with defer-ence and courtesy everywhere we went.

I chafed constantly over the fact that I didn't know a word of Spanish, and an experience one afternoon cemented my determination to try to learn the language. The Banking Committee members had scheduled closed meetings with Cuban banking officials. Because I had nothing to do, I decided to check out downtown Havana, courtesy of Smith, who offered me a car and driver.

Without any Spanish, in a society closed to Americans, all I could do was wander the streets and the shops, trying to gain what impres-sions I could, feeling isolated from the Cubans around me.

One vivid impression was in the Cuban version of a department store. There was a huge pile of cheap black high-top tennis shoes from China—with a low price and no buyers. Near-by, a throng of people jostled for position at a jewelry counter. People elbowed each other aside in their eagerness to buy whatever was offered. It confirmed what we had been told about Cubans: that they had enormous savings in cash because they had little on which to spend their money.

My frustration at not being able to speak Spanish nagged at me for some time afterward. Determined to learn the language, I cooked up a deal with The Journal's editors to let me take intensive training. I contributed two weeks of vacation time and my own air fare (flying on Sharlene's passes and discounted fares), and The Journal contributed two weeks of time off, as well as the tuition and room and board. I went to Cuernevaca, Mexico, for a month in 1980 and another month in 1981, where I immersed myself in Spanish. I couldn't get away for a long time after that and finally did a third month in San Andreas, Costa Rica, a suburb of San Juan.

Each time, I lived with a local family and attended classes in the mornings, then studied and practiced in the afternoons and evenings. My pronunciation was excellent; but try as I might I never did achieve my goal of being able to function as a reporter speaking Spanish. Some people, I think, have a facility for languages; I didn't. It was a great dis-appointment. As always, when I was gone Sharlene took care of the home front.

The climax of the 1978 Cuba trip was a reception for the Codel members at the Palace of the Revolution, hosted by Castro himself. We all arrived early at the cavernous lobby, where open bars and groaning tables of food greeted us. It was a stark contrast to the living conditions of the Cuban people, but that's not unusual. Diplomats and lawmakers from even the poorest countries usually can be counted upon to throw lavish parties.

Castro arrived with his interpreter, a gorgeous young woman with violet eyes, who hovered near him constantly. We guests first went through a receiving line of sorts, and when I got to Castro I talked with him about Cuban cigars. At the time, I smoked cigars, but they were Muriel Coronellas, cheap drug store issue, which cost about 8 cents apiece.

I told Castro that I had seen some Cuban cigars, but they were all of the large variety. The cigars I smoked were small, short smokes, and I asked Castro if small Cuban cigars were available. He or his interpreter must have misunderstood, or only listened to part of what I had said. Castro motioned to an aide and spoke a few words to him. He disappeared and returned a minute or so later with a giant, Churchill-sized Cohiba cigar, Castro's personal brand. He gave it to me. I later smoked it at the party that celebrated my inauguration as the 1978 president of the National Press Club.

After the formalities, members of the delegation gathered around Castro and started asking him questions. I instinctively reached for my reporter's notebook, but thought better of it when I saw one of Castro's plainclothes security guards glaring at me. I had been warned earlier by one of our escorts that the Cubans had decided that the reception would be off-the-record, and I would not be permitted to take notes.

But then Rep. Silvio Conte of Massachusetts, the senior Republican on the Banking Committee, whipped out his tape recorder and a microphone and started taping the exchange between Castro and himself, as well as questions to Castro by others.

Then Peggy Stanton, the wife of Rep. William Stanton, a Republican committee member from Ohio, also took out a tape recorder and started recording the conversations. I took out my notebook, but one of the security guards tapped me on the shoulder and motioned me to put it back in my pocket. I took that to mean that committee members and their spouses were not to be bothered, but that a reporter had no such immunity.

I knew the woman slightly, but as Peggy Smeeton, the daughter of a Marquette University business professor. She had done a bit of journalism in Milwaukee before marrying the Ohio congressman.

I was frustrated and furious. It was a Saturday, and I had made arrangements to call The Journal's national desk to file a Sunday story. I could only hear snatches of the conversations, but it was Castro, and he was talking to U.S. members of Congress, and I was the only reporter there, so it had to be a story of some sort.

On the bus back to the hotel, I explained my dilemma to Mrs. Stanton and asked if I could borrow her tape to get some notes for a story. She hesitated, then informed me sweetly that she wasn't about to share her tape with me because she was thinking of possibly using it to write an article herself, which she planned to free lance somewhere. I was enraged, but stifled it. As far as I know, she never wrote a word.

However, there was still Silvio Conte. I had met him briefly on the plane, but he seemed a decent guy.

He'd gone on ahead, in a car with Reuss. I found him sunbathing by the pool, told him my problem, and asked if I could borrow his tape, which he had made for the radio broadcast he did for his constituents back home. He didn't even hesitate. Sure, he said, and he gave me the key to his room to retrieve the tape recorder.

There were enough quotes on the tape to put together a story for The Journal. It ran on page one that Sunday—an exclusive from their man in Cuba.

Feeling self-satisfied, I headed down to the hotel lobby and bumped into one of the escorts, who told me that Conte was hopping mad because I had forgotten to return his key and he'd been locked out of his room until a spare was delivered. Red-faced, I found him at the pool and profusely apologized. He laughed it off.

For many years on Capitol Hill, Conte and I always exchanged affectionate hellos when we bumped into each other. It was as if that episode had started a friendship, even though we never saw each other socially. I interviewed him several times and he was always available.

ON TO COLOMBIA

The next stop was Bogota, Colombia, where Reuss, his wife, Margie, and I dropped off while the rest of the Codel went on to other Latin American countries. I would have liked to have gone with them, but the whole rationale for my being on the trip was to shadow our local congressman. The trip turned out to be memorable anyway.

From Bogota, we flew to Pasto, in the central part of the country. Reuss wanted to see American foreign aid at work, and Jim Megellas, director of the U.S. Agency for International Development in Columbia, handled the arrangements. We went off into the mountains for a look at a pick and shovel road. It was a basic sort of aid: the U.S. government paid local workers to go out and hand-carve a crude road from the mountain wilderness, connecting isolated communities with the main road to Pasto.

The idea of the pick and shovel road was to enable the people of San Vicente to reach the main road so they could catch a bus to Pasto and sell the charcoal they had painstakingly made in their hamlet, which was little more than a collection of huts in a jungle so thick nobody could see even the closest neighbor.

We were big news in San Vicente. Practically everybody came out to see the powerful American congressman. Work stopped on the road, and the head of the village invited us in for lunch.

Lunch turned out to be the most succulent treat the village had to offer: roast guinea pig. Well, we couldn't insult our hosts by not at least trying a couple of bites. Reuss, as he did with everything else, attacked his pig with gusto, gnawing off a couple of bites. I was more tentative. I picked at the skin and nibbled a bit. We'd done our duty, and the village leaders accepted our protestations that we were not really hungry and had to move on.

I was so moved by the whole episode that I gave one of the leaders 200 pesos, saying I wanted to contribute to a party for the village. He was delighted. He said with that amount of money, they would be able to buy several chickens for a big fiesta.

Our next stop was the Sibunduoy Valley, where we first visited an Indian tribe whose men dressed in brown robes and bowl-cut their hair exactly like the Franciscan missionaries who had come and converted them hundreds of years before. Then we went to see the Kamsa Indians, whose tribal government was a matriarchy.

Once again, we were received in a small cottage, this time by Dolores Muchavisoy, the chief whose official title was civic action president. However, there was no food. Bowls of a frothy white liquid called chicha, with a noticeable alcoholic content, were passed around. We, of course, sipped along with everybody else.

Ms. Muchavisoy gave Reuss a beautiful, multi-colored, hand-made wool blanket, similar to a poncho. I admired it so much that she sent one of her aides off for another one, which she gave me. I still have it.

On the way back to Pasto, I asked one of our Colombian escorts about the chicha. "You don't want to know," he said. "Yes, I do," I said. He told me that it was the tribe's basic alcoholic beverage. It was made by the old women, who sat around a large bowl or bucket and chewed corn. When it was well masticated, they spat it into the bowl. It needed a few weeks to ferment before it was drinkable.

The escort also told me a marvelous inside joke about Colombia. He said that Saint Peter was taking notes as God was describing a country he wanted to create. "I want it to have access to two oceans," he said. Peter wrote it down. "I want it to have beautiful beaches, and fertile plains, and majestic mountains," Peter wrote that down, too. "I want it to have a variety of climates, all of them hospitable." Peter started to write; then said, "But God, don't you think you're giving this one country too much?"

"Don't worry," God replied. "I'm going to put Colombians there to run it."

HIS OWN INDIANS

Our final stop in Colombia was Leticia, on the Amazon River in the west. That's where we met Mike Tsalikis, a Greek-American and a friend of Megellas's who maintained an Indian Tribe to attract tourists. He also was an animal trapper, ran a motel and a restaurant, was one of the town's leading citizens, and was rumored to have more than nodding acquaintances with drug runners.

Tsalikis showed us a great time. We went up the Amazon in a boat to visit Mike's tribe, which lived right on the river bank. Ordinarily, these Indians, whose men hunted with blow guns and whose women went bare-breasted, would have lived many miles in the deepest jungle, away from any corrupting influences brought by white entrepreneurs. But Tsalikis had cut a deal with them. He promised they would never go hungry and they would always have access to medical care. So they moved the whole tribe out of the jungle to the river bank so Mike could show them off to his boatloads of tourists. In return, on any given day you would see groups of tribe members waiting outside the medical clinic in Leticia—the women modestly covered for their foray into civilization.

Though back home I was strictly a reporter—we always had photographers with us if the story called for it—on a trip like this I carried
a camera and took my own photographs. In Leticia, one of the more
memorable moments came when Tsalikis brought out a pet boa con-
strictor and draped it around Reuss's neck. The doughty congressman,
undaunted, played with it for at least 10 minutes while I snapped pictures. I figured they had to be page one for sure. Here was the Banking
Committee chairman, given to pin-striped dark suits in his meetings
with international financiers, playing with a big snake. But the film
didn't thread properly in the camera, and I didn't get a single picture.

I did get a lot of other pictures, however, and they ran with the series
of stories I later wrote for The Journal. The trip was a success for both
me and Reuss. Once again, this time in Cuba and Colombia, I had
adventures that a lot of people would pay big money to experience.

For Reuss, it was the adventure as well. He was always up for almost
anything that had to do with outdoors and nature. For years, he had
worked to develop the Ice Age Trail in Wisconsin, and he and Margie,
both years older than me, easily out-hiked me on the trails in Colombia. They always carried a sense of excitement at new experiences.

In later years, I traveled south and north of the border for a series
of stories on Mexico, another series on Central America and Panama,
and one on Texas. The Texas articles came about because I was on the
team covering the 1984 Republican convention in Dallas, which had
little news because it was simply a coronation of Ronald Reagan for
his second term. The editors in Milwaukee envisioned me twiddling
my thumbs, so told me to bail out of the convention and travel around
Texas for the series.

It was great fun. I visited all of the so-called "five states of Texas,"
interviewing a lot of characters, including Maury Maverick Jr., a de-
scendant of Samuel Maverick, a founder of Texas whose unbranded
cattle became known as "mavericks."

Another interview, in Austin, was with Don Graham, who had written a book called *Cowboys and Cadillacs*, an account of how Hollywood
looked at Texas. He was as funny as his book, decrying the influx of
high-tech companies infesting the corridor between Austin and San
Antonio. He called it "the Californication of Texas."

The series on Central America in 1983 provided some harrowing
moments, especially in El Salvador, which still experienced remnants
of its civil war. I took a car trip from San Salvador to Sonsonate with

a photographer from the St. Louis Post-Dispatch and a reporter from Baton Rouge, La. On the way, at a shallow river crossing, we were stopped by a group of five kids dressed in military fatigues and carrying AK-47 assault rifles.

I don't think any of them was more than 14 years old, and there was nobody in charge. Our car had adhesive tape all over it spelling out the letters "TV," and our driver did a lot of fast talking before they finally let us pass. But we were scared silly. The road and the area for miles around the crossing were deserted—I remember not even hearing birds—and there would have been nothing to prevent those kids from simply blowing all of us away. Later I would interview women who showed me photographs of their dead sons, thumbs tied together behind them and shot in the back of the head, allegedly by government soldiers.

For the Mexico series in 1982, I promoted an advance scouting trip. As a high school graduation present, I had given my oldest son, Matt, a month in a Spanish-language school in Cuernavaca, where I had studied earlier. I went down to pick him up at the end of his studies, and we bummed around Mexico in a rented Volkswagen Bug, staying wherever we could find lodging, and often sitting on the motel bed in some obscure town, singing songs while he played the guitar. Later I returned for more travel and interviews.

The nine-part series was so well received The Journal reprinted it in a booklet, which was widely distributed. Illustrating the opening article was a photograph of a Mexican farmer with a sack of grain on his lap, riding a burro. The credit line said, "Photo by Matthew Aukofer." It was his first newspaper byline, but not the last.

1. *The Aukofer family, circa 1955. I'm at the right in back, next to my parents.*
Brother John is at the left. In front, from left: CiCi, Dottie, Tessie, Margie and Clare.

2. *The Air Force Reservist.*

3. *Father Matthew Gottschalk, OFM Cap.*

4.a. *I receive the first scholarship awarded by the Milwaukee professional chapter of Sigma Delta Chi. From left: Marquette Journalism Dean Jeremiah L. O'Sullivan, Edward R. Johnson of the Milwaukee Sentinel, me and Walter Kante, the chapter's secretary-treasurer. (George A. Wolpert photo.)*

4.b. *Another presentation of the $200 scholarship check at the Milwaukee Press Club. From left: me; Edmund (Ted) Carpenter, director of the Marquette University News Bureau; Paul McMahon and James Meyer of The Milwaukee Journal, and Richard H. Leonard, chairman of the scholarship committee who later became The Journal's editor.*
(George A. Wolpert photo.)

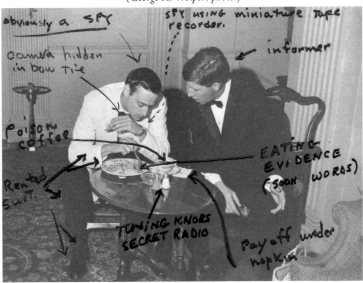

5. *This is a gag photo given to me by Journal Women's Section staffers Barbara Schmoll and Sandra Cota. It shows me (at left) undercover at a debutante party.*
(© Richard Bauer, The Milwaukee Journal.)

6. *In May, 1964, driving a formula vee, I pull into the pits at a driver's school operated by The Sports car Club of America at the Lynndale Farms road racing course in Pewaukee. (Sherman A. Gessert Jr., The Milwaukee Journal)*

7. *April 3, 1964. Alabama Gov. George C. Wallace leaves the Marquette campus, where he had made a speech at the Dental School. I'm at the left with the notebook. (AP photo)*

8. *Apr. 8, 1964. A Wallace rally in Milwaukee. I'm at the right, in the foreground. (James L. Stanfield, The Milwaukee Journal)*

UCPI20901—12/9/65—MILWAUKEE—Police move civil rights demonstrators so a car could pass the entrance to the MacDowell school construction sire as Robert Bundy, 20, sits on the ground chained to the gate that allowed construction equipment to enter the site. A hole was cut in another part of the fence to let cement trucks enter.

9. Dec. 9, 1965. Civil rights demonstrators, including Father James E. Groppi (in sunglasses), block the MacDowell school construction site, arguing that it would be another segregated school. I'm right behind Groppi. (Photographer unknown)

30. Mar. 20, 1984.
An interview in the
Oval Office with
President Ronald
Reagan. I'm the one
leaning forward, asking
the question. Others,
clockwise from left,
are: Andrew Miller,
Kansas City Star;
Paul Bedard, St. Louis
Globe-Democrat;
Jerry Watson, Chicago
Sun-Times; Tom
Ottenad, St. Louis
Post-Dispatch; Gary
Schuster, Detroit
News, and David
Phelps, Minneapolis
Star Tribune.
(White House photo)

31. October, 1984. At the Press Club with Joe Slevin (left) and Arthur Wiese. (Stan Jennings)

32. Christmas, 1985. Sharlene and I greet the Reagans at the White House press Christmas party. (White House photo

33. May, 1985. With Henry Keys at the Press Club. (Stan Jennings)

34. October, 1985. At the National Press Foundation's "Business Beat" conference at the University of California-Berkeley, with Ray Enderle of Sun Oil Co.

35. April 12, 1986. An all-Marquette group at the dinner at which I received the Marquette University Merit Award. My son, Joe, and daughter, Becky, both MU graduates (students when the photo was taken), with MU President Father John P. Raynor.

36. December, 1987. NBC's David Brinkley at the reception before receiving the National Press Club's Fourth Estate Award. Sharlene greets his wife, Susan. (Stan Jennings)

37. August, 1990. A group of news people and Saudi Arabian officials on a tour of the Saudi commercial city of Jubail. I'm second from the left in the second row. Third from the left in the front row is Christiane Amanpour, later with CNN to become one of the most famous foreign correspondents in the world.

38. *August, 1990. I sit in at the command console on an AWACs surveillance plane flying over Saudi Arabia.*

39. *September, 1995. With Admiral William P. Lawrence (center) and John Seigenthaler of the Freedom Forum First Amendment Center at the rollout of "America's Team: the Odd Couple."*

40. *With Bill and Hillary Clinton at the 1993 White House press Christmas party. (White House photo)*

41. *August, 1996. With portrait artist George Pollard of Kenosha, at the unveiling of the portrait of Rep. Les Aspin, chairman of the House Armed Services Committee.*

42. 1998. George Pollard's portrait.

43. Dec. 10, 2001. *As chairman of the Press Club's Speakers Committee, I get to sit next to actress Goldie Hawn at the head table.*

44. May 6, 2002. *Still Speakers Committee chairman, this time my head table partner is actress Raquel Welch.*

45. Sept. 22, 2003. Former Sen. Gaylord Nelson's last major speech is at the National Press Club, arranged by me as the Speakers Committee chairman. Afterward, we pose with Wisconsin Rep. David R. Obey (left) and columnist Robert Novak (right).

46. Nov. 19, 2003. I'm chairman of the Fourth Estate Dinner Committee when the award goes to NBC's Tom Brokaw, who greets me and Sharlene at the reception.

10

IMPEACHMENTS

There have been only three impeachment proceedings against presidents in American history. I covered two of them.

President Richard M. Nixon was not impeached. He resigned the presidency on Aug. 9, 1974, before the House could vote on three articles of impeachment that had been cleared by the House Judiciary Committee. Clinton was impeached, but acquitted on Feb. 12, 1999, when the Senate could not muster a majority on either of two articles of impeachment. A two-thirds vote in the Senate is required to convict a president and remove him from office. It was a lot closer in 1868, when the Senate acquitted President Andrew Johnson by the margin of one vote.

Had Nixon not resigned, he certainly would have been impeached and likely convicted and removed from office after a trial in the U.S. Senate. After Nixon admitted that, in 1972, he had ordered the FBI to stop investigating the break-in at Democratic Party headquarters in the Watergate office building, all 10 members of the Judiciary Committee who had voted against impeachment said they would reverse their votes. Republican leaders—among them, Wisconsin's Melvin R. Laird, then working as Nixon's domestic adviser—told him there was no support to sustain his presidency.

Along with a horde of other reporters, I stood in the East Room of the White House when Nixon announced his resignation to the nation on Aug. 9. Though I was a witness to history, it was not the best vantage point. Everyone watching on television saw Nixon's face close up, and watched as he boarded the presidential helicopter for the final time.

It had been exactly three months since I started covering the Nixon impeachment hearings on May 9, 1974. It was one of the most hectic times I had ever experienced as a reporter, but it was an assignment I eagerly sought.

Though The Milwaukee Journal had only a two-person bureau in Washington, I argued that The Journal was one of the country's great newspapers and should have its own man covering what likely would

be the biggest story of the century—certainly the biggest involving
Washington and the national government.

I didn't have to argue very hard. The editors and Jack Kole, my bureau chief and partner, were receptive from the start. I was surprised
that Jack didn't take the story for himself. In our four years together,
he occasionally had exercised his prerogative to take the big stories,
especially if they involved politics. There were times when it annoyed
me when Jack grabbed a big story in which I had an interest, but it was
not a source of friction between us. I would have done the same thing
in his place.

Like many other reporters, I was a passive witness to the events that
unfolded after five men were arrested for breaking into the headquarters of the Democratic National Committee at the Watergate on June
17, 1972.

I covered the Senate Watergate hearings on an occasional basis,
which meant that I mostly winged it. Each time I covered a hearing,
I boned up on the background events that it focused on, just enough
to flesh out the story of the day. Unlike the reporters who covered the
hearings every day, I did not have a firm grasp of the details that made
up the fabric of Watergate. It was a classic case of the general assignment reporter who parachuted occasionally into a big story.

But the House Judiciary Committee's impeachment hearings were
another matter. From the start, I was the daily—and only—reporter
covering for The Milwaukee Journal. And I had support, and tremendous backup, in the person of Carl Schwartz, a young copy editor on
the National Desk. He was assigned to be the other half of the impeachment team and, as such, steeped himself in every aspect of the
story. Schwartz was a big, amiable man who was as good an editor as I
ever worked with.

I kidded a lot in later years that it was a good thing I had taken
Hallway Standing 101 and Lurking 102 in journalism school. That
was because all of the substantive hearings in the Judiciary Committee
on Nixon's impeachment were conducted behind closed doors. The
reporters covering the story had no choice but to hang out in the hallway outside the Judiciary Committee room on the first floor of the
Rayburn Office Building, waiting for a roll call vote in the House that
would send all the committee members scurrying out of the hearing
room to cast their votes.

Lounging in the hallway wasn't all bad. There were a lot of fine looking young women working on Capitol Hill, and it seemed that almost all of them, at some point, satisfied their curiosity by strolling past the Judiciary Committee room. So the girl watching broke up the boredom while the overwhelmingly male clutch of reporters waited for the bells and buzzers to sound for a roll call vote.

CHASING THE STORY

Then, like a bunch of dogs yapping at passing cars, the reporters trailed the members down the hallways, into the elevators, onto the subway cars and up the Capitol elevators to the House chamber. Some of the members talked freely about what had gone on in the hearings, some dropped snippets of information, and some refused to speak at all.

The wire services, TV networks and the bigger newspapers—the Washington Post, New York Times and Los Angeles Times—had platoons of their top reporters covering the story. It was daunting to a reporter like me, basically working alone.

I did have two major sources: Democrat Bob Kastenmeier and Republican Harold Froehlich, both of Wisconsin. They talked to me, but guardedly. Typically Wisconsin in their approach, they had integrity that some of the other members did not possess. They were not leakers, unlike some of the members who parceled out information to reporters for personal or political motives.

The committee chairman, Rep. Peter W. Rodino Jr., a New Jersey Democrat, had more than 100 staff members working on the impeachment. One of them was a young lawyer named Hillary Rodham, later First Lady of the United States and a senator from New York. Another staffer on the sub-committee was William P. Dixon. We became close, and often played poker with mutual friends.

Dixon was a bright, super-savvy politico, so knowledgeable and immersed in the insider's game that I sometimes didn't understand what he was talking about. He was a good source on matters that were above board, and was usually helpful, but like his boss, he did not leak information or tell tales out of school. Dixon later worked on the vice presidential nominations of Nelson Rockefeller and Gerald Ford, and joined the committee staff of Milwaukee Democrat Henry S. Reuss, when Reuss was chairman of the House Banking Committee. (He was on the Codel that took me to Cuba and Colombia).

Dixon moved from the committee to a position as alternate executive director for the U.S. at the World Bank, and managed the Democratic National Convention in New York in 1980, which was another great story for me because former Wisconsin Gov. Patrick J. Lucey resigned as deputy campaign manager for Sen. Edward M. Kennedy of Massachusetts. Later he abandoned the Democratic Party to become the vice presidential running mate to maverick Republican John Anderson, who ran an independent campaign for the presidency. Dixon's last Washington assignment was as chief of staff to Democratic Sen. Gary Hart of Colorado, when Hart made a run to become his party's presidential nominee in 1984.

Hart was done in by the public exposure of an affair he had with a young woman, Donna Rice, after he had dared the news media to follow him around. A photograph of him sitting with Rice on a boat named "Monkey Business" ran in newspapers and magazines all over the country.

Dixon hired my son, Matthew, who had majored in political science at Lawrence University in Appleton, for an entry-level job in Hart's Washington office. He thought Matt had political potential, so sent him off to work on the state Senate campaign of a Democrat in Colorado. The candidate lost, but Matt gained valuable experience in running a campaign, and he later went to work for Hart as a low-paid staff member working on the Iowa caucuses.

Everyone had visions of getting jobs in the White House, so sure were they that Hart would win the nomination and the presidency. As a result, the disillusionment that set in after the disclosure of the candidate's affair with Rice was deep and long-lasting. Matt went into a funk that sent him back to working construction until he finally returned to the government and political world as a reporter for the Lynchburg (Va.) News & Advance, and later for newsletters, including Kiplinger. Dixon left Washington for Wisconsin, swearing he would never again set foot in the nation's capital. He settled in Madison, served for a time as the state's banking commissioner, then went into private practice as a trial lawyer who represented individuals against government and big corporations.

Most days, I worked 12 to 14 hours covering the Nixon impeachment hearings, and almost as many on some weekends. Working for an afternoon newspaper was both an advantage and a disadvantage. The advantage was that I'd get a look at the major newspapers' stories first thing in the morning. The disadvantage was that I would have to come up with something new to top up my story in that afternoon's Journal.

Schwartz and I soon developed a routine. After chasing committee members down hallways and doing telephone interviews in the evening with my two committee members and others, I filed overnight some of what I had as what we called A-matter—basically the bottom half of the story. Then I got up very early, in time to be at my desk in the Senate Press Gallery at about 7 a.m., which was 6 a.m. in Milwaukee. Schwartz, already at the national desk, had reviewed my submission, as well as all the wire copy from the AP, UPI and the supplemental services provided by the New York Times, Washington Post and others.

We went over the salient points. If the wires had something I did not, Schwartz asked if I could provide it. If I could, I simply wrote and filed it as an addition to my earlier A-matter. If it was something I did not have, Schwartz would break it out as a separate story or include it in my story with attribution to the source.

Then I was off to scare up something new to top that day's story. If it was Monday, we wanted to have "Monday" in the lead sentence or paragraph of the story. It was the same every day. My best source for something new usually came from James St. Clair, the respected Boston lawyer who was representing Nixon. Every morning, shortly before 9 a.m., he arrived by car at the "horseshoe" driveway on the east side of the Rayburn Building. I usually met him at the door and walked with him the 100 yards or so to the committee room. Almost always, I was the only reporter dogging his tracks, and he was unfailingly affable. More often than not, he'd give me just enough—a quote or a snippet of information about how he thought the hearings were going—to enable me to put a new lede on that day's story. We were all aware that our fresh information was not necessarily the most important element in the story; just the newest. But that's the curse of the afternoon newspaper.

The House Press Gallery press room in the Rayburn Building soon became too crowded to handle all the reporters covering the story. So Rodino loaned the news media a hearing room on the floor above the Judiciary Committee room. Each reporter was assigned a small work space—enough for a chair, a typewriter and a bit of elbow room. But the newspapers had to share the room with the television and radio networks and stations, so frequently I'd sit writing something while a network reporter like ABC's Sam Donaldson stood on a chair nearby doing a "stand-up" with lights in his face and a microphone in hand. The story was particularly difficult for the TV reporters because there were so many names, titles and details that they could not squeeze them all into their 30-second or one-minute spots. We often laughed at the TV reporters doing and re-doing their stand-ups to cover the main points of the day, but I felt sorry for them, too, because they were so constricted. I didn't feel too sorry, however. After all, we were all covering the biggest story most of us had ever experienced.

GUTSY "FAT HAROLD"

On Aug. 24, the Judiciary Committee voted to impeach Nixon and put him on trial in the Senate. It approved three articles of impeachment, and rejected two others. But the three that were approved accused the president of, among other things, obstruction of justice, abuse of power, misuse of government agencies and a refusal to comply with subpoenas from the committee. The first two articles, encompassing the major charges, were approved on bipartisan votes of 27 to 11 and 28 to 10, with six Republicans joining all of the committee's Democrats on the first vote, and seven joining them on the second.

Among the Republicans was Wisconsin's Harold Froehlich, who had sometimes derisively been called, behind his back, "Fat Harold." He had been a Wisconsin assemblyman before being elected to Congress, and had been regularly pilloried by The Milwaukee Journal's liberal cartoonist and editorial writers for his right-wing stands on issues. But as a member of Congress, he turned out to be as principled as any member I covered. On the Judiciary Committee, though skeptical of the accusations against Nixon and inclined to support him as a fellow conservative Republican, he never had what could be regarded as a knee-jerk reaction to disclosures about the president's conduct in the Watergate affair. Instead, Froehlich insisted that he would make up his mind based on the evidence.

In the end, he voted for those two articles of impeachment, and it likely cost him his job. He served only one term in the House, and then was defeated for re-election. Froehlich went on to become a respected judge in Appleton, and years later we reminisced over the telephone about his role in the Nixon impeachment hearings. He expressed no regrets, and I told him how much I had admired him.

The House took a recess after the impeachment votes, and I headed to Wisconsin with my family in our '70 Chevy Kingswood Estate station wagon. Sharlene and I, after a few years in Washington, had devised a system for making the 800-mile journey. We piled all of our luggage in a weatherproof carrier on top of the car, folded the back two rows of seats, put the kids in their pajamas and dumped them in back with pillows, blankets and a tape player with a tape I had recorded of songs that appealed to children, like Harry Bellafonte's "Mama, Look a Boo-Boo," and the Kingston Trio's "Zombie Jamboree."

We usually set off about 7 p.m., and endured a couple of hours of the kids arguing and horsing around in back. There was no thought in those days of securing them in car seats; they simply rolled and flopped around back there, with us shouting at them to behave, until they finally put their heads down and went to sleep. They'd wake up about 8 a.m., after we'd traversed the Pennsylvania, Ohio and Indiana Turnpikes, we'd stop for breakfast near Chicago, get them dressed, and cruise the last hour and a half into Milwaukee.

Our two weeks there were almost up when Jack Kole called to say that that Nixon planned to resign. I immediately jumped into our car and drove back, making the 800 miles in about 12 hours. Sharlene and the kids flew back later, using her United Airlines passes.

I got back in time to be in the White House press room the evening of Aug. 8, when Nixon went on television to tell the nation that he would resign the next day. Like everyone else, the reporters watched it on the tube, and that evening there occurred a historical oddity.

The press room was crowded with reporters before the televised speech, when suddenly the door to the west wing was closed and locked. I was heading out the door to the north lawn and the northwest entrance on Pennsylvania Avenue when that door was locked, too, and a couple of uniformed Secret Service men stationed themselves outside. Nobody had any idea what was going on.

Standing next to me at the door was Trudy Feldman, a regular member of the White House press corps. I knew who she was because she was acquainted with Dick Leonard, The Journal's editor. But I had no idea who she wrote for. She was not highly regarded by members of the press corps, who considered her to be an embarrassment and little more than a hanger-on, in the same category as Naomi Nover, who represented the Nover News Service after her husband, Barnet

Nover, died. Like everyone else in the room, Feldman wondered what was happening.

Word soon circulated throughout the press room that the doors had been locked because Nixon wanted to take one last, solitary walk around the White House grounds, without interruption. Time passed, the doors were unlocked, and we watched the president announce his resignation.

The next day, I returned to the press room well before Nixon's scheduled farewell speech. As we milled around, waiting for our escort to the East Room, Feldman came up to me, acting perplexed. She said she wanted my advice. Obviously not remembering me from the night before, she asked if I had been there during the lockdown. I said I had. She said she had a terrible ethical problem. The night before, she said, she happened to get out the north door before it was locked and was out on the White House grounds when she bumped into Nixon on his walk and had a brief chat with him. She wanted to know if I thought she should write the story or respect his privacy and not report the encounter.

I was dumbfounded. She had made up the entire thing, and I knew it because I had been standing right next to her inside the door during the lockdown, a fact I reminded her of. I don't think she was even embarrassed. She simply walked away, likely to tell someone else of her bogus encounter with the disgraced president.

THE CLINTON IMPEACHMENT

For me, the Clinton impeachment was almost a reprise of the Nixon story. Once again, I had two Wisconsin members on the House Judiciary Committee, except their status was exactly reversed. In the Nixon impeachment hearings in 1974, Kastenmeier was the No. 2 Democrat after Rodino, who was chairman by virtue of the fact that Democrats were in a majority in the House.

Republicans had taken over by the time of the Clinton impeachment in 1998, so the committee had a GOP chairman, Rep. Henry Hyde of Illinois. I liked and respected Hyde, who was the leader of the anti-abortion forces in the House and by far its most eloquent spokesman. I privately agreed with him on abortion, though not always with every legislative or constitutional solution he favored. I always admired any lawmaker who stood on principle on an issue, regardless of whether I happened to agree. Kastenmeier, for example, was a staunch advocate of abortion rights, and I liked and respected him as well. In fact, Kastenmeier and Hyde were friends.

Hyde, from northern Illinois, was always accessible to me. He usually didn't remember my name, but he knew that I worked for a Milwaukee newspaper, and I'd had occasion to seek him out for interviews on a number of stories prior to the time he took over as chairman of the Judiciary Committee. Hyde's accessibility did not change after he took over as chairman and the committee launched its impeachment inquiry into Clinton's conduct in the Monica Lewinsky affair. For me, he became an important source, though usually for a couple of quotes in a larger story.

Another good source for me was Rep. John Conyers Jr., a Democrat from Michigan who was the top-ranked Democrat on the committee. Like Hyde, Conyers did not remember my name, so I always had to remind him that we had interviewed Teamsters leader James Hoffa in the Lewisburg federal prison many years before. Because of that bond, Conyers was always available to talk to me, even when I had to track him down back in his home district in Detroit.

But my main men on the Clinton impeachment were Rep. F. James Sensenbrenner Jr., a principled conservative from Menomonee Falls who was the No. 2 Republican on the committee, and Rep. Tom Barrett, a liberal Democrat from Milwaukee. Barrett was the most junior member of the committee, having been named to it only two months before the impeachment inquiry. Years later, he went on to become mayor of Milwaukee.

Unlike the Nixon impeachment inquiry, in which most of the committee members genuinely seemed to be seeking the truth—both the Democrats' counsel, John Doar, and the Republicans' counsel, Albert Jenner, agreed that Nixon was guilty of obstruction of justice—the Clinton impeachment was mired in politics from the start. Many of the Democrats, including Barrett, agreed that Clinton had engaged in reprehensible conduct, but they did not believe it deserved impeachment and removal from office.

From the opening statement before the committee by Kenneth Starr, the independent counsel who had investigated Clinton, the arguments for and against impeachment mostly broke down along party lines. At one point in the proceedings, I wrote, "Nobody expects any of the committee's 21 Republicans to change their minds and vote against impeachment. Nobody expects any of the 16 Democrats to change their minds and vote to impeach." And they didn't.

Barrett, however, won the respect of many of his Democratic colleagues—and likely even some Republicans—by trying to steer a middle course. He introduced a resolution to censure Clinton as an alternative to impeachment. But he never got a vote on it.

For me, coverage of the Clinton impeachment hearings was far easier than it had been covering the proceedings in the same room 24 years earlier. Most of the Clinton proceedings were open to the press, and after the hearings got under way, it was even fairly easy to find a seat. Perhaps because the public, according to polls, did not favor impeachment, or perhaps because so many people believed that the entire exercise was politically motivated, the Clinton hearings did not attract hordes of people waiting in line to witness history. In fact, on some days, the empty seats in the Judiciary Committee hearing room outnumbered those that were occupied.

In the end, the committee voted on party lines to impeach Clinton, accusing him of perjury and obstruction of justice. It happened on Saturday, Dec. 12, 1998, and it was huge. I had my byline on the line story in the Sunday Journal, and the three-line headline across the top of the page was a full four inches deep.

A week later, on Dec. 19, the full House voted to impeach Clinton, and The Journal's headline, in giant capital letters, screamed "IMPEACHED" in a type size we used to joke was reserved for the end of the world. But it was an angry and bitter day for me because my byline was not on the story.

Never mind that I had covered the impeachment proceedings from the beginning, doing the main story as well as local-angle sidebars along the way, or that the previous week I had covered the committee's vote to impeach.

I was blindsided. The House vote came on a Saturday, too late for the Saturday afternoon paper. I covered the debate and the vote, as I had all along, and then prepared to walk across the third floor of the Capitol to sit down at my computer in the Senate Press Gallery to write the Sunday story, visions of my byline on the biggest news event I had covered since the Nixon impeachment.

LOSING THE BIG STORY

As usual, I called the national desk first from the House Press Gallery to give Carl Schwartz, the national editor, a heads-up on the story. Schwartz told me that, on orders from editor Martin Kaiser, I would not be writing the main story. Instead, I was to write a local reaction story.

I was furious, devastated and sick to my stomach all at once, and I told Schwartz I wanted to plead my case personally. He transferred me to Kaiser. I told him I had covered this story from the start, it was mine, and I deserved to write the main story. He was calm but firm. Nope, he wanted me to round up local reaction. I told him he could get any reporter in the room to do that sort of simple-minded piece over the phone.

My protests were to no avail. I hung up the phone, shaking, red-faced and using every cuss word I had ever learned. I briefly contemplated quitting; then thought better of it. I also contemplated refusing to do the reaction story; then thought better of that, too. In the end, I did my duty. Fuming the entire time, I got on the phone and rounded up comments from Wisconsin's senators and representatives.

The story wound up on page one. But it had a one-column head underneath the main story. It was one of the most maddening things I had ever experienced in all my years as a reporter, but there wasn't anything I could do about it. There was only one slight consolation. The Journal used the Knight Ridder news service's account for the main story. It carried a triple byline. Two of the reporters—David Hess and Steven Thomma—were friends and poker-playing buddies of mine. But I still get angry when I think about what happened, and I don't believe I've ever quite forgiven Kaiser, though overall I think he became a good editor in the years afterward.

I think my angry reaction to getting sidelined on that story may have influenced the fact that nothing of the sort happened after Clinton's trial in the Senate, which I also covered.

The Senate trial had strong local angles for us as well as its national significance. Chief Justice William H. Rehnquist of the United States Supreme Court, presided over the trial, and Rep. F. James Sensenbrenner Jr. was one of the House managers, or prosecutors. Both were Republicans, and both had Wisconsin ties. Rehnquist had grown up in Shorewood, a suburb just north of Milwaukee, and Sensenbrenner had his home in Menomonee Falls, a Milwaukee suburb west of town.

In many ways, the trial was easy to cover, except for when the Senate went behind closed doors for its deliberations. At the time, I had been a denizen of the Senate Press Gallery for many years. I had my own desk and computer, telephone, television set, fax and copy machine, and a couple of file drawers. My desk was only about 25 yards from the daily press entrance to the Senate chamber, and I had a choice front-row seat in the press gallery overlooking the senators' desks. It was a simple matter to cover the proceedings and walk back to my desk to file the story.

When Clinton was acquitted on Feb. 12, 1999, there was no question of who wrote the main story. Interestingly, though my lede said Clinton had been acquitted when the Senate could not muster even a majority on either impeachment count, the banner headline focused on Clinton's remorse and his call for reconciliation. There was a page one sidebar that focused on Wisconsin's two Democratic senators, Herb Kohl and Russ Feingold, who voted for acquittal, but it was reported and written by my sidekick in the Washington bureau, Craig Gilbert.

HELP FROM MY FRIENDS

July 24, 1974, likely was the most important day in President Richard M. Nixon's life. It was the day the United States Supreme Court ruled unanimously that he had to turn over his secret White House tapes to a special prosecutor. It led directly to his resignation as president.

I had been covering the impeachment hearings in the House Judiciary Committee, and I also had developed the Supreme Court as a part-time beat, so I knew my way around there. We were expecting the decision that day—though we had no idea what it would say—and were looking forward to it because, like most of the high court's decisions, it would happen on our time. The Journal then was one of a few quality afternoon newspapers left in the nation. Supreme Court decisions usually were handed down shortly after 10 a.m.—9 a.m. central time, and the editors had decided to hold our first edition past its usual 9:30 a.m. closing.

Just to be on the safe side, I went to the court's pressroom early, shortly after 9 a.m., only to find—to my horror—that every telephone within several city blocks already was tied up. I was not a regular reporter at the Supreme Court, so I did not have my own workspace or telephone. The pay phones in the pressroom were already taken over by minions from the television networks and other newspapers. They were on line, connected directly to their newsrooms.

I should have expected that would happen, but naively had not. There were no cell phones in those days, so I was incommunicado with my desk and The Journal, with no way of filing my story on deadline. I could have sprinted across to the press galleries in the U.S. Capitol after the decision came down, but that would have cost 10 or 15 minutes, and I still had no way to talk to anybody in Milwaukee before that. I was beginning to panic when I spotted Warren Weaver, the great reporter for The New York Times, who had been covering the high court. I didn't know him very well; just enough to engage in a bit of banter and casual conversation, but I told him of my plight.

Without hesitating, he offered the use of his telephone in The New York Times's cubicle on the northeast side of the press room. He said he would not have to file his story until early afternoon, so I could use his phone. In addition to being a superb reporter and writer, Weaver was a kindly soul with a great sense of humor.

So on the day of Nixon's denouement, I was backed by none other than the best newspaper in the country. Weaver offered his desk as well, and stayed away while I worked. I called the national desk shortly before 10 a.m., filled in the editor, who transferred me to Rosemary Kozak, the best professional I ever knew at taking stories on deadline. She could type as fast as I could dictate, and she was so smart and informed you rarely had to spell anything for her.

We kept the line open. Shortly after 10, as expected, the decision was announced in the somber Supreme Court chamber. Downstairs, I stood in the press office with the reporters from the wire services, TV networks and p.m. newspapers. As soon as I snatched my copy from an outstretched hand, I quickly noted that the decision was unanimous. I scanned the summary head notes as I walked into the press room next door and learned that the decision had gone against Nixon. In the Times cubicle seconds later, I picked up the telephone and told Rosemary that the decision was unanimous and that Nixon had lost—the idea being to get the desk working on a headline. Then I told her I needed a few minutes.

I spent about 20 minutes skimming through the decision for significant passages and started dictating the story. Another 20 minutes and we were done. Rosemary had flawlessly taken down a story about 40 inches long. The editors rammed it into the first edition. Then, between editions, I went over the decision again and found little to add or change, and the desk plugged in some reaction from the White House. The story ran all editions much as I had originally dictated it. I felt the adrenaline rush that most reporters experience at one time or another. Filing a big story on deadline is like getting high.

But I couldn't have done it without Warren Weaver. He, along with many others along my journalistic travels, epitomized the song by the Beatles, "A Little Help from My Friends." When I retired after 40 years with The Milwaukee Journal, I was proud of the fact that I had done my entire career as a newspaperman and, more than that, as a reporter. But it would never have happened without a lot of help along the way from family and friends.

Over the years, as detailed elsewhere, I had help from my family, friends, foremen and co-workers in the printing trade, the dean and professors at the Marquette University College of Journalism, and Dick Leonard and other editors and reporters at The Milwaukee Journal.

THE AUTHOR

My best friend and helpmate always was Sharlene. First there was the nine-month fellowship at Northwestern University in 1966-67, when I was away five days a week and Sharlene was left to take care of the family and everything that went with that monumental undertaking

The routine rarely varied. I left Monday morning for the two-hour drive to Evanston, Ill., where the Medill School of Journalism had rented me a small efficiency apartment. I stayed the week to attend classes and work on a book on freedom of assembly; then headed for home late Friday afternoon.

Sharlene was pregnant with our fourth child, Joseph, when I started the fellowship, and she somehow took care of that and the other three kids all week while I was away. Around the holidays in 1966, the kids all came down with chicken pox, and later so did Sharlene. We moved in temporarily with my mother in Milwaukee so she could watch the kids when Sharlene was hospitalized. The disease produced a painful kidney infection, and she still had the chicken pox when Joseph was born.

I barely missed any of the fellowship. As soon as she was back on her feet, Sharlene was home taking care of Joseph and the other kids while I was back in Evanston during the week. As tough as it was on her, it produced some romantic moments. Always a great cook, Sharlene then was something of a disciple of Julia Child's succulent French sauces. On Sunday nights before my return to Evanston, we put the three older kids to bed and she cooked steaks with baked potatoes, tasty sauces and a salad. We ate late off the coffee table, sitting on the couch in the living room, with Joe lying in a bassinet near-by.

I returned from the fellowship to cover "the long, hot summer of 1967," which included the Detroit and Milwaukee riots as well as almost daily civil rights demonstrations, mostly over open housing. Once again, I was away a lot, out of town or on night assignments, while Sharlene kept the family propped up.

Late in the year, I received what I believed was an incredible offer. A local attorney, James Shellow, who was the pro bono lawyer for Father James E. Groppi, the militant civil rights Catholic priest, came to me with the news that Random House in New York wanted a book by Groppi. The priest was a revolutionary, not a writer, and Shellow asked if I would write the "as told to" book, along the lines of what Malcolm X had done with Alex Haley. The advance was to be $10,000, which we would split, and we would split the royalties. Needless to say, I didn't hesitate.

I went out and bought a tape recorder, on credit, for $120. I figured maybe 30 or 35 hours with Groppi on tape would give me the basis for the book, and I could fill in the details from clips in The Journal library and other sources. Suddenly I had the sort of access to Groppi that I had coveted as the civil rights beat reporter covering him. I went to a private Mass he celebrated at St. Boniface Catholic Church one evening for the children of the NAACP Youth Council. Before the Mass, I met him in the rectory and was mildly shocked—as a traditional Catholic—when just before donning his vestments he reached into the refrigerator and grabbed a chunk of summer sausage and wolfed it down. In those days, Catholics were forbidden to eat anything from midnight until receiving Communion.

I taped the Mass, and it was remarkable, with Groppi engaging in questions and answers with the children about human and civil rights. A few days later I sat down with Groppi for our first interview, and I blew it.

With my linear reporter's mindset, I decided to question him chronologically, starting with his childhood as the son of an Italian immigrant grocer on Milwaukee's South Side—something about which he had no interest in talking. What I should have done was to get him into a free-flowing discussion about his passion in life, which was about ministering to and seeking justice for the oppressed, mainly black people. But the damage was done.

We struggled through the interview, though Groppi was clearly agitated, and he rebuffed my subsequent attempts to sit down for further interviews. Finally, I spoke to Shellow about it. He had a talk with Groppi and came back to tell me that the priest had lost interest in the project and did not want to continue. I was angry at this flouting of an agreement, even though no contract had been signed. I even tossed in the fact that I was out $120 for a tape recorder I did not need. To his credit, Groppi bought the tape recorder from me, paying me the full $120 in cash from his own pocket.

I was upset at missing out on a chance to do a book that might have become a big seller, not to mention the fat advance and the royalties that would come. But again there was help from a friend.

This time it came from a peripatetic Irishman, Gary MacEoin, who was a writer of books and articles on the Catholic Church, the papacy and Latin America. With a leprechaun's mischievous sense of humor, he was an engaging debater and conversationalist on almost any topic imaginable, especially when glasses of good Scotch whiskey were available. I met him quite by accident because my sister, Dorothy, had married his only child, Don. They later divorced.

WRITING A BOOK

Because of his world-wide travels and writing, MacEoin seemed to know everybody in the Catholic book publishing world, including the Bruce Publishing Co. in Milwaukee. He told me that Bruce was trying to get out of its old rut of selling only religiously-oriented texts to Catholic school and church libraries, and wanted to do some publishing on social issues in an effort to become "relevant and meaningful."

In short order, I had a contract with Bruce to write a book on civil rights in Wisconsin—obviously with a strong chapter or two on Father Groppi and the civil rights protests in Milwaukee, which recently had been the one of the biggest stories in the country. That would help sales, but even that did not particularly matter. MacEoin told me that Bruce had a virtual lock on the thousands of Catholic school and church libraries around the country, which would automatically assure many thousands of sales in addition to retail sales at book stores. My advance was $1,500, but I was salivating at the thought of more bucks from royalties.

I started on the book right after Christmas, 1967, and delivered the finished manuscript on Apr. 1, 1968, Sharlene's 30th birthday. Once again, she held the family together while I worked. Fortunately, in early 1968 the black power movement had taken hold and, to the editors and me as well, it seemed to make more sense to have Negro reporters covering the movement. So I spent most of my time working as a substitute assistant city editor, making assignments for reporters on the staff. It meant I didn't do any writing at the office, so I wasn't written out when I worked on the book at the end of the day.

Every day, on my lunch break and after working hours, I researched clips in the library—most of them stories I had written. I was struck at how difficult it would be for a historian to depend on stories written for an afternoon newspaper. The reason was that a p.m. always covered a day and a half at a time on a big story—the previous day plus whatever could be found to top up the running story before a mid-day deadline. Sometimes there was a new lede for every edition. So I took to looking at the Sentinel's clips to establish the sequence of events, then using my own and other Journal stories for the facts because we never trusted the Sentinel even though The Journal now owned it.

I usually arrived at home around 4:30 p.m., played with the kids some and then sat down to dinner at 5. Sharlene not only did the cooking, but the cleanup as well with some help from Juliann, then almost 7 years old. I went immediately upstairs to the spare bedroom, where I had a desk set up, and wrote until 9:30 or 10. On days off, I wrote all day and put in a few hours on Sunday. I also took my two weeks of vacation during that time and wrote every day.

I didn't think much of my effort at the time, regarding the manuscript as little more than a slam-bang rewrite job. But the editors at Bruce had no complaints and, in retrospect, the book is a fairly decent account of the tense civil rights days in Milwaukee in the 1960s. At least one Bruce representative wanted to give the book a provocative title, like "Milwaukee Is Not for Burning," or some other such grabber. But I thought that was irresponsible given my usual optimism. I firmly believed that Milwaukee would pull out of its troubles, mainly because of its stalwart black people. So I titled it *City with a Chance*. The dust cover design, however, was supposed to represent a revolver pointed directly at the reader. Fortunately, the artist didn't know much about guns so all it looked like was a bunch of circles.

When the book came out in September, Bruce and The Journal sponsored a reception at the Milwaukee Press Club. I was puffed up and the center of attention, a published author. But the most important thing was the dedication in the front of the book.

It said, "To Sharlene, who took care of everything else."

Unfortunately, the book went nowhere. Bruce put a half-page ad in the Sunday New York Times Book Review section, and there were a few reviews done here and there, including in The Journal and Sentinel, but Bruce could not sustain itself. The old-line Milwaukee Catholic book publisher was sold to Crowell, Collier and Macmillan in New

York City. The anticipated sales of thousands of copies to Catholic churches and libraries never materialized, and Macmillan had no interest in *City with a Chance*. The last I heard, the leftover copies had been remaindered and were sitting in a warehouse in New Jersey.

CHICKEN JOURNAL

Though I almost always was the recipient of help from many people, there was one exception to prove the rule. That was when I put myself on the line to help my newspaper keep publishing, then was rewarded with a pedantic, penny-pinching response.

It happened in 1962, when for the only time in its history The Journal was besieged by a strike that could have shut it down. It was wrenching for me because my former union, Local 23 of the International Typographical Union, called the strike. But there was one big difference as far as I was concerned. It was the mailers, not my brothers from the composing room. For some unfathomable reason, the mailers—largely unskilled laborers who mostly bundled newspapers and loaded them on trucks—had been allowed into the proud Typographical Union, where the compositors were skilled tradesmen and often, as with proofreaders, highly educated. No doubt admitting the mailers had given the union even more power in a strike situation, but their presence always galled me. I didn't think they belonged in my union any more than the Teamsters would.

When the strike started, my former composing room colleagues had no choice. All but a few of them honored the picket lines, and some picketed with the mailers. My first decision was whether to cross the picket lines. Though I no longer worked at the trade, I carried the union's honorary withdrawal card, which would enable me at any time to re-join any local and go back to work as a journeyman. I decided quickly that I would cross the lines, partly because of my strong belief that The Journal should continue to publish, and also because of my disdain for the mailers.

But it was not that simple. On the first day of the strike, Harvey Schwandner, the assistant managing editor, who earlier had been a skilled and fearsome city editor, came and asked me if I would work in the composing room during the strike. The request figuratively knocked the wind out of me. Deciding to cross the picket lines to continue to work as a reporter had been a reasonably easy decision, but this was something quite different. It meant that I would be work-

ing at the very jobs my brother compositors had left to go on strike. I
would be something between a scab—a nonunion strikebreaker—and
a rat—a union member who crossed a picket line to work. I asked
Schwandner if I could think about it overnight.

I talked it over with Sharlene and agonized over the request. In the
end, I decided that I was now a newspaperman and not a printer, and
I believed as a matter of principle that newspapers were at least as
important as trash collection, and should not be shut down for any
reason. But the matter of the mailers also loomed large. I might have
decided otherwise if the compositors had been on strike. The next day,
I told Schwandner I would do whatever I could.

For the next month, I was one of only a few skilled tradesmen in
the composing room. I ran the Ludlow and the Linotype head letter
machine, and took time to give some rudimentary training in typesetting and page makeup to the would-be printers who showed up to
volunteer, including a number of them from the Fourth Floor editorial department. More than once, I saved eager reporters and editors
from burns or injury as they clumsily operated the Ludlow or used the
high-powered table saws. I was everywhere, I worked hard 10 hours a
day, and I enjoyed it immensely. I felt as if I were an important cog in
the machine that kept The Journal publishing, which helped break the
strike after about a month. Though the papers were set in typewriter type and looked awful at first, the appearance gradually improved
when tele-typesetters were installed. They ran the Linotypes and In-
tertypes with perforated tape, like a player-piano. The Journal never
missed a day, and the settlement included amnesty from the union
for those of us who had worked in the composing room. So I kept my
honorary withdrawal card.

Early on, there came the question of pay. Among those in the composing room were fly boys from the pressroom and other low-skilled
workers. So the bean counters decreed that anyone working at a skilled
job would be paid the union wage for that job, regardless of the hours.
The reasoning was that an unskilled worker would be earning more
than at his regular job, and did not deserve time and a half for overtime. Reporters and editors who already made more than union scale
also would receive their regular salaries, but again with straight time
pay for overtime work because they also lacked the skills of the trade.
The few compositors who crossed the picket lines continued as before,
with union wages and time and a half for overtime.

I was in a unique position. Although I had all the skills of the other compositors, I was now a reporter with a salary less than the union compositors' scale (I had started as a reporter at $35 a week less than my wages as a printer, and I had not yet caught up to my old pay scale). So I fell into the category of people who were paid the higher union wages. But I soon learned to my chagrin that I was being paid at the straight time rate when I worked overtime. I mentioned it to the managing editor, Arville Schaleben, arguing that because of my skills I should be treated the same as the other compositors, with time and a half for overtime at the union rate.

In truth, I didn't care. I was having fun, I felt important, and I was making plenty of money because of all the overtime. It was more a matter of principle. I was risking the enmity of my union brethren, and perhaps jeopardizing my future with the Typographical Union if I ever decided to return to the trade—something I had believed would always be there as a fallback, an insurance policy. For all those reasons, I believed I should be treated as a union compositor. But I would have been perfectly happy if The Journal had simply given me a bonus of $50 or $100 and a thank you to recognize my work.

Several months passed, and I was back to work in the newsroom when Schwandner summoned me to his office. He told me we were going down to the third floor to see Donald B. Abert, the publisher and son-in-law of Harry Grant, the legendary editor and publisher who had started the employee ownership program in 1936.

We sat down and listened to Abert torturously explain how The Journal had resolved my complaint about overtime. He said the payroll department had gone through every one of my time cards for the duration of the strike, and had adjusted my pay accordingly. But he also said that because I was a reporter and not a union member, the decision had been made (I noted the passive voice) to pay me union wages for regular hours, and time and a half for overtime, but at my reporter's salary. He had a check all prepared for the additional amount. I was stunned and, later, furious at what I considered a chicken-shit solution. The check amounted to something over a hundred dollars.

I would have been happy if Abert had thanked me and handed me a bonus check, or had invented some other simple remuneration for my special circumstances. The nitpicking, bean-counter approach not only was unfair, but was unworthy of The Journal, I thought. Even the hard-bitten Schwandner was embarrassed and angry at the way the situation had been handled. He apologized to me as we made our way back up to the fourth floor, saying he and Schaleben had raised the issue with the bosses, but had no say in the outcome. It was the only time I ever saw Schwandner, who went on to become editor of the Milwaukee Sentinel, look sheepish.

But my anger didn't last long. I was back to being a reporter, even though at that time I still had my share of obits.

HELPERS IN WASHINGTON

Over the years, after I moved to Washington in June of 1970, I continued to get a lot of help from my colleagues, including many of them who were not friends, but simply reporters I met covering stories. With a few exceptions here and there, there's a great give and take among reporters when they're not competing directly with each other. In some places, this is derided as "herd journalism" or "pack journalism." But those terms mainly refer to the phenomenon of the major news media jumping on a big story like the O.J. Simpson trial, Anna Nicole Smith's death or President Clinton's sorry sex adventures, and there is no question that those sordid spectacles reflect poorly on the entire craft, though more on the electronic practitioners.

But on day-to-day coverage of the news, especially in Washington, the news capital of the world, reporters co-operate with each other. Of course, no reporter working an exclusive story would share it with colleagues, or seek their help. But when you're covering a running story—important legislation in the House or Senate, for example—it makes sense to help each other out. You can't be everywhere at once, so the reporters who catch a senator in a hallway can share what they know with the reporter who went to the press conference. It gives an individual reporter extra sets of eyes and ears, and it makes for better stories all around, which in the end benefits the readers.

As a primarily regional reporter in Washington, which meant that I mostly covered the local and state angles for The Milwaukee Journal, I worked some of those big stories—including the Nixon and Clinton impeachment proceedings—and shared information with my fellow reporters. But there was an additional benefit as well. If I covered a Senate hearing, for example, and heard something that might be a story for another regional reporter, I'd take extra notes and pick up copies of the testimony, and pass them on. They'd do the same for me.

In many instances, another reporter would tip me off to a local-angle story I didn't know existed.

Several examples stand out. For all of my time in Washington, I covered the U.S. Supreme Court. Well, I didn't really cover it because I had too many other duties on Capitol Hill, at agencies and departments, and occasionally at the White House. What I did was part-time regional coverage. I tracked the cases that came out of Wisconsin or had particular interest for Wisconsin readers. But sometimes I'd get tied up on other stories, or I'd be away, and I'd get behind at the court.

That was where Glen Elsasser came through. A genial identical twin, as subdued as he was competent, he covered the court for the Chicago Tribune. Over the years, he was as important to my Supreme Court coverage as Warren Weaver of The New York Times had been on the Nixon tapes case. Whenever Glen came across any story with a Wisconsin angle, he'd give me a call to tip me off. More often than not, it was something of which I was unaware, and would have missed but for his generous soul.

There were others at the court who never hesitated to help out with background information on stories about which I was sometimes ignorant: erudite Lyle Denniston of the Washington Star and Baltimore Sun, and relentless Richard Carelli of the AP, who were the fastest guns I ever saw on a court story; restless Joan Biskupic of The Washington Post and USA TODAY (who had once worked as a copy kid on The Journal and said she had sorted my mail); sweet Linda Greenhouse of The New York Times, one of the best at understanding the court; laid-back Steve Wehrlein of The Wall Street Journal, and tough Toni House, a former Washington Star reporter who was the press officer for the Supreme Court.

As on Capitol Hill, these superb reporters—some of whom also were lawyers—often got into bull sessions on the cases they were covering, offering different interpretations of points of law or the Constitution, and analyzing how an individual justice might vote. It was collegiality, not collusion. Those informal conversations doubtless contributed to more informed stories that enlightened readers of their publications.

THE BREMER TRIAL

Toni House had helped me at an earlier time, long before she became the Supreme Court's press officer. It was August, 1971, at the trial in Upper Marlboro, Md., of Arthur Bremer, who had shot Alabama Gov. George C. Wallace at a shopping center in Laurel, Md., paralyzing him for life. Bremer was from Milwaukee, so he was a natural local-angle story for The Journal. I got the assignment to cover the trial, and it turned out to be one of best—and most fun—stories I'd ever covered, partly because of Toni and Anne Groer.

The two were young suburban reporters for Washington papers— Toni for the Star and Anne for the Daily News, a Scripps Howard paper. They covered Prince Georges County, of which Upper Marlboro was the county seat. Though they competed, they were friends, and like good reporters anywhere on a geographic beat, they knew everybody—every judge, every bailiff, every clerk, and likely every secretary and cop in the vicinity.

I knew nobody. But shortly after I arrived to cover the trial, I met Toni and Anne, and immediately fell in love with them. They were savvy, funny and irreverent, the sort of brass-balls female reporters who had always captivated me. And even though they were younger—I was 36—they decided to mother me. Throughout the trial, I was "with" them. It meant that I got waved past the security checkpoints. I got a front-row seat in the courtroom. I got introduced to the judge, as well as others who could provide good information. In short, I was an insider, not someone outside with his nose pressed against the glass.

Even better was the way the trial broke. It started on a Monday morning and ended on Friday afternoon. Each day, it ran from about 9 a.m. to 4:30 p.m. Best of all, almost all of the important news broke on my time. The Journal was a p.m. newspaper, which meant I had to file for every edition in the morning, then for the upstate edition in the afternoon. Every day, I'd have a new lede for each edition in the morning. Then things would drone on in the afternoon.

At the end of the day, I'd go over my notes and telephone the Reuters bureau in Washington. Always on the lookout for extra money, I had signed on as a stringer for Reuters. I was mostly ignorant of its U.S. outlets, but knew it supplied the British tabloids, among others. So I'd sift through my notes to pick out the most savory salacious details from the trial, and I'd dictate them to a Reuters rewrite man in the bureau. The editors there loved it, and I was paid $110 for my week's efforts. I used the money later to buy a tailor-made black suit with wide lapels and a red lining.

Early in the morning, before the trial started, I'd write the leftovers from the previous day—what The Journal called A-matter—then I'd go into the courtroom to look for the first edition story. Invariably, I got a new lede for almost every edition, and Anne and Toni would keep watch while I left to go phone it in. Toni, of course, had to leave as well because the Star also was a p.m., but her deadlines were different. Invariably, virtually nothing would happen while I was away, and then I'd get something else for the next edition.

I almost felt sorry for the reporter for the Milwaukee Sentinel, Keith Spore, who had been sent from Milwaukee to cover the story. I got all of the news breaks, except one, for The Journal. Even the guilty verdict came on Friday morning. The only thing left for Spore and the Sentinel was the sentencing, which came Friday afternoon. By then, I didn't care. I was flying high—thanks to circumstances and Toni and Anne. In the end, Spore did all right. He became editor of the Milwaukee Sentinel and, later, publisher of the Milwaukee Journal Sentinel.

NEWSLETTER HELPERS

Over the years in Washington, I became acutely aware of the limitations of a professional cream skimmer like myself. Just covering the Wisconsin congressional delegation meant that I had to have at least a nodding acquaintance with everything from dairy price supports and copyright law to urban and foreign affairs. Like others, I soon came to rely on my colleagues who were beat reporters, and therefore experts in their fields. One time, I was covering a tax bill in the House Ways and Means Committee and getting regular explanations from a sharp reporter for The Wall Street Journal. Though his name slipped from my memory, I never forgot one thing he told me. He said I'd never understand tax legislation unless I did my own income taxes. Up to that time, I had been a regular customer of any number of tax preparers. After that, I started doing my own taxes.

I also gained a great deal of respect for newsletter reporters, who covered federal agencies and departments, as well as different subjects, with a relentless scrutiny and expertise they never received from the mainstream news media. As soon as I became aware of the newsletter editors and reporters, I came to rely on them. Whenever I came across a story with subject matter with which I was unfamiliar, I'd check to see if was covered by a newsletter. Then I'd call the reporter or editor to get background.

It never failed. They all were happy to help, and they often knew more about the agency than the people who worked there. A prime example was Art Amolsch, who plumbed the depths of the Federal Trade Commission with his newsletter, FTC Watch. From time to time over the years I was in Washington, and mostly when Janet Steiger, the widow of Wisconsin Rep. William A. Steiger, was a member and then chairman of the commission, I relied on Art to give me the insider's take on events there. More than one person there told me Art knew more about the FTC than most of the commissioners.

Although I have sometimes been mouse-trapped by fellow reporters who interviewed me and then wound up quoting me in a story—the late David Rosenbaum of The New York Times was one—I never believed in interviewing colleagues for attribution. Though beat reporters like Art are extremely knowledgeable, they do not make decisions or policy. I relied on them strictly for background, and always assured them they would not be quoted, especially because the background information sometimes would include the reporter's opinions about sources in the agency.

But newsletter reporters were not the only colleagues I counted on. There were many occasions, as at the United States Supreme Court, when I could count on reporters for newspapers, magazines, radio and television to give me a fill, as we used to say. I returned the favor when it was something another reporter needed. For example, when a national publication did a profile on one of my guys, as when Les Aspin became chairman of the House Armed Services Committee, or Clement J. Zablocki took over the House Foreign Affairs Committee, I was only too happy to provide as much help as I could—even to getting the reporter clips from The Milwaukee Journal library.

So I got a lot of help not only from my friends, but from reporters and editors I barely knew or did not know at all. In 1986, a couple of the latter even helped get me nominated for a Pulitzer Prize. The Journal sent me to Managua, Nicaragua, to cover the trial of Eugene Hasenfus, a 45-year-old minor mercenary for the CIA who helped deliver supplies to the Nicaraguan Contra rebels. He had been captured by Sandinista government troops after the plane on which he was working as a cargo kicker was shot down. Hasenfus was just barely a local story for us because he was from Marinette, Wis., which is up north of Green Bay just across the border from Menominee, Mich. But that was enough for The Journal's editors. Like politics, news is mainly local.

I had been to Nicaragua before, in 1983, when I traveled throughout the five countries of Central America, as well as Panama, for a series of stories. At that time, I had most everything well arranged in advance, thanks to help from Zablocki, who plugged me into the U.S. embassies in those countries and even helped me get interviews, among them Sandinista government officials and Violetta Chamorro, the widow of Pedro Joaquin Chamorro, the publisher of La Prensa, the newspaper that had opposed the pre-Sandinista dictator, Anastasio Somoza. Chamorro was assassinated in 1978 and his death solidified national opposition to Somoza. By the time I arrived, Violetta Chamorro was a symbol of the opposition to the Sandinistas. One of her sons, Pedro, was co-director of La Prensa, which was heavily censored and opposed the Sandinistas. Another son, Carlos, was director of Barricada, the official Sandinista newspaper.

A PULITZER FIZZLE

But the Hasenfus trial was a different story. On my first visit, I did interviews and gathered information, and wrote the series after I returned home. This time I had to file daily stories from the trial, as well as sidebars about the country. I could have worked from my hotel room, but everything became a whole lot easier after I met Edward Cody, a veteran foreign correspondent for The Washington Post, who was fluent in Spanish, French and Arabic. He had an arrangement to work out of the Managua Bureau of ABC News, where he had a small office. He took me there and introduced me to John Martin, the ABC correspondent who was the Managua bureau chief.

One thing about networks: On a big story, they never do anything on the cheap. Martin had set up a full-blown bureau in a house on a Managua side street. He had telephones. He had food and drink. He had satellite technicians. He had cash, because Diners Club was the only legal credit card. He had cars and drivers. He had gofers. He had an office manager who doubled as a money-changer on the black market, where the exchange rate was the most favorable. And now he had me.

Martin, as pleasant a man as I ever met in the news business, threw the doors open and invited me in. He gave me a place to work, and offered me the use of any of the facilities. I gratefully accepted the work space and the use of his telephones—though I charged my calls to The Journal—and I took advantage of the money exchange. But I did not want to wear out my welcome, so I didn't eat the food or use the cars and drivers.

I even felt bad when I got a minor scoop by co-operating with one of Martin's competitors. But it happened by accident. Hasenfus was charged with terrorism, violating public security and associating with criminals. (He later was convicted, sentenced to 30 years in prison, quickly released and sent home). But while awaiting the verdict from the Sandinista tribunal, he was allowed a family visit. His wife, Sally, and brother, William, were allowed inside the tribunal headquarters with his Nicaraguan attorney, Enrique Sotelo Borgen, and an interpreter.

As always, tribunal functionaries stopped reporters and television crews from entering the building, except for a Sandinista government TV crew. But I had covered the trial every day and apparently was a familiar face. I managed to slip inside, along with Jamie Gangel, a correspondent for NBC news. Hasenfus and the others were seated at a table in a small meeting area, and Gangel and I and crouched down and observed the scene as best as we could. I could see, but not hear; she could hear fragments of the conversation, but could not see. Between the two of us, we cobbled together a decent story with descriptions and indirect quotes.

It wasn't a major story, but I made the front page with it. I never did learn what NBC did with Gangel's story, especially because it didn't have any pictures. That fact made me feel a bit better about helping one of Martin's competitors. But because I had worked together with Jamie on the story, I did not tell Martin about it, though I felt conflicted because of all the help he had given me. In the end, I doubt it made much difference. Years later, I was proud to sponsor Martin for membership in the National Press Club.

On the days when there was no trial to cover, I did other stories about Managua, Nicaragua and the Nicaraguan people. The Journal's editors considered the entire package worthy of a nomination for the Pulitzer Prize, and actually did enter the required maximum number of stories. But the entry was put together by a mid-level Journal editor who selected mostly local stories, which I believed doomed my chances. Some of my best work, I thought, was not even in the Pulitzer submission.

But I did receive the 1986 Richard S. Davis Award—the highest honor The Journal paid to one of its own reporters. It was named for the legendary reporter who was the consensus choice as one of the best reporters and the finest writer in The Journal's history. It wasn't a Pulitzer, but recognition by one's peers is maybe more fulfilling. I've noticed over the years that hardly anyone ever remembers Pulitzer winners—except for their families, friends and peers.

I did receive one other major award that, to members of the Society of Professional Journalists, is the rough equivalent of a Pulitzer Prize. It was the bronze medallion that went with the Sigma Delta Chi Distinguished Service Award for Washington Correspondence. The award was for stories I wrote in 1992, when a confidential source gave me the logs of the VIP 89th Military Airlift Wing at Andrews Air Force Base. I wrote one story detailing Secretary of State James A. Baker's use of military aircraft for private purposes, and another that, among other things, disclosed that Vice President Dan Quayle and his wife, Marilyn, had taken separate military planes to a funeral in Norway.

The source also provided me with travel logs for the comptroller general of the United States, who headed the General Accounting Office, which was the watchdog, or investigative arm, of Congress. There was no serious scandal there, but the story focused on the question of who watches the watchdog. The stories drove people there nuts. I heard that the GAO people at one point even speculated that I had been sneaking in the building at night, posing as a janitor to root through wastebaskets. It wasn't so. I simply had a well-placed source.

Another friend who propped me up along the way was Jack Kole, my colleague and The Milwaukee Journal's Washington bureau chief for 18 of my 30 years there. Though he was the bureau chief and I was the Indian, we never operated in a boss-subordinate fashion. Jack was about as laid-back as anyone I ever worked with, and he supported my forays into journalism politics. In 1978, for example, when I was president of the National Press Club, he basically took over The Journal's Washington coverage. I produced maybe a story a week, while he took care of all the other stories.

THE EDITORS OF DESTRUCTION

In 2002, when Sig Gissler was appointed administrator of the Pulitzer Prizes, a press release identified him as the former editor of The Milwaukee Journal and cited his stature as a journalist. It neglected to mention that he had been fired.

Gissler served as The Journal's editor from 1985 to 1993—or, rather, The Journal served him. In eight years, he and his handpicked managing editor, Steve Hannah, egos unfurled, presided over the decline of a great newspaper.

In the 1970s and early 1980s, when Gissler was an editorial writer and later the editorial page editor, Jack Kole and I were writing an opinion column on national issues, in addition to our reporting duties. It ran weekly in the Sunday editorial section and we alternated writing it, so it became a biweekly chore—at least for me.

The column came about because of Irwin Maier, The Journal Company's chairman. Though he never, to my knowledge, interfered in The Journal's daily news coverage, he maintained that if The Journal ran opinion columns from Washington, it should feature the opinions of its own people, who had a better understanding of Wisconsin and its people. As military folks would say, the editors knew whom to salute and when.

Occasionally over the years, as Jack and I did the column, we heard from Joe Shoquist, the managing editor, that there were complaints back in Milwaukee that the columns were "more liberal" than The Journal's editorial page. He did not identify who had made the complaints. But it soon became obvious that these passive-voice mutterings were directed at Jack, who was a professed liberal and usually wrote on politics and economics. I was less political and eclectic in my choice of subjects, and therefore harder to pin down.

We did not learn where the complaints came from, though we strongly suspected Gissler, the editorial page editor, who once described himself to me as a "militant moderate"—whatever that means.

Before he was named to the top job, Gissler had been bumped up from editorial page editor to associate editor. It was obvious to a lot of people in the newsroom that he was being groomed for higher things. At that time, I had high hopes for him. I did not know him well, but he had been pleasant to me and I supposed he was a decent enough editorial page editor. That's because I had little first-hand knowledge; I was only a casual reader of the editorial pages.

Though Dick Leonard had been my mentor, I didn't have strong feelings either way about Gissler replacing him. Leonard had held the job for many years, and had come in for criticism in the newsroom, mainly for being a detached and absentee editor. Gissler, I supposed, was to be the catalyst for maintaining and even improving The Journal's national reputation.

I even got excited—and taken in—when Gissler traveled to Washington while he was associate editor, partly to pick my brains. We spent the better part of an afternoon and early evening in a hotel bar, discussing The Journal and my perceptions of what was good and what was wrong with it, as well as what could be done to produce a better newspaper. Gissler oozed sincerity and seemed genuinely interested in taking into account what I had to say. But that disappeared soon after he was named editor.

I had my first inkling of what was to come when, on one of my periodic trips back to Milwaukee, he invited me and Sharlene to dinner at his home. There were five of us that evening: Gissler; his wife, Mary; Sharlene and me, and Steve Hannah. Gissler dominated the conversation, with occasional verbal reinforcement from Hannah. They talked expansively about their plans for The Journal. But there was something disturbing about the way Gissler talked—as if The Journal were now his personal fiefdom. He even talked about dispensing expense money as if it came from his own pocket.

I remarked about it to Sharlene on our way back to our motel, observing that it seemed our new editors had the bit in their teeth.

Though I didn't make much more of it at the time, I wasn't far off the mark. Gissler and Hannah soon became the founts of all knowledge on how the paper should be run. As far as I knew, they didn't consult anybody; I certainly was never asked again, nor did I see any of the suggestions I had given Gissler implemented in any way.

From our 800 mile distance in Washington, Jack and I learned through the grapevine that the paper was now driven by two egos and the whim of the day. An example: Beth Slocum, our fine assistant managing editor for features, told me that Gissler and Hannah had gone off on a weekend "retreat" at Hannah's summer cottage, where they pored over women's magazines and discussed them. When they returned, she said, Gissler had decided he knew exactly what women wanted in a Sunday features section and ordered her to follow his formula. She had no say in the matter.

At first, the upheavals in Milwaukee had no impact on Jack and me. But inevitably, the editors' spotlight swept onto the Washington bureau, and we soon became the guilty parties—guilty of not producing enough stories, guilty of doing too many national rather than local stories, guilty of not taking detailed directions from Milwaukee, even though such directions were notable mainly by their absence.

At one point, the dismal twins issued a decree. Henceforth, the Washington bureau reporters were to spend 90% of their time on local stories and only 10% on national stories. There was no basis whatever for inventing such a formula.

None of this bothered me much because almost everything I did had some sort of local angle. I mainly worked Capitol Hill and the Wisconsin delegation, believing that The Journal had a responsibility to keep its readers informed about what their elected officials were doing. But Jack balked and made himself the target. He had integrity and pride, and had been a reporter and then bureau chief in Washington in earlier times, when the bureau reported directly to the managing editor and was considered on a par with that level of supervision.

Soon the twins started running a number on Jack. At one point, he was ordered to spend half of his time in Washington on local business stories—a ridiculous formulation that betrayed a complete lack of understanding of Washington news, never mind that there weren't that many such stories that The Journal would even consider running.

At one point, Hannah decided to place the Washington bureau under the supervision of the state editor, Dan Hanley, who also knew nothing about Washington. When I asked Hannah why, he replied, "Dan's a good soldier. He knows how to follow orders."

On a personal level, Hanley was a decent enough guy. But he took his sergeant's duties seriously and became a constant pain—ordering us, for example, to pursue stories that required us to make long-distance telephone calls to Wisconsin, when those stories could as well have been handled back in the home office at less expense in time and resources.

The tragic comedy of the situation came home for me when a story I had written involving our two Milwaukee congressmen was trimmed in a way that made it totally lopsided, without any of the balance and fairness we always carefully sought. Furious, I vented my spleen at Hanley over the telephone. He explained that the story had to be chopped when he was up in the composing room supervising the page makeup.

I didn't buy it, because the trim had been so substantial—fully one-third to one-fourth of the story. That's not the sort of cut you make in the composing room, unless you had screwed up and completely mis-read the page dummy. I did the story again for the next day to make sure we got the other side in the paper.

Many months later, Hanley did a "performance review" on me—another of the control-freak innovations from Gissler and Hannah. Though it ticked me off to be subjected to such humiliation, there actually wasn't much to it, except for this criticism from Hanley: "Needs to have more understanding of editors who must trim stories in the composing room."

As humorist Dave Barry would say, I'm not making this up.

THE CATCH 22

Matters came to a head for Jack in his "Catch 22" situation after he balked at the order to produce a steady diet of Wisconsin business stories. He could hardly have done otherwise—the stories didn't exist or, if they did, they were of a caliber that would never get in the paper.

The editors summoned Jack back to Milwaukee for consultations, where they told him he was being ordered back there to become a reporter on the business news desk—this after 18 years as the Washington bureau chief covering the White House, Congress, national political conventions and reporting and writing countless national and local stories. I learned later that Jack tried to plead his case with Tom McCollow, then the chairman of The Journal Company. McCollow had been Jack's guest of honor at the 1985 Gridiron dinner. Jack was the Gridiron president in the club's 100th anniversary year, and Mc-Collow had been seated at the head table next to President Ronald Reagan.

He reacted like a star-struck teenager, so impressed that he wrote a lengthy, poorly written, account of the evening for his friends and acquaintances. Of course, somebody got hold of it and a copy found its way to Washington. It was as fawningly obsequious as anything I've ever read.

Yet when Jack trekked to the third floor to plead his case, McCollow turned him down cold. So Jack did the only thing he could under the circumstances. I don't know what was said, though it was probably something on the order of, "Take this job and shove it." Jack took an early retirement.

Throughout the Gissler-Hannah vendetta against Jack, I tried to keep a low profile, figuring I likely would be next on the list. But my anger against the two editors outweighed whatever fear I had. I figured it was Jack and me against Gissler and Hannah, so whenever there were meetings or communications, I did my best to argue our case and to try to show them how ridiculous their demands were. I know Jack understood that. But his wife, Betty, did not. She believed I was part of the conspiracy to oust Jack—and said so one night after too many drinks at a dinner party at our home.

A BRIGHT SPOT

There was one bright spot in the Gissler and Hannah hobbling of our great newspaper. Hannah hired Rem Rieder as the assistant managing editor for news. Rieder was a solid newsman. He had been deputy metro editor of the Washington Post, and before that was city editor and national editor of the Miami Herald. Best of all, he understood how news happened in the nation's capital. He became a welcome buffer between the bureau and the Milwaukee editors.

From the outset, Rieder was interested in the big story of the day and showcasing his Washington reporters, especially me. On almost a daily basis, we'd try to figure out what our best shot was to make page one, which of course he controlled. I'd go to work on the story, often plugging in the obligatory local angle and, voila! The story would wind up on the front page. I don't believe I ever had such a high concentration of page one stories in such a short period of time as I did in those years.

Even with Rieder as buffer, there were occasionally silly orders from the home office. One came when the AP moved an investigative story, many months in the making, which involved a Milwaukee mortgage banker. The business news editor, Dale Buss, who had come to us from The Wall Street Journal and should have known better, called and told me he wanted me to duplicate the AP story so we could have our own piece. This was about 9 a.m., only hours from our final deadline for that afternoon's paper.

I told him it could not be done, that the best I could do was to seek fresh comment from the mortgage banker. But he insisted. I appealed to Rieder, who understood but apparently was under the gun from the editors. He called back, sheepishly, and asked me to do what I could.

Furious, I nevertheless managed to cobble together a pale imitation of the AP story for the final edition. It had little that was new or original, and it was only about 15 inches long. After I filed it, I called Buss to tell him it had arrived. He seemed pleased and then, in one of the most stupefying questions I've ever heard from a supposedly experienced editor, said: "Did you write it inverted pyramid style?"

As I said, I'm not making this up.

Unfortunately, Rieder did not last. Family ties forced him to resign and return to the east coast. Years later he became the editor of the American Journalism Review at the University of Maryland.

After Gissler and Hannah forced Jack into retirement, I expected to be next. Sure enough, they ordered me back to Milwaukee for a consultation. To my surprise, they wanted to keep me, but wholly on their terms. We spent most of an afternoon in Gissler's office, sometimes shouting at each other, with the two of them basically telling me what they wanted from me—which, in truth, was not much different from what I had been doing.

I had always taken the position that, as a Washington reporter, I should give The Journal stories it could not get anywhere else. That meant primarily covering the Wisconsin stories and not duplicating the wire services.

The meeting continued at the bar in Turner Hall a half block from The Journal building—this time with just Hannah and me. Several more hours passed until I was finally able to return to my motel room, exhausted but happy that I still had a job in Washington.

But I couldn't sleep that night. All I had heard was what Gissler and Hannah wanted from me, even though they had expressed almost no criticism of my performance.

I had learned from my experiences with trying to build a new National Press Building while I was president of the National Press Club that it's always a good idea to get something on the record after a meeting so the adversaries—and even the allies—could not change signals later.

After any meeting on our proposed new building, Henry Keys, the Press Building's executive director, always wrote a memo summarizing the discussion and his understanding of whatever had been agreed upon, which he sent to all of the participants.

Lying in my Milwaukee motel bed that night, I resolved to do the same thing with Gissler and Hannah, so they couldn't play games with me later. Moreover, I was getting angrier by the minute. All I had heard was what they wanted from me. Nothing had been said about what they would do for me. About 2 a.m., I crawled out of bed, sat down at my Radio Shack "Trash 80" portable computer and wrote a long memo summarizing our meeting. I ended by telling them what I wanted. They had recently abolished the bureau chief's title in the Madison bureau, the better to pull its strings from Milwaukee, and I figured Washington was next.

BUREAU CHIEF TO EDITOR?

I wrote that titles were important in Washington—even if they were not to me personally—and that I wanted the title of Washington bureau chief. In view of my new responsibilities, I said I also wanted a $100 a week raise.

We met again at The Journal the next morning, this time with other editors present—no doubt so everybody would be clear about my marching orders. To my surprise, there was little to talk about. Hannah also had produced a memo, which did not differ substantially from mine—except, of course, for the part about the pay raise and the title.

The meeting was over quickly. Gissler gulped and said he'd have to think about my demands. Two weeks later, after I had inquired several times, he telephoned to say he had approved the title and a $50 raise. I felt as if I'd won the lottery.

Despite the fact that I came through that episode largely unscathed, I retained a low-level animosity toward Gissler and Hannah that uncharacteristically did not subside with time. Though I had tacitly supported Gissler's ascension to the editor's chair, I couldn't help but conclude that he was a midget compared to Leonard, even though I had been among Leonard's critics. In the space of eight years, as I saw it from my 800-mile distance, Gissler and Hannah had taken one of the nation's great newspapers to second-rate status. I was not privy to the reasons for Gissler's firing, but somebody else obviously had come to a similar conclusion.

With the search on for a new editor, I saw an opportunity and decided to pursue it. Over the years I had been in Washington, there were occasional feelers about whether I would consider returning to Milwaukee in some capacity. I didn't seriously encourage them, saying cavalierly that the only jobs I would consider were managing editor or editor. But with Gissler gone, I decided to go for the big prize.

I first consulted my mentor, Leonard, who, though retired, still retained a lively interest in the paper. He encouraged me, and even volunteered to be my advocate, especially with his friend Bob Wills, the Sentinel editor who by then had been promoted to publisher of both newspapers.

With some chutzpah, I telephoned Gene Roberts, a professor at the University of Maryland who had been the Pulitzer Prize-winning editor at the Philadelphia Inquirer, and asked if he would advise me. Though we had never met or even spoke, he graciously accepted, and we had a long lunch at an Asian restaurant near his home in Northwest Washington. One piece of advice that stood out was when he told me that if I got the job, the first thing I should do is to find a good, empathetic local columnist.

I wrote a lengthy memo to McCollow, outlining why I believed I would be a good editor who could bring the paper back over an interim period because I was only six or seven years from retirement. Sharlene and I figured we could keep our home in Annandale and rent an apartment in downtown Milwaukee for the duration. But by the time the new editor was ready to be chosen, Robert Kahlor had become chairman of the board.

Kahlor and I had similar backgrounds. We had both started on the mechanical side of the newspaper business, though he came up through those ranks, where I had switched to the editorial side. I thought Kahlor had been unduly impressed by Gissler, whom I regarded as a pseudo-intellectual.

I did not sense that Kahlor was as impressed with me as he was with Gissler, regarding me as little more than an upstart back-shop guy. Whether those impressions had any basis in reality I do not know, but I nevertheless believed them. In the end, Kahlor chose Mary Jo Meisner, a 40-something star who had worked at the Washington Post and was the managing editor of the Fort Worth Star-Telegram.

I was disappointed, but not overly so. I figured I was a long shot under the best of circumstances and, as one who had been supportive of women's rights, I could not argue with the historic decision to name this young woman as The Journal's first female editor. Moreover, it wasn't exactly as if I were out on the street. I was still The Journal's Washington bureau chief—a fun job because I was a reporter, not a bureaucrat or administrator.

A minor footnote: During the search for a new editor, Hannah came to Washington and we had drinks at the Washington Hotel. He also was a candidate for the job, though without much hope, and he said that if I got the job, he would be interested in replacing me as The Journal's Washington bureau chief.

It gave me no satisfaction later when Meisner also was summarily fired as editor. We had hit it off fairly well in our infrequent encounters, and she did not interfere with the Washington bureau. Without her, I almost certainly would not have spent the 1994-'95 academic year at the Freedom Forum First Amendment Center in Nashville.

When the opportunity came for the fellowship to study the relationship between the news media and the military, Meisner approved it without hesitation, even though it was taking her Washington bureau chief away for nine months. But my request had two things going for it. It was not a presidential election year, when the bureau might have been expected to be covering campaigns, and by then my sidekick in the bureau was Patrick Jasperse, as talented and hard-working a reporter as I ever knew.

Even as a summer intern, Patrick had out-performed some veteran Journal reporters, and though I did not know him personally, I had read his stories, so he was my only recommendation as Jack's replacement in the Washington bureau. Before Gissler and Hannah approved the request, however, I spent many months as The Journal's only man in Washington.

While I was in Nashville with the Freedom Forum, Patrick performed with distinction, right through the beginning of the Newt Gingrich-led Republican revolution in the House and the trauma of the decision in Milwaukee to kill The Journal and Sentinel and start a new newspaper, The Milwaukee Journal Sentinel, in April, 1995.

At the request of Carl Schwartz, my Nixon impeachment editor who was then the news editor, I took a two-week break from my stint in Nashville to go to Milwaukee, where I wrote two big stories for The

Journal's final edition. One was a compilation of the big stories The Journal had covered over its more than 100-year history. The other was The Journal's obituary.

Thirty-four years and 10 months earlier, I had started out writing obits as a young Journal reporter. Now I was writing my newspaper's obituary. It doesn't get much sadder than that.

13

THE STANDING COMMITTEE

I never regarded myself as a political reporter, though I covered my share of political stories, as well as presidential nominating conventions from 1972 through 1996. But I never had the scholarly interest of some of my contemporaries, who could recall eye-glazing minutiae from ancient and obscure campaigns. My colleague in The Milwaukee Journal's Washington bureau was one example. To Jack Kole, politics was part of his being. My later sidekicks, Patrick Jasperse and Craig Gilbert, also were superb political reporters.

But I was a fairly decent politician. Chris Lecos, an iconoclastic Journal reporter who was a close friend of both mine and Jack's, used to say that Jack knew more about politics than I could ever learn, but I was a better politician.

Three years after moving to Washington, I had my first taste of it. The Standing Committee of Correspondents was a five-member elected body of Capitol Hill Correspondents that was responsible for running the Senate and House press galleries for daily newspapers and wire services.

There were four such committees on the Hill—one each for the daily press and wire services, the periodicals, the radio and TV correspondents, and the still photographers. Among them, they oversaw the staff and seven press gallery work areas that served journalists who covered Congress—three on the Senate side and three on the House side for the reporters, producers and technicians, and one combined office on the Senate side for the still shooters.

The Standing Committee was mostly invisible, even to accredited gallery members. It met regularly to pass on credential applications and to occasionally deal with complaints either by or against reporters chasing stories in the Capitol complex. Congress had long before ceded its authority over press passes to the correspondents themselves. The idea was that the politicians should not get involved in deciding who could and could not cover Congress.

Over the years, the Standing Committee—and the other committees that supervised the other galleries—had been empowered not only to issue press passes but to hire and fire the gallery staff as well, despite the fact that they were congressional employees. Because of the jealously guarded prerogatives of the Senate and House, as well as the fact that the various galleries came into being at different times, the galleries were subject to different masters.

In the House, for example, the daily press gallery operated under the purview of the office of the Speaker, while the other galleries were nominally supervised by the House Administration Committee. In the Senate, the Sergeant at Arms and, ultimately, the Rules Committee, were in charge.

In practice, however, the congressional authorities—though they controlled the budgets and payrolls of the galleries—left most of the decisions to the committees of correspondents. In the daily press gallery, elections were held each December. Two-year terms were staggered, with three of the five members elected one year, and two the next.

Interest in the committee intensified in the December before the quadrennial presidential election year, when the national political conventions were held. That was because the Standing Committee was in charge of issuing daily press and wire service credentials for the Democratic and Republican conventions. It also parceled out convention work spaces and press stand seats for the news organizations that covered the proceedings.

Not surprisingly, the big news organizations—the wire services, the local newspapers and the big bureaus—flexed their muscles at such times. Because all of their staff members were eligible for congressional press passes, there were a lot of copy editors, supervisors, bureau chiefs and others who had press cards but almost never showed up on Capitol Hill.

Except for the Standing Committee elections before a presidential election year, that is. Then they would turn out in droves to vote to make sure they elected Standing Committee members to protect their interests in credentials and work space at the conventions. The AP, the Washington Post and other big news organizations would field candidates that were shoo-ins simply because of the numbers of eligible voters their organizations could turn out. It was classic machine politics.

That meant that regional reporters like me, with no big base of voters, had no chance of being elected to the Standing Committee before a presidential election year. So we were relegated to the crumbs—those off-years when there was no national election. Even then, however, the competition sometimes was fairly lively.

It didn't take a two-by-four upside my head to learn, fairly quickly, that the members of the Standing Committee had a certain status with the staff of the Senate and House daily press galleries. They were career bureaucrats and had an uncanny knack of knowing just what to kiss and when.

THE POLITICAL CAMPAIGN

So I determined to run for the committee in 1973, just three and a half years after I had arrived in Washington. Two seats were open for the 1974-'75 term, and one was a lock. Lee Bandy, the correspondent for The State in Columbia, S.C., was a good ol' boy who'd been around a long time, was a great political reporter, worked exclusively on the Hill and was popular with his colleagues.

There were two other candidates—Joe Ganley of the Gannett Newspapers and Bruce Winter of the Baltimore Sun. Ganley was an amiable and mild-mannered older guy who had no particular ambitions but was running because his bosses had encouraged it. Winter, on the other hand, was a brash young reporter who had been around and knew a lot of people.

The conventional wisdom was that the two seats would go to Bandy and Winter, with Bandy leading the ticket. By custom, that would make him chairman of the committee, with also-ran Winter taking over as the committee's secretary. Ganley and I would return to obscurity.

But with Jack Kole's support and encouragement, I determined to make a race of it. While my two opponents, Winter and Ganley, did virtually nothing, I campaigned all over town. So did Bandy. Even though he had the lock, the old pol didn't take it for granted.

It was great fun. I visited every major bureau in town, getting permission from the bureau chief to walk around and meet people. I shook hands and passed out crude little printed biogs of myself. The fun was in meeting all those reporters and editors—some of whom were famous—and seeing where they lived and worked every day. At The New York Times, I even walked into the office of Clifton Daniel, who was famous not only for heading the bureau but for marrying Margaret, the daughter of President Harry S. Truman.

Though I did my best not to show it, I was intimidated. Daniel had the demeanor and dress of a sophisticated and powerful guy. But he was friendly and smiling, said he doubted whether he would personally troop up to Capitol Hill to vote, but said if he did I'd have his vote.

It went that way all over. I met people I would come to know closely over the years in Washington. Many years later, when I finally got elected to the Gridiron Club, I already knew every member personally—something that had been required in the early days of the club but had come to be honored mostly in the breach.

I even visited the foreign bureaus, reckoning that the Japanese contingent, for example, had a substantial voting bloc, which it did. Not many of them turned out, but a few did, and I bet I got their votes.

But we didn't take anything for granted. Kole had a Volkswagen microbus, and we enlisted his wife, Betty, and my wife, Sharlene, to drive it as a shuttle bus on election day. We offered rides to voters at the National Press Building and carted them up to the Capitol to vote. I even pressed my '64 Volkswagen Karmann-Ghia convertible into service. Shortly before the polls closed at 5 p.m., and after the wives had gone home for the day, I drove to the Press Building, picked up three reporters from the Knight Ridder bureau and drove them up to the Hill.

As expected, Bandy led the ticket and Ganley was a distant fourth. But I beat Winter by 10 votes. It was exhilarating; the first time I'd ever won a contested election for anything. And the reaction was amazing. Press gallery staff members who had barely acknowledged my existence before suddenly discovered something else to kiss. Following custom, Bandy became the committee chairman and I was elected secretary, which meant that I was available to sign the occasional check when Bandy was away.

There wasn't much to the job except for the famed—among the cognoscenti—Strout incident, which became not only a crusade for me but an example of how hilariously wrongheaded journalists can become when they attempt to function in the same way as the legislators they so often ridicule.

Richard Strout was a revered correspondent for the Christian Science Monitor who also wrote the TRB column in the New Republic. He was an old man who'd been around forever and made no pretense of being an objective reporter. He was an unabashed and respected liberal, proud of his principles and his integrity. He also had little use for people who tried to tell him what his ethics should be.

Strout told me that he had taken trips abroad that were sponsored by foundations and other institutions. Working for a shallow-pockets outfit like the Monitor, he said, he would never have been able to travel anywhere without such outside help.

I used to see Strout fairly regularly on Capitol Hill when we covered the same hearings. Of course, I knew who he was. He usually recognized me, but never remembered my name, although sometimes he would recall that I worked for The Milwaukee Journal, the great liberal dowager of the Midwest. He had a knack for never missing anything important, even when he dozed off. He'd snooze through some of the droning testimony at a hearing, yet he'd always snap to attention when something important or newsworthy came up. It was amazing.

At a hearing one day, his eyes popped open just as I happened to be looking at him. Not the least embarrassed, he looked at me and said, "You know, they used to call me veteran. Now they call me venerable. God, it's an infirmity to grow old."

THE STROUT EPISODE

Strout had run afoul of the Standing Committee just before I joined it. In a burst of ethical fervor, the committee—headed by Pulitzer-prize winner Bill Eaton of the Chicago Daily News—had voted for a new rule that forbade any member of the daily press gallery to appear for pay on programs sponsored by the government. It was directed specifically at a few correspondents, including Strout, who had participated in Voice of America programs.

Usually, the programs were in a press conference format. A government official, or member of Congress, would submit to questions by a group of reporters. They expressed no opinions, and simply asked questions as they would at any news conference. The programs were broadcast exclusively overseas. They were never heard in the U.S. For taking the time to participate, the reporters received $50.

Strout, who had appeared on some of the programs, was incensed when the Standing Committee passed the new rule. It was not the money; he was insulted that anyone would question his ethics or integrity over a small payment for something as innocuous as asking a few questions. He protested, and even wrote an article about the matter for The New York Times. It was all to no avail. The committee would not budge.

Nor would Strout. Because he refused to abide by the new rule, he was threatened with a loss of his press pass. But that was no problem. He simply went down the hall to the periodical press gallery, where he received a new pass by virtue of his position with the New Republic. The periodical gallery had no such rule.

I was immediately sympathetic to Strout's position. At a minimum, it seemed to me that the Standing Committee, in issuing credentials, functioned as an agent of the U.S. Congress. I did not believe that the Congress, or any of its agents, had the right to dictate the ethics of members of the press corps because that was a matter between the correspondent and his or her publication. A newspaper, as a private business, could enforce an ethics code on its employees and fire them if they didn't comply. On the other hand, for an agent of Congress to dictate ethics to an individual reporter, I believed, was a violation of the First Amendment.

Of course, a set of minimum basic rules had been laid out by Congress when it set up the correspondents' committees. These were mostly common-sense qualifications for members and prohibitions against lobbying or engaging in advertising. When they had been violated in the past, the Standing Committee had usually dealt with the miscreants on a case-by-case basis.

When I first sought to get the committee to repeal the "Strout rule," my motion failed for lack of a second. Later, a sympathetic Bandy gave me the second so we could discuss the issue, which we did. Then my motion failed on a 4-1 vote.

In 1978, however, a more enlightened—to my way of thinking—committee did revisit the issue and repealed the Strout rule. It remained off the books until 1986, when The Washington Post carried a brief item about correspondents appearing on Voice of America broadcasts. It was a bogus revelation about something that had been going on legally.

Members of the Standing Committee were scandalized. The committee asked the daily press gallery staff to research whether there was any prohibition of such egregious conduct. Somehow, along the way, somebody read the situation entirely backward, and the committee was informed that the Strout rule still existed, which it didn't.

Then the committee instructed Bob Petersen, the superintendent of the Senate Press Gallery, to investigate and get the names of the supposed miscreants who were appearing on the VOA broadcasts. He did, and the committee—over the signature of the chairman, Mike Shanahan, of McClatchy Newspapers—sent letters to the offenders' bureau chiefs, warning that they could lose their Capitol Hill press passes unless they ceased and desisted from their unethical actions.

When I heard what had happened, I laughed. But as ridiculous as it was, I didn't want to let it lie. So I wrote a hyperbolic letter to the Standing Committee, accusing it of McCarthyism in ordering Petersen to get the names of the alleged perpetrators, and the committee itself of libeling the correspondents by accusing them of violating a nonexistent rule.

That and protests from others forced the Standing Committee to conduct a hearing on the committee's actions. I tried to keep the hearing focused on the issue: that the committee had wrongly accused innocent gallery members. But the hearing wound up as a debate on the Strout rule itself.

In the end, instead of apologizing to the people it had wronged, the Standing Committee re-instituted the rule!

I threw up my hands and resolved never to get involved in Standing Committee affairs again. It reinforced my growing conviction that journalists, despite their standing as the Fourth Estate, should stick to reporting and writing because they are woefully incompetent when it comes to running anything of even passing importance.

14

PRESS CLUB DAYS

Though it has had its ups and downs, the National Press Club is the best and most successful of any press club in the world, and I was proud to be its president in 1978—even though I got there by stepping over a colleague who probably deserved it more than I.

I was first exposed to the club in 1965, when my wife Sharlene and I visited Washington to receive an award for a traffic safety story. Con Eklund, The Milwaukee Journal's bureau chief, took me to one of the NPC's famed newsmaker lunches. The speaker was Hubert Humphrey, the vice-president of the United States. The place was packed and I felt like a rube from the sticks, impressed and privileged to be in the same room with so lofty a figure.

Thirteen years later, I was the president of the Club. The second day after my inaugural party, which featured Vice-president Walter F. Mondale, and Wisconsin Sen. Gaylord Nelson as the master of ceremonies, I attended another jam-packed newsmaker lunch. This time, I ran the show and the speaker was President Anwar el-Sadat of Egypt, who was the biggest newsmaker in the world at that moment, having proposed peace with Israel and its prime minister, Menachem Begin.

It was a heady event. Every corner of the club's ballroom, every square inch of the balconies, was filled with spectators, to the point where the District of Columbia fire marshal threatened to shut down the event. In the audience, pleased and proud, was the editor of The Journal, Dick Leonard, who had been active himself in journalism organizations and understood that it was not a bad thing to have his own guy as the Press Club president, even though my productivity as one of his Washington reporters would suffer for a year.

Throughout my term, I stood at the podium more than 50 times with such world figures as Begin, President Carter, First Lady Rosalynn Carter, Mondale, King Hassan of Morocco, Prime Minister Morarji Desai of India, as well as other prime ministers and assorted famous people, including actors Peter O'Toole, Carol Channing and and Deborah Kerr, authors James Michener and Alex Haley, evangelist Billy Graham, Playboy magazine's Hugh Hefner, Washington Redskins coach Jack Pardee, and Vernon Jordan, the president of the Urban League who would later become even more famous as a close confidant of President Bill Clinton.

I was the smiling host, but credit for the stellar lineup of speakers was due to Joseph Slevin, a financial newsman who ran his own newsletter in the National Press Building and was my Speakers Committee chairman. As far as I could tell, there was no committee. Slevin did it all by himself, and I basically gave him carte blanche to invite anybody he saw fit. The only disagreement we had during the year was when former President Richard M. Nixon was suggested as a speaker, and Slevin balked, saying he didn't want a crook up there on the podium. Because Slevin had done such a great job, I acquiesced and Nixon was not invited. Slevin became the NPC president himself in 1981, and later we became unfortunately estranged when I helped engineer his ouster as president of the National Press Foundation.

When Carter spoke at the Press Club in March, 1978, the detailed planning was excruciating, and the normal format for a club luncheon had to be substantially altered to accommodate the president's 45-minute visit, including his 15-minute speech. After he spoke, I asked questions that had been submitted on cards by people in the audience, checking my watch constantly to keep to the agreed-upon schedule.

As I sorted through the questions, a note was passed to me from Rex Granum, a deputy press secretary, saying that because Carter's speech had run longer than expected, I could take an extra five or six minutes for questions. At almost the same time, another note arrived from Walt Wurfel, another deputy press secretary, saying we were running overtime.

I did the only thing that made sense. I sent Granum's note to Wurfel and took the extra six minutes.

URINE IN A BOTTLE?

Earlier, as the press club's vice-president in 1977, I presided at a lunch for Mary Martin, who had starred as Peter Pan on Broadway. When it came time to go to the ballroom, she took my hand and, like two kids, we skipped together down the hallway, me with a foolish grin on my face and she acting as if this were an everyday thing.

The most exasperating speakers had I had to deal with that year were India's Desai and Mangosuthu Gatsha Buthelezei, head of the Kwa Zulu nation in South Africa. Desai, who served as prime minister for two years between terms of Indira Ghandi, was 82 and didn't suffer fools—including me. It started with word from the Indian embassy that Desai required a special meal consisting of fruits and six peeled cloves of garlic. We were also told that there could be no alcohol in Desai's presence, and no smoking.

That was all fine, except one of the news magazines had reported that Desai, as part of his daily religious practices, drank his own urine. It caused some consternation and snickering at the reception before the lunch because, to comply with the ban on alcohol, the press club staff provided the bartenders with apple juice, served from unlabeled carafes. Quite a few guests declined a pre-lunch cocktail.

With his penchant for chewing garlic, Desai could practically clear a room with his breath. Anybody who got close soon backed off, like courtiers bowing before the king. At the lunch, he reinforced his secret weapon as he blithely chewed on the fruit and garlic cloves before standing up to speak.

Press club newsmaker lunches follow a longstanding ritual: reception from noon to 12:30, lunch from 12:30 to 1 p.m., introduction of the head table and the speaker, the speech, and a question session. Finished promptly at 2 p.m. Questions are written on cards by people in the audience and sorted by the club president, who presides. I always came prepared with my own set of questions, just in case the audience didn't come through.

There were plenty for Desai, but he dismissed a number of them with one-word answers. Once he turned from the microphone to me and said, "Who asks such a foolish question?" I cringed but soldiered on. Unfortunately, I ran out of questions, including all of my own, about 10 minutes before the program was scheduled to end. I had no choice. I gave Desai his certificate of appreciation and ended the program. As I walked off the dais with Desai, he asked why the Press Club had disrespected the prime minister of India by cutting the program short. I mumbled an apology and hot-footed it out of there.

Buthelezei posed a different problem. As the head of a black South African tribal organization more conservative than Nelson Mandela's African National Congress, he was working on compromises with the country's white rulers. His trip to the U.S. was his big shot at developing legitimacy. He was affable and friendly, and then proceeded to stand up and talk for about an hour and 15 minutes, well past the club's traditional 2 p.m. deadline—so established because Press Club speeches were carried live on National Public Radio.

By the time Buthelezei finished talking, the only people left in the club's ballroom were members of his entourage and several of the head table guests. By that time, the damage had been done, so I figured, what the hell. I asked him a couple of questions, thinking I could at least preserve the luncheon format. He went on for another 20 minutes or so.

I don't think I ever became blasé about so much exposure to famous people. I got used to it, but I don't think any of it impressed me as much as those early ones with Sadat and Humphrey.

Part of my job as host was to introduce the speakers at the newsmaker lunches. I hated long, dull introductions that essentially were recitations from official biographies, so I wrote my own. I sought to keep each introduction light and irreverent, and I tried to include a nugget about the speaker that would be news to the audience and also delight the speaker. My sources were the speaker's spouse, close friends and associates. It took a lot of work, though the introductions usually ran less than two double-spaced typewritten pages. But they went over well.

HAPPY, BARBARA AND PETER

An incident at the Press Club, in 1977 when I was the club vice president, taught me a lesson about how famous and rich people, and sometimes even intelligent ones, make assumptions about others. The occasion was a club lunch with Nelson Rockefeller, who had just finished his term as vice president after having been dumped by President Gerald Ford.

His ouster had happened prior to the Republican National Convention in 1976. Ford, the nation's only unelected president, faced a tough battle, which he ultimately lost, for re-election against Jimmy Carter, the Georgia peanut farmer and nuclear engineer. Rockefeller had been Ford's appointed vice-president, but was regarded as too liberal to satisfy the GOP's conservative wing. So the president dumped him in favor of Robert Dole, who 18 years later ran for the presidency against Bill Clinton.

But in 1976 Rockefeller was still the vice-president, and attended the convention in Kansas City, putting on a brave face and making the rounds in a last hurrah. The Journal wanted it covered, and assigned me to spend the day with him. In the story, I wrote, "Rockefeller is 68 now, and he is both a heartbeat and a light year away from the one job he wanted most."

Surprisingly, I was the only reporter in the Rockefeller entourage, which included his wife, Happy. Because I was in the trailing group, I spent a good deal of time with Mrs. Rockefeller, who helped me with names and other information. It was a lot of fun. We traveled to caucuses and other events, and wound up at a party hosted by Katharine Graham, the publisher of The Washington Post.

Among the guests was Barbara Walters, the television personality. I introduced myself and we chatted amiably. Later I wrote in a diary I kept at the time: "Spent the day with Rockefeller and had a good time. I was the only reporter with him. Happy very pleasant. Met a bunch of celebs, including Barb Walters, at Kay Graham lunch. Walters very pleasant and very sexy."

Eleven years later, at a Press Club dinner honoring ABC's David Brinkley with the club's Fourth Estate Award, I ran into Walters again. We chatted briefly, and I recalled that we had met in 1976 at the Katharine Graham party for Rockefeller. "Oh," she said. "Were we intimate?"

It was at that same 1987 dinner that I reinforced my impression that celebrities weren't necessarily pompous asses. At the reception, I encountered Peter Jennings, the ABC anchor. The previous year, my wife, Sharlene, and I had met Jennings at one of the cocktail parties following the Gridiron dinner, the most prestigious journalism event in Washington.

The Gridiron Club, founded in 1885, was an organization of leading newspaper journalists, including bureau chiefs, reporters, editors and columnists. Its one reason for being was to run an annual dinner where the club members, augmented by a few "limited" members with singing talent, lampooned politicians and government officials. The white-tie dinner, capped at about 600 persons, traditionally hosted prominent figures from the news media and entertainment, politics and government, including the president, vice-president, congressional leaders and members of the U.S. Supreme Court.

I was not yet a member, but attended many of the dinners over the years as a guest of either Con Eklund, whom I had replaced in The Journal's Washington bureau, and my partner, Jack Kole, who served as the Gridiron's president in its 100th anniversary year in 1985. In fact, I attended so many of the dinners in those years that some people thought I was a member. After Jack retired, I quietly got myself nominated and became a Gridiron member in 1991. I was proud of the fact that when I joined I knew every member of the club personally—something that has rarely happened in the years since. When I retired in 2000, I already had done the politicking to get my successor as bureau chief, Craig Gilbert, invited into the club to ensure continuity in the Gridiron for The Journal.

The Gridiron is an elite group, and would have even more famous members if it did not limit the membership. In a two-person bureau, I would have had no chance at membership if Jack had not taken his early retirement. For example, Robert Novak became a member, but not Rowland Evans. Jack Germond also was invited, but not his sidekick, Jules Witcover.

I was awed to be a member, along with people I liked and admired, like my close friend Art Wiese, Novak, Germond, Hedrick Smith of The New York Times and public television, Charles Lewis of Hearst Newspapers, David Broder of The Washington Post, Al Cromley of the Daily Oklahoman, Ann McFeatters of Scripps Howard, Albert Hunt of The Wall Street Journal, Georgie Anne Geyer of Universal Press Syndicate, Susan Page of USA TODAY, and, when the club later admitted television and magazine correspondents, Bob Schieffer of CBS News and Tim Russert of NBC.

Despite its exclusive air, the club is cordial and collegial. The unspoken assumption is that if an individual was good enough to get into the club, he or she is deserving of respect and even affection from then on, regardless of whether the person retires, leaves town or abandons the news business for public relations or other pursuits.

In my first Gridiron show, Media General's John Hall, the music chairman and later a friend and neighbor of mine, assigned to me a solo singing number, to the tune of "Twinkle, Twinkle Little Star"—obviously chosen to prevent me from screwing up the melody. It was the first time I had ever sung on stage before an audience—and my audience included the president of the United States. It was an auspicious if dubious debut.

There were usually several post-dinner cocktail parties to which Gridiron members brought spouses and other guests who had not been at the dinner. Sharlene, who did not enjoy cocktail parties, especially when she didn't know anyone, came anyway in 1986, and decided it was worth it because we met Jennings. She was a big fan. We made small talk with him for about five or ten minutes, then we all moved on.

Sharlene was floored when we encountered Jennings again about an hour later. "Hi, Sharlene," he said. She couldn't believe that he had remembered her name.

When I met Jennings at the 1987 Fourth Estate reception for Brinkley, I reminded him of that incident and told him how much he had impressed my wife. Then I had a flash of inspiration. Sharlene already had gone into the ballroom with Nanette Wiese to take her reserved seat at our table. I asked Jennings if he'd go up to her and address her by name, as if he still remembered her. He grinned and agreed.

We moved into the ballroom and I pointed her out. Not only did he go up and say hello, he went down on one knee, took her hand and said, "Sharlene, it's so good to see you again." It took her only seconds to tumble to the gag. She looked around and shouted, "Frank!" We all laughed and Jennings had proved himself a good sport. I had other encounters with him in later years—as seatmates on a military plane to Montgomery, Ala., where we both spoke at a media-military conference at the Air War College, and together at the head table at a National Press Foundation dinner—and found him as unpretentious as ever.

The lesson about how people, especially the famous who are insulated from the hoi polloi, came when Rockefeller spoke at the Press Club in 1977 after he had left the vice-presidency. Happy was with him, and she recognized me as "that nice young man" she had met at the 1976 GOP convention. But this setting was different, and our conversation soon lagged. Trying to keep things going, I made a comment about the suit she was wearing. I told her it was gorgeous and commented, "My wife likes things like that."

"Oh," she replied enthusiastically. "It's a Halston. Why don't you give me your address and I'll send him out to show her a few things."

Right. Maybe the designer Halston himself goes to the homes of Happy and her friends to show his megabucks creations, but to our tiny split foyer in Annandale, with no garage and the cracked concrete driveway? No way! It was an interesting insight. Happy simply assumed that the person she was talking to was somebody like herself.

I had a similar encounter once with Henry Kissinger, when he was the national security adviser to Nixon. We were at a cocktail party and unaccountably wound up talking to each other. I didn't know how to make conversation with the famous statesman, so I asked a reporter's questions, based on the current news, as if I'd been interviewing him. I don't believe I expressed a single thought or an opinion.

This went on for maybe 10 minutes or so; then Kissinger decided he had to move on. He shook my hand and said he had enjoyed our conversation. "It's rare to encounter somebody with your grasp of the issues," he said.

Kissinger had been listening to himself.

PRESS CLUB POLITICS

I started in National Press Club politics by accident. When I arrived in Washington in 1970, the club had ebbed in respect in the journalism community. It was perceived by many mainstream news people as having been taken over by flacks and hacks. The president in 1969 had been John W. (Pat) Heffernan, the respected Washington bureau chief of Reuters and the only foreigner to ever serve as president. But he was succeeded in 1970 by Michael Hudoba of Sports Afield Magazine and, in 1971, by Vernon R. Louviere of Nation's Business, the magazine of the U.S. Chamber of Commerce. Both were nice guys, but they were not regarded by mainstream journalists as legitimate newsmen.

It provoked a revolt, and reform forces in 1972 engineered the election of Warren Rogers, a onetime reporter for the New York Herald-Tribune, then with the Chicago Tribune-New York News Syndicate. He was succeeded by Donald R. Larrabee, who ran the Griffin-Larrabee News Bureau, serving newspapers in New England. I didn't know Larrabee then, but we became friends and close associates later on.

The pendulum swung back in 1974 with the election of Clyde W. LaMotte, who wrote for oil industry newsletters. He was forced to resign in mid-term because of a free trip he took to Iran, courtesy of the Shah, Mohammed Reza Pahlavi. The vice-president, Kenneth M. Scheibel, took over. Scheibel, who had his own small news bureau, was an unelected president, the only one in the Press Club's history.

After that, there came a string of presidents from prominent news organizations, starting with William Broom, the Ridder (later Knight

Ridder) News Bureau chief. He was followed by Robert Ames Alden of the Washington Post, who also was the founding president of the National Press Foundation, and Robert Farrell, the bureau chief for McGraw-Hill publications, my immediate predecessor.

I had been only peripherally involved in club operations. I served briefly on the membership committee, which considered applications for membership, and I was a member of the awards committee, where I chaired a subcommittee that developed an awards program for regional reporters. But I harbored no particular aspirations.

THE CAMPAIGN FOR WOMEN

I did get involved in one campaign early on: To admit women to membership. The Press Club had admitted its first black member back in 1954, but still held out against women. It was humiliating for women reporters (or "news hens" as Time Magazine had referred to them), who were forced to sit up in the balcony (the club's version of the back of the bus) whenever they wanted to cover one of the prestigious Press Club speakers.

Older members were bitterly opposed, but the tide had turned by 1971. Along with other young members, I helped beat the bushes to make certain that the pro forces were out in numbers at the annual membership meeting where the resolution came up, and we won. The club's male members voted to admit women.

Several of us grabbed two women reporters who were there covering the story—Lynn Langway of the Chicago Daily News and Elaine Shannon of The Tennessean in Nashville—and ushered them into the men's bar and bought them each a drink. The bartenders were startled, but complied as we loudly proclaimed the results of the membership meeting a few minutes before.

Alas, the dinosaurs recovered, if only briefly. One evening a few days later, my wife and I and another couple went down to the club for drinks and a sandwich. We walked into the men's bar and ordered drinks, but the bartender refused to serve us. He said the club's board of governors had not certified the vote by the membership. Some diehards die very hard. By 1982, we had our first woman president, Vivian Vahlberg of the Daily Oklahoman. I served as co-chairman of her inaugural party.

But six years earlier I had no particular ambition for holding office in the Press Club. I was dragooned into it. Clark Hoyt, a reporter for

Knight Ridder News Service who ultimately became one of its top executives before it was ignominiously sold to McClatchy, had spent a year in 1975 as financial secretary—the same year I was serving out my term on Capitol Hill as secretary of the Standing Committee of Correspondents. Financial secretary was the fifth officer, after the president, vice-president, secretary and treasurer. There also were seven board members, for a total of 12. The financial secretary's office didn't present much of a job—the main responsibility was dunning club members who hadn't paid their bills or dues—and the details were mainly handled by the paid staff anyway.

Hoyt said the club needed to continue its efforts to get more mainstream news people in offices and on the board. Nobody else was interested in financial secretary, so I would run unopposed. I agreed, but without much enthusiasm. (In 2007, Hoyt became the ombudsman for The New York Times).

There wasn't much going on in 1976. We had a new president, Jimmy Carter, and, like other presidents before him, he graciously accepted his free National Press Club membership card. The club president, Robert Ames Alden of the Washington Post, trooped over to the White House with other club officers to make the presentation and pose for pictures. Two years later, as president, I did the same thing.

Boring board meetings were enlivened somewhat by the presence of Don Byrne of Traffic World magazine, who usually fortified himself at the bar before displaying his often unreasonable belligerence at the meetings. Byrne eventually went on the wagon, stayed there and distinguished himself as the club president in 1983 during what may have been the most difficult year the club ever had—renovation of the Press Building, when the entire club, under construction, was a disaster zone.

TEXAS POLITICS LESSON

It was also a time when I learned something about Texas politics because I met a man who would become a lifelong friend. His name was Arthur E. F. Wiese Jr., the brash and talented young bureau chief for the Houston Post. He was 11 years my junior, and I have no idea why we connected so thoroughly, but we did. Like others of my close friends, we were opposites in many ways. I was a Wisconsin progressive, with a lower-case p because as a newsman I never affiliated with any political party or organization, and Art was a Texas Republican, which in some ways was more liberal than the Democrats there, but still conservative. Not surprisingly, we occasionally differed on issues that came before the Press Club board.

That's when I learned that Texans take their politics personally. In the traditional Wisconsin way, where opposing politicians could battle all day in the legislature and then go out for beers and dinner together in the evening, I usually could separate my emotions from the issues. So I was never particularly bothered if another Press Club board member voted on the other side.

Not Arthur. After one particularly intense board meeting, with a close vote on which we voted on opposite sides, he confronted me in a hallway after the meeting. His face red and looking as if he were about to explode, he demanded, "How could you do this to me?" I laughed, but he was serious, and stalked off. Fortunately, he was not a man to hold a grudge.

Another member of the board was the treasurer, Richard Maloy, the bureau chief for Thomson newspapers. He was a likeable guy, mild-mannered individually and in small groups who also could become acerbic in Press Club board meetings, especially when it came to the club's loosely-guarded finances. He had been on the board for some years, and it was common knowledge that had aspirations for the presidency.

In those days, there was a "ladder" to the presidency. You paid your dues by serving on the board, or as an officer, and then you ran for vice-president. If elected, you were virtually certain to be elected president the following year. Everybody expected Maloy to run for vice-president for 1977.

I had not given any thought to continuing in the club's leadership, until one day Sharlene and I were visiting our close friends in Annandale, Alvin and Dotty Fuchsman. Fitting nicely into the stereotype of the ambitious Jewish mother, Dotty asked me what my Press Club plans were. I replied that I had done my duty by serving as financial secretary, and didn't have any plans beyond that. She said it was ridiculous for me to get involved as an officer and not aspire to the top job.

I dismissed the idea initially, but it got me thinking and I decided to seek advice from Frank Holeman. As an associate editor of the New York Daily News, he had been the club president—its youngest ever—way back in 1956, and had played a leading role in 1954 in the club's admission of its first black member. In 1976, he ran the Washington

office of the Tire Industry Safety Council, an association of the major
U.S. tire manufacturers. His office was near The Milwaukee Journal's
on the seventh floor of the Press Building, and I had gotten to know
him fairly well.

Holeman, a tall, gangly and amiable man who laughed readily at
jokes, was trusted by everybody. He was regarded as one of the club's
premier historians and raconteurs, and an honest broker among fac-
tions. Once he left the news business, he never voted again in a Press
Club election. As a past president, he continued to have the franchise,
but never exercised it. He reveled in the fact that he had a fat expense
account from the tire industry, and he used it liberally to help the club
in whatever way he could. Many years later, after his death, the club's
main lounge was named for him.

EYE ON THE PRIZE

I invited Frank to lunch to discuss my future in press club politics. Of
course, at his insistence, it turned out to be at the upscale Three Con-
tinents restaurant in the Washington Hotel, a block from the Press
Club. And, of course, he insisted on paying. He was well aware of what
young regional reporters earned in Washington.

I told him about my conversation with Dotty Fuchsman, and how
I had been thinking about making a run for the presidency. The first
step, of course, would be to run for vice-president. In typical Holeman
fashion, he neither encouraged nor discouraged me. But he did tell me
what I would have to do if I decided to make the run. The first thing,
he said, would be to line up support among the club's past presidents,
whose endorsements would carry some votes. He also suggested that
I go out and campaign, and not ignore the foreign bureaus, especially
the Japanese, the largest foreign journalism contingent in town.

There were a number of Japanese news bureaus in the Press Building, all of which paid for Press Club memberships for their staffs. The
correspondents, whose spoken English was not very good because they
were rotated back to Japan every few years, had a reputation as vacuum
cleaners who ingested every piece of information in Washington that
related to Japan. They also enjoyed gathering at the Press Club bar at
the end of the work day for relaxation and conversation. For me, they
represented a substantial voting bloc.

I repeated my successful campaign a few years earlier for the Standing Committee of Correspondents. I visited every bureau in town,

handing out a simple, half-page flyer with my photograph and asking Press Club members to vote for me. They did.

I'm fairly certain I blindsided Dick Maloy. By the time he announced for the vice-presidency, I had already gotten the approval of my editor, Dick Leonard, lined up support among the past presidents and circulated my nominating petitions. I felt a bit guilty about denying him an office he deserved more than I did, based on his years of service in the club's leadership. But I was ambitious.

In some ways, it was a classic political campaign. Maloy focused on the issue of Press Club finances, putting out detailed position papers that argued for the club to engage competent outside management to stem losses and put the club on a sound financial footing. I, on the other hand, ran a bland campaign that basically said I was a nice guy who would work for a brighter future for the club. Without naming him, I said Maloy's drastic measures were premature.

In retrospect, I compared the election to the campaign of President Lyndon B. Johnson against Sen. Barry Goldwater in 1964. Goldwater took a hard line favoring military action against communism, with his most remembered slogan, "Extremism in the defense of liberty is no vice." Johnson, on the other hand, argued for moderation. He was re-elected in a landslide and later, in the Vietnam War, basically did what Goldwater had been advocating.

I did the same thing to Maloy. He was advocating specific courses of action which, while not particularly radical, were a recipe for substantial change. I was blandly asking club members to wait awhile and see if those measures would be necessary. And, as I half-expected, they were. The club eventually did what Maloy had advocated. But I got elected.

"Maloy took his loss very well," I wrote in my tiny diary. "I think we're still on good terms. It's nice being a winner. Called other winners to congratulate them. Pushing Von Bergen for chairman of the board of governors."

Drew Von Bergen, a reporter for United Press International, did get that position, then got on the ladder himself and served as president in 1980. As vice-president in 1977, I had persuaded my friend, Wiese, to become my running mate when I ran for the presidency. He did, and later succeeded me as president in 1979. The ladder system worked for them as it had for me. When I ran for president, I was unopposed.

It was an incredibly hectic year. Fortunately, with Dick Leonard as
editor of The Journal, and Jack Kole as my bureau chief, there were
few journalistic demands on my time. We had a two-person bureau,
a chief and an Indian as I used to describe it, and I was the Indian.
Jack took over and basically did all the coverage himself. I managed, at
most, to eke out one story and one column a week.

PAPER BOY AND PROSTITUTE

Despite my lofty status, I also worked as a newspaper delivery boy
during my presidential year. My sons, Matt and Joe, consecutively had
the Washington Post route in our neighborhood, and I helped them
out. I refused to drive the car, except on Sundays when the paper was
fat, but I was out every morning for about four years with a bag over
my shoulder, delivering papers on part of the route. Though it never
happened, I thought it would have made a fun feature story for a local
suburban newspaper: "National Press Club President Works as Carrier Boy for Washington Post."

Several years earlier, I had written in my diary, "Started 6:30 helping
Matt deliver papers, finished day covering State of Union. Guess that's
a compleat newspaperman."

The cool thing about being president of the National Press Club is
that you are regarded by the non-news community in Washington as
the representative of the press corps. So you temporarily become famous and sought-after within a small group of press-sensitive people.
It brought me and Sharlene invitations to the White House and foreign embassies, to receptions of associations and political organizations, as well as assorted entertainment events. And it brought me, for
the first and only time in my life, an offer of a prostitute.

The press counselor for the Iranian embassy paid a courtesy call on
me, as others did, shortly after my election. He was a furtive sort who
tended to avoid eye contact and seemed to be constantly wiping sweat
from his face. He offered his help and services, for which I simply expressed a noncommittal thanks. I treated him with reasonable courtesy, given the fact that he worked for the shah of Iran, Mohammed
Reza Pahlavi, whose regime had been part of the scandal that caused a
former press club president, Clyde LaMotte, to resign in mid-term.

One Friday afternoon, the shah's press counselor showed up at my
office with a young blonde woman in tow. I was working on a Sunday
story and was not happy to see him. Sweating profusely, he introduced

me to the woman, who was chewing gum and obviously bored. He told me she was a wonderful young lady who would be happy to do anything I wanted. And wasn't she beautiful?

Naïve as I was, it took several minutes to realize that he was offering me a prostitute. I didn't like him much in the first place, and the whole episode was distasteful, if not disgusting. He obsequiously backed out of the office, wiping the sweat off his face.

At the start of my presidential year, Sharlene and I looked forward to the social invitations, which included an East Room concert at the White House conducted by the National Symphony Orchestra's Mstislav Rostropovich, and a Kennedy Center concert by Nana Mouskouri, the Greek diva. We were especially excited about the embassy parties, believing that we would learn about other cultures—and especially get to sample their foods. No such luck. There was a tedious sameness about almost all of the parties. You never got to sit with your spouse, which irritated Sharlene because she had to make conversation with total strangers, often with accents that made them nearly impossible to understand.

Even the food and drink, and often the bartenders and waiters, were the same. All the embassies, it seemed, used Ridgewell's, the top Washington caterer. It got to the point where we'd walk in and the bartender would say, "The usual, sir?" The main course almost always was the same: Sliced beef tenderloin, with vegetables and potatoes, served from a silver tray by a waiter expertly wielding two large serving spoons as if they were chopsticks.

There was one notable exception, at the Embassy of Poland. At the time, Poland was still a Communist country, part of the Soviet-dominated Eastern bloc. The ambassador and his wife, who later defected, invited us and many others to a chamber opera—the only time I've ever attended one. The performers were famed Polish opera stars who had been touring the United States. They performed the opera in a large embassy ballroom, with no sets and accompanied by a string quartet.

After the performance, which I didn't understand but which was wonderful nonetheless, we all trooped into another large room for a buffet dinner that—hooray!—had been prepared by the embassy staff. It was all native Polish stuff, including pirogues and some other things I recognized from my youth in Milwaukee, but also bigos, a

Polish hunter's stew I had never heard about. It was so delicious I ate nothing else once I tasted it.

After dinner, the ambassador's wife, who was a former singer herself and a huge fan of Broadway musicals, gathered the opera singers around the piano, where they sang show tunes until the early morning hours. We stayed until the end.

Realizing that my limited fame was temporary, and as a regional reporter for Wisconsin with no need of international sources, I didn't make much of an attempt to maintain relationships with the embassy people I met during that year. But I wish I had, if only because it might have made subsequent foreign travel more interesting. For example, partly because of Sharlene's Greek heritage, we became friendly with a young man who was the first secretary at the Embassy of Greece.

GREECE AND ENGLAND

Coincidentally, we had planned a trip to Greece with our four kids, flying on passes that Sharlene had obtained because of her employment as a reservations agent with United Airlines. When the first secretary learned we were going, he asked if we would deliver a silver snuff box to a friend of his in Athens. We readily agreed.

In Athens, we called the friend, who turned out to be an admiral in the Greek Navy. He invited us out to dinner, we got a baby sitter at the hotel for the kids, and he sent a chauffeur-driven Mercedes-Benz to pick us up. We had cocktails with the admiral and his wife at their classically-furnished mansion, then went to dinner at what the admiral described as "a real Greek restaurant" at the foot of the Acropolis, a hole in the wall with delicious food, where they threw plates into the fireplace. It was the sort of memorable time that would never have happened except for the Press Club presidency.

Years earlier, in 1971, Sharlene and I had a similar experience in London that happened because of my Press Club membership. The club sponsored a charter flight there, but without any guided tours. We were on our own, and found a bed and breakfast in Russell Square for $10 a night. There was a pub across the way that was frequented by chauffeurs, and we had a rousing good time with them one evening.

I was hot to see the Press Club of London, then on Fleet Street. So we went there one evening, and I showed my National Press Club membership card to take advantage of the clubs' reciprocal privileges. Once again, we were an instant hit with the regulars at the bar, which included the club treasurer. But a problem soon developed. The club had a rule that, at 10 p.m., anyone who was not a member would have to leave. The rule was adopted to make certain there would be room in the bar for the flood of reporters and editors who made their way there after putting the newspapers to bed on Fleet Street.

Under the rule, I could stay, but Sharlene would have to leave. At that point, the club treasurer stood up on a table and moved to make Sharlene a temporary member for the evening. It passed by acclamation, and we spent another couple of happy hours with our new British friends. Unlike the pubs, the Press Club bar could stay open after 11 p.m.

Our friend the treasurer invited us back the next morning for what he said would be a memorable experience, which it was. He took us to St. Bride's Church, adjacent to the Press Club, where the rector took us on a tour of the church's basement charnel house. It consisted of room after room, lighted by bare bulbs hanging from ceiling cords, containing piles of skulls, arm and leg bones, pelvises, hands and other skeleton parts, all neatly sorted by type and stacked in bins constructed of unpainted wood.

The rector explained that there had not been enough cemetery space in the city in medieval times, so after a decent interval bones were dug up to free up space, and then the bones were stored in the churches, as we had witnessed there in St. Bride's.

CUBA NIGHT

Despite my lofty position later as Press Club president and my experiences as a newspaper reporter, I was still fairly naïve. I demonstrated that trait when I received a proposal from the head of the Cuban Interests Section in Washington, Ramon Sanchez-Parodi. He had come to introduce himself early in my term, and I was intrigued because I had been to Cuba on a reporting trip just before my inauguration. Now he came to me proposing a Cuba Night at the club

Nation and state nights were a staple of the club's entertainment activities. We even had a Wisconsin state night just before I finished my term as president. Typically, the event was arranged with input from the club and an embassy or a state society. Party-goers were rewarded with favors, food and drink. Some of these events were quite lavish before the club, embarrassed by the appearance of being on the take, asserted an ethics code and cut back on the largesse.

I told Sanchez-Parodi that I had no objection to a Cuba Night, as long as it focused on culture and not politics. Because of my reporting trip to Cuba, I was well aware of the trade embargo and the contentious relations between the U.S. and Cuba. He readily agreed.

It wasn't long before the proverbial stuff hit the fan. The Cuban-American community in Miami was outraged that the National Press Club would do an event that promoted Fidel Castro's Cuba, despite the fact that the club's entertainment committee had been ordered to avoid politics and strictly stick to Cuban history and culture. A delegation, representing a cross-section of Cuban exiles, from housewives to professional people, traveled from Miami to ask me to cancel the event. I refused, saying that to do so would, in itself, be a political statement.

The right wing jumped all over me. Lester Kinsolving, a tub-thumping pseudo-journalist and occasional clergyman who made a nuisance of himself at the White House, wrote a column excoriating me and the club, as did Reed Irvine, another rabid right-wing polemicist who headed Accuracy in Media, which purported to be a journalism criticism outfit but which ranted repeatedly about how the media supposedly promoted liberal causes to the detriment of conservative ideology.

The Cubans, who had promised to keep the event on the up and up, also blindsided me. Among other things, the Cuban Interests Section had committed to bring in a musical group from Havana. A brief item in the Record, the Press Club newsletter, announced the name of the group, "Giron."

Once again, I had footprints on my chest. Playa Giron, which means the Giron beach, is the Cuban name for the Bay of Pigs, the site of the abortive U.S. and Cuban expatriate invasion of Cuba in 1961. Furious, I called Sanchez-Parodi and said that I would cancel the event unless they kept the band home or changed its name, which I suspected had been cobbled up just for the party anyway. They chose the latter and Cuba Night was a resounding success, complete with Cuban cuisine, music and cigars. The cigars were OK because they were given away, not sold in violation of the embargo.

Overshadowing the embarrassment of Cuba Night was the Fourth Estate Award dinner, also in December, 1978. The award, the club's most prestigious, was given for a lifetime of achievement in journalism. Its first recipient, in 1973, was "the most trusted man in America,"

Walter Cronkite. In my presidential year, it went to the respected former editor of the Wall Street Journal, Vermont Royster.

Twenty-five years later, and for five years afterward, I served as chairman of the dinner. In 2003, the award went to NBC's Tom Brokaw; in 2004, when the recipient was my joke-swapping Gridiron Club buddy, columnist Bill Raspberry of the Washington Post; in 2005, when the award went to Austin Kiplinger of the Kiplinger Letters; in 2006, when the recipient was TV newsman and educator Marvin Kalb, and in 2007, when it came full circle with the award going to the former Wall Street Journal managing editor, Paul Steiger.

The Fourth Estate Dinner had evolved into one of the premier events of the National Press Club, black tie and all. With Royster as the recipient, we drew a who's who of prominent journalists, including James "Scotty" Reston of The New York Times, Herblock of the Washington Post, columnists James J. Kilpatrick and Elizabeth Drew, and Murray Gart, editor of the Washington Star.

A SLAM DUNK

If we were impressed, so was Royster. He took the occasion to deliver a thoughtful and hard-hitting speech about trust, responsibility and the relationship between the press and government, with words that ring true decades later. It was so timely and well-received that the National Press Foundation reprinted and widely distributed it.

After the event, Royster wrote me a letter, saying it had been overwhelming and an impressive affair. "I would like to add," he wrote, "that I hope the club will continue to grant its Fourth Estate Award on the same basis; that is, to those who in the opinion of the club have made a lifetime contribution to the press. It is that aspect of the Award that makes it special. It is for that reason that I will value it more than any other, including the Pulitzer."

Slam dunk for us. Royster already had won two Pulitzer prizes.

I also served as chairman of the Speakers Committee for two years starting with the administration of Dick Ryan in 2001. Unlike Slevin's one-man show back in 1978, I had a committee of about 30 Press Club members to help me out, and I got to sit at the head table next to the speakers.

One time the guest was Bud Selig, the Milwaukeean who was the commissioner of baseball. I spent some time chatting with his wife,

Sue, who told me: "He talks to himself all the time. He's crazy ... ever since he got so interested in politics. I can't stand it any more."

The biggest event for me, of course, was my inauguration as president of the Press Club in February. Traditionally, the club president actually assumes office at the club's annual membership meeting. That is followed by an inaugural party done strictly for fun.

My inaugural was a black-tie dinner, with its own array of principals. Wisconsin Sen. Gaylord Nelson, the father of Earth Day, agreed to be the master of ceremonies, and he persuaded his old friend, Vice-President Walter F. Mondale, formerly a senator from Minnesota, to attend and conduct my mock swearing-in. Rep. Dave Obey, the northern Wisconsin Democrat and a dedicated blues harp player, provided bluegrass entertainment with Scott Lilly on the guitar and John Holum on the banjo. Obey would later become chairman of the House Appropriations Committee, with Lilly as the committee's chief of staff, and Holum would eventually head the U.S. Arms Control Agency.

(Three years earlier, Obey and his group had played at my home in Annandale at the surprise 40th birthday party that Sharlene organized for me. Sitting in with his 12-string guitar was Sen. James Abourezk, a South Dakota Democrat and the only Arab-American in the U.S. Senate).

Besides Mondale, the Jimmy Carter White House also contributed Midge Costanza, the assistant to the president for public liaison, who did a hilarious stand-up comedy routine, and Jack Watson, another assistant to the president. Rep. William A. Steiger of Wisconsin was the only Republican on the program. Tragically, Steiger, one of the country's most promising young politicians, died at age 40 the following December of a heart attack brought on by diabetes.

The Steigers were close to the Bush family, and George H. W. Bush, who would become president, was godfather to Steiger's son, Billy. The congressman's wife, Janet, with her own special talents, went on to become chairman of the U.S. Postal Rate Commission and chairman of the Federal Trade Commission.

In the audience were other members of the Wisconsin congressional delegation, including Sen. William Proxmire, Rep. Clement J. Zablocki and Rep. Bob Kastenmeier. The entire power structure of The Journal Company also was in attendance—Board Chairman Donald Abert, President Thomas McCollow, Executive Senior Vice-President Warren Heyse, Senior Vice-President Joseph Flanagan, and all the top editors: Richard Leonard, editor; Joseph Shoquist, managing editor; Harry Hill and George Lockwood, assistant managing editors; Sig Gissler, editorial page editor, and, of course, my partner Jack Kole, the Washington bureau chief, who introduced Nelson and all of The Journal brass.

SCOOPED BY MY MOTHER

Also in attendance was Robert Wills, who had been the assistant city editor of The Journal when I started back in 1960 and rose to become editor of the Milwaukee Sentinel, the former Hearst paper that was purchased by The Journal Company in 1962.

My whole family came to the inaugural party, including my 67-year-old mother, Wanda. With only an 8th grade education, she had decided late in life that her kids' writing talent had to come from somewhere. So she took writing courses at a senior citizen center in Milwaukee and, with the help of my sister, Tessie, a high-school English teacher, actually sold stories to local weekly newspapers and the daily Sentinel, which was The Journal's competitor even though both papers were under the same employee ownership.

In a perverse bit of one-upmanship, Wills hired my mother to write a story about the inaugural. So the Sentinel carried a bigger story than my own paper and, because it was a morning paper, Ma scooped The Journal.

The party itself was one long laugh track from start to finish. I celebrated by smoking the giant Cohiba cigar that Fidel Castro had given to me when I had met him a few weeks earlier at the Palace of the Revolution in Havana.

Nelson set the tone by saying he would observe the number one rule of Jack Anderson, the muckraking national columnist: "If you can't say something good about someone, let's hear it."

Costanza summed up the evening when she said, "Frank, as you are being sworn in tonight as president of this organization, please keep in mind that the nation doesn't care. ... The good news, judging from the track record of this organization, is that no one will ever hear about it."

I wrote my own oath of office for Mondale, but he had the temerity to edit it and insert some of his own comments. It went this way:

"Frank Aukofer, now that you have proved, once and for all, that a vice president can amount to something, do you solemnly swear to discharge the duties of the presidency of the National Press Club, including the continuation—no matter what—of the 25 cent short beer?

"Will you promise to maintain a high quality flow of qualified speakers at Press Club events, especially Democrats from Minnesota and Wisconsin? Do you promise to continue to seek détente with, if not a total armed takeover of, the Washington Press Club, the Capital Press Club, and any and all such competitors?

"Do you swear to uphold the First Amendment to the Constitution, while ignoring the Second, Sixth any others that conflict with the freedom of the press? Do you solemnly pledge to never again have Senator Nelson as the emcee for a Press Club event, or to allow Obey to play his harmonica within the confines of this building?

"If you do so swear, by the authority vested in me by the tap room regulars, I pronounce you president of the National Press Club, so help us God."

THE EMPLOYEES CELEBRATE

There were two events of note toward the end of my presidency. One was Wisconsin night, patterned after the club's nation nights. It was a celebration of my home state and its culture, and an array of my news sources and other people I had covered were among the attendees. Sen. William Proxmire commented to the assembly that I was the only president in Washington history from the state of Wisconsin.

The evening put a hefty crimp in the Press Club's finances. Unknown to the management, but well known to anybody from the state, Wisconsin people drink brandy. Brandy with sweet white soda, brandy with ginger ale, brandy old-fashioneds, brandy Manhattans. Any alcoholic drink made with whiskey anywhere else is made with brandy in Wisconsin. I had done a story around that time about how Wisconsin was second in the nation in brandy consumption behind California, which had about five times the population.

There was one problem. The Press Club's bars did not stock the inexpensive California brands favored in Wisconsin. So the bartenders had no choice but to trot out the expensive Napoleon brandies from France, and even the Armanacs when that ran low. That made for some expensive brandy and sweet. The Wisconsin brandy drinkers never had it so good.

The other event was a party we ran for the club's employees. I discovered that I had some money left in my presidential expense account toward the end of the year, so I ordered an appreciation party for all the folks who propped up the club on a daily basis—the office workers, waiters, cooks, kitchen helpers and dishwashers.

We held it in the old East Lounge, and we did it up as fancy as any reception the club would host for anybody else. There were heavy hors d'oeuvres at a groaning center table, and an open bar. I rounded up past presidents and officers and members of the club's board of governors, who donned aprons to serve as waiters and bartenders, and we had recorded music for dancing.

Our guests dribbled in slowly, and at first they mostly sat shyly on the chairs lining the walls. So we went to them, asking if we could get them a drink or fix them plates of food. Soon the party was in full howl. One guy kept coming to the bar for his own special drink, scotch and vodka, which was blithely served by Rick Zimmerman of Cleveland's Plain Dealer. One of the club's assistant managers told me later that they found the guy passed out in a stairwell early the next morning.

The party was a rousing success. Even many years later, employees came up to me to comment about what a great time it was and what a wonderful thing I and the club had done. Some of those who told me that had not even worked for the club back then and obviously had not attended. The party had become part of the club lore in the back of the house.

There are many stories that contribute to the lore of the club, and one of its best raconteurs was the late Frank Holeman. There were only a few in which I was involved.

One had to do with the unofficial "Press Club within the club," open to every member but presided over on Saturday mornings by Kim Gregory, who worked for CBS News. On weekends, he was on call in case a big story broke, and had to be handy, but not in the office. So he spent most Saturday mornings in the Press Club bar, where he often treated the denizens to snacks and other food he and his wife prepared at home and brought in.

Once a year, Gregory set out the Alferd (sic) Packer Memorial Lunch. It honored a man who had been convicted of cannibalism in Colorado in 1874. The fare consisted mostly of uncooked food, including raw beef and onions, and Gregory decorated the bar with bones and other items honoring cannibalism.

In those days, Jack Kole and I alternated working Saturdays to finish up Sunday stories and be available in the bureau in case there was breaking news, so I often went up to the bar in the morning to sample Gregory's cornucopia.

Two of the regulars on Saturday mornings were Stan Weston and Tommy Sand, who worked for the Secretary of Agriculture. At the time, the Agriculture Department was building a new employee cafeteria in its main building in Southwest Washington.

When the sparkling new cafeteria opened, it featured a brass plaque over the entrance that said "Alferd Packer Memorial Grill." It stayed there for a few weeks until someone decided to find out what made Packer so prominent that a federal government cafeteria was named for him.

Needless to say, there was a huge outcry and a rib-tickling page-one story in the Washington Star, quoting officials as saying that it was outrageous—and even probably illegal—to name a federal cafeteria for a convicted cannibal. So one night, the plaque simply disappeared and the story went away.

Mysteriously, the plaque reappeared in the Press Club bar, where it remains to this day. Nobody ever confessed to anything, but we all had our suspicions. After Weston died, Gregory had his name engraved at the bottom of the plaque, under Packer's name.

On another occasion, The Journal's editor, Dick Leonard, who was active in international journalism organizations, brought a group of editors of Japanese newspapers to Washington for briefings and tours. Part of the agenda was a standup cocktail party at the Press Club, and Leonard invited me and other Washington-based journalists to come and mingle with the editors.

During the reception, one of the regulars from the club's bar, obviously tipsy, lurched into the room and wandered around. Several of us considered asking him to leave, but we didn't want to cause a scene, so we just kept an eye on him.

He soon learned that he was with a group of Japanese editors, and he had a point to make. He snagged one of them, a little guy at least a foot shorter than he was, and backed him up against a wall, then blearily demanded, "What is the best language to use for international business dealings?" Clearly, he expected the answer to be, "English."

Instead, the Japanese editor bowed slightly and said, "Ah, yes, sir, the language of your customer."

The barfly sputtered a few epithets and stalked out of the room.

15

THE NATIONAL PRESS BUILDING

This was the dream: We were going to build a brand-new National Press Building, combined with a 1,066-room convention hotel and 40,000 square feet of space for a new National Press Club. It would be so successful that the club would be awash in money, to the point where it likely would be able to eliminate dues for active members—that is, members of the working press, many of whom could not afford the existing dues.

Though it had been in the works for years, it all came to a head the year I was the Press Club's president. In those days, the president wore more than one hat. He was also president of the National Press Building Corp., which ran the Press Building. The club had built the building back in 1927, without having to put up any money, and it had survived, though shakily at times. In 1978, the club owned 77% of the building, which produced little or no revenue. But the club got 28,000 of its 35,000 square feet of space from its own corporation for $1 a year.

In the aftermath of the assassination of the Rev. Martin Luther King Jr. in 1968, Washington was struck by riots that terrified many of its residents, as well as those in the suburbs. People stopped going downtown, and office buildings lost tenants. The historic Willard Hotel, across 14th St. from the National Press Building, shut down and stood as a vacant monument to urban deterioration.

There was some talk of moving the Press Club to a new location to escape the blight. But the club had no money and no concrete plan, and the consensus was that the location was great—just a three-block walk to the White House—and that the area would eventually come back. So the membership sat back passively until the presidency of Warren Rogers in 1972, when the club assumed direct control of the Press Building. Though the club was the majority owner, the building had been run for many years by a tight cabal of trustees, who were effectively ousted after the 1970 president, Michael Hudoba, engineered a change to reduce trustees' terms from five years to one year.

That enabled the club to take over the building and start planning for the future.

The sparkplug in all this was Henry Keys, an Australian who had been a World War II war correspondent in the Pacific theater for the Sydney Australian and the Straits Times of Singapore. He had covered China for London's Daily Express, including Mao Tse-Tung's Long March in 1948. He also had interviewed the revered Indian mahatma, Mohandas K. Ghandi, whom he described privately as "a little brown man in a wretched dirty diaper." Eventually, Keys worked in London, and then Washington, as the foreign editor for United Press International, and became active in the Press Club. With the backing of Rogers and other Press Club leaders, Keys's National Press Building Committee produced a report in November, 1972, that outlined a new management scheme for the building.

More importantly, the report noted presciently that the Press Building likely would be included in nascent plans to redevelop Pennsylvania Avenue between the White House and the Capitol, which had become an alleyway of decrepit shops and souvenir stands—certainly not a great venue for the quadrennial presidential inaugural parade.

"Within the next year or so," Keys wrote in the 1972 report, "policy decisions will have to be taken as to the future of the building. For example, there is now a prospect that under the Pennsylvania Avenue Development scheme, the building may be subject to condemnation procedures, acquired and demolished.

"We have now to work at deciding our policy in regard to this. We cannot be taken by surprise. We must be ready to move swiftly to secure, build indeed, new premises should such come about.

"If we must rebuild, or if we decide at some not too distant date that we need a new building anyway, we will be better off than our forerunners (who) constructed the building up in 1927; this time we will have some cash invested in it to begin with. . . .

"The one thing of which we are convinced is that a Club such as ours cannot survive unless it has very substantial investments, returning substantial income."

That was Henry Keys. Though some dispute it, I and others, including my successor as president, Arthur E. F. Wiese Jr., and Bill Hickman, who served as president of the building corporation, argue fervently that Keys and his cadre saved the National Press Club. As this is written, the club is on a sound financial footing, with its future assured through at least 2070, when we will all be gone. It would not have happened without the vision, tenacity and politicking of Keys. Even though he failed—as did we all—to build the new National Press Building, the effort set in motion all of the subsequent harrowing financial schemes that resulted in the renovation of the old Press Building and the guarantee of a long-term home for the club.

I was blissfully unaware of all that had gone before when I was elected vice president of the Press Club for 1977. By then the club had hired Keys, who had retired from UPI, as the executive director of the building corporation, and he was hell bent on his crusade to give the club a "high-revenue-earning facility"—that is, a new building—to secure its future. When Keys retired a second time and moved back to Australia years later, the building corporation board gratefully voted him a generous pension, with benefits also for his wife, Maidie. Subsequent officers and board members, ignorant of what had happened, criticized the pension as a giveaway, and tried to rescind it.

Keys was a consummate conniver, but it had nothing to do with personal gain and everything to do with the Press Club. In a letter to Wiese in April, 1987, Keys wrote from retirement in Australia, "Oh, yes, I politicked all right, but never, ever against or for individuals, only for the project. … The objective of my efforts was always to make the club completely independent, with money the last of its concerns."

Wiese wrote back in October of that year: "When you took on this thankless task, we had a building and ground worth less than the debt against it. Now, through your Herculean efforts and those of Bill (Hickman), we could be about to realize a total package of income from the sale price, ground rent and club rental forgiveness worth well in excess of $300 million."

Ah, the project. Keys hooked up with John Portman, the famed architect and developer from Atlanta, who had designed Peachtree Plaza there, as well as the Renaissance Center in Detroit and many other hotel-based developments that invariably featured giant indoor atriums.

Portman came up with his grand plan, estimated to cost $165 million in 1978 dollars: the 1,066-room convention hotel, with the new National Press Building occupying the top five floors, a total of 600,000 square feet. The new Press Club would have 40,000 square feet of space facing south on the two top floors, with a view of the Washington Monument.

Naively, as it turned out, we thought it was a sure-fire plan. How could anybody resist such a grand new landmark in the nation's capital, housing the press corps and the finest press club in the world? At one point, the biggest question in our minds was whether the new hotel would be able to charge $100 a night for a room.

But we had not reckoned with the serpentine ways of Washington politics, both national and, more importantly, local. In retrospect, we were all babes in the woods, and especially me. None of us, including the officers and board members of the Press Club, as well as the members of the building corporation board, stood to gain a nickel in any of the financing and construction. Our only concern, reflecting Keys, was assuring the future of the Press Club, and I think we all believed that the purity of our motives would carry the day.

We had a couple of things going for us. My predecessor as club president, Bob Farrell, bureau chief for McGraw Hill, had gone to Capitol Hill to testify on behalf of the Pennsylvania Avenue Development Corporation, which was threatened with funding starvation. And Keys had developed a personal relationship with the corporation's chairman, Elwood Quesada, who looked favorably upon both the Press Club and the Portman project.

A big stumbling block was the National Theater, which would have to be torn down to accommodate the new building/hotel complex. The theater was housed in an old building that had no architectural merit and, though the theater board argued that it was the oldest continuously-operating theater in the country, it had been dark for many years early in the 20th century.

Keys made a number of proposals to the theater and its board, all of which were rejected. In one effort to satisfy the constantly vacillating theater representatives, Portman included a new, 1,500-seat theater in the complex, which would have been built at no cost to the theater board. Several of us met with Maurice Tobin, the theater board chairman, and the vice chairman, Gerson Nordlinger. To our surprise, they agreed to the plan and said they would take it to their board for approval.

We were elated. It was the last real obstacle, we thought, to getting the Portman project approved. Our elation was short-lived, however. Later that same day, Tobin and Nordlinger held a press conference to reject the proposal, accusing the Press Club once again of trying to kill the venerable old National Theater. We were dumbstruck.

At a subsequent meeting some time afterward, Nordlinger, a wealthy circulator in Washington's high society, took me aside. In a comment that would have been worthy of a seamy, class-conscious novel in the Old South, he said, "I want you to know that I am not a coward." I was too startled to even reply.

In addition to the duplicitous dithering of the theater representatives, we faced other formidable obstacles. At one point, they enlisted the iconic stage actress, Helen Hayes, to denounce the Press Club for trying to destroy the National Theater. And we didn't fare any better with our colleagues at The Washington Post, which pummeled us regularly in stories and editorials, saying at one point that our project was "a scheme that would send the theater packing." In fact, we had laid five separate proposals before the National Theater Board, all to include a new theater in the building or to help with a new or renovated theater near-by.

The most annoying thing about the Post's editorials was their inaccuracy. They were full of errors about the project and the Press Club's role in helping to redevelop Pennsylvania Avenue. As newsmen, we knew that trying to change the Post's mind would be fruitless, but we resolved to at least try to persuade the editorial writer to get the facts straight.

Farrell arranged a meeting at the Post with Philip Geyelin, the editorial page editor, and four of us trooped over there one day: Me, Farrell, Wiese and Keys. But Geyelin bailed out on us. When we arrived, he was nowhere to be seen, and we were directed to meet with the editorial writer who had been writing the damaging editorials.

Her name was Pat Matthews and, as we subsequently learned, she had no previous newspaper experience, having worked on the staff of a Maryland congressman before joining the Post. She also had what we regarded as a clear conflict of interest: She was a member of the Washington Society for the Performing Arts.

Nevertheless, we laid out our case, saying that we understood the editorial function of a newspaper and were not there to try to change the newspaper's stand on the National Theater issue. We only wanted to get the facts straight. Disagree with us, we said, but at least use accurate information. Here's the information. You can check it out yourself. We left satisfied that we had at least made our point.

When the next editorial appeared, it was as if we had never met with Ms. Matthews. It contained all of the same faulty information as all of the previous editorials. We were honestly shocked to be so blown off by this insensitive woman. I wrote her a long, bitter letter about her lack of journalistic ethics, but I never heard back.

It was a great lesson for me about bucking an institution as powerful and entrenched as the Washington Post. The old adage, "Never argue with someone who buys his ink by the barrel," even worked against kin in the news craft.

There were other obstacles. The Washington Fine Arts Commission didn't like the project. There were rumblings that J. Carter Brown, the director of the National Gallery of Art, was opposed, though he didn't say so publicly. A private group, "Don't Tear It Down," threatened to sue. The city government was indifferent. Portman said he had never encountered a situation with more layers of authority that needed to be persuaded or mollified.

Still, we thought we had a chance. Keys had Quesada on his side, though he met stubborn resistance from the Pennsylvania Avenue Development Corp.'s hired gun, executive director W. Anderson Barnes. I thought I was fairly persuasive with anybody I had an opportunity to buttonhole, but I was juggling my building corporation and Press Club duties with trying to pretend I was still a working reporter for The Milwaukee Journal.

When the PADC met to consider the project, both Portman and I testified. I thought it went well. But the vote was 6 to 3 against us, and that was that. We even lost one of the people I thought was most sympathetic to us—Joseph Danzansky, the chairman of the Giant food store chain.

It was another lesson for me. Most people in the news business are convinced that they can easily step into a public relations position and do a credible job. But PR is a specialized profession, and we had little expertise in it. We all thought that our project was a slam dunk on the merits. But if we had it to do over, I would have hired top lobbyists and public relations professionals to carry the arguments. Even then, given the Washington political maze, it might not have been enough.

In the end, the Press Club went through the trauma—for the second time—of renovating the press building in place. It was horrible. Most of us likened the building to "greater downtown Beirut," which at the time was being laid waste in Lebanon's civil war. I remember standing in the men's room on the seventh floor, looking up at a big hole that stretched all the way to the sky, with pieces of electrical cable and pipes hanging out of the blasted concrete.

For the Press Club, the most traumatic year was 1983, when the club quarters were transformed into a maze of temporary floors and plaster-board walls. Still, the club continued to operate under the presidency of Don Byrne. In earlier times, Byrne had been perhaps the most difficult of all board members, frequently arriving drunk at meetings and belligerently accusing other board members of all sorts of perceived infractions. But he got on the wagon during his presidency and guided the club through its most difficult year with good humor and calm. Like others before and since, Byrne rose to the task.

Through successive presidents and boards, Wiese and I, along with Hickman and others, did what we could to protect the reputation of Keys, who had gone back to rediscover Australia before both he and Maidie died. As with any organization that elects its officers and board members annually, the Press Club seldom has any institutional memory, which is why some of us have done our best to set the record straight.

16

THE NATIONAL PRESS FOUNDATION

By virtue of my standing as president of the Press Club and president of the National Press Building Corp., I also was a member of the board of the National Press Foundation. It had been organized as a nonprofit, tax-exempt entity back in 1976 by club members led by the president, Robert Ames Alden.

The club needed such a creature because it occasionally received bequests or other contributions and had no way to handle them. It came to a head when jazz icon Louis (Satchmo) Armstrong performed at the club's inauguration of Louisianan Vernon Louviere as president in 1971. The club produced and sold an LP album that was a live recording of the brief concert, with the proceeds earmarked for journalism scholarships. To dispense the scholarship money in an orderly, tax-free way, the club needed a tax-exempt channel.

The National Press Foundation's charter required its board of directors to have a majority of its members drawn from the officers and board members of the National Press Club. That assured Press Club control, but it also contributed to indecision and stagnation, aggravated by the fact that most of the board members thought they could run a successful foundation by relying solely on the news community.

Robert Farrell, the Washington bureau chief for McGraw-Hill/Business Week, was president of the Press Club in 1977, and took over the Foundation in 1978, the year I was the club president. I became a foundation board member. He served a second term in 1979, by which time it had become obvious that the foundation was in danger of losing its federal tax-exempt status because, essentially, it wasn't giving away money or doing much of anything. It also had to contend with strong-minded members of its own board like Earl Richert of Scripps Howard and Sol Taishoff of Broadcasting Magazine who believed that it was somehow sinful to take money from anybody but individuals or legitimate news organizations.

That was a prescription for starvation because newspapers tended to put their charitable contributions into their own communities, and the big chains and broadcasters were not noted for their empathy. Farrell and others of us recognized that. So Farrell appointed me as chairman of a special committee (I would later dub it "The Shit or Get off the Pot Committee") to recommend a new direction.

We came back with a report that had two major recommendations: Sever all ties with the Press Club, while retaining a historical affinity for it, and open board membership to non-news members, especially those who worked for other foundations or big corporations that could contribute money to our cause, which was to improve the quality of American journalism. The idea was to become an independent entity, raise a whole lot more money for as-yet-undetermined programs, and remove the dead weight that came with a constant stream of uninformed new board members drawn from the Press Club officers and governors, who were elected annually and seldom had any institutional memory.

LARRABEE TAKES OVER

Surprisingly, there was little opposition to the plan, and the NPF board adopted it. Then they elected me to succeed Farrell as president, starting in 1980. At the same time, the board asked Donald R. Larrabee to serve as the foundation's paid executive director, succeeding L. David LeRoy of U.S. News & World Report, who had served as the club president back in 1967.

Larrabee was another past president of the Press Club, a solid newsman and consummate gentleman who had owned and operated the Griffin-Larrabee News Service on Capitol Hill, which served newspapers in New England. Though the news service was mostly unknown outside of Washington, Larrabee seemed to know just about everybody of importance in town, and he had trained some fine young reporters who went on to major publications. Eventually, he left the news business to take over the Washington office of the State of Maine. The office, in the National Press Building, was staffed by Larrabee and his wife, Mary Beth. They literally worked in the smoke-filled room of political lore because Mary Beth was a heavy cigarette smoker and Don was fond of cigars. Tragically, years later Mary Beth came down with Alzheimer's disease, and Don affectionately nursed her until her death.

Larrabee was supposed to be paid $10,000 a year for his part-time efforts as the NPF's executive director. As far as I know, he never took a nickel, though he and Mary Beth worked harder than anybody to get our newly-chartered foundation up and running.

We had a lot of fun with it, especially because our new board mostly let the two of us do whatever we wanted. We figured we needed some big names to give the board some credibility. Don, as usual, had a contact who got us an appointment, and we went up to New York City and persuaded Walter Cronkite, "the most trusted man in America," to become a member of our board. Though he never participated, his name was pure gold, and he continues on the board to this day.

Without much money, we put up a great front, dreaming up grants and programs to demonstrate that the foundation was actively promoting quality journalism. Borrowing from an old joke, I called it the white Cadillac school of philanthropy, figuring if we drove a white Cadillac and wore a snappy white suit, nobody would know how poor we were.

Among other things, we helped fund a how-to book for regional reporters to cover Washington, and another on jailhouse journalism. We established a program to send working news people to Mexico to study Spanish (an idea that came after I went there myself to try to learn the language). And we established the Center for Journalistic Achievement in the National Press Building.

The center was nothing but a few exhibits in what once had been a dress shop on F St. It came at a time when the National Press Building Corp., having lost its bid to build a new press building and convention hotel, was in the process of renovating the old Press Building. The rejection of the club's grand plan, among the biggest disappointments in its history, came in 1978, when I was president. The Pennsylvania Avenue Development Corp. rejected our bid in favor of another, less ambitious developer.

We had all these simultaneous responsibilities. While I was president of the Press Club, I was also chairman of the National Press Building board of directors. Later, I was still a member of that board while I was president of the National Press Foundation.

THE JOURNALISM CENTER

During the run-up to the renovation of the old press building, Henry Keys, the building corporation's executive director, learned that he would have the dress shop on F St. vacant for about a year. That would not do. Boarded up stores are not much help when you're trying to attract investors and tenants—especially during a renovation.

So Keys offered the empty premises to the Foundation, and Larrabee and I blithely accepted. We named it the Center for Journalistic Achievement and went out to strong-arm the journalism community to give the center some semblance of respectability. We designed a logo for the foundation, which consisted of the NPF initials, upside-down and backwards, as a typesetter would see them. That was my doing; my old trade as a hot-type compositor was near death, though not world-wide, and I wanted to preserve the memory. The logo survived until 2007, when the foundation killed it after I left the board.

Our biggest coup was Larrabee's discovery of a working Intertype machine, which the Baltimore News-American not only donated, but also agreed to ship the multi-ton monster to our center in Washington. I was thrilled. It was just like one of the typesetting machines I had operated as an apprentice and journeyman compositor back in the 1950s in Milwaukee.

We never did fire it up. But we did get it installed as our centerpiece display in the center, and it looked wonderful. Larrabee learned that Cronkite was going to be in town, and we invited him over. We got great photographs of him sitting at the Intertype machine in our nifty Center for Journalistic Achievement.

There were other displays as well, from the local newspapers and news magazines, so that the center actually looked something like a room in a museum. We offered the facilities to journalism organizations for meetings and other events, and a few actually were held. We had free rent and free utilities, courtesy of Keys and the building corporation, and were convinced the foundation was on its way. Unfortunately, the center was grossly underutilized, and it died when the renovations crept to that quarter of the building.

I don't know what ever happened to the Intertype. I wish I'd paid attention and figured out a way to store it somewhere. It was in actual working condition, and would have been a far better addition years later to The Freedom Forum's Newseum, which obtained and displayed a real clunker of an old Linotype machine that sat there forlornly, with parts missing.

I spent five years as the Foundation's president and, after we restructured, its chairman. We had some successes, particularly the Business Beat. It happened after I put my oldest and best friend, Ray Enderle, on the board. A Marquette journalism graduate and onetime newsman who had worked on the Wall Street Journal and the Philadelphia Bulletin, he was the corporate communications manager for the Sun Oil Co. in Philadelphia. Coincidentally, he had known Larrabee years before when Larrabee provided Washington news to the New Bedford (Mass.) Standard-Times and Enderle was a reporter there.

We plotted to devise something that would be acceptable to the foundation's board and also extract some money from Sun Oil. At the time, few newspapers had anything resembling good coverage of business and economics, and one of the big gripes in corporate America was what the executives saw as journalistic incompetence in covering their issues. There were exceptions, of course, like the Wall Street Journal and New York Times, but for the most part papers were still back in the era of the "markets desk."

A good way to get some bang for the buck, we figured, was to get at the source. So we devised conferences on business and economic news reporting aimed at journalism professors and deans, the idea being to get them to establish courses and perhaps even curricula back at their institutions.

Ultimately, we held four conferences—three regional and one national—at Princeton University, the University of California at Berkeley, the University of Missouri and in Asheville, N.C. All of them were designed and operated by Enderle's crack staff members, who were experts in running fast-paced and interesting conferences. We brought in big-name reporters and editors from USA TODAY, The Wall Street Journal, The New York Times, Forbes Magazine and other top publications. They dispensed their wisdom to a total of about 110 professors and deans that we invited in from colleges and universities all over the country.

Though we had no way to measure our success, some of the participants went back home and established business and economics reporting courses. I think we also had an impact on the news atmosphere because in the succeeding years, business news went through a revolution and became, at many publications, as important as any of the news sections of the papers.

There were disappointments, too. Some of the professors and deans griped that they had to share hotel rooms (two to a room). Others displayed utter incompetence. They didn't even keep up with the news. Others couldn't write and, worse, couldn't even spell. A few simply blew off the conference sessions and went touring or treated the whole event as a vacation.

Overall, however, the conferences succeeded in helping create an awareness of the importance of quality reporting of economics and business news. Throughout, Sun Oil—because of Enderle's understanding of the journalism community—kept a low profile. Its only reward was a small italic line in the Business Beat programs saying it had sponsored the conferences. We gave one of our more prestigious awards, for distinguished contributions to journalism, to Theodore Burtis, Sun's chairman.

OUR BANKER BUDDY

The award, which also went to Larrabee and Leo Bernstein before the board decided to use it for big-name journalists as part of our fund-raising efforts, was presented at our fledgling annual awards dinner. I had mentioned the possibility of a big dinner several times, and we had kicked it around some, but it didn't jell until Bernstein offered it as his own idea.

Leo was a piece of work. A banker and financier who had his hand in all sorts of ventures, he had wealth, contacts and only one big flaw: he loved journalism and members of the press corps. At one point in the National Press Club's naïve and bumbling efforts to improve its financial situation, he had personally signed a promissory note for several hundred thousand dollars to keep the club afloat. He was a natural for membership on the Press Foundation board when we detached it from the club.

Leo had properties everywhere, it seemed. He owned the longest continuously-operating inn in the United States in Middletown, Va., at the end of I-66, and he was the only Jewish member of the local Methodist church board. He also owned an antique emporium and a couple of hotels in Strasburg, Va. He furnished his hotels and inns with antiques, all of which were for sale. For many years, he played host to the foundation board members and their spouses at the NPF's annual meeting in Middletown, Strasburg and at a modern motel he also owned in Luray, Va.

At a board meeting at the Women's National Bank—yep, another Bernstein venture—Leo suddenly blurted out, "Why don't we have a big annual fund-raising dinner?" His excitement was infectious and soon the whole board was persuaded. The idea had instant appeal because everybody knew that Leo knew a lot of people with money, who could be persuaded to part with some of it for a fancy, black-tie event.

We held our first awards dinner in 1983, with our first big award. It was named for Sol Taishoff, the founder of Broadcasting Magazine, who had been a member of our board. Sol was a crusty, instantly likeable old guy with a mischievous sense of humor. After he died, we put his son, Larry, on the board. He was a dim light compared to his father, but he supported the foundation, endowed the Taishoff award, and we had to put him at the head table for virtually every awards dinner for many years. He died in 2006.

We gave the first Sol Taishoff award to Ted Koppel of ABC News and, as the foundation's chairman, I was the master of ceremonies and sat next to him at the head table. My biggest coup was persuading Koppel to donate $2,500 of the $5,000 Taishoff prize money back to the foundation. He would have given it all back, but wanted to send half of it to an ABC fund named for the late Frank Reynolds, an ABC newsman.

The next year we gave the Taishoff award to John Chancellor of NBC News, and again I was the master of ceremonies and sat next to him. Slyly, I thought, I mentioned in our conversation at the head table that Koppel had donated some of his prize money back to the foundation and the rest to the Frank Reynolds fund.

"I can't," Chancellor said. "My wife's already spent it."

With only the Taishoff award as our centerpiece, we were having trouble getting print news organizations to buy tables at the dinner. It came to a head in a conversation I had with Dan Thomasson, the opinionated and profane Washington editor for Scripps Howard News Service. "Why should I support a TV dinner?" he growled.

EDITOR OF THE YEAR

So we invented a print award, Editor of the Year. In its first year, 1985, it went to Bill Dwyre, the sports editor of the Los Angeles Times. For me, it was particularly gratifying because Dwyre had been the sports editor of The Milwaukee Journal before he decamped to the City of Angels. The award was well deserved. Dwyre had led a team of more than 200 reporters and editors to publish large special sections every day throughout the 1984 Olympic Games. It was an astonishing journalistic feat.

In introducing Bill at the awards dinner, I recalled that the last time he had covered the Olympics was as a Milwaukee Journal reporter in 1976, in Montreal. "And then he did it all by himself," I said.

Those first couple of years, we gave the Distinguished Contributions to Journalism Awards to our own people—to Bernstein and Larrabee, as well as Burtis. But we switched, beginning in 1986. Always on the lookout for ways to enhance the dinner and raise more money, the board decided to devote the award to major journalism figures as a way to boost attendance.

John J. Johnson, founder of the Johnson Publishing Co. in Chicago (Ebony, Jet), was the first recipient. In later years, the award went to such journalism stars as A. M. Rosenthal of The New York Times, Fred W. Friendly of Columbia University, Eugene L. Roberts Jr. of the Philadelphia Inquirer, Robert and Nancy Maynard of the Oakland Tribune, John Seigenthaler of The Tennessean in Nashville, media Atty. Richard M. Schmidt Jr., David S. Broder of The Washington Post, Nat Hentoff of The Village Voice, William Safire of The New York Times, advice columnists Ann Landers and Abigail Van Buren, columnist Carl Rowan, cartoonist Herb Block, The Freedom Forum's Allen H. Neuharth, reporter and columnist Helen Thomas of Hearst Newspapers, Katharine Graham of The Washington Post (posthumously), Eugene Patterson, editor emeritus of the St. Petersburg Times; Benjamin Bradlee, the famed Watergate executive editor of The Washington Post; investigative reporter Seymour Hersh, then of the New Yorker; syndicated columnist Jack Germond of the Baltimore Sun, and beloved humor columnist Art Buchwald.

The Editor of the Year Award sometimes went to an editor for lifetime achievement; other times, it was for outstanding work in the face of adversity or a huge story. For Mike Pride, it was the Concord Monitor's coverage of the Challenger shuttle explosion and the death of Astronaut Christa McAuliffe, and for Mike Jacobs it was the heroic effort to keep the Grand Forks Herald publishing after it was inundated by a flood. For Ed Kelley, it was The Daily Oklahoman's coverage of the 1995 bombing of the federal building in Oklahoma City that killed 168 people and wounded 500 more, and ultimately sent terrorist bomber Timothy McVeigh to the death chamber.

Other Editors of the Year included John C. Quinn, USA TODAY; Richard A. Oppel, The Charlotte Observer; N. Christian Anderson, The Orange County Register; Norman Pearlstine, The Wall Street

Journal; Janet Chusmir, The Miami Herald; Burl Osborne, The Dallas Morning News; Tina Brown, The New Yorker Magazine; Geneva Overholser, The Des Moines Register; Shelby Coffey III, The Los Angeles Times; Jim Amoss, The New Orleans Times-Picayune; John Carroll, The Baltimore Sun; James P. Willse, The Star-Ledger of Newark; Howard A. Tyner, The Chicago Tribune; Paul E. Steiger, The Wall Street Journal; Howell Raines, The New York Times; Sandra Mims Rowe, The Oregonian; Martin Baron, The Boston Globe; Roy Royhab, the Blade, and David Remnick, The New Yorker.

Steiger was not present for his award because of the kidnapping and murder by terrorists of one of his reporters, Daniel Pearl. The dinner turned into a tribute to Pearl and other reporters who put their lives on the line to cover stories. As I was leaving, I bumped into Howell Raines, the executive editor of The New York Times, who commented that it had been an inspirational evening. Raines himself received the Editor of the Year Award the next year, in 2003. Fortunately for him, it came before the scandal that tarnished The Times and resulted in Raines's resignation over story fabrications by a young African-American reporter, Jayson Blair.

After Koppel and Chancellor, the Taishoff Award went to a glittering array of famous broadcast personalities: Don Hewitt of "60 Minutes" at CBS; Robert MacNeil and Jim Lehrer of the News Hour on public television; Ted Turner of CNN; Brian P. Lamb of C-SPAN; David Brinkley of ABC; Roone Arledge of ABC News; Ken Burns, who produced the memorable Civil War series on public TV; Ed Bradley of CBS; Barbara Walters of ABC; Bernard Shaw of CNN; Jane Pauley of NBC; Dan Rather of CBS; Sam Donaldson of ABC; Nina Totenberg of National Public Radio; Judy Woodruff of CNN; Peter Jennings of ABC; Bob Schieffer of CBS; Cokie Roberts of ABC; Brit Hume of Fox News; Tim Russert of NBC News; Charles Osgood of CBS News, and Gwen Ifill of PBS.

At the Jennings dinner in 2001, the NPF's leaders decided to seat me at the head table between Jennings and Donaldson—because of my longevity on the board, I supposed. I couldn't think of anything special I had done to deserve the honor, and my queries brought mostly vague responses. In any case, I had a good time. The three of us had just gotten into a discussion of what sort of work we might want to do instead of what we were doing. Donaldson confided that he'd always had a hankering to be a classical music critic for a newspaper. Before we could pry something out of Jennings, we were interrupted by well-wishers coming up to the head table and never did get an answer out of him.

THE HOLEMAN DICTUM

The foundation's early years were not without some bitterness and heartache. In my previous iterations as president of the Press Club and the Press Building Corp., I had learned a lot about working with boards of directors. Mainly, I followed the Frank Holeman dictum. Frank, who worked for a time as a volunteer with the NPF and earlier had advised me about Press Club politics, was the youngest president of the National Press Club back in 1956, when he was with the New York Daily News. When I first met him in 1970, he had gone into public relations and lobbying as the head of the Washington office of the Tire Industry Safety Council.

Frank was tall, maybe 6 feet 8 inches, and he had an ambling, har-rumphing manner about him, but always with a grin or a joke. He'd buy a drink at the drop of an excuse, and was personally fond of a Gibson straight up—essentially a gin martini with tiny onions instead of olives. The drink became known around the club as a "Holeman."

Over the years, Holeman had become the one of the most respected former presidents of the club—along with Larrabee and John Cosgrove. He was a mentor to seemingly everybody, including myself. He refused to vote in any club election, even though he had that right in perpetuity as a past president, and he was always available to mediate any dispute or help solve any problem. Sometimes he took sides, but in such a gentle and unassuming fashion that he never angered or alienated anybody.

Holeman also was a master at getting things done. He had an uncanny knack for quietly lining up support for whatever was needed—including opening the club to women members—so that the vote at the board or membership meeting usually was a foregone conclusion, despite what bitter debate might precede it. In the club, he told me one time, "You never want to let democracy run rampant." He was only half kidding.

I was mostly successful in following the Holeman dictum at the club, on the building corporation board with the impish Henry Keys, and at the foundation, with one exception. I was not able to prevent Joseph Slevin from assuming the title of president of the foundation.

At the outset, I was an enthusiastic supporter. Slevin was a handsome, dignified, respected and well-dressed newsman who ran his own newsletter, the Daily Bond Buyer, out of an office in the Press Building. He had an air of class and sophistication—and a hint of arrogance—about him, appearing more like a successful banker than a reporter. When I was president of the Press Club in 1978, he took on the chairmanship of the Speakers Committee—arguably the second most-important position in the club, and did an incredible job at it.

With the National Press Foundation growing, Larrabee's part-time job as executive director was getting to be a burden, and we all decided that the best thing would be to have a full-time staff director. Slevin, by then a board member by virtue of having served as Press Club president in 1981, was an immediate and popular candidate, but he had two conditions: He wanted to continue publishing his newsletter, and he wanted the title of president.

The idea of him continuing as a part-time journalist while running the foundation's operations had a lot of appeal because we all believed that it would enhance his credibility both inside and outside the journalism community. The title was something else. I was the president and had no problem with having my title switched to chairman. But I had detected in Slevin a tendency toward self-aggrandizement. I had a nagging fear that he would become its public face and convert the National Press Foundation into the "Joe Slevin National Press Foundation."

When the board hired Slevin, I was able to temporarily put off the question of his title, and he started as executive director. But he eventually wore the board down, and the members voted—with only a few of us in dissent—to give him the title. It was one of the few battles I ever lost while operating under the Holeman dictum.

My fears were validated. Slevin became increasingly arrogant and disdainful of the board. He started running the foundation as he had the Speakers Committee when I was president. It was a one-man show, and I soon concluded that he was more interested in attending receptions and events as the president of the foundation than in fund raising and developing ideas and programs for the board. So along with a few others on the board, including my good friend, Art Wiese, I started a quiet campaign to oust Slevin.

It was a tough sell. Most of the board members were not as close to the situation as I was, and they didn't share my concerns about Slevin's conduct. But I kept plugging away, and the end came at a board meeting where board members expressed concern about several initiatives Slevin had taken without consulting the board, as well as ignoring some of the board's wishes. Arrogantly, I thought, Slevin said he was doing his job as he saw it and was not required to consult the board on every move.

Bernie Goodrich, one of the board members who had supported Slevin, was astounded, and said so. Bernie was a one-time Washington Star reporter who had made a solid career as one of the top public relations men in Washington, in a variety of jobs. I had put him on the board because he was respected in both the journalism and public relations communities, and he had contacts everywhere.

When Bernie turned on Slevin, it was all over. He carried wavering board members, who now decided that Slevin had become highhanded in his relations with the board. We voted to ask him for his resignation—in effect, firing him. I had mixed feelings about the entire exercise. I had a lot of respect for Joe; he was a past president of the Press Club, and he had done a great job for me as Speakers chairman. But I also firmly believed that the National Press Foundation should not become a personality-driven organization. For many years, Slevin treated me as if I were invisible, never speaking to me. But without mentioning anything that had gone before, we reconciled in a pleasant conversation in 2004.

He even attended one of our so-called Long Gray Line lunches. Years before, wielding his fat expense account, Holeman had invited groups of Press Club past presidents to lunch with the immediate past president, to welcome him or her to "the long gray line." After Holeman's death, several of us re-instituted the practice, and I later took it over. At some of our lunches, we had as many as 25 past presidents. Slevin died in 2005, and I spoke at his memorial service at the press club without mentioning our rift.

Over the years, the NPF grew in stature and net worth, and it absorbed the old Washington Journalism Center, which for many years sponsored in-career training conferences for journalists. That brought Austin Kiplinger into the fold because he and the Kiplinger publications, founded by his father, had been solid supporters of the center. The orientation of the NPF gradually moved to encompass the mission of the center, and the foundation's distinguished contributions to journalism award was re-named for Austin's father. In 2005, Austin received the National Press Club's Fourth Estate Award for a lifetime of contributions to journalism.

One of our early and enthusiastic supporters was Joseph L. Allbritton, a Texan who at various times owned the Washington Star, the Riggs National Bank and the WJLA television station, channel 7. We put George Beveridge Jr., the editorial page editor of the Star, on the board and, after his death, named the Editor of the Year Award for him. Many years later, after I left the board, I was disappointed when the foundation decided to rename it for Benjamin C. Bradlee, The Washington Post's famed Watergate editor. But I understood. Bradlee was a better draw for raising money.

Today, the National Press Foundation is a thriving nonprofit foundation that works to improve the quality of journalism not only in America, but world-wide. Though I likely would have done some things differently, I am proud of it. My only regret is that, with its big-name board of directors, it has drifted away from its parent, the National Press Club, and the two have sometimes been at odds. I've said on a number of occasions, only half jokingly, that it has reached the stratospheric point where it likely would not name either Larrabee or me to the board of directors.

THE CAR COLUMNIST

Ibecame a car nut in 1960, about the time I started as reporter. That led to a career-long sideline of writing about automobiles, which stretched into retirement. What triggered it was my clunky 1957 Ford. I had bought it new, on credit, while I was in college and working as a compositor. It was a gray two-door Custom, the bottom of the line, with a six-cylinder engine, three-speed column shift and no options except an AM radio. It cost $2,350.

But it was a new car, and I was happy with it despite some feelings of guilt because my father, then 47 and only five years away from dying, had never owned a new car in his life. We always had clunkers, and the one rare time when Pop managed to find a decent used car, a 1946 Pontiac, my brother John wrecked it. I once loaned my Ford to my dad for a brief vacation trip, one of the few he and my mother ever made.

But by the time the summer of 1960 rolled around, my Ford was a clunker, too. In retrospect, it was probably something fairly simple, like shock absorber bushings, but the car clanked and rattled every time I hit a bump. It drove me crazy. So I went looking.

I knew Volkswagens were sturdy cars. A close friend in college, John Doyle, had a 1957 model, and it had never given him any trouble. But I was more intrigued by the Saab 93 from Sweden. The Saab had front-wheel drive at a time when all American cars had rear drive, but it also was small and economical. Power came from a three-cylinder, two-cycle engine—you had to add oil to the gasoline, just like on a lawn mower.

The only Saab dealership in town was the Lee Garage. George Pritzl was the owner, salesman, service manager and likely even the chief window washer. He was an affable, big man, maybe 250 pounds, and when he jumped up and sat on the top of the open driver's door to demonstrate the Saab's safety and strength, I was hooked.

The 93F cost just over $2,000 with the German Blaupunkt AM radio that replaced the glove compartment because there was no place else to put it. That was a couple of hundred dollars more than a VW

Beetle, but it was cool and a more useful car, with a large trunk that opened into the back seat area if you removed the rear seatback.

On the early August night of my bachelor party at an inner city tavern my father frequented, Sharlene drove me there in the Saab and dropped me off. It was raining hard. A few minutes later, she showed up at the party, wet and miserable. She had gotten only a few blocks when another car hit the Saab at one of those residential intersections where there are no stop signs.

We were only a couple of days from our wedding on Aug. 6, 1960, and had planned a honeymoon on Cape Cod and a trip to New Bedford, Mass., where I was to be best man at the wedding of my best friend, Ray Enderle, to Denise Cormier.

We had the car towed to the Lee Garage, where the next day Pritzl ascertained that the only thing damaged in the collision was the left front fender. He didn't have a white left front fender in his parts inventory, so he took one off a brand-new car that had just come in and installed it on my car in time for our wedding. Years later, when the engine quit at about 50,000 miles, he installed a new one for $200, with no labor charges. So who says all car dealers are charlatans and crooks?

At The Journal as a rookie reporter, I was so eager I was constantly volunteering to do anything and everything. If I had a couple of hours or an afternoon with nothing to do—as often happened on a p.m. newspaper—I would volunteer to work on the local copy desk, editing stories and writing headlines. Or I'd see if anybody needed a feature story done.

I wrote my first automobile feature in 1961—a roundup of the British sports cars available in the United States—and soon became typecast. That was typical at The Journal in those days. If you wrote a big takeout or a series on a given topic, you became the expert—and sometimes even the beat reporter—for that area. One of my chores became writing the regular stories we carried on local and state automobile sales. They weren't bad—a lot of statistical stuff—but I was happy to do anything.

What really launched me as an automobile writer was a story I did about a young automotive entrepreneur who had started selling race cars based on Volkswagens. Harold Zimdars, a talented mechanic and former Porsche race car driver, had a small garage on the South Side of Milwaukee, where he repaired and restored old Porsches.

Zimdars became the local distributor for Autodynamics, a manufacturer of Formula Vee race car kits in Marblehead, Mass., and I did a story about it. It was a fairly routine feature, with a photograph, but Harold and his wife, Valerie, would say many times over the years that the story gave a tremendous boost to Zimdars Motors, which years later evolved into several large and profitable new car dealerships.

After that first foray, we cooked up a dream assignment. Zimdars offered to loan me his Formula Vee, powered by a VW engine, and get me into an upcoming driving school sponsored by the Sports Car Club of America. At the time, the SCCA was the main organization for amateur road racing around the country.

I took the idea to Don Trenary, the acerbic editor of The Sunday Journal's Men's and Recreation Section. Though often difficult, Trenary was another one of those extremely talented Journal staffers, a fine reporter and editor, and a writer of uncommon grace. I always seemed to get along with people like him. I suppose it was because I respected their talent, was deferential and wanted to learn as much as I could from them—just as I had with the veterans in the composing room when I was a printer's apprentice.

Trenary went for the idea and The Journal picked up the tab for the two-day SCCA driving school, which was held at a new road-racing course called Lynndale Farms near Pewaukee, about 15 miles west of Milwaukee.

For two days, I lived my Walter Mitty life as a race driver, hurtling down the main straightaway at more than 100 miles and hour and doing my best to brake, shift and steer properly to clip the apexes of the curves. As in most road-racing then, there were several classes of cars on the track, with the Formula Vees among the slowest.

The climax came at the end of the second day, when we had an actual race of about four laps. I was determined to do well, and despite the fact that several of the other Vees were faster in the straights, I came to the final lap in the lead because I had done better in the corners and turns. But the faster cars were gaining on me as I came down the main straightaway and into the first turn.

I braked, downshifted and got back on the gas, but clumsily. The car started spinning and careened off the track backwards into the infield. I was shaking and angry at myself, but the Vee was still running, so I shifted back into first gear and, with a wave from a corner worker, drove back out on the track. I finished last, but at least I wasn't a DNF (did not finish), which is humiliating for a race driver.

The story, with color pictures, ran on the front page of the Men's Section. The SCCA leaders liked it so much they asked for permission to reprint it, and for years afterward gave a reprint to every person who completed a driving school and received an SCCA racing license. I had my license, too, though I never used it.

Over the next few years I expanded my motoring coverage, and even included motorcycles. I started with a feature about learning how to ride a motorcycle, with lessons from a local dealer on a little Honda with a 50 cubic centimeter engine. The story ran big in the news columns, with a full page of photographs.

Later I tried motorcycle racing for a feature in our Sunday magazine. I rode cross-country, participated in off-road motocross events, and did flat-track dirt racing, called scrambles. My first scrambles turned out to be memorable. With a Journal photographer's lens trained on me and the other riders gunning their engines for the standing start of the race, I popped the clutch when the checkered flag went down.

The 250 Yamaha went out from under me and straight up in the air. But I managed to hang onto the handlebars, throttled the engine back, got it back down and took off. I finished last, no surprise. The worst part was that the photographer captured the moment, so I had to endure a raft of ribbing back at the office. Fortunately, the picture didn't run in the paper. At least I had kept my racing record intact—two last-place finishes.

Eventually, I worked my way into writing reviews of new cars, and that opened up an entire world that had been unknown to me—a world in which the car companies courted and even wined and dined a cadre of journalists, writers, advertising people and assorted hangers-on who constituted the automobile press corps.

Of course, The Journal was above all that. As one of the top newspapers in the country, and even without a formal ethics code, The Journal had high standards. Reporters on assignment rode first-class on airplanes and stayed in the best hotels. Though we were allowed to accept things of insignificant value—cases of beer from the Milwaukee breweries were delivered to all staffers' homes on their birthdays, and every ice-skating revue, circus or other show that came to town dropped off free tickets at the city desk for distribution to the staff. But the paper always paid its own way on bigger events.

So when I went to an American Motors press preview at a posh resort in southeastern Wisconsin, The Journal insisted on paying all my expenses. It drove the public relations people nuts. As now, the car companies picked up the tab for everything—air fare, hotel and meals—and even gifts for the auto writers.

I was surprised by the extent of the largesse, which included prizes for competing in autocrosses and other events dreamed up by the public relations people. Even more surprising—and disgusting—was to listen to a few of the "journalists," some of whom worked for ad departments or tiny Midwestern radio stations, gripe about the food, drink and accommodations.

Fortunately, I went to only a couple of such events. The Journal wouldn't let me take a freebie, and it wouldn't pay to send me to most of the press previews. The American Motors event was an exception because it was nearby, and a home state enterprise.

But I was still fairly naïve about such matters. One day, a call came from a Volvo public relations man. He invited me and my wife to join four other automotive journalists and their spouses to travel to Sweden for the introduction of a new model. We were to visit the factory and receive briefings on the car. Then each couple would get one of the cars for two weeks. We could arrange to drop the car at any one of five cities in Europe, and Volvo would fly us home from there. Expense money for meals and hotels would be provided.

I was so excited I could barely contain myself. With such an opportunity, I could write a whole raft of stories—about the car, of course, but also travel stories from the places we would visit. And it wouldn't cost me or The Journal a penny.

I went to see Arville Schaleben, who was then the managing editor, had hired me and who, until the day he died, never learned to spell my last name—he always wrote it as "Aukhofer"—despite his reputation as a premier journalist of his time. He listened quietly to my breathless rhetoric about all the great stories I would produce at no cost to the paper. Then, coldly, he said, "If we think it's worth sending you, we'll pay the expenses. I don't think this is worth it."

I was devastated. But it was a lesson learned. The lesson was buttressed by the subsequent experiences of our aviation reporter, Ed Williams, who was in love with airplanes. He kept a book with all the details of every airplane he had ever flown himself or as a passenger—

not only dates and times, but specifications of the aircraft themselves, right down to the fuel consumption.

Williams had a pilot's license, and one day took all of my kids for their first airplane rides out at Milwaukee's Timmerman Field. The plane was a Cessna. After the flights, he gave the kids certificates attesting to their first flights.

But The Journal considered aviation a minor, part-time beat and mostly refused to send Williams anywhere. He finessed the situation by taking vacation time and paying his own expenses for air shows and other aviation events. Then he'd come back and tell the editors he had a story. Almost invariably, they'd accept it and run it, and he'd get at least some expense money.

I, too, had a part-time gig with automobiles for several years. I wrote features and car reviews in between covering civil rights, general assignment and rewrite. In 1966, I got what I regarded as a dream assignment: I was to put out one of our periodic automobile sections.

I was determined to do a great artistic job, and this time the editors couldn't refuse my travel request, which was to go to Detroit with a photographer to learn about and shoot all the new American cars. Reasoning that most of the car companies showed their wares in advertisements anyway, I wanted to get creative pictures of the cars that would not necessarily show the car but would have artistic merit and give us an attractive section.

Allan Scott, one of The Journal's fine photographers, came with me. We worked hard, and Scott came up with creative color photography of taillights, grilles and other standout features that was as artistically beautiful as it was different. But none of the photographs was ever published.

Civil rights waylaid me. Dick Leonard, who was then the managing editor, called me into his office and offered me a Ford Foundation fellowship at Northwestern University. But I had to leave fairly quickly, which meant I wouldn't be able to put out the automobile section. It was turned over to the business desk, which had handled such sections in the past. To my anger and chagrin, the section that eventually came out was full of wire copy and public relations photos. Not a single one of Scott's stunning photographs was used.

The fellowship also meant that I had to give up the automobile beat, which I did willingly, although I knew I would miss it.

My time away from automobile writing would last nine years. In 1975, after completing the fellowship, covering the civil rights beat, working as an assistant city editor and getting transferred to The Journal's Washington Bureau, I had a telephone conversation with Joseph W. Shoquist, the managing editor, an automobile enthusiast who favored German cars. We did not have a car review column at the time, and Shoquist suggested that perhaps I might do one.

I was delighted but wary. At various times, The Journal's car reviews had been written by the business news reporter who covered the automobile industry. It was logical, and we did have a reporter covering the beat at the time. Wouldn't it make sense, I asked Shoquist, to have him do the column?

"No," Shoquist replied, "he doesn't know anything about cars, and he can't write."

In subsequent discussions and memos, I remembered my earlier experiences with auto coverage. So I told Shoquist I wanted to free-lance the column to The Journal. He asked why, and I told him that, from his perspective, he could pre-empt critics in the newsroom who might gripe that I was writing about cars when I should be covering Washington stories. From my standpoint, I said, I could make a little extra money—The Journal didn't pay overtime to anyone who was out of town, even in its bureaus—and it would free me to sell the column to non-competing outlets elsewhere. There also was precedent: reporters always earned free-lance money for Journal book reviews, magazine articles or other stories they did on their own time.

What was in the back of my mind, however, was that as a free lance I would not be subject to The Journal's stringent standards and could attend some of the industry-sponsored press previews and other events on my own time as long as I was not identified as a Journal representative.

Some of my mainstream newspaper colleagues are horrified by the way automotive journalism operates, and I can't say I blame them. How can you maintain credibility and fairness if you're writing about a product or an event where the manufacturer pays all the expenses and even sometimes gives gifts to the writers?

Initially, it wasn't much of a problem. I was too new and simply didn't get invited to the press previews. I did, however, get a new car every week from the press fleets and wrote about them in my weekly column, as did virtually every automobile writer for other publications and broadcast outlets. As far as I know, only Consumer Reports actually buys the cars it tests, although it sometimes has sent representatives to automotive events.

Over the years, and despite my misgivings, I came to terms with the system, which would be virtually impossible to operate any other way. For example, if an automobile company wanted to conduct a press introduction for a new model and invited several hundred journalists at their own expense, only a few would attend. That's because most of the writers are free lances, or work for small news organizations that cannot afford the travel and other expenses. As a result, no car company would go to the expense of an elaborate press introduction for only a couple of journalists from The New York Times, USA TODAY or The Wall Street Journal. And there is no guarantee that even those wealthy publications would send anybody. Likely they would not, because it would lop off a big chunk of their budgets. There are as many as 30 or 40 of these events in a year.

So the answer for the car companies is to foot the bill for the whole thing, while allowing those few upstanding news organizations to pay their own way if they wish. The press introductions are expensive, but the cost is small compared to the billions of dollars it often costs to develop a new car or truck model. And in fact some of the news organizations that insist on paying their own way often skip the press previews and buy articles from free-lances who do take the freebies. So there is an element of hypocrisy even on the news side.

Another mitigating argument is that all the car companies do the same thing to introduce their new cars, so there's no advantage to any of them—or any special way to co-opt the journalists who are invited to the events.

Moreover, the system is not terribly sophisticated. The car companies make no distinction among mainstream reporters, and television and radio journalists, who work for the editorial side of news organizations, and those who basically serve advertising departments. In the latter case, as might be expected, a discouraging word about the product is hardly ever heard. In the former, there is sometimes criticism of the sort you'd find in movie reviews or sports columns, but the car company representatives take a sophisticated approach and rarely complain.

Of course, they have total control over the journalists and pseudo-journalists—and even stock market analysts—they invite to their press previews, and presumably could—and probably do—freeze out people whose criticisms they don't like.

In the later years before my retirement in 2000 as the Milwaukee Journal Sentinel's Washington bureau chief, I started attending some of the press events. But I went on my own time and never was identified as a Journal representative. I had hooked up with the Artists & Writers Syndicate, a small business in Washington owned by veteran syndicate operatives Philip and Marjorie Steitz, and was identified as their auto columnist.

At first, we called the column Keys to Wheels. I partnered with a close friend, Bill Rechin, the cartoon artist who drew the "Crock" and "Out of Bounds" comic strips that ran in newspapers around the country. He drew cartoons to go with my car columns, the thought being that it would make the feature more attractive to editors. Alas, that was not the case. It never seemed to make much difference. But Rechin and I collaborated for years before we called it quits. Later I re-named the column DriveWays, and it went under that name at the Scripps Howard News Service.

In 1995, something ominous happened. The powers at Journal Communications decided to kill off both The Milwaukee Journal and the company's morning paper, the Milwaukee Sentinel, which it had bought from Hearst in 1962, mainly because the Sentinel lost money. At the editors' request, I took a leave from my military-media fellowship and returned to The Journal newsroom for several weeks to write my newspaper's obituary, along with a sidebar on the many big stories it had covered over the years.

The new Milwaukee Journal Sentinel (two words, no hyphen) appeared just before my 60th birthday while I was back in Nashville writing America's Team: The Odd Couple, with Vice Admiral William Lawrence.

With the staffs of The Journal and Sentinel now merged, there was a question of which car column would survive. My column had been appearing in the Sunday Journal Lifestyle section, while the Sentinel's column had been running on the business pages. The Journal's features editor, Beth Slocum, did not survive the staff merger—she was summarily ousted—and the Sentinel's business editor became the new paper's business editor. Not surprisingly, he decided to keep his own guy's car column. That meant I was out as well.

Even though by then I was selling my car column elsewhere—
mainly to The Washington Times—I didn't want to be left out of the
newspaper where my column had run for 20 years. So I went to talk
the situation over with George Stanley, the business editor who later
became the managing editor. I tried to argue that my column should
be the one to run in the new newspaper, both on merit and longevity.
Alas, it was to no avail.

Though Stanley had committed to running the column by Mark
Savage, whose writing I considered infantile, he compromised and
agreed to continue to buy my column for the periodic automobile
sections that the Journal Sentinel would continue to publish. Moreover, he said my columns could run when Savage was on vacation. We
shook hands on it and, though I wasn't totally satisfied, at least I wasn't
frozen out of the newspaper where I had spent 35 years.

My editor at The First Amendment Center in Nashville, Natilee
Duning, was the wife of the editor of The Tennessean, Frank Sutherland. Wary of the goings-on back in Milwaukee—I had been required,
along with everybody else, to re-apply for my job as Washington Bureau Chief—I went to see Sutherland about possibly taking an early
retirement from the Journal Sentinel and going to work part-time for
The Tennessean back in Washington. Wouldn't work, he said. The
Tennessean was a Gannett newspaper and was required to use its
Washington news bureau. But he had heard about my column, and
said he wanted to see it. He bought it and The Tennessean has run it
weekly from 1995 on.

Later, I also worked out an agreement with Scripps Howard News
Service in Washington, where the editor was Peter Copeland, who
had been a sidekick of mine in the Pentagon press pool that covered
Desert Shield in the Persian Gulf War. It uses the DriveWays column as one of several pre-packaged features that go out to newspapers
around the country. So with that, the Journal Sentinel, The Tennessean and the Washington Times, I had enough outlets to comfortably
maintain my bona fides as an automotive columnist. After my retirement from the Journal Sentinel in June, 2000, I continued the column
and maintained my identity as the columnist for the Scripps Howard
wire service and the Artists & Writers Syndicate.

It's not lucrative. I earn a few bucks, but mainly it enables me to
continue to indulge my interest in motor vehicles, as well as to keep me

in test cars and trucks every week of the year. Almost everybody who finds out about that has the same question: "How do I get a job like that?"

There aren't many of us, perhaps a few hundred journalists in all. They are an odd amalgam of staffers for magazines and newspapers, some of whom work for the editorial side and others who work only with ad departments, web site and broadcast writers, free lances who sell their stuff wherever they can, and a few who attend press events and never write anything at all.

Almost invariably, the press introductions follow the same formula. The location is usually a luxury hotel, sometimes with four or five stars, in places like Kona in Hawaii, San Francisco, San Diego, Phoenix, Washington, Seattle, Anchorage, Los Angeles and any number of European cities. Occasionally, the car companies invite journalists to venues in Europe, Africa and Asia.

On domestic events, the journalists usually travel in one day, and sit down to a nice dinner with the "internals"—the name for the public relations people, executives and engineers. The next morning, they sit through a briefing about the new car. Then they pair up for a "ride and drive" on routes set up by the public relations people. Another dinner that evening, and then the journalists travel home the following day. Sometimes, the journalists find gifts in their hotel rooms—everything from ball caps to briefcases and MP3 players.

There sometimes is time for sightseeing or other activities, but mostly the trips involve work—if you consider driving new cars around the countryside work. Columnists like me get material for columns, and the other journalists—print, radio, television and Internet—get material for their stories, videos and actualities, often including interviews with top automobile company executives.

Because the automobile manufacturers foot the bills for all the travel, hotel and meals, they control who gets invited. Among the journalists and fellow travelers, the constant topic of discussion is the mystery of which of them are on the different manufacturers' invitation lists. Obviously, the enthusiast magazines and the big newspapers, along with the writers who serve them, are on all the lists. Some of the lesser lights, who may only have a web site somewhere or a small publication, have to take whatever scraps are left.

It's a journalistic anomaly. But once again, it fits that old Winston Churchill definition of democracy. It's the worst possible way to do it—except for all the others.

18

RELIGION AND POLITICS

Call me Father Aukofer.

I baptized four of my grandchildren—not because I'm a religious fanatic, or even a particularly devout Roman Catholic. I did it as a form of insurance, following on something I heard many years ago about Blaise Pascal, the 17th-century French mathematician and philosopher.

As I recall it, Pascal did not believe that anyone could prove the existence of God. He said you had to bet on it. The idea was that if you lived a moral, unselfish life, you would be a happier person than one who lived an immoral, selfish life. That fit with what I had learned in college about the philosopher Aristotle, who was a nonbeliever but had come to the same conclusion.

Pascal reasoned that if you bet there was a God—and you lived your life accordingly, you would have a happier life regardless. And if God existed, you would please Him or Her and go to heaven.

You were fine on two counts. Even if you were a non-believer, you would have a happier life. But if you did not believe in God, and therefore lived a life of utter selfishness and disregard for any moral code, you would be unhappy in any case. And if God existed, you also would be condemned for all eternity.

Somewhere along the way at Marquette University, I assented to an intellectual proof for the existence of a First Cause in the universe. It could be, as the Harvard Lampoon once posited, a cosmic muffin. Or it could be the loving, merciful and sometimes vengeful God of the Judeo-Christian heritage.

I am a Roman Catholic because of the accident of my birth. Had my parents been Indians, I might as easily have been a Hindu. Or if they had been Saudi Arabian, I might have grown up a Wahhabi Muslim.

But if I learned anything in 40 years as a newspaperman, it is that no one in humankind has a lock on the truth, or exclusively has the ear of the First Cause. My conviction is that, if anything, we all have pieces of it—from the isolated native in a jungle somewhere to the Archbishop of Canterbury.

That's a hard thing for many people to swallow. It's a matter of belief. If you believe that your religion—be it Christian, Jewish, Muslim, Buddhist, Hindu, Shinto or whatever—is the truth, the absolute truth, you exist in an invisible—and in many ways secure—comfort zone.

Though I sometimes envy it, I do not have that comfort. I believe that the First Cause—God, if you will—takes care of all of His creations. He could send His only begotten Son to be crucified for all, but also provide the prophet Muhammad for the Muslims and Abraham and the prophets for the Jews. After all, if this is an all-knowing, all-seeing, all-powerful God, nothing is beyond possibility or imagination.

As a Catholic, though my faith is riddled with doubts—a friend once referred to me as a Christian agnostic—I believe that it is a simple matter for God to delegate to a priest the power to turn that wafer of unleavened bread into the Body of Christ, and that wine into the Blood of Christ. From a philosophical standpoint, it's a matter of changing the substance while retaining the form.

But in the end, I don't really know. That's where the agnostic part comes in. I don't know whether the Catholics or the Muslims, or the Buddhists or the Holy Rollers, have got it right. Only God knows. And if God has revealed all of it to any single human or institution, I haven't seen it. My suspicion is that all of us have shards of the mosaic.

Two of my four children—Juliann and Matthew—stayed with the Catholic Church, though not without some wavering. I was the same. The two younger kids—Becky and Joseph—wound up as born-again Christians, devout and dedicated but no longer formally Catholic.

Given my conviction that God provides many paths to paradise for all of mankind, I could not condemn their rejection of Catholicism. But it did bother me that their new churches did not include infant baptism. So to be on the safe side—in case God had given an edge to Catholics—I felt it would be prudent to baptize Becky's Cole, and Joe's Aliya, Lucas and AnnaLyn. (Becky's Zoe had been baptized in the Church before her parents switched).

We couldn't do the baptisms in a Catholic church with a priest because the Church requires the parents to promise to rear the child as a Catholic. When I consulted our pastor, Father Tuck (formally Father Horace Grinnell), of St. Anthony of Padua parish in Falls Church,

Va., he said anyone could perform the rite, and it would be just as valid as if the Pope himself had done it.

So I edited the script of the rite to remove the overtly Catholic stuff, and I put on a suit, shirt and tie, and baptized each of the kids at different times, with Sharlene doing the organizing and the older grandchildren—Alyssa, Rachel, Hanna and Zoe—assuming different roles. At the last baptism, of AnnaLyn in 2005, Rachel and Hanna sang a song, and Alyssa, a budding journalist at 16, delivered the homily, which she wrote. Aliya held the basin as I poured the water over AnnaLyn's head. Matt's son, Seth, then 16 months old, chugged around looking cute. All of us agree that our family rituals are more impressive, emotional and with deeper meaning than you'd find in a standard church baptism.

Alyssa's beautiful homily deserves mention because it tells something about our family. I quote it here in its entirety:

Dear AnnaLyn,
I'll admit, when grandma asked me to write a tribute to you, I was completely lost. I had no clue what I was supposed to write. I've never written a tribute to or about anyone or anything. However, I agreed to write this because I feel like it's an important part of your baptism service. So here it goes my best attempt at writing a tribute for you, my youngest cousin.
Being born into a family as close as ours is a privilege, and when you get a little older, you'll understand exactly what I mean. It's not often that you find a family where every member knows practically everything about everybody. It's even rarer to find a family who knows everything about everyone and still offers you unconditional love. You are only beginning to understand this special family bond, and I know from experience that it will only strengthen as you grow older.
Since you're the youngest cousin, and I'm the oldest, we will always have a bond that's different than that of any of the other cousins. When you're my age, 16, you'll be heading into your junior year in high school, preparing for various school projects and extracurricular endeavors. Meanwhile, I'll be 32 years old, and I just might have some kids of my own. The age difference between us, though quite large, will make our relationship as cousins even more interesting. You'll be able to keep me up to date on what the latest and hippest trends are,

while I'll be able to offer you an experienced ear to listen to whatever problems and successes that life holds for you in the future.

Our family is a special blend of countless different things. Among these are emotions, successes, failures and many, many joyful moments. Though everyone in our family is different, different religions, different parenting styles, different likes and dislikes, there is one bond that keeps our family close and content: love.

Webster's dictionary defines love as a strong tender affection or deep devotion. However after living in this family, you'll find that love is much more than that. Love is having tea parties at grandma's house and playing no licks and just kisses with grandpa. Love is when Uncle Matt checks to see if "your clothes fit," then he tickles you so much you can't breathe. Love is naming waves "Larry" with Uncle Joe (your dad), being trendy with Aunt Becky or painting with Aunt Juli (my mom). Love is what we have in this family.

Though I don't know what the future holds for you, AnnaLyn, I do know a few things. I know that you'll be talented and successful. Whether you're a singer like Rachel, a poet like Hanna, a car nut like Lucas, a girly-girl like Aliya, an artist like Zoe, an athlete like Cole, inquisitive like Seth, or a writer like me is still uncertain, but I know that in whatever you do, you'll be successful and happy. I also know that no matter how hard you search you will never be able to find the kind of love that we have in this family, and for that reason, I know that you will have an amazing life.

It is my sincere hope that you will grow up and live the kind of life I have lived with this family, because if you do, you will never feel alone, upset or unloved. In this family, love is unrestricted, and it will undoubtedly provide you with affection and support that will last you a life time.

I viewed the baptisms basically as cheap insurance. If Becky and Nick, and Joe and Joanne, were right, and baptism was not needed until adulthood, no harm done. But if the Catholics were right, the kids were assured a shot at heaven if something happened to them while they were young. Moreover, it was a way of relieving a grandfather's anxiety.

My attitudes and beliefs toward religion and politics percolated during my years at Marquette and as a reporter. If, as I am convinced, no human can know the mind of God and the absolute truth of life and the universe, it is quite likely that some of us know part of it.

My ideas developed over years of observing the lives of other people, and also watching—and being repelled by—those who believed they possessed absolute truth exclusively.

I believe that the worst sin is intolerance, because it makes God narrow-minded and petty, which He most assuredly cannot be. While it may seem arrogant of me to assert my theory of God as the truth, I only argue it is logical. If we are indeed created in the image and likeness of God, how could Muslims be favored over Christians, or Christians over Hindus or Jews?

As a newspaperman, I always tried to steer clear of ideology—religious or political. Convinced that my view of the universe likely was no better or worse—or more accurate—than anyone else's, I always strived as a reporter to accurately communicate the convictions of those I covered.

It had a practical purpose as well. It gave me credibility with the people I covered. If I accurately conveyed their points of view, I was seen as sympathetic and sometimes even as an advocate, though I was not. I always thought it presumptuous to impose my own views. In Washington, I'm sure the conservatives I covered believed I was sympathetic to their views, and the liberals also regarded me that way.

The people who have always annoyed me the most—to the point of anger—have been those who purport to possess all the truth. They are the arrogant know-it-alls, whether they proselytize for the right or the left. I have no more sympathy for the left-wing fanatics than I do for the right-wing zealots.

At the same time, I recognize that those same people often are in the vanguard of change, especially when they battle against injustice and tyranny.

I may be appalled at the rigidity of an Alexander Solzhenitsyn, but recognize his bravery and role in helping bring about the fall of evil in the form of Soviet communism.

No one can escape politics, especially in a democracy. But as a reporter, I always tried to give every side a fair shake. Reporters often are accused of being liberal, which is true in the sense that most of them are exposed to different ideas, politics, cultures and people—to the point where they develop a broad tolerance.

Publishers and editors, however, don't get out as much. They spend most of their time dealing with subordinates, so tend to be more conservative, in the lower-case sense. Yet in my experience, editors and reporters for mainstream newspapers always sought to make certain that news stories were, if not objective, at least fair to all of the parties involved. If there were six or seven legitimate, competing points of view, the goal always was to represent them accurately.

That's not to say that reporters don't have opinions. Many are as opinionated—especially on subjects they are covering—as anyone else in society. But most of them are professionals who strive for credibility with their sources, be they left or right politically, and most of them succeed. I have read beautiful down-the-middle stories by reporters who were personally politically liberal or conservative, but through long force of habit could not bring themselves to consciously slant a story.

In fact, one of the toughest things I did as a Washington reporter was writing opinion columns. In the 1980s, the chairman of The Journal, Irwin Maier, wanted the Washington bureau to contribute opinion columns. He said it was more meaningful for Journal subscribers in Wisconsin to read opinions by one of their own, rather than those of some East Coaster.

But in the hustle and bustle of daily news coverage in Washington, a reporter often does not stop to form an opinion on a political issue. Usually, he is too busy gathering information and writing stories on the issue and the proponents' and opponents' views. There is little time for reflection before moving on to the next story. At least that's the case with generalists. Beat reporters tend to have strong views on running stories they cover because they become experts in the subject matter. But they, too, strive to maintain equilibrium in their stories. At a minimum, it's common sense. Why slant a story and alienate half of your sources?

After many years in Washington, I came to the conclusion that there were few issues of moral moment. Abortion is one, and perhaps capital punishment. For the most part, however, the stories are about issues about which reasonable men and women of good will disagree. There's no question that they often disagree strongly, and even attempt to cast arguments in moral terms, but in the end it's simply a matter of political priorities.

Usually, it's a two-step process. Do we need to balance the budget? Do we want welfare reform? Once that decision is made, the question becomes a matter of how it should be done, and what priorities should be incorporated. Again, these are matters about which reasonable people disagree, based on their politics or ideology, and a good reporter doesn't get involved in deciding which side is right. At least, I never did.

None of this means that reporters take everything at face value. Experience causes red flags to pop up in a reporter's head, giving him the sense to spot lies, misrepresentations and political motives, and take those into account when writing the story.

Not all of these generalizations apply. Reporters are like anyone else. They have different talents, skills, interests and passions. Some of the best reporters are great at investigations and bring a sense of outrage to their craft, others are superb writers who can evoke emotions with a few words, and still others can bore a reader to sleep with factual recitations.

In our craft, we have our share of self-promoters, prima donnas and miscreants. But I think the percentage is smaller than in the general population. As imperfect as it is, daily journalism still provides the public with the most accurate information available, and it is—as has often been said—the first draft of history.

19

ADMIRATION

Anewspaper reporter, especially a generalist like me, gets to meet a lot of interesting people. In interviews, I'd often ask the person who they most admired. It was a good gimmick to gain some insights into the person's character. If someone admired Al Capone, it was one thing; if the admired person was Mother Teresa ... well, you get the idea.

I had the tables turned on me when I was the subject of an interview in the Newseum's television studio in Arlington. The audience consisted of a group of older folks on an Elderhostel trip. Elderhostel is an international program that arranges trips for affinity groups of people 50 and older. These folks had decided to learn about the news business, and the Newseum was on their agenda.

During a question session, one of them asked me to name the people I admired most. That was easy. I quickly named Father Matthew Gottschalk, the Capuchin priest in Milwaukee who worked with the poor and outcasts, and Gaylord Nelson, father of Earth Day, who had served Wisconsin as both governor and U.S. senator. But in a follow-up, the questioner threw me a curve. Was there any woman among my most admired?

I was stumped, but only because my brain was focused on people I had covered over the years. There had been many memorable women, but none I could put on my most-admired list. I was barely in my car on the way home when it hit me.

It was not anybody I had ever covered, but someone with whom I had lived for about 40 years—my wife, Sharlene. Now that's likely a standard answer from anybody who has been married as long as we have, and ordinarily it would have more to do with love, familiarity and comfort than any dispassionate assessment. However, by any objective standards, I could unashamedly rate Sharlene as the woman I most admired.

Four children, punctuated by one miscarriage, came along in less than seven years. It was Sharlene's great competence and love that made it possible for me to focus on my career.

In 1965, we had three kids, Sharlene was pregnant with our fourth and attending night school not far from our home in Cedarsburg. One evening when I was out of town on assignment, she tragically miscarried while at school. Despite the shock and trauma, she somehow drove herself home and did not tell me until I had returned.

She has known adversity in her life and in every instance, conquered it. Her childhood was a chaotic mix of limited attention by her oft-married working mother and loving care from her revered grandmother. Determined to make a life for herself, she broke away after high school and moved to Chicago, where she started a promising career as an airline agent. But she returned home when her mother became ill, took a job in a dress shop and studied to be a cosmetologist. That was when we met. We dated for about a year before we married.

She has an uncanny knack for relating to other people's feelings and troubles, to the point where I cannot think of a single person in my life or hers who does not like or love her. Among my relatives and friends, I am convinced, most like Sharlene better than they do me. In some cases, I am certain that I am tolerated because of her.

Any time Sharlene has been faced with a challenge, no matter how unpleasant, she has met it with a courage that inspires me and our children.

When the kids grew old enough to take to amusement parks, she confessed that she was terrified of roller coasters and those sky rides in chairs that resemble ski lifts. Nobody would have blamed her if she'd simply sat on the sidelines. But she wanted to be with the kids, so one time she repeatedly rode a roller coaster a dozen or more times, each time coming off shaken, with tears streaming down her face, until she had conquered her fear. She did the same thing when we started skiing. She simply rode the chair lift until it no longer frightened her.

After we moved to Washington, Sharlene kept me going as a newsman by returning to her earlier occupation as an airline agent. She joined United Airlines as a reservations agent and worked there for more than 21 years before retiring. Without her contribution, I would have been forced—like some of my colleagues—to seek a less-interesting, better-paying job, maybe in public relations, to get the kids through college. She worked all sorts of night and weekend shifts in those years, which allowed me to follow my professional dreams.

We were in our forties, living in Annandale, Va., with four kids in school, when Sharlene learned she had breast cancer. We sat on the living room couch, held hands and cried. She didn't cry after that, at least not in my presence. She had a modified radical mastectomy and, later, reconstructive surgery. Fortunately, there was no lymph gland involvement, so no chemotherapy or radiation was needed. She met this challenge with courage and determination as she had every other difficulty in her life.

Later, Sharlene decided to put her empathy to good use with Haven of Northern Virginia, a volunteer organization that provides services to the grieving. She worked one-on-one with clients and facilitated groups for people who had lost spouses, as well as survivors of suicide victims. She also invented an annual generic memorial service for anyone who wanted to attend, and arranged the readings and music to make certain there wasn't a dry eye in the house.

For Sharlene, conquering challenges and self-improvement are not New Year's resolutions. They are a way of life, and they show up in countless small ways constantly. That's why I can stand back and say that I can classify her as my most-admired woman because, as I often say, half jokingly, I'm a newspaperman trained in objectivity and truth.

I don't remember exactly when I met Father Matthew Gottschalk, but it likely was in 1964 when he and a group of young seminarians picketed the Marquette University dental school, where Alabama Gov. George Corley Wallace was making a speech. He was on a foray into Wisconsin to test whether his racist and segregationist message—he, of course, labeled it populist—as a prospective presidential candidate would resonate with the state's voters.

Gottschalk is a Capuchin priest who has spent his entire life serving the poor, the dispossessed and the outcasts of society as a parish priest and pastor in Milwaukee's inner city. He also has been a behind-the-scenes force for civil rights and was a founder and later the director of the House of Peace, a nonprofit, tax-exempt organization that helps the poor with housing, clothing, food and anything else they might need, physical or spiritual.

One of Gottschalk's pastoral services was as the confessor and spiritual counselor for Father James E. Groppi, the mercurial Milwaukee priest who became a leader of the city's civil rights movement in the 1960s. Because I covered most of those events, I encountered Gottschalk on many occasions. He rarely made news himself, preferring the background, but his influence and contributions were apparent to anyone with half an eye.

Gottschalk is a man's man, as strong as he is gentle, with a faith that remained constant as many of his disillusioned fellow priests and ministers, including Groppi, left the Church. I came to regard him, and I still do, as a living saint.

You couldn't apply the saintly description to Gaylord Nelson, the other man on my short most-admired list. He didn't have the same sort of beliefs as Gottschalk, having once told me with a twinkle that if he had a religion, it was something similar to that of a Unitarian who believed in one God at most.

But there are similarities between the two men. Nelson became a high-ranking elected official and national leader on environmental protection, who never—as far as I could tell in several decades of covering him—did anything for personal gain. His lifestyle was as middle-class as the reporters who covered him. After he lost his re-election bid for the Senate in 1980, he accepted a modest salary from the Wilderness Society to continue his environmental advocacy.

A progressive Democrat, Nelson's inclinations always were to introduce and champion legislation to help working people and the poor—not unlike Gottschalk. Yet despite the lofty offices he held, and the important people he counted among his friends, he was a regular guy with a self-effacing sense of humor who liked nothing better than knocking back a few scotch whiskeys or bloody marys and swapping jokes and political stories with friends and acquaintances.

Nelson's wife, Carrie Lee, whom he met when both were in the U.S. Army in World War II, was a sometimes-profane iconoclast whose blunt honesty endeared her to many despite her barbed tongue. Like Nelson, her humor trumped any self-importance she might have picked up over the years. On their golden wedding anniversary, Nelson recalled that Carrie Lee had once said the reason they had gotten along so well for so many years was that both were in love with the same man.

EPILOGUE
FORTUNATE SON

As I write this, I have passed my 72nd birthday. When I set out to write this memoir, I was 65 and recently retired from 40 years as a newspaperman.

I was full of ideas then, convinced that my four decades of adventure would be of interest to whoever might read these words. In my imagination, it could have become of interest to those thousands of people who determine a best-seller.

I have been proud and gratified to have the good fortune to be a newspaper reporter. But I am aware of my circumstances. I am not famous, like some of my journalism colleagues and friends who have had memoirs published. I have been a good reporter and, I think, an honest one, with an attitude that most of the people I covered and wrote about were basically good and trying to do the right thing as they saw it. Some did not fit that view, and they appear in places in this book.

I also believe that I am a good writer, but not one with any literary pretensions. I cannot immerse myself in and expose the depths and frailties of human nature, nor can I do a credible job of inventing characters and events. Whenever I have had flashes of what might be called great writing, it has always been the people and the facts that determined them. It amazes me that some reporters, to their disgrace and infamy, have been able to make up news stories and pass them off as factual. For me, that would be difficult if not impossible.

In my lifetime, I have been uncommonly fortunate. I had flawed but dedicated parents, a good brother and five fine sisters who were—like me—far from ideal, and we were not particularly close. Though we did not always share affection, there always was underlying love. I also had close relationships with some of my cousins, so family was always important in my life, and especially my wife, my four children, their spouses and my 10 wonderful grandchildren.

Many people rose up along the way to help me. An uncle, Paul Butzen, an accountant by profession, was not always popular in the Aukofer family. But he was proud of me and encouraged me because

I was the first in the family to go to college. He also taught me how to hold a pool cue and to eventually shoot a decent stick. Others are mentioned throughout this book.

In the 1990s, I met George Pollard, a renowned artist from Kenosha, Wis., who had painted portraits of many members of Congress, including those of Rep. F. James Sensenbrenner Jr. as chairman of the House Science Committee and Rep. Les Aspin as chairman of the House Armed Services Committee. At the unveiling of Aspin's portrait in 1996, I chatted with Pollard, about whom I had done a story earlier, and he said he wanted to do a portrait of me. I had a nice smile, he said.

I told him I couldn't afford his fees, but he said he would do it gratis because he wanted to use my portrait in some of his promotional materials. So I traveled to Pollard's home in Kenosha in 1998 and sat in his studio while he shot maybe 70 or 80 photographs of me. He combined that with photographs of episodes from my days as a reporter and produced a wonderful portrait similar to those he had done for sports stars.

It is often written that adversity and failure are necessary to breed character and success. While I think that may have been true in some cases, I haven't had that experience. I far prefer the blessings that—for some unfathomable reason—have been bestowed on me.

I could have, for example, had an unhappy marriage, as has so often happened, and especially to those who made it secondary to their careers. I used to say, with youthful certitude, that a woman could make a man more of a man or less of a man. Fortunately, I never experienced the latter. And I had an exciting job with never a slow day.

When I received the By-Line Award for lifetime achievement from the Marquette University College of Journalism in 1992, I delivered an acceptance speech in which I compared newspaper reporting to a mother telling her child, "I'll give you an ice cream cone if you'll go outside and play instead of staying in the house to do the chores."

I concluded by saying, "If you don't mind, I'd like to go out and play some more."

It's been a great run, and it continues.

APPENDICES

PORTRAIT OF A DETERMINED WOMAN
(MAY 8, 1977)

I'd like to tell you about my mother, the writer. A few months before her 66th birthday, she got her first byline. That's not bad, considering she never made it past eighth grade and spent most of her life rearing seven children and taking care of some of her 19 grandchildren.

But then, she always was a determined woman. She tells the story of her father whipping her with a wire coat hanger because she registered to attend public high school. He was an old-fashioned Polish father; he ran a coal yard, a saloon and a dry goods store on Milwaukee's South Side, and didn't believe girls needed more than an eighth grade education to change diapers.

The grade school she attended in those days was Catholic and Polish, in that order, and no English was spoken. Which is why even today you hear a lot of older South Siders who were born there speaking with heavy Polish accents. But not my mother.

She was determined to break away; nowadays people would call her ambitious. I believe she is still. But she was sidetracked. Her mother and stepmother both died, and she had to help take care of the family and her father, who lived long enough to keep her out of high school and to see a couple of his grandchildren.

However, she eventually did escape ... sort of. She met and married a young man from across the viaduct on the other side of the Menomonee River Valley. He was from a German family, but enough removed from the old ways so that the only time they spoke German was when they drank beer and played skat and sheepshead at Pewaukee Lake.

They had good times at Pewaukee Lake, where there were three cottages side by side, all inhabited by cousins and other relatives and each one with a bar in the basement so everyone could go from cottage to cottage to celebrate. Many gallons of beer disappeared, especially on Granddad's birthday over the Fourth of July each year, when the children sometimes would find their fathers sleeping on the lawn the next morning.

But mostly there were hard times. Ma and Pa were married in 1934—when the Great Depression was at its worst. Pop had a trade—he was a printer—but they didn't need many printers then, so he usually found work only one week in five. It was not considered proper to accept welfare, so they borrowed to get by.

And the babies came, with regularity, usually less than two years apart, until there were seven in all. Later my mother would laugh and say they were all rhythm babies because in those days the Catholic Church was the same as it is now—no artificial birth control. Except in those days, Catholics did what they were told.

There never was any money, even after the war started and people were working again. Ma remembers the time Pa gave her a nickel candy bar for a birthday present, and the older ones among us remember vividly how we all practically lived on potatoes during one particularly tough period.

They kept trying, though. They went into debt to buy an old barn of a house which needed a full restoration just to make it livable, and in later years they went into debt again so Pop could go into the printing business. He worked second shift on his regular pressman's job and spent days and Saturdays in his little print shop, doing beautiful four-color work on platen presses. His product was admired by anyone who knew anything about it. But Pa was as bad at business as he was good at printing, and later they moved the shop into our basement to save the rent.

Money was always a problem and led to arguments and fights, sometimes made sharper by drinking and often brought on by Pa's insistence on maintaining his one relaxation in life—his daily stops for brandy and beer at his favorite taverns. Ma went along sometimes but mostly she stayed home and harassed her children about everything from their playmates to their morals.

She always yearned to do the fine things of life—like going out to dinner and dancing and shows. But that was seldom possible.

Cancer took Pa at the age of 52, wasting him away in a matter of six months, and leaving Ma with most of her family still at home, including three daughters still in elementary and high school. By dying, Pa lifted the family out of debt for the first time. The insurance paid off the house and the bills.

But even with Social Security for the girls, it was still a struggle and Ma kept up the printing business as best she could, teaching herself as she went along. She sold wedding invitations and printed jobs herself for long-time customers. When she locked the type in a form for the press, it was enough to put Rube Goldberg to shame, but the jobs got done. As she grew older, the customers dwindled and the work became too much, and eventually she sold the two platen presses and the galleys and sticks and fonts of foundry type—and the business was no more.

Though printer's ink flowed through all of us, we children went different ways, as children do. Cici is a genius at accounting and numbers, John is an electronics whiz and Margie with her three kids is going to be a truck driver. Four of us wound up writing in one way or another: Dottie with a newspaper in Europe, Clare as a magazine editor and Tessie doing free-lancing. I followed Pop into the printing trade but wound up as a newspaper reporter.

I guess Ma figured the talent had to come from somewhere ... and probably from her side of the family. I don't know about the writing, but I do know about the ambition. If any of us has any ambition for anything, it had to come from Ma. She never stopped trying.

That was why, even after a couple of illnesses laid her low to the point of almost flattening her permanently, she decided to try writing. Never mind a lack of education and a lifetime spent at household chores. She was going to be a writer. She tried it on her own and also in classes at the Washington Park Senior Citizens Center.

Like any smart writer, Ma writes about things she knows, which is mostly her life and her family. A while ago, she won second place in a writing competition at the senior citizens center. But the big story was a reminiscence about how the family always trooped downtown to watch the Schusters' big Christmas parade, with Billie the Brownie and Santa Claus and Me-tik the Eskimo. She had the darndest time finding out how Me-tik spelled his name.

Not long before Christmas, she sent the story to Post Newspapers and they ran it in the first column under an eight column headline with a boldface byline saying, "By Wanda Aukofer."

My mother, the writer.

THE HOSTAGES RELEASED
(JAN. 21, 1981)

Washington, D.C.—The temptation is to call it the end of a long national nightmare. Lord knows, a lot of commentators will refer to it that way. But it had long since ceased to be a nightmare, downgraded instead to one of those dreams you can only partly remember when you wake up.

Time has a way of dulling things. How long ago was it? A year? Two years? What difference does it make? A whole lot, if it was your son, husband, brother or sister marking time God knows where, surrounded by religious fanatics whose minds you could never begin to understand. But for many Americans, the only reminder was Walter Cronkite's regular, "And that's the way it is ... the umpteenth day of captivity for the hostages in Iran."

Still, even if we were not directly involved, the hostages touched every American in some way. Many of us cried when we saw them bravely greeting us last Christmas on the films provided by the Iranian government. But before the tears had a chance to dry we were angry because it had been more than a year and they were spending their second holiday season in captivity.

More than a year! Could anyone have imagined? No, never. We were all sucked in, from President Carter on down. It would all be over in a few days, we thought. The Iranian government, such as it was, would never allow a bunch of militant hoodlums to defy international agreements on diplomatic security. Such madness would turn every nation in the world against Iran.

But it didn't. And even if it had, it wouldn't have made any difference. Americans had no notion of how deeply the bitterness had soaked into the souls of the people in the streets of Tehran and Qom and those other cities whose names we were only beginning to learn.

Or how their hearts yearned for revolution, regardless of the cost, and how that revolution was deified in the person of one man, a sinister-looking old cleric with a beard, Ayatollah Ruholla Khomeini.

Khomeini supported the militants, and that was that. No government, no United Nations, no international court at the Hague in The Netherlands could prevail. The Iranians wanted their shah back. Shah

Mohammed Reza Pahlavi, whom they had deified in a different way, was the devil incarnate, responsible for the wounds that had festered into revolution.

They held the United States responsible, too. It was the United States that had admitted the exiled shah into the country for medical treatment. It was the United States that had propped him up, given him guns and tanks and combat airplanes, even used its Central Intelligence Agency to put him back on the Peacock Throne in 1953 after Mohammed Mossadegh had almost taken it away.

Officials in Washington were dimly aware that all was not well. From time to time before the revolution, bands of Iranian students had taken to the streets to march and shout, "Death to the Shah," their faces swathed in cloth to conceal them from SAVAK, the Shah's dreaded secret police.

For Washington, a city calloused by protests, it was all very ho-hum. More interesting were the glittering receptions hosted by Ambassador Ardeshir Zamedi at the Iranian embassy. He gave the best parties in town. The shah sold us oil (we even forgave him for quadrupling the price in 1973), and we sold the shah arms and ammunition, all in the interest of Middle East security.

In those days, the shah was worried more about image than revolution. His government commissioned a public opinion poll by a respected US firm to find out what American opinion leaders thought of Iran, the shah, his family and their relationships with the United States. But he was looking in the wrong direction. Soon he watched from exile as Khomeini's firing squads, led by lesser ayatollahs and other clerics, soiled the walls of Iran's cities with the blood of the shah's men—and even some lowly prostitutes and other offenders who had been tainted by western ways.

The horror was tinged with comedy. We uttered mock groans when the ayatollah banned booze and his minions dumped all that good Scotch and Bourbon whiskey down a sewer, and we chuckled when he outlawed popular music. Even today, when letters arrive from a 15-year-old boy in Tehran who had lived most of his life in the United States before the American government sent him home in retaliation, the plea is for some forbidden cassettes.

We rattled out sabers, but always half-heartedly. A few weeks after the Americans were kidnapped, a prominent senator said the seizing an American embassy was an act of war, and that in due course the US would take military action. But we continued to hope that some way would be found out of the mess. We faithfully supported our president and we linked arms in an Auld Lang Syne of patriotism that had not been seen since World War II.

And by God, we weren't going to be dragged down to their level, no matter what. So when Iranian students marched to support the militants holding the hostages, we provided them with police protection against our own people. And when the president acted to deport Iranian nationals, it was only against those who were here illegally—and always with maddening due process. The rest, except for the diplomats ousted when we broke diplomatic relations, could stay. In a way, we were like Mammy Yokum in the old Li'l Abner comic strip, who always said that good was better than bad because it was nicer.

But Mammy could fight, and we reached that point, too. But we botched it. Eight young American volunteers, airmen and marines, died for their country in an unmarked Iranian desert trying to rescue the hostages. Because he had quietly fought against such a desperate course, Secretary of State Cyrus Vance resigned, to be replaced by Sen. Edmund S. Muskie, also a man of compassion and deep emotion, who could sympathize with failure.

That was the nadir of our national melancholy. But there were highs, too. Early on, the ayatollah, obviously seeking the debilitation of our national resolve, released 13 of the hostages—five women and eight black men. Islam, he said, believed in special rights for women and recognized the American tyranny against blacks. Nobody was fooled, but it did serve to keep us sucked in, hoping for an early release of the other hostages.

But how thrilled we all were when our friends, the Canadians, people like us, managed to cloak six Americans in their flag and sneak them out of Tehran. To be a Canadian in those days was to become an instant and authentic hero, worthy of standing ovations everywhere, and to this day many Americans wear the red maple leaf in their lapels.

Richard Queen came home, too, smiling and shyly handsome, looking so vulnerable, weakened as he was by multiple sclerosis. Again the Khomeini line was that it was done out of compassion, to show the American people the humanity of the revolutionary Iranians. But where, we asked, was the compassion for the suffering of the innocent 53, and again our anger welled up.

We were forced to endure the bizarre, the constant emotional ups and downs, the threats of executions and trials, the right hand in Iran not knowing or caring what the left hand was saying or doing, the conflicting signals from the militants and the men in government whose names nobody could pronounce, the aloofness of the ayatollah himself, the frustration because no one seemed to be in charge of anything except making sure of the continued bondage of the Americans.

We witnessed the grandstand play of an obscure Idaho congressman, George Hansen, who defied his president and traveled to Iran. It won him a visit with some of the hostages, but nothing more, and we watched the sometimes puzzling, sometimes infuriating meanderings of Mrs. Barbara Timm of Oak Creek, a mother who marched to her own sometimes staccato cadence as she tried on her own to win the release of her son. She, too, won an audience with her son, but also the anger of some Americans when she appeared on Iranian television to denounce the tragic rescue mission.

Most of the other members of the hostages' families tried to stay relatively obscure, a difficult task because they were hounded constantly by the press, who decided early on that they were public property. The families displayed saintly patience and forbearance, and provided the nation with a focus for its frustration and grief.

Always, throughout the maddening events that hammered away at us from the screens of our television sets and the pages of our newspapers, we stretched for tidbits like the shah's death in Cairo in July. Surely, we thought, that would mean something. No point in demanding the return of a corpse. Perhaps the war with Iraq would do it. Iran needed help it could not get while it held our people. But, as always, we assumed that the heads of the militants contained a brand of logic similar to our own. We learned, only slowly, that it was not so.

Ronald Reagan was elected president on the first anniversary of the capture of the hostages, and some of us felt a little better, a little tougher. The old jokes came back. What's flat and glows in the dark? Iran after Reagan's inaugural. But we didn't really believe it. The families of some of the hostages, however, were beginning to conclude that perhaps our national honor would demand the sacrifice that none allowed themselves to think about. No apologies, the president's man had said.

As with any epic experience, we have learned much, and we will learn more as time passes. Even out of a national trauma, there is always some positive result. Once we recoiled in fear and anger at the actions of civil rights militants and anti-war protesters. But many of us also stopped to think about it, and we changed.

We will think about Iran, too. No longer will we view the shahs of the world as secure plantation bosses with their happy bands of darkies. No longer will we dismiss the deeply held religious beliefs of others as the ravings of the lunatic fringe. We will learn about them, try to understand and be prepared. And although it does not diminish our anger at the act, we understand a little better that desperation sometimes drives people to do crazy things.

Though we still pride ourselves on being the most powerful nation on the planet, we know something more about our own vulnerability. We learned in Vietnam that we were not invincible. Oil price inflation taught us that we were not an island. And Iran has taught us that the time has indeed passed when any nation, large or small, can with impunity tell any other nation how to act. Our destinies are all too tangled.

What now? There will be investigations, analyses, some recriminations. the journalists, the instant chroniclers of history, will in a year or so write stories about how the experience changed the lives of the hostages and their families, and how some of them were psychologically scarred, perhaps permanently. The historians will stitch Iran into the fabric of greater events.

Most of us will do what we have been doing all along, with some sense of relief and, for some of us, a vague foreboding. What next?

LOST AND LOADED AND JUST LIKE HOME
JANUARY, 1982
(ONE STORY IN A SERIES ON MEXICO)

Jojutla, Mexico—There is only the dim light from a waning moon to give us some idea of where we are. That and the dazzle of oncoming headlights as the Volkswagen chunks its way over the potholes of the country road. We are lost.

The Swiss in the right front seat is holding on with one hand, white-knuckled and furiously smoking a cigarette with the other. He is tense because our host—and the driver of this Volkswagen with the bad clutch—has had too much brandy and beer.

Our host is like a moth, drawn to every pair of oncoming headlights, most of which are attached to huge buses and trucks. The Volkswagen gradually drifts leftward until, at the instant when a head-on collision seems unavoidable, the steering wheel is jerked to the right and the bug resumes its meandering on the right side of the highway.

Fortunately, though the engine is roaring at high revolutions, we are not traveling very fast—perhaps 25 to 30 mph—because the clutch slips so badly. To get up a hill earlier, we had to get out and push.

I am alone in the back seat, a can of beer in one hand and a silly grin on my face, totally relaxed. I am back in my childhood and I know nothing can happen to me.

A REUNION

Out here, in the middle of the night in the middle of nowhere in the state of Morelos, where Emiliano Zapata rode with his young rebels during the Revolution 65 years ago, I should be somewhat apprehensive. But the situation is so similar to 35 years ago in the middle of Milwaukee that I cannot be anything but comfortable. The brandy and beer help, of course.

Our host—I will call him Ramon in this story because I do not want to embarrass him by using his real name—has become something of a friend. He is about my age, 46, and he is a good example of the still small number of people in Mexico who have passed from the vast plain of poverty into the foothills of the middle class.

I have a sense of something already seen because Ramon's situation is so similar to what I experienced as a boy in Milwaukee—right down to the brandy and beer and driving down the highway with what my father used to refer to as a snootful.

Unlike four out of 10 Mexicans, Ramon has a steady job—as a mechanic on a ranch near Cuautla, an hour's drive from his home in Cuernavaca, a city of about 300,000 people 50 miles or so south of Mexico City.

HOUSEFUL OF FEMALES

He lives with 10 females—his wife, eight daughters ranging in age from 11 to 24, and a granddaughter. His oldest daughter, who has an off-and-on again relationship with her husband, is pregnant again, so soon there will be an even dozen in the family.

They own their home—a two-story house and a small cottage surrounded, as are most city properties in this part of Mexico, with a wall. But the family rents the cottage and the second floor of their home for extra income. So mom and pop and the eight daughters and the granddaughter live downstairs, which consists of two bedrooms, a bathroom, a small kitchen, a dining area and a front hallway that serves as a living room.

The family also buys and sells honey to earn a few extra pesos, and two of the daughters, who are now out of high school, work as secretaries. The family's diet is mostly vegetarian, partly because meat is expensive but also because Ramon's wife is a health food enthusiast. She has taken a course in cooking such things as a soybean meat substitute that looks and tastes a little like veal.

I know the family fairly well because I lived upstairs with two other students there last year while I was in a school trying to learn Spanish. I know also that Ramon, though he has the Mexican male's macho pride in having so large a family, is part of the change that is slowly happening in his country. On a holiday morning, when his wife was suffering from her varicose veins, I found him up early scrubbing pots and pans in the kitchen.

In my family in Milwaukee, we had seven children and never enough money. My father worked as a pressman and had a small job printing shop on the side to earn extra money. Like Ramon, his chief form of entertainment was meeting his friends for brandy and beer in local taverns.

Although in later years I recognized the folly of it, as a child I trusted my father completely when he insisted he could drive a car even if he could not walk from drinking. They were always old cars, too, sometimes with bad clutches and brakes. Oddly, Ramon's Volkswagen reminds me this night of Pop's creaky 1936 Hudson Terraplane.

The Swiss, a young man in his 20s who is studying Spanish and is living with Ramon's family this year, has not had the benefit of my childhood experiences, which is why he puffs constantly on his cigarette and appears ready to leap from the Volkswagen at any second.

We have become lost while returning from an event near the small town of Jojutla that provided another of those jarring contrasts that are so much a part of modern Mexico. One of Ramon's teen-age daughters is attending a sort of vocational school in Zacatepec, where she is studying to become a travel agent.

DRIVING A CHALLENGE

The school has decided to select a queen from among the top six students in the class, and Ramon invited the Swiss and myself, along with a crowd of assorted relatives, to attend.

It had taken nearly an hour and a half, in the late afternoon, to make the drive from Cuernavaca to Jojutla, including three or four stops to ask directions and pick up a six-pack. Driving anywhere in Mexico is a challenge because there are not many signs to tell motorists where to go, which is one of the reasons tourists are advised never to drive at night. Moreover, directions provided by local residents are usually only more or less accurate.

Eventually we found Jojutla, and it was typical of many smaller towns in this part of Mexico: tiny shops and stores in concrete buildings with faded and peeling paint; shacks constructed of whatever on dusty, unpaved streets pockmarked with potholes; children and dogs playing, and groups of people just hanging around. If there was any wealth in this sleepy town, it did not present itself to the world.

ENTERED ANOTHER WORLD

But then we drove down one of the narrow streets toward the outskirts of town, rounded a bend and passed into another world. Beyond a wrought-iron gate, like one on a wealthy estate in the United States, was El Rollo, a luxurious swim club.

The club, in the middle of nowhere with miles of poverty in every direction, had six swimming pools, each of a different shape and size, with diving boards, bridges, islands and slides for playing and relaxing in the sun. Tree-shaded walkways meandered to bathhouses and refreshment stands. In the center of the complex stood a huge, open-air pavilion decorated like a night club or discotheque.

This was where the competition for the queen of the travel agents' class was held, and it operated like a Miss America pageant in the United States, except that there was no swimsuit competition. There was an emcee from a local radio station, full of jokes and cute things to say that embarrassed the contestants; a panel of judges, and a makeshift runway to the stage.

The young women were all stunningly beautiful in their long evening gowns, but also a bit awkward and shy parading in front of the audience as their family and friends whistled, led cheers and whooped it up. Each contestant also had to recite a prepared travel agent's sales pitch about the history and attractions of the state of Morelos, and then the judges asked questions to test the contestants' poise and knowledge.

"WE WUZ ROBBED"

In the audience, sweating waiters hustled to keep up with the demand for buckets of ice and bottles of liquor and soft drinks. Tequila, brandy and beer—Mexico brews some of the best beer in the world—are alcoholic staples, and brandy appears to be as popular in Mexico as it is in Wisconsin.

Although clearly she was the prettiest and most poised in the group, Ramon's daughter did not win, and I was on my feet good-naturedly yelling, "We wuz robbed" in Spanish, much to the delight of her sisters and friends.

With the competition over, the monotonous beat of recorded disco music came thudding over the sound system, and the contestants and their young friends crowded onto the floor. Disco dancing is very popular in Mexico, but usually very expensive. Here it was a no-cost extra and everybody wanted to take advantage of it.

MOST EVERYBODY . . .

Everybody, that is, except for some middle-aged dinosaurs like myself and Ramon. After trying one number with one of Ramon's daughters, emboldened by the brandy in my belly, I gave up.

Now we are trying to find our way back to Cuernavaca through bleak little towns without street lights and only low-wattage bare bulbs on buildings here and there to light the way. Occasionally I can see into some of the tiny homes or shacks along the road and I am grateful that I do not live out here with little money and no prospects. But I also am grateful to have experienced a small slice of Mexican life on this warm night.

Eventually, after several stops in the darkness for directions and relief, Ramon finds the road to Cuernavaca, as I was confident he would. My father always got us home, too.

JA! AUKOFER!
(JUNE 2, 1991)

Growing up, I had one of those names that kids can twist and that get you in fights on the playground. But I was stubborn about it. Though I hated having to defend my family honor, I never wanted to be called anything else. In fact, I was disdainful of movie stars who changed their names.

Later, as experience replaced childhood defiance, I learned that what you were called was not as important as what you did. If you accomplished something, people would learn how to pronounce and spell your name and treat it with respect, so you could be a Marlon or Sylvester and still be a big movie star. Or, if you were a ballplayer, people would prize your autograph even if it said Yasztremski or Dalrymple.

As an adult, I became proud of the fact that I epitomized the roots of my home town of Milwaukee—German on my father's side and Polish on my mother's. Before she married, my mother Wanda was a Kaminski, a fairly common name in Poland.

Though members of my father's side of the family were stubbornly proud of our name, we were never much on heritage. My grandfather, Frank X. Aukofer, had immigrated to the United States with his father in the late 19th century and, like many immigrants of the period, sought to become Americanized as rapidly as possible. He was born on the Fourth of July, which always was the occasion for a big party at the family cottage on Pewaukee Lake.

All we ever knew about Grandpa was that he came from somewhere in Bavaria. A printer, he died back in 1945, when I was 10.

Even his only surviving child, my Aunt Clare, now in her 80s, did not know his father's name or the name of his home town when I interviewed her last year, trying to learn more about the family.

Over the years, I had made a few casual inquiries, hoping to find out whether my last name meant anything in translation. The closest guess came from a university professor of German, who told me that the name might have been changed from Au-hofer, which meant a man who owned a farm near a stream.

Last November, my wife and I took a short vacation trip to Germany, and decided to drive a big counterclockwise loop through Bavaria, up to Berlin and back to Frankfurt. I had no notion of seeking out my ancestors; I wouldn't have known where to start even if I had been so inclined.

But through an unlikely series of coincidences, we found the Aukofer family. We also learned that the name had no particular meaning in German, but that it had been traced back to the 13th century.

But I'm getting ahead of myself. . . .

The biggest coincidence was a total lack of hotel rooms in Munich. We were following our noses, without reservations or even a definite route, and arrived in Munich late one evening to learn at the tourist office that everything in town was booked. So we got back on the road and headed north toward Berlin. We found a wonderful little guest house in a town called Reichertshausen, where we ate a delicious meal of pork, sauerkraut and noodles, and stayed the night.

The next morning, we moseyed on north again and, on a whim, decided to poke around for a few hours in Nurnberg. Christmas was near and the downtown was decorated for the holidays. We found a gift shop where we bought nutcracker dolls for our daughters.

Without stopping to see any of the tourist attractions, we drove back out of town toward the autobahn to Berlin. Rounding a turn, I looked up and saw a big sign on the side of a construction shed near some railroad tracks.

"L. Aukofer," it said.

I was blown away. In a split second, I had gone from uncertainty about whether my family name was a bastardization of something else to the knowledge that it was a real name.

We pulled into the construction site and saw the L. Aukofer sign everywhere, but no people. So we parked the car and started looking around. One of the construction trailers was wide open, and inside was a stack of four cases of beer. On the end of each green case, in white letters, "the brand name: "Aukofer Brau."

So there not only was an Aukofer construction company, but there also was an Aukofer brewery. I was so excited I was trembling.

In short order, a rugged, blue-eyed man in his 50s strode up. "Are you Aukofer?" I yelled.

"Ja, ja," he said, and I immediately assumed he was a cousin. He could have been, too. He had the Aukofer laugh wrinkles around his eyes. As it turned out, he was the foreman on the job and must have thought that I was asking if he worked for Aukofer. He spoke no Eng-

lish and we spoke no German, but he placed a telephone call to the
L. Aukofer headquarters in Regensburg, where the chief switchboard
operator, Helma Trout, spoke English.

Between that and a lot of gesturing, we learned that not only was
there a construction company in the medieval city of Regensburg,
there was the J. Aukofer brewery and hotel in Kelheim, a small city on
the Danube River about 45 minutes southwest of Regensburg.

We left the construction site with hearty handshakes from the foreman, four bottles of Aukofer beer and tears in my eyes.

Our entire itinerary changed in seconds as we sped off down the
autobahn toward Regensburg. We arrived on a Friday afternoon, only
to learn that the L. (for Luitpold) Aukofer construction company was
closed for the weekend.

But it was obvious that at least one Aukofer had prospered. There
was a 10-story office building, a fleet of Mercedes-Benz trucks and a
huge dormitory for construction workers.

So it was back in the car and off to Kelheim. After some poking
around, we found the hotel and brewery, right outside the old walled
city, which was still surrounded by a moat. On a mountaintop that
overlooked the city was a huge monument, called the Rescue Hall,
which must be three or four times the size of the Jefferson Memorial
in Washington. It had been built by King Ludwig I to commemorate
Bavaria's victory in the "rescue war" against Napoleon around 1814. A
picture of the monument is incorporated into the Aukofer beer label.

The brewery and hotel and the farming of a substantial tract of land
around Kelheim are family operations. Head of the Aukofer family is
Johann, now in his 80s, who mostly sits in the office and counts the
money. He is the brother of the late Luitpold, whose widow, Doro-
thea, now runs the construction company in Regensburg. Johann's
son, Hans, and daughter-in-law, Anna, run the hotel, brewery and
farm. Both Johann and Hans are German versions of John, my only
brother's name and obviously popular in the Bavarian branch of the
family as well.

Among those who help out at the hotel are Franz (Frank) Aukofer, a
banker in nearby Essing; his wife, Herta, and their daughter, Barbara. A
son, Franz, is an apprentice brewer under the tutelage of his Uncle Hans.

Barbara, 20, speaks excellent English and was our interpreter during
our brief stay. When we had dinner in the hotel dining room, Barbara
brought us a copy of the Aukofer family tree.

It focused only on the branches of the family in the immediate area, so there was no indication of where my grandfather fit in. My own opinion, from looking at it, was that his father—my great-grandfather—might have been a brother of Hans's great-grandfather, Joseph. My grandfather had a brother named Joseph, and that also is the name of my youngest son.

Hans proudly gave us a brewery tour on Saturday.

Like many local breweries in Bavaria, the Aukofer brewery is small by US standards. It produces 350,000 gallons of beer a year, along with lemonade and other soft drinks. As Hans put it, in Bavaria "you only have to sell within sight of your chimney." The brewery dates back to 1874 and produces a half dozen varieties, from Pilsner to a dark festival brew. The beer was uniformly delicious and would sell at premium prices in this country.

Kelheim is a summertime tourist area for Germans and Austrians, who visit Rescue Hall and ride tour boats on the blue Danube.

As we were leaving Saturday afternoon, we picked out souvenirs—a dozen Aukofer Pilsner glasses for ourselves and beer mugs bearing the family name for our children. When we tried to pay, we were politely refused.

We also brought back six bottles of Aukofer beer, which we poured out like fine champagne for our family at a big Thanksgiving dinner.

But there remained the mystery of where the American and German families converged. Although I was convinced we had to be related, there was no proof. The only document I had was my grandfather's baptismal certificate, which was written in Old German and therefore was unintelligible even to most Germans. I made a copy of it and sent it off to Barbara.

A few weeks later, her reply came back, affirming my link to Kelheim.

It said that my grandfather, Franz Xavier Aukofer, had been born July 4, 1868, in the hamlet of Waldorf near Kelheim, and had been baptized the next day in the local parish church according to the Catholic rite. His godfather was Andreas Aukofer, a mason of Munich.

The document was certified by the Catholic rectory of Kelheim. Most importantly, it said my grandfather was the "legitimate son of the brewer Franz Aukofer, mercenary of Wallddorf, and his spouse Anna."

LESSONS FLUSHED FROM A POKER HAND
(MARCH 26, 1995)

W hen the twins turned 5 years old, I figured as a responsible grandfather it was time to teach them poker.

As anyone who plays can testify, poker teaches valuable lessons of life: Make the most of what you have; don't let the opposition know when your confidence is wavering; learn to assess the character and honesty of people around you; and, when you are unbeatable, don't press your advantage to the point of making enemies. And, of course, play the cards you are dealt.

You win and lose with courtesy and honor, though you may seethe behind your poker face.

It occurred to me only later that poker also could reinforce old-fashioned societal roles that would not benefit my granddaughters. In poker, the king always beats the queen. But I have a fix ready (more on that later).

Alyssa and Rachel Navarrete learned to play poker during our family vacation at a beach house in Duck, on the Outer Banks of North Carolina. Their sister, Hanna, sat on my lap for a couple of hands. But she was just 3 and more interested in playing with the chips, although one day she did show her developing card sense by loudly announcing that I had a pair of queens.

I had prepared the twins the week before. We sat down with a deck of cards and I showed them what beat what, from the deuce through the ace. When I started a review during our first session at the beach, they informed me impatiently that they already knew that part. So we went on, and that same day we were playing. We have continued since.

They quickly learned all the hands, up to and including a royal flush. I taught them about calling and raising, and even that when you check it's a bet, but a bet of nothing.

They learned poker clichés like "down and dirty," and giggled and shouted, "Pot's light" whenever they caught anyone who forgot to ante or meet a bet or a raise.

In dealer's choice, it was fun to say gruffly, "Name your poison, kid," and have one of these wonderfully confident and intelligent girls reply firmly: "Five-card stud, roll your own," or "Five-card draw." They liked roll-your-own more than standard five-card stud because it meant they could have more "secret cards." For the same reason, they liked five-card draw.

One day, when the girls were covered with goose pimples and shivering in their towels after spending too much time in the pool, one shouted:

"Grandpa, let's go home and play five-card stud."

Adult heads jerked around in astonishment. I grinned and proudly escorted my diminutive gamblers away.

We haven't played much for real money, mainly because they don't have much regard for its value. We each have our own color chips, and we take them back after every hand. They don't take too well to losing anyway, and having to give up their chips just rubs it in.

One day, I folded a flush in the face of Rachel's pair of eights, mainly because both Alyssa and I were winning steadily and Rachel was getting discouraged.

Later, of course, I'll teach them that compassion doesn't have much of a place in poker. They'll also learn how to bluff and more about when to stay and when to drop.

But I have this nagging thought about the fact that the king always beats the queen.

I remember when the twins were 4 and learning about presidents from their mom, my daughter Juliann, and Alyssa tearfully argued with the family that a girl could never be president. Everyone assured her that was not so, that a girl could be anything she wanted. But Alyssa, with impeccable logic, insisted that there never had been a girl president, and therefore concluded that girls could only be first ladies.

There's not much to be done about poker, either. But I plan a countermeasure. Next I'm going to teach the girls to play sheepshead.

Though I've lived in the Washington (D.C.) area for 25 years, I'm a Milwaukee native and learned the game as a boy.

For the uninitiated, sheepshead—also known as schafskopf—is an old German game derived from another old German game, skat. In the U.S., it's mostly unknown outside of Wisconsin. It's played with 32 cards—sevens and up—and, unlike in bridge, the trump are permanent. There are 14 trump cards in all.

But the crucial thing for Alyssa and Rachel, and perhaps for females everywhere, is that the highest cards in the game are the four queens.

And of the queens, the two black ones—clubs first, then spades—are the most powerful, followed by the queen of hearts and the queen of diamonds. Think of it. Two black queens at the top of the power heap. It's enough to make a diversity manager's day.

Kings are almost inconsequential. Except for the king of diamonds, a low trump card, they have almost no power. They are worth only four points apiece, and in rank beat only the lowly nines, eights and sevens.

Jacks fare better. After the queens, the jacks—my granddaughters think of them as princes in the royal family—are the next highest trump cards. The order of power is the same: clubs, spades, hearts and diamonds. But it is clear they are subservient to the queens.

In sheepshead, you must amass points to win, so aces (11 points) and tens (10 points) are important. Kings are worth four points, the powerful queens three and the jacks two. The nines, eights and sevens are worthless.

It is not a difficult game to learn, although playing it well takes awareness and skill. It was the first card game my grandmother taught me at age 10, perhaps unintentionally planting the seeds of feminism. So I am quite certain my granddaughters will pick it up quickly.

Between poker and sheepshead, Alyssa and Rachel will gain valuable insights for life. They already know that despite the fact that the king always beats the queen in poker, they can beat their old grandpa or anyone else in a given hand.

And if that's not enough, there's always sheepshead and the four powerful queens.

THE OBITUARY OF THE MILWAUKEE JOURNAL
(MARCH 31, 1995)

This is the last breath of The Milwaukee Journal. After today, after 112 years and 106 days, The Journal will exist no more.

In its place, on Sunday, comes a new newspaper, the Milwaukee Journal Sentinel, an amalgam of two old institutions that were sometimes admired, sometimes vilified, but also respected. The new entity no doubt will face the same attitudes.

The late Ray Kenney, who bridged the 4th St. gap and worked at different times as business editor of both the morning Sentinel and afternoon Journal, used to grouse about the way newspapers described their own demise.

They always say a newspaper died, he complained, where if it were any other business, it would be said to have collapsed, or folded, or merged, or simply gone out of business.

At the risk of offending a departed colleague, it will be recorded here that The Milwaukee Journal died today.

The reason that can be said is that, like human beings, all newspapers have personalities, complex and sometimes inscrutable, but always on display.

A lot of people have the notion that newspapers are simple things, like a club, that can be wielded easily and swung left or right to advance a political or other agenda.

The fact is they are collections of people with all manner of beliefs, values, ambitions and talents. It is that cohort, combined with the history and tradition left by earlier collectives, that determines a newspaper's personality.

In the case of The Journal, you can pick almost any adjective out of the dictionary and it will apply at some point in the newspaper's history.

It has been great, accomplished, courageous and innovative. It has also been careless, mendacious, second-rate and cowardly. Such is the nature of people, and such is the nature of newspapers.

But like other institutions that strive to serve the public—and, in the American way, make a profit as well—its guiding principles and its intentions have always been lofty, even if some of its people failed from time to time.

For decades, The Journal was ranked among the finest newspapers in the nation. In 1960 and 1961, for example, three separate surveys ranked The Journal among the top five.

In 1960, a survey of 335 daily newspaper editors ranked The Journal No. 3, behind The New York Times and The Christian Science Monitor. In 1961, a survey of 311 publishers ranked The Journal No. 4, behind The New York Times, St. Louis Post-Dispatch and The Christian Science Monitor. In the same year, a survey of 125 deans and professors of journalism ranked The Journal No. 5, behind The New York Times, The Christian Science Monitor, The Wall Street Journal, and St. Louis Post-Dispatch.

In 1954, Time magazine did a cover story on The Journal's fiercely independent publisher, Harry J. Grant. In an interview, he told Time:

> The Journal must be our fair lady. We must have freedom, freedom, freedom—not to be willful, or bigoted, or swell-headed, or to give us delusions of grandeur—but so that The Journal can act entirely as it thinks best for our community. The Journal is above our frailties. The Journal's job is to serve the public. It can't be anything else.

Of course, not everyone has agreed with The Journal's perception of what is best for the community. Some even ban the newspaper from their homes, even as others eagerly anticipate its smorgasbord of information. But that is the nature of American democracy, with a First Amendment to the Constitution that guarantees everyone's freedom of expression—be it a big newspaper or an individual shouting on a street corner.

In his "warts and all" history in 1982, to mark The Journal's 100th birthday, Robert W. Wells provided the best modern analysis of The Journal's developing personality over the years.

In a foreword, Donald B. Abert, then chairman of The Journal Company, remarked about the difficulty of squeezing that lifetime between the covers of a book.

"Writing the history of a century-old newspaper," Abert wrote, "is no ordinary literary assignment. Consider its dimensions. The writer must compress a hundred years of activity into a book equivalent in word-count to a single daily issue of the paper."

It is even more daunting to attempt such a feat in a single story, even one long enough to tire a determined reader.

But such is the nature of newspapers. On any given day, there never is enough space for all the stories the editors and reporters would like to send on to the readers.

And there never is enough space for all the obituaries—even The Journal's own.

So what is available will, of necessity, be a skimming of the cream, a tiny taste of what The Journal was all about for 112-plus years.

SOME STRONG INDIVIDUALS

As with any community institution, The Journal's personality has been defined by a few strong individuals, much as a nation's history is defined by its queens, kings, presidents and prime ministers—weak and strong, capable and incompetent.

For almost 95 of its 112 years, The Journal was dominated by three men—Lucius W. Nieman, Harry J. Grant and Irwin Maier.

It was Nieman who is regarded as the founder of The Journal, even though he did not actually start it.

The Daily Journal was first published on Nov. 16, 1882, by a now-forgotten Democratic congressman from Milwaukee, Peter V. Deuster, who also was editor of the Seebote, a leading German-language newspaper.

But the paper lost money immediately and, only 25 days later, on Dec. 11, Deuster sold out to Nieman, a native of Sauk County who had worked as a typesetter at the Waukesha Freeman and later as a reporter and editor at the Milwaukee Sentinel. The new publisher was just two days shy of his 25th birthday.

Nieman started with a pledge to his readers: The Journal, he wrote, "will oppose every political 'machine' and cabal, venal politicians of every stripe, every form of oppression, and at the same time give all the news for 2 cents."

Later he would drop the price to a penny, and he dropped his pledge of non-partisanship for a time to become a party organ—the "Official State Paper" of the Wisconsin Democratic Party—but eventually put The Journal back on its independent track.

Before the turn of the century, Nieman's Journal broke precedent
and tradition, hiring first a woman editorial writer, then a woman reporter. He leased Wisconsin's first typesetting machines, called Linotypes, hired a Washington correspondent and printed color on Page
One.

MANY JOURNAL FIRSTS

Fast forward to 1945, when The Journal became the first newspaper
in the country to run a color photograph of a news event. From 1947
to 1960, the newspaper led the world in volume of color advertisements. Its photographers set the standard for every publication in the
country.

Nieman's most tenacious crusade came during World War I, when
The Journal defended patriotism. That would be considered quaint
and naïve today, but it was courageous at a time when Milwaukee
was overwhelmingly pro-German. Among other things, The Journal
sneaked reporters into pro-German meetings and translated articles
in German newspapers to expose propaganda on behalf of the kaiser's
Germany.

In 1919, the effort won the Pulitzer Prize for Public Service for The
Journal. It was a prize that previously had been awarded only to The
New York Times.

Based on that accomplishment, the promotion manager came up
with a new slogan that defined The Journal's personality for many
years: "First By Merit."

There were other attributes that helped establish The Journal's image over the years. The most prominent of these were the editorial-
page feature, the front-page editorial cartoon, the front-page editorial,
the Peach Sheet and the Green Sheet.

The Green Sheet started before World War I as a sports features
section. Later, in 1920, it became the daily repository of scandalous
and sensational news—a way of competing with William Randolph
Hearst, who owned the Wisconsin News.

The Green Sheet, which generations of Wisconsin families fought
over on weekday afternoons, continued as The Journal's features and
comics repository until last year.

The Peach, which was part of the paper from 1913 to 1967, was
given away free or wrapped around the final edition of The Journal

each afternoon to provide readers with late-breaking news, sports and final stock-market quotations.

Front-page editorials and cartoons also set The Journal apart from other newspapers.

Unlike Nieman, Harry grant was primarily a businessman who knew how to make money. In its heyday, in the mid-1950s, The Journal was the fattest newspaper in the nation, running up to 100 pages a day and 400 pages on Sunday, and carrying more advertising than any paper in the world.

Grant's greatest achievement, as publisher and board chairman, grew out of his dogged determination to maintain The Journal's independence. After Nieman died in 1935, he turned the ownership of the company over to its employees.

Today, the employees of Journal Communications, Inc., a diversified company with interests around the world, own more than 90% of the stock.

Grant's successor as board chairman, only the third in The Journal's history, was Irwin Maier, another powerful personality who shaped The Journal and whose career paralleled much of Grant's.

Unlike Grant, who maintained an arm's length relationship with movers and shakers in the Wisconsin community, Maier was a man of involvement. He was a founder and prime mover in the Greater Milwaukee Committee and became a leader in virtually every civic improvement and movement, from construction of the Performing Arts Center to the re-establishment of major league baseball in the city.

Despite that, Maier had the same determination as had Grant to keep The Journal free from outside influences. In a 1968 letter to Editor Richard H. Leonard, Maier re-emphasized that no story should be put in or kept out of the paper based on whether the chairman approved or disapproved of it.

Maier's dedication to the Milwaukee community and the ideal of competitive journalism led to The Journal Company's purchase of the Sentinel in 1962. The Hearst paper had been closed down by a strike and likely would not have survived.

It was Maier who named Leonard as The Journal's sixth editor in 1967, thrusting him into the turmoil of the civil rights movement and riots that erupted that summer in cities around the country, including Milwaukee.

At 45, Leonard was the youngest editor since Nieman's early days. He held the job for more than 18 years, a period in which he fostered a change in The Journal's personality from a newspaper of the majority community to one of affirmative action and sensitivity toward minorities.

After Maier stepped down as chairman in 1977, he was succeeded by Donald B. Abert, who in turn was succeeded by Thomas McCollow in 1983 and Robert A. Kahlor in 1992.

Sig Gissler was named editor in 1985, followed by Mary Jo Meisner in 1993.

Kahlor became board chairman in September, 1992, and it is he who presides over The Journal's final personality change.

In a history of The Journal published in 1963, Arthur Ochs "Punch" Sulzberger, a onetime cub reporter on The Journal and now chairman of The New York Times Co., wrote that there had been only a handful of newspapers, like The Journal, that had become synonymous with their cities.

"To think of Milwaukee without The Journal," he wrote, "is like trying to think of New York without Broadway, San Francisco without the Golden Gate, Washington without the Capitol—clearly impossible."

That impossibility has arrived, but not without at least one bright spot. Though it is easy to think of a newspaper as having a personality, as The Journal clearly has demonstrated, it is more difficult to prove that it has a soul.

Yet because of its history of independence, quality journalism and service to its readers—but mostly because of the people who continue to shape it—there is much about the personality and the soul of The Milwaukee Journal that will live on in the new Journal Sentinel.

30

FOR A LITTLE ONE WHO HAS SADLY FALLEN ASLEEP
(AUGUST 2, 1998)

Washington—The tears of happiness were rudely followed by tears of pain.

It would have been our fifth grandchild, the first-born of our youngest, Joseph, and his wife, Joanne. Though married less than three years, they had dated since their sophomore year in high school.

Not long into the pregnancy, our euphoria was shattered. The doctors had determined that the baby had serious afflictions. A lymph gland disorder called cystic hygroma and, apparently, missing heart chambers.

The child, the doctors said, also could be born with Turner's syndrome, a genetic defect that could result in physical and mental impairment.

In our family, as well as Joanne's there was no question of what to do. We would all welcome and love the child, no matter what.

After their initial shock and grief, the kids found spiritual solace. Joe sent along an e-mail, in which he said he and Joanne were at peace. He included a biblical psalm (Psalms 139:13-16):

> *Truly you have formed*
> *my inmost being;*
> *you knit me in my mother's womb*
> *I give you thanks that*
> *I am fearfully, wonderfully made;*
> *wonderful are your works.*
> *My soul also you knew full well;*
> *nor was my frame unknown to you*
> *when I was made in secret,*
> *when I was fashioned*
> *in the depths of the earth.*
> *Your eyes have seen my actions;*
> *in your book, they are all written;*
> *my days were limited*
> *before one of them existed.*

The doctors also had said it was likely that Joanne would lose the baby. That happened in the 17th week. She felt a softening, a vague absence of substance and shape.

It was soon confirmed. There was no life left in her womb. After 13 hours of painful labor, she delivered the remains.

Although many features were recognizable, there was no way to determine the sex. So they named their little one Baby A. The nurse wrapped it in a blanket.

Then there were choices. They could leave Baby at the hospital or perhaps have it cremated.

But that wouldn't do. They talked it over with Joanne's parents, who had driven all night from their home in northern Virginia to Joe and Joanne's home in Lilburn, Ga., a suburb of Atlanta. (We were out of town and did not immediately learn what had happened).

Many years ago, Joanne's father had bought four plots in a cemetery near his home. He offered one.

They went to a local funeral home and bought a tiny coffin, 17 inches long. Before driving home to Northern Virginia, they placed Baby A inside, along with photographs of themselves and a small gold cross that Joanne had worn every day.

The brief graveside service, on a hazy, humid morning last week, was conducted by the pastor of the church attended by Joanne's parents. Among other things, he quoted from St. Paul (1 Thessalonians 4:13-15):

We do not want you
to be unaware, brothers,
about those who have fallen asleep,
so that you may not grieve
like the rest, who have no hope.
For if we believe
that Jesus died and rose,
so too will God, through Jesus,
bring with him
those who have fallen asleep.
Indeed, we tell you this,
on the word of the Lord,
that we who are alive,
who are left until

the coming of the Lord,
will surely not precede
those who have fallen asleep.

Four generations from both families gathered to grieve at the grave: Parents, grandparents, brothers and sisters, and nieces, nephews and friends of Joe and Joanne, about 30 in all.

There were 11 cars in Baby A's funeral procession.

FAREWELL TO AN AMERICAN HERO
(JAN. 15, 2006)

Not many of us ever witness the farewell to a hero.
Unless it's a president or chief justice, it's not something that makes the national news. Only the people who attend get to experience what it's all about.

The nation and, in particular, the United States Navy, gave a hero's sendoff to Vice Admiral William Porter Lawrence at the U.S. Naval Academy.

The local newspaper and television in Annapolis, Md., covered the story.

But that was about it.

Of course, every man and woman serving in harm's way, and especially those who give their lives or are wounded, deserves the title of hero.

But Admiral Lawrence was special. He spent his life in the service of his country, including six years in a brutal prison camp in Vietnam.

Like most of you, I had never heard of him. We were brought together by the Freedom Forum, a foundation that promotes free speech, free press and free spirit.

We spent nine months together in 1994-'95 on fellowships at the foundation's First Amendment Center in Nashville, Bill's home town.

Together, we tried to reconcile the disparate goals and means of America's mighty military and its unfettered journalism. The result was a book on the military-media relationship titled *America's Team: The Odd Couple.*

Among other things, it recommended the embedding of reporters with military units, which is practiced to this day.

When I first met Bill, I was struck by his reluctance to make eye contact—until I understood. When we'd sit and talk, he usually focused somewhere near my kneecaps.

It took awhile for me to figure out that it was a lingering residue of his dealings with guards and interrogators during his six years in Hoa Lo, the infamous French-built North Vietnamese prison camp, which Bill and his fellow prisoners nicknamed the "Hanoi Hilton."

They were there at his funeral—24 of them, now mostly old men, some hobbling on canes and staffs, led by Sen. John McCain, the Arizona Republican and still a possible presidential candidate.

Despite our disparate backgrounds—a Milwaukee kid who became a newspaper reporter and a Nashville boy who excelled at sports and academics and nearly became an astronaut—Bill and I became close.

With more tragedy and suffering, it intensified into what Bill's wife, Diane, said simply was love.

A month after the book was published in September of 1995, Bill suffered a massive stroke at the Naval Hospital in Bethesda, Md., where he had gone to have a heart valve replaced.

It was the same valve that had produced a murmur that lost him a shot at the astronaut corps with John Glenn and Alan Shepard. Instead, he became a test pilot and the first naval aviator to fly at twice the speed of sound in the 1950s.

Later he became a squadron commander in Vietnam. He bailed out of his crippled F-4 Phantom fighter in June, 1967, and spent six years as a prisoner of war.

With him in the Hanoi Hilton were McCain and future Admiral James B. Stockdale, who later became H. Ross Perot's running mate in Perot's maverick bid for the presidency.

There are so many interlocking relationships.

Perot and Bill had been classmates at the Naval Academy, where they collaborated on a codification of the honor code.

McCain's physical therapist after his release from Hoa Lo was Diane.

At the funeral, he said she had restored a knee that the doctors said would never function again—using, he said to laughter, some of the same tactics as had his North Vietnamese captors.

McCain introduced Diane to Bill, and she became his lifeline for 31 years, though she later said he never really got over the fact that his first wife left him while he was a POW.

When I met Bill, he was retired from the Navy. He suffered from depression, and his own honor code forced him to disclose it.

But he had served as commander of the famed Third Fleet and, from 1978 to 1981, was superintendent of the Naval Academy, at a time when women were first graduating.

His daughter, Wendy, was one of them. She now is a Navy captain and an astronaut who has logged more than 1,200 hours in space.

The 1995 stroke nearly killed Bill, and he likely would have been a wheelchair-bound invalid but for Diane.

She used the same harsh and loving tactics on him as she had on McCain, and Bill responded. He could no longer play tennis or drive a car, but he could walk under his own power and function as a human being.

Bill spent a lot of time on the telephone. We spoke often, and got together at home or Navy events like the Navy-Air Force football game, where courtesy of Bill I got to ride to the stadium on the Academy superintendent's bus, with a police escort.

I was always struck by the respect the military community paid to Bill. Everywhere we sat together, old friends, acquaintances and strangers, officers and enlisted men and women, lined up to pay their respects to this man who had suffered so much he aged before his time.

Recently, my wife and I were on a foreign trip, and we went on a tour of the Hoa Lo prison in Hanoi, now a memorial that features McCain's flight suit and boots in a glass case.

We were excited to return and tell Bill we had seen where he and the others were imprisoned.

But he died, at home, at age 75, on Dec. 2, 2005. He told Diane he was feeling poorly and stayed in bed. She was baking Christmas cookies and found him when she went to check on him.

Bill was cremated, and his remains were in a polished wooden box carried by the honor guard into the Naval Academy chapel, which holds 2,500 and was nearly full for the Dec. 14 funeral.

Perot and McCain, with the 23 other former POWs standing behind him, delivered the eulogies along with two of Bill's doctors, another fellow prisoner of war, Capt. Ned Shuman, and the chief of naval operations, Adm. Michael G. Mullen.

Perot read a tribute from President Bush.

The words were all about a lifetime of integrity, duty, bravery and unflinching honor, often in the face of torture and unrelenting adversity.

Once, in solitary confinement in the hole in Hoa Lo, Bill composed—in his head because there was nothing with which to write—a poem about his native Tennessee, remembering the iambic pentameter he had learned as a schoolboy.

His fourth-grade teacher, Mrs. Lipscomb Davis, a spry 90-year-old, marched to the pulpit and read the poem. After Bill was released from the prison in 1973, the Tennessee legislature adopted it as the official state poem.

After the service, the mourners followed an honor guard more than a mile on a bitterly cold day to the hillside cemetery overlooking the Naval Academy.

Walking at the head of the procession, behind Diane's car, were Mullen; Marine Gen. Peter Pace, the chairman of the Joint Chiefs of Staff; Vice Admiral Rodney P. Rempt, the academy superintendent; Capt. Wendy Lawrence, and Bill's other two children, William Jr. and Dr. Laurie M. Lawrence, a Nashville physician, and me.

On the hillside, the throng prayed with the academy chaplain, listened to the mournful playing of Taps, heard the crack of honor guard rifles and trembled to the crashes of a 15-gun cannon salute.

Four Navy F-18 warplanes roared overhead in "the missing man" tribute to a fallen warrior.

That is how we honor a hero.

INDEX